# Labour Law

CORE TEXT SERIES

# Labour Law

**Series Editor: Nicola Padfield**

1st Edition

**Richard Benny**
*Senior Lecturer in Law, University of Surrey*

**Stephen Hardy**
*Senior Lecturer in Law, University of Manchester*

**Robert Upex**
*Professor of Law and Head of Law Department, University of Surrey*

OXFORD
UNIVERSITY PRESS

# OXFORD
## UNIVERSITY PRESS

Great Clarendon Street, Oxford OX2 6DP

Oxford University Press is a department of the University of Oxford.
It furthers the University's objective of excellence in research, scholarship,
and education by publishing worldwide in

Oxford New York

Auckland Bangkok Buenos Aires Cape Town Chennai
Dar es Salaam Delhi Hong Kong Istanbul Karachi Kolkata
Kuala Lumpur Madrid Melbourne Mexico City Mumbai Nairobi
São Paulo Shanghai Taipei Tokyo Toronto

Oxford is a registered trade mark of Oxford University Press
in the UK and in certain other countries

Published in the United States
by Oxford University Press Inc., New York

British Library Cataloguing in Publication Data
Data available

Library of Congress Cataloging in Publication Data
Data available

ISBN 0–406–97116–1

1 3 5 7 9 10 8 6 4 2

Typeset in Gill Sans by Kerrypress Ltd, Luton, **www.kerrypress.co.uk**
Printed in Great Britain by William Clowes Ltd, Suffolk

# Preface

Labour Law is now so vast a field that it is easy to forget that as recently as 40 years ago it was still commonly called the law of 'master and servant'. The main matters to concern lawyers in those days related to personal injuries suffered by 'servants' and to industrial disputes. The enactment of the Contracts of Employment Act 1963 and the Redundancy Payments Act 1965 (still to be found in modified form in the Employment Rights Act 1996) represented the first steps towards what Professor Wedderburn has called a 'floor of rights'. Viewed from the perspective of 2004 those Acts may seem very tentative, but at the time they were significant, particularly the 1965 Act. The other significant event of the late 1960's was the establishment of the what came to be called the 'Donovan Commission'. Its Report effectively opened the modern era of Labour Law.

Although there has been an enormous volume of legislation since the enactment (and subsequent repeal) of the Industrial Relations Act 1971, the contract of employment (or 'contract of service', as it used to be quaintly called) remains at the centre of the relationship between the individual and his or her employer. Some would argue that in the modern era of Labour Law the importance of the contractual relationship is overstated. Indeed, Kahn-Freund (one of the major figures in this field) suggested many years ago that the relationship was becoming status based rather than contract based. Nevertheless, the development of the implied term of trust and confidence over the last 30 years suggests that there is plenty of life left in the notion of the contract of employment.

The other major contributor to the modern face of Labour Law is the United Kingdom's membership of the European Union. The UK joined the EEC (as it used to be called) on 1 January 1973. Over the succeeding 30 years, the influence of Europe has been profound. The impact of directives and the case-law of the European Court of Justice has influenced our domestic legislative processes and necessitated the introduction of legislation which otherwise might have taken longer to see the light of day. It has also had an impact on the way the courts interpret legislation, particularly legislation introduced in response to initiatives from Europe.

Labour Law in 2004 is a subject so large that it is difficult to teach the subject to undergraduates within the space of one academic year. This books is intended as an introductory text to this vast and continually developing subject. Overall, this text should be treated by the student as a useful course companion, seeking to give concise guidance and user-friendly access to the key points, principles and cases in this overwhelmingly complex, though exciting, subject which deals ultimately with the interaction of employer responsibilities and employee rights in the workplace.

The authors would like to thank their families, friends, efficient researcher Mark Butler, the editor of this series (Nicola Padfield) and publishers (especially the extremely patient Julia Burns) for their support, guidance and encouragement throughout. We offer our apologies to our friends and families for our absences, physically and mentally, during the writing of this text. This book is dedicated to the numerous students to whom we have taught labour law over the years and from whom we have learnt.

As Kahn-Freund once said, 'labour law is a discipline, only determined by its relations ...' (1954) Readers are invited to enjoy their relation with this discipline and text.

*Robert Upex*
*Richard Benny*
*Stephen Hardy*
London, August 2004

# Contents

# Table of Statutes

xiii

# Table of Statutory Instruments

# Table of European Legislation Conventions

# Table of Cases

PARA

**Decisions of the European Court of Justice are listed below
numerically. These decisions are also included in the
preceding alphabetical list.**

# CHAPTER ONE

# Introducing Labour Law

## Summary

This chapter introduces labour law as a discipline. The key points are:

- description of the main institutions;
- explanation of the underlying ideologies; and
- list of the sources of labour law.

**1.1**   Labour law is one of the most dynamic and interesting areas of the law. The study of this area offers an intellectually stimulating and challenging field for undergraduate students on law degrees and those following related programmes, such as business and management degrees. It is usually offered as an optional subject (sometimes called an 'elective') within degree programmes. In recent years the pace of change, both in terms of legislative and case-law developments, has been very fast indeed, and students of the subject should be aware that it is a demanding field of study, requiring diligence in keeping abreast of this fast pace of change.

**1.2**   As well as forming a discrete part of the law with its own specific case-law and legislation, labour law also involves the study of several other, related areas of the law such as the law of tort, eg concerning the vicarious liability of employers; statutory torts under the discrimination statutes; and the duty of care placed upon employers, employees and others in the tort of negligence. It also comprises a part of contract law, since the employment relationship is based upon a specialised contractual relationship, ie one with its own specific features, particularly with reference to implied terms (see Chapter 3).

## Definitions

**1.3** Essentially, labour law concerns the regulation of the workplace, ie those parts of the law dealing with: (1) the relationship between employees (and, in some cases, workers) on the one hand and employers on the other; (2) the relationship between trade unions (or groups of trade unions) and employers (or employers' associations); and (3) the relationship between trade unions and their members, and trade unions *inter se*.

**1.4** The first category of relationship identified above is often called 'individual labour law', while the second and third categories are often termed 'collective labour law'. Labour law is also known as employment law and, sometimes, industrial law (this latter term derives from the 1960s although the phrase is still current eg as embodied in the title of one of the leading journals in the field, the *Industrial Law Journal*, which was founded in that decade). Generally, these categorisations all mean the same thing, ie the relationships identified in (1), (2) and (3) in para. 1.3 above.

**1.5** However, labour law covers a wide range of topics within these categories, including: the law of dismissal (both unfair and wrongful – see Chapters 5 and 6); discrimination law (sex (including equal pay), gender reassignment, race, disability, religion or belief, sexual orientation and, from October 2006, age discrimination – see Chapter 4); 'family friendly' policies under which flexible working, parental leave and enhanced maternity leave provisions have been introduced – see Chapter 7; working time and the national minimum wage – discussed in Chapter 2; enhanced protection of what was formerly called the 'atypical workforce', comprising part-time workers and fixed term employees; and the protection of employees upon the transfers of a business or a part of one – see Chapter 9.

**1.6** One particularly complex area concerns the basic division between employees who work under a contract *of* service, and the self-employed (sometimes called 'independent contractors'), who work under a contract *for* services. The categorisation of an individual as one or the other may be important, particularly for claims for personal injuries sustained in the workplace context, where employees may claim under the employer's compulsory liability insurance covering employees, but the self-employed are not covered under this insurance. Somewhat confusingly, some rights are granted only to employees, eg the right to claim unfair dismissal, whereas other rights cover both employees *and* 'workers', the latter being a broader category including employees *and* those working under a contract whereby they agree to provide their own services personally), eg those provisions under the discrimination statutes giving individual employees and workers the right to claim. These issues are discussed in Chapter 3.

**1.7** Numerous other key definitions are dealt with in the following chapters, including those on the collective labour law side, eg that for trade unions (Chapter 9).

**1.8** As in many other areas of the law, the significance of European Union (EU) law has been immense within the field of labour law. All lawyers within the UK are also European Union (EU) lawyers, since EU law not only forms an important part of our laws, but it has also had a major influence on labour law in this Member State. Several of the most important developments in domestic labour law have come about as a result of developments at EU level. These are discussed in more detail in Chapter 2.

**1.9** Finally, students of labour law should be aware of the specialist publications in this area, not least the two main sets of specialist law reports, the Industrial Cases Reports (ICR), published by the Incorporated Council of Law Reporting, and the Industrial Relations Law Reports (IRLR), a privately published series containing, in addition to labour law reports, a very interesting *Highlights* section, written by the editor, Michael Rubinstein. It should be remembered that the most important labour law cases will also be reported in the general series of reports, such as the Law Reports, the Weekly Law Reports and the All England Law Reports. Other important titles include the *Industrial Law Journal* (ILJ), the *Industrial Relations Law Bulletin* (IRLB), the *IDS Brief* and the *International Journal of Comparative Labour Law and Industrial Relations* (IJCLLIR). Furthermore, many articles on labour law are published in the general law journals such as the *Modern Law Review* and the *Law Quarterly Review*. In addition to these sources, a wide range of relevant material is accessible on the internet from government bodies and other organisations.

## Institutions

**1.10** When studying labour law, it is essential to have knowledge of the key institutions (and, to some extent, the personnel working within them) comprising the institutional framework of the subject. The following section outlines these key institutions.

### Advisory, Conciliation and Arbitration Service

**1.11** The Advisory, Conciliation and Arbitration Service (ACAS) is a key organisation in labour law. It was established in 1974, and received statutory status under the Employment Protection Act 1975 (EPA 1975), although the main statutory provisions relating to ACAS are now contained within the Trade Union and Labour Relations (Consolidation) Act 1992 (TULRCA 1992). It has a head office in London and regional offices around the country, with offices in Scotland and Wales. It is an independent organisation and not a government body, although it receives government funding, since its functions are carried out on behalf of the Crown (see TULRCA 1992, s 247(3)), and it has close links with the Department for Trade and Industry. It has the general duty 'to promote the improvement of industrial relations' (TULRCA 1992, s 209). Its constitution is specified in TULRCA 1992, ss 247–253: it is governed by a council, chaired by an appointee of the Secretary of State for Trade and Industry, with a tripartite structure: it has nine members in total, three representing employers, three representing trade unions, and three independent members.

### ADVICE – ACAS

**1.12** ACAS' advisory function is one of the most important aspects of its work, providing free advice on a wide range of employment matters by way, inter alia, of telephone helplines and publications. It also publishes advisory handbooks (for example, *Discipline at Work*) and booklets and organises training events and seminars.

## CONCILIATION – ACAS

**1.13** Conciliation is a way of resolving disputes without recourse to law. It involves bringing together the parties in dispute to help them reach an agreement by themselves. ACAS provides both individual and collective conciliation: on the individual level, it offers a conciliation service through its Conciliation Officers to employees in dispute with their employer or former employer, as is the case in unfair dismissal claims (the vast majority of employment tribunal applications are referred to a Conciliation Officer who seeks to explore whether the dispute may be settled without the need for a tribunal hearing); on the collective level, ACAS offers a voluntary channel by which the parties (an employer and one or more trade unions) may resolve their dispute. Under TULRCA 1992, s 210, ACAS has the right to offer its conciliation services to the parties, or the parties may request them.

## ARBITRATION – ACAS

**1.14** Arbitration is a voluntary process at the collective level whereby the parties to a dispute agree to submit to the decision of an arbitrator, although the decision itself is not legally binding (it is expected, however, that having agreed to submit to this process, the parties will observe the terms of any decision arising from it). Under TULRCA 1992, s 212, 'Where a trade dispute exists or is apprehended ACAS may, at the request of one or more of the parties to the dispute and with the consent of all the parties to the dispute,' refer the matters in dispute to arbitration. Arbitration should be considered by ACAS only after consideration has been given to whether conciliation or negotiation could resolve the dispute (these should be attempted before arbitration is offered). Arbitration is carried out through the Central Arbitration Committee (see below) or by an arbitrator selected from a panel of names kept by ACAS.

**1.15**  Under the Employment Rights (Dispute Resolution) Act 1998, a new section was inserted in TULRCA 1992, s 212A which allowed ACAS to introduce a new voluntary arbitration scheme for certain *individual* disputes and, in 2001, ACAS introduced such a scheme for unfair dismissal disputes. This was intended to be speedier and less legalistic than going to the employment tribunal, and the hearing is held in private. However, the parties must waive their rights to have their case heard by an employment tribunal, and they must agree in writing to this process. However, there are severe limitations to the scheme: first, only disputes concerning whether the dismissal was unfair may be arbitrated in this way, ie if other issues arise, such as whether there was a dismissal in the first place, or whether the applicant qualified to make such a claim, the scheme cannot be used; second, there is no appeal from the arbitrator's decision; third, arbitrators do not have to pay regard to legal principles, but rather to general principles of fairness, which may lead to uncertainty and a lack of trust in the whole process.

## CODES OF PRACTICE – ACAS

**1.16**  ACAS has power to issue codes of practice giving practical guidance 'for the purpose of promoting the improvement of industrial relations' (TULRCA 1992, s 199). These codes are not legally binding but they may be taken into account by Employment Tribunals (TULRCA 1992, s 207). ACAS has issued the following very important and useful codes of practice on: Disciplinary and Grievance Procedures; Disclosure of Information to Trade Unions for Collective Bargaining Purposes; and Time Off for Union Duties and Activities.

### Central Arbitration Committee

**1.17**  The Central Arbitration Committee (CAC) was established in 1975 under the Employment Protection Act 1975, although the relevant statutory provisions are now contained in TULRCA 1992, ss 259–265. It comprises ten members appointed by the Secretary of State for Trade and Industry, with a chair and a number of deputy chairs. Originally, the CAC's main roles were: (i) to provide arbitration in collective disputes referred to it by ACAS under TULRCA 1992, s 212(1)(b); and (ii) in relation to disputes where trade unions complained that an employer had failed to disclose information required for collective bargaining or selection for redundancy purposes. However, since 6 June 2000 when the Employment Relations Act 1999, s 25 came into force, the CAC's most important role concerns the compulsory recognition procedure concerning recognition of trade unions by employers for collective bargaining purposes, as set out in TULRCA 1992, Sch A1. This is considered further in Chapter 10.

## Certification Officer

**1.18**  The office of Certification Officer (CO) was created in 1975. The office is now governed by TULRCA 1992, s 254. The CO is appointed by the Secretary of State after consultation with ACAS. One of the CO's main roles is to decide whether a trade union is independent, ie not associated with employers or employers' associations (see TULRCA 1992, s 5). If it is independent, the CO will issue a certificate of independence, from which a number of important things flow. For example, only members of an independent trade union are protected in law from dismissal or a detriment on grounds of their union activities. Among other duties of the CO is the maintenance of a list of independent trade unions, keeping records of the membership and financial returns of trade unions, and keeping copies of union rules. The CO also has powers, inter alia, to adjudicate complaints relating to the election of trade union officials, and complaints concerning political expenditure by unions.

## Discrimination Commissions – the Equal Opportunities Commission, the Commission for Racial Equality, and the Disability Rights Commission

**1.19**  There are currently three commissions in the field of discrimination law: the Equal Opportunities Commission (EOC); the Commission on Racial Equality (CRE); and the Disability Rights Commission (DRC). The EOC covers sex discrimination and equal pay, the CRE deals with race discrimination and the DRC covers disability discrimination. Recently, the idea of having three separate commissions covering discrimination law has been reviewed, and the Government proposed a single commission in a White Paper of May 2004 (*Fairness for all: a New Commission for Equality and Human Rights*: Cm 6185). The White Paper proposes that the new body would be called the Commission for Equality and Human Rights. The EOC, CRE and DRC would be merged into this Commission, which would also promote human rights and have responsibility for the operation of the new equality regulations on religion or belief and sexual orientation. There is also pressure on the Government to create a single discrimination statute, instead of the three main discrimination statutes.

## EQUAL OPPORTUNITIES COMMISSION (EOC) AND THE COMMISSION FOR RACIAL EQUALITY (CRE)

**1.20** These two Commissions were established under the Sex Discrimination Act 1975 (SDA 1975), s 53 and the Race Relations Act 1976 (RRA 1976) respectively. They have similar powers and duties under both statutes, so it is appropriate to take them together in this discussion. Both have a statutory duty to work towards the elimination of discrimination and to promote equal opportunities. They also have a duty to keep the working of the relevant legislation under review, ie the SDA 1975 and the Equal Pay Act 1970 (EqPA 1970) in the case of the EOC, and the RRA 1976 in the case of the CRE, and to make proposals to the Secretary of State for amending them (SDA 1975, s 53; RRA 1976, s 43). They have numerous other functions, one of which is to provide advice and legal aid to individuals who have cause for complaint concerning discrimination. They will provide legal aid if a question of principle is involved or the case is too complex for the applicant to deal with it unaided (SDA 1975, s 75; RRA 1976, s 66). This is a vitally important part of their functions, not least because legal aid is not available in the Employment Tribunals. They may also undertake and/or fund research and educational activities (SDA 1975, s 54; RRA 1976, s 45). They may issue codes of practice (SDA 1975, s 56A; RRA 1976, s 47), and have done so (for the EOC, see the Codes of Practice on Sex Discrimination, Equal Opportunity Policies, Procedures and Practices in Employment (1985); and the Code of Practice on Equal Pay (1997), and for the RRA 1976, see the Code of Practice for the elimination of racial discrimination (1983); and the Code of Practice on the Duty to Promote Racial Equality (2002)). These codes do not have statutory force but they are admissible in evidence and may be taken into account by tribunals and courts in determining any question under the relevant statutes, ie the SDA 1975 and the EqPA 1970 (SDA 1975, s 56A(10)); RRA 1976, s 47(10).

## FORMAL INVESTIGATIONS

**1.21**  The EOC and the CRE also have the power to conduct a formal investigation 'for any purpose connected with the carrying out of (((its) duties', (SDA 1975, s 57(1); RRA 1976, s 48(1)), but only where they have reasonable suspicion that unlawful acts of discrimination are taking place (see *Prestige Group plc, Re, Commission For Racial Equality v Prestige Group plc* (1984), a case on a CRE investigation under the RRA 1976). Formal investigations must be conducted under the provisions of the relevant regulations, ie the Sex Discrimination (Formal Investigations) Regulations 1975, SI 1975/1993, and the Race Relations (Formal Investigations) Regulations 1975, SI 1977/841. If, following a formal investigation, the EOC or the CRE become satisfied that a person is committing or has committed, inter alia, any unlawful discriminatory acts or practices, they may issue a non-discrimination notice to employers (SDA 1975, s 67; RRA 1976, s 58(2)). The notice may require the person not to commit any such acts and, where this involves changes in any practices or arrangements, to inform the EOC/CRE that he has effected such changes and what they are (SDA 1975, s 67(2); RRA 1976, s 58(2)). A person may appeal against any requirement of the notice (SDA 1975, s 68; RRA 1976, s 59).

## DISCRIMINATORY ADVERTISEMENTS

**1.22**  It is unlawful to publish discriminatory advertisements (SDA 1975, s 38; RRA 1976, s 29), and the EOC/CRE have the power to prosecute both the publisher and the person who placed the advertisement, provided they did so knowingly or recklessly (SDA 1975, s 72; RRA 1976, s 63).

## USEFUL WEBSITES

**1.23**  Both the EOC and the CRE have user-friendly Websites containing a wealth of information. They are a useful research tool and well worth looking up. Their addresses are: for the CRE – www.cre.gov.uk, and for the EOC – www.eoc.org.uk.

## THE DISABILITY RIGHTS COMMISSION

**1.24** The Disability Rights Commission (DRC) was established under the Disability Rights Commission Act 1999 (DRCA 1999). The DRCA abolished the National Disability Council (NDC) which was set up under the Disability Discrimination Act 1995 (DDA 1995), the NDC being a body without enforcement or investigatory powers, unlike the EOC and the CRE. Its powers and duties mirror to some extent those of the other two Commissions, but they are by no means exactly the same. From its creation on 25 April 2000 the DRC's main duties have been to work towards eliminating discrimination against disabled people; to promote equal opportunities for disabled people; to keep the DDA 1995 under review; to provide information and advice to disabled people, employers and service providers. It has the power to issue codes of practice (DDA 1995, s 53A) and to support individuals seeking to enforce their rights (DRCA 1999, s 7). It has similar powers to the other two Commissions in terms of conducting investigations and issuing non-discrimination notices (DRCA 1999, ss 3, 4).

**1.25** One of the differences between the DRC and the other two Commissions is that the DRC has the power to refrain from taking enforcement action if the discriminator agrees to enter into a legally binding agreement not to commit any further unlawful acts and to take the action specified in the agreement (DRCA 1999, s 5). Another point of divergence is that, unlike the EOC and the CRE, the DRC currently has no power in relation to taking action concerning discriminatory advertisements (ie placing of which is not in itself unlawful under the DDA 1995), there being a power given to individuals to enforce their rights under the DDA 1995, ss 8 and 11. However, upon the coming into force of the DDA 1995 (Amendment) Regulations 2003, SI 2003/1673 (the Amendment Regs) on 1 October 2004, it will be unlawful to place a discriminatory advertisement, and the DRC will have the exclusive power of enforcement (see the Amendment Regs, regs 15 and 16; DDA 1995, ss 16B, 17B)(1)).

## International Labour Organisation

**1.26** The International Labour Organisation (ILO) was created by the League of Nations under the Treaty of Versailles in 1919, although it is now a specialised agency with links to the United Nations. It has a tripartite structure, comprising representatives of employees, employers, and governments. It is a significant organisation in the field of labour law in that it seeks to promote the improvement of international labour standards by the adoption of fair working conditions through the Member States (MS) ratifying its Conventions (ie treaties). It also issues Recommendations. It has numerous Conventions, for example ILO Convention (No. 87) on freedom of association and protection of the right to organise (1948), and ILO Convention (No. 98) on the right to organise and collective bargaining (1949). Once a MS ratifies an ILO Convention, the normal obligations of international law apply, ie the MS has a duty to change its national law to ensure compliance with its international law obligations. It is possible for a MS to withdraw from its obligations under a Convention by denouncing it (a formal process whereby the MS gives notice, after which it is no longer bound by it). One of the weaknesses of the ILO Conventions is that there is no enforcement body to ensure a MS's compliance with any ILO Conventions. It is worth noting that ILO Convention No. 100 (1951) on equal pay for work of equal value was the precursor to our Equal Pay Act 1970 and to Art 141 (former Art 119) of the EC Treaty.

## Employment Tribunals

### INTRODUCTION

**1.27** Employment tribunals (ETs) were called industrial tribunals until 1 August 1998, when their name was changed under the Employment Rights (Dispute Resolution) Act 1998. They were first established under the Industrial Training Act 1964 to consider employers' appeals against training levies, and their jurisdiction was extended under the Redundancy Payments Act 1965 to consider claims relating to redundancy payments. However, their workload has increased massively since 1972, when they were given jurisdiction in unfair dismissal claims, which account for a large part of their workload. Their jurisdiction covers both English and Scots law, as well as EU law.

**1.28** Their jurisdiction extends, inter alia, to claims relating to: discrimination (ie sex, race, disability, sexual orientation, religion or belief and, from October 2006, age discrimination) and equal pay; breach of contract claims arising out of or outstanding upon the termination of the employment relationship (up to £25,000); redundancy payments; unlawful deductions from wages; working time; the national minimum wage; infringement of the rights of part-time workers and fixed-term employees. They also have jurisdiction across a wide range of other matters, for example, claims concerning a right to: written particulars of employment; guarantee payments; time off for public duties; written reasons for dismissal; and maternity, paternity, parental and adoption leave.

**1.29** The Annual Report of the Employment Tribunals Service (the ETS Report) reported that in the year 2002–2003 there were approximately 100,000 applications to the ET, of which approximately 26% were for unfair dismissal. Unlawful deductions from wages claims accounted for 23% of applications, while breach of contract and discrimination claims comprised 17% and 12% of applications respectively. It should be noted that not all applications reach the hearing stage: the ETS Report recorded that, in the year 2002–2003, 39% were settled with the assistance of an ACAS conciliator (see below), 31% were withdrawn, 13% were successful at the hearing, 11% were unsuccessful and 6% were 'disposed of otherwise'.

**1.30** Although ET decisions do not create precedent, ETs are important as the first-instance forum in which an enormous range of employment-related matters are adjudicated. However, they are not courts of law, and they cannot enforce their orders: the successful party must take enforcement proceedings in the County Court. Originally, they were seen as a way of providing speedy, accessible, and relatively inexpensive resolutions of disputes, without the need for legal representation of the parties, in a hearing relatively free of the formal, legalistic approach of the courts. Despite this, over the years ETs have become rather more formal, with rules of procedure etc. Legal representation of the parties is a feature of many hearings. The latter development could be explained by the fact that labour law has both proliferated and become increasingly complex over the years. However, they are still fairly inexpensive when compared to the cost of litigation in the ordinary civil courts, and hearings usually come on within a reasonably short time when compared to the listing times for cases in the courts: the ETS Report states that 74% of applications are heard within six months of the application being lodged. Many are heard within three to four months of this date.

## CONSTITUTION AND COMPOSITION OF ETS

**1.31** The primary legislation governing ETs is the Employment Tribunals Act 1996 (ETA), although their constitution and rules of procedure are contained in the Employment Tribunals (Constitution and Rules of Procedure) Regulations 2004 (SI 2004/1861) (the ET Regulations), in force from 1 October 2004. ETs consist of a three-member panel, ie a legally-qualified Chairman, and two lay members (sometimes called 'wing members'), who are not legally qualified. The Chairman, who is appointed by the Lord Chancellor as either full-time or part-time, must be a barrister or solicitor of at least seven years' standing, while the lay members (who are all part-time) are chosen after consulting organisations representing employees and those representing employers. This means that the lay members have experience of each side of industry, ie management and labour, and together provide what is sometimes called an 'industrial jury'.

**1.32** A challenge was mounted recently (see *Smith v Secretary of State for Trade and Industry* (2000)) against the composition of ETs and the method of appointment of lay members under the Human Rights Act 1998 (HRA 1998), arguing that these breached Article 6 of the European Convention on Human Rights (the Convention), which confers a right to a fair and public hearing before an independent and impartial tribunal in the determination of civil rights. As lay members are paid by the Department for Trade and Industry (DTI), the argument was that ETs did not have jurisdiction in cases where the DTI was one of the parties. The EAT in *Smith* did not reach a conclusion on this claim, but gave permission to appeal to the Court of Appeal (CA) (no appeal was made).

**1.33** However, following subsequent changes to the method of appointment of part-time Chairmen and lay members in 2000, which mean that all such appointments are for a fixed term, renewable automatically except on specified grounds, the Employment Appeal

Tribunal (EAT) has stated that these are sufficient to ensure the independence of lay members, so there is no breach of Article 6 of the Convention (see *Scanfuture UK Ltd v Secretary of State for Trade and Industry* (2001).

**1.34** Where there is a three-member panel, ET decisions are by a majority, which means that lay members may out-vote the Chairman, although an ET may sit with only one lay member where both or all parties agree, in which case the Chairman has the casting vote. Some ET proceedings may be heard by a Chairman sitting alone in certain circumstances, for example where both or all parties have given their written consent to this, in breach of contract claims and on certain interlocutory matters.

## ADMINISTRATION OF EMPLOYMENT TRIBUNALS

**1.35** The President of the Employment Tribunals (a judicial officer appointed by the Lord Chancellor) is responsible for their running, assisted by a Central Office of Employment Tribunals (COET) in London (there is also one in Glasgow for Scotland, with a President of Employment Tribunals for Scotland) which keeps a public register of all ET applications and decisions. The system is divided into regions, with a number of Regional Offices of Employment Tribunals (ROETs), each with a Regional Chairman, and ETs sit at these regional centres and at a number of permanent centres. Applications are lodged at the appropriate local ET.

**1.36** The Employment Tribunal Service (ETS), which is part of the DTI, has responsibility for the overall administration of ETs. It has a Director appointed by, and who reports to, the Secretary of State for Trade and Industry.

## PROCEDURE

**1.37** Only an outline of the procedure of the ETs can be given here. Essentially, ETs have an overriding objective which is 'to deal with cases justly'. This means dealing with cases, 'so far as practicable', so as to ensure that the parties are on an equal footing, saving expense (legal aid is not available in ETs), dealing with cases in ways proportionate to their complexity, and ensuring that they are dealt with expeditiously and fairly. There is no requirement to use any special form to commence proceedings in the ET, although there is a standard form which may be lodged as the originating application within the relevant time limit. In unfair dismissal and discrimination cases, for example, this is three months, whereas it is six months in redundancy payments claims and equal pay claims. The ET has discretion to extend this limit.

**1.38** ETs have the power to strike out a 'misconceived' claim (or defence – known as the Notice of Appearance). This is defined as those with 'no reasonable prospect of success'. The idea is that hopeless claims are not allowed to proceed to the hearing. Similarly, it may strike out 'scandalous …or vexatious' claims. A copy of the claim is sent to the respondent employer, together with the response form on which the respondent may set out its response, which must be made within 21 days, although the ET may extend this limit where it was not reasonably practicable to respond in the time stipulated. A copy of the claim is also sent to ACAS, with a view to possible settlement before the hearing with the assistance of an ACAS conciliation officer.

**1.39** ETs may make orders for discovery (or disclosure as it is now called under the Civil Procedure Rules (CPR)) and/or inspection of documents, further particulars of the claim or the notice of appearance, or to provide written answers to any question. They may also order a pre-hearing review (PHR), either on the application of one of the parties, or of their own motion, where it appears that an aspect of the claim or defence is unlikely to succeed. PHRs may be heard by a Chairman sitting alone. Where the ET decides that the aspect of the claim in question is unlikely to succeed, it can impose a condition that a party pays a deposit of up to £500 within 21 days before being allowed to continue with the proceedings. Further, the party upon whom such a condition is imposed is warned that an order for costs could be made against them at the full hearing, together with forfeiture of the deposit.

## THE HEARING

**1.40** Although ETs are allowed to regulate their own procedure, their proceedings tend to be quite formal, akin to civil court proceedings. If possible, the parties should agree in advance of the hearing the documents to be used before the ET, usually contained within a Bundle of Documents, for ease of reference. The party with the burden of proof starts, eg in an unfair dismissal case where the employer accepts that a dismissal has taken place, this will be the employer. However, in a constructive unfair dismissal case, where the fact of dismissal is in dispute, it is the employee who starts. Witnesses give evidence on oath and undergo examination-in-chief and cross-examination. When all witnesses have given their evidence, closing submissions are made by each side, and the ET retires to consider its decision.

**1.41** The ET may reserve its decision until a later date or give its decision orally at the conclusion of the hearing, with the written decision setting out summary reasons being sent out some time later. However, the parties may request full written reasons either at the hearing or within 21 days of dispatch of the summary reasons. In discrimination and equal pay cases, full written reasons are provided.

## Costs

**1.42** Although costs are not normally awarded by the ET, it does have power to make a costs order against a party (or a party's representative) where in bringing the proceedings the party or the representative has 'acted vexatiously, abusively, disruptively or otherwise unreasonably, or the bringing or conducting of the proceedings by a party has been misconceived', up to a maximum of £10,000 (rule 14). The ETS Report states that, in the year ended 31 March 2002, ETs awarded costs in 636 cases, comprising 169 awards to the employee and 467 awards to the employer. The average costs award was £983.

**1.43** ETs may review their decisions, either of their own motion or upon the application of a party within 14 days of promulgation. There are very limited grounds for review, eg a clerical error, or that the decision was made in the absence of one party. An appeal may be made to the Employment Appeal Tribunal on a point of law within six seeks of the promulgation of the decision.

### Employment Appeal Tribunal

**1.44** The Employment Appeal Tribunal (EAT) was established in 1975 under the Employment Protection Act 1975 (EPA 1975), although it is now regulated by the ETA and regulations made thereunder. As stated in para. 1.28, it hears appeals from the ETs on points of law (not fact). A President is appointed for a term of three years from the ranks of High Court judges. Its composition is similar to that of ETs, in that it has two lay members drawn from employers and employees organisations (although these tend to be fairly senior members with wide experience, compared to lay members of the ET), but the Chairman is a High Court judge or circuit judge. Part-time recorders who also appear as counsel in the EAT are not allowed to sit as Chairmen of the EAT following the House of Lords in *Lawal v Northern Spirit Ltd* (2003) that this practice tended to undermine public confidence in the judicial system. As in the ET, the judge may be outvoted by the lay members. A judge sitting alone in the EAT may hear appeals from a single-member ET (EPA 1975, s 28(4)), and the EAT may consist of the Chairman and one lay member where the parties agree to this. Unlike the ET, legal aid is available in the EAT. As appeals are made to the EAT on points of law, it is much more usual for the parties to have legal representation in this forum. Although proceedings are not quite as formal or legalistic as in the High Court, they are more formal than in the ETs.

**1.45** The EAT is a court of record and, as such, its decisions must be followed by ETs and inferior courts. However, different divisions of the EAT are not obliged to follow their own decisions, which can lead to confusion at ET level about what is the correct legal analysis to be applied. The English EAT sits in London (the Scottish EAT sits in Edinburgh). Appeals from the EAT are to the Court of Appeal and then to the House of Lords.

## Court of Appeal and House of Lords

**1.46** Once a case is appealed from the EAT to the Court of Appeal and beyond, it leaves the specialist tribunals set up to deal with labour law matters and moves into the ordinary civil court system. Clearly, cases reaching these higher courts are of wider public interest and, in appeals to the House of Lords, they must concern a matter of public importance.

## European Court of Justice

**1.47** The European Court of Justice (ECJ) has been immensely significant in the development of labour law within the UK, particularly in the field of sex discrimination and equal pay. Any court or tribunal, including ETs, from within the jurisdiction may refer a case to the ECJ under Article 234 for a ruling on the correct interpretation of EU law, or on its applicability within the domestic legal system. Although this topic is dealt with in more detail in Chapter 2, it should be noted here that the ECJ's rulings on, for example, whether directives have been correctly implemented by the Member States, or whether English labour law complies with our obligations under EU law, have been immensely significant in the field of labour law. The ECJ does not decide the issue before the domestic court or tribunal; it simply provides a ruling on the questions put to it by the domestic court, and it is for that court to decide the matter in the light of the ruling given by the ECJ.

## Low Pay Commission

**1.48** The Low Pay Commission (LPC) was set up in May 1997, although it was given statutory status by the National Minimum Wage Act 1998 (NMWA 1998), s 8, which came into force on 1 November 1998. Its main functions are (i) to monitor the national minimum wage (NMW) and evaluate its impact and (ii) to make recommendations to the Government on changes of rates. With reference to (i) above, it carries out this function with particular reference to: the effect on pay, employment and competitiveness in low-paying sectors of the economy and small firms; the effect of the NMW on different groups of workers; the effect on pay structures; and the interaction between the NMW and the tax and benefit systems. With reference to (ii) above, the LPC must consult such people and organisations as it thinks fit before making any recommendations. The LPC's recommendations, including the setting of NMW rates, are generally accepted by the Government but they are not always: in 2001 and 2002 the LPC recommended that the adult rate be paid to 21 year olds, but the Government rejected this recommendation on both occasions.

# Ideologies

**1.49** Labour law may be seen, at its simplest, as the legal rules regulating the workplace, but it may also be seen in a wider context: as *Deakin and Morris* (2001), p 1, comment:

> ... a broader perspective would see labour law as the normative framework for the existence and operation of all the institutions of the labour market: the business enterprise, trade unions, employers' associations and, in its capacity as regulator and as employer, the state.

**1.50** A number of ideologies have been used to analyse this field. For example, one way of viewing labour law is to see it through the *conflictual* model, ie as a struggle between labour and capital (a broadly Marxist approach), while the theories of the current Labour Government underpin a 'partnership' approach to the subject (the *consensual* model), ie management and labour working together, the so-called 'third way', which is essentially an attempt to improve labour standards (including an encouragement to trade union recognition in the workplace) while maintaining a 'flexible and efficient labour market' (see the White Paper, *Fairness at Work*, Cmnd 3968, para 1.8). The 'labour *versus* capital' analysis of labour law is what is being described by *Collins, Ewing and McColgan* (2001), p 1, in the following passage:

> From a political perspective the employment relation lies at the centre of a fundamental conflict of interest that is intrinsic to capitalist societies. The conflict lies between the owners of capital, who invest in productive activities, and the workers, who supply the necessary labour. Employers seek to maximise the return on their investments, whereas the workers seek the highest price available for their labour, which digs into the employer's profits. As in other contractual relations, however, the parties ultimately share a common interest in the successful achievement of production and profits through the combination of capital and labour.

**1.51** Another way of analysing labour law is to see it as a balance between regulation and de-regulation, the former often associated with governments of the political left, the latter with Conservative administrations, such as that of former Prime Ministers Thatcher and Major in the 1980s and much of the 1990s. These approaches are a reflection of a deeper ideological debate on the labour market between, on the one hand, those holding the interventionists' stance and, on the other, those adhering to the abstentionists' (or non-interventionists') point of view (a classic example of the latter being the laissez-faire approach taken in the nineteenth century). The interplay of these approaches has been one of the characteristic features of labour law over the last few decades.

**1.52** There are many other ways of analysing labour law. For example, it could be seen as the conflict between collectivist and individualistic approaches, ie between securing what is best for the majority of workers on the one hand, and ensuring the protection and enhancement of the rights of individual employees (as against the majority) on the other. It may also be subjected to a purely economic analysis, ie as an economic transaction between a worker and the employer. In this analysis, labour is simply a unit of production, to be bought and sold, and with a market value: this is to view labour as a commodity. This approach is fundamentally opposed to those who argue that workers have innate human rights, which is not reflected in the economic theory in which they are simply a commodity (for an argument supporting this viewpoint, see P. O'Higgins, 'Labour is not a commodity', (1997) 26 *Industrial Law Journal* 225)). Yet another approach would be to analyse labour law from the feminist perspective. This argues that labour law is gender-biased in that it is the product of largely male-dominated institutions such as the courts, tribunals and Parliament. This perspective suggests that labour law fails adequately to represent, protect or advance the interests of women (for an interesting text using this approach, see A. Morris and T. O'Donnell, *Feminist Perspectives on Employment Law* (1999)).

**1.53** It will be seen from the above summary that the study of labour law will be enriched if one keeps in mind the various ideologies that may be employed to analyse this area of the law.

## Sources of Labour Law

**1.54** The sources of labour law are essentially legislation and case-law. In terms of legislation, there is, at the national level, a body of both primary and secondary legislation comprising the statutory regulation of this area of law. At the European Union level, there are Treaty provisions, Directives and Regulations regulating the labour law of the Member States. At the international level, there are, for example, ILO Conventions which the signatory states are expected to observe. The case-law from both national courts and the ECJ is important in terms of the interpretation of this legislation. Case-law is also important in that the employment relationship is based upon the contract of employment, so contract principles derived from the case-law form an important part of the subject. In labour law, the main sources of law derived from cases come from the decisions of the EAT, High Court, Court of Appeal and House of Lords at domestic level, and the decisions of the ECJ and the European Court of Human Rights (ECHR) at the European level.

**1.55**  In addition to these two main sources of labour law there is a range of less formal 'sources', in the sense that these may have an influence on how the formal law is interpreted, applied and changed. These informal sources include: the Codes of Practice and reports issued by the EOC, CRE, DRC and the Health and Safety Executive; EU Commission Recommendations; the Social Policy Agenda and the Social dialogue at EU level (see Chapter 2 for a discussion of this area); and ILO Recommendations. At the workplace level, informal, *voluntary* sources of law include collective and workforce agreements, works rules (ie the workplace rules, often contained in rule books or handbooks, issued by management to employees), and internal codes of practice and policies adopted by individual employers. However, although these sources form the 'core' of the subject, there is a whole raft of 'soft law' that may act as a source of law.

**1.56**  Students of labour law should be aware of these formal and informal sources of law, and of their interplay at the various levels, eg workplace, national, European and international.

## Key Legislation

**1.57**  Students of labour law should have knowledge of the centrally important provisions contained in the key legislation which form the legislative backbone of the subject. The primary legislation is the main focus of this section, although secondary legislation, mainly in the form of statutory instruments, forms an important part of the regulation in this area. In the sphere of individual labour law, the Employment Rights Act 1996 is the primary legislation regulating, inter alia, the law relating to: unfair dismissal; redundancy; notice rights; protection of wages; 'whistle-blowing'; time off work; and maternity, adoption and parental leave. At the collective level, the Trade Union and Labour Relations (Consolidation) Act 1992 concerns, inter alia, the law governing trade unions, their relationship with their members and employers, industrial action, and collective bargaining, including the important area of the statutory recognition of trade unions contained in Schedule A1 of the Act. Certain aspects of wages have been regulated by the National Minimum Wage Act 1998, which stipulates the minimum wage for certain categories of worker in any pay reference period.

**1.58** Other important secondary legislation includes: the Transfer of Undertakings (Protection of Employment) Regulations 1981 (SI 1981/1794) (TUPE), which safeguard certain employment rights upon the transfer of a business (or part of a business) as a going concern – these Regulations were supposed to implement the Acquired Rights Directive (Directive 77/187/EC) (the ARD); the Working Time Regulations 1998 (SI 1998/1833), which regulate working time, daily and weekly rest periods and rest breaks, annual leave, and night work – these Regulations implement the Working Time Directive (Directive 93/104/EC, which was amended by Directive 2000/34/EC – the 'Horizontal Amending Directive': the original Directive 93/104/EC is soon to be consolidated by Directive 2003/88/EC, in force from 2 August 2004) (the WTD); and the National Minimum Wage Regulations 1999 (SI 1999/584), which contain detailed provisions concerning the minimum wage.

**1.59** In the field of discrimination law, the key statutes are the Sex Discrimination Act 1975, the Race Relations Act 1976, and the Disability Discrimination Act 1995, covering sex, race and disability discrimination respectively. It should be noted that these statutes regulate a wider area than labour law as they include the provision of goods, services and facilities. Generally, the student of labour law need only concentrate on the employment parts of these statutes. The Equal Pay Act 1970 should be considered alongside the SDA 1975 in any study of sex discrimination law, as this statute concerns the elimination of sex discrimination from pay structures. Important (and recent) secondary legislation in the discrimination field are the Employment Equality Regulations. There are two sets of these: the Employment Equality (Religion or Belief) Regulations 2003 (SI 2003/1660), and the Employment Equality (Sexual Orientation) Regulations 2003 (SI 2003/1661), which implement part of the Equal Treatment Framework Directive (Directive 2000/78).

**1.60** Other important pieces of legislation in labour law are: the Health and Safety at Work etc Act 1974; the Human Rights Act 1998; and the various Employment Acts.

**1.61** At EU level, Article 141 (former Article 119) of the Treaty, the provision concerning equal pay for equal work or work of equal value, has been immensely significant in the development of equal pay law at the domestic level. Furthermore, several Directives have been centrally important in domestic law, eg:

- the Equal Treatment Directive (Directive 76/207/EC); (the ETD);

- the Equal Pay Directive (Directive 75/117/EC) (the EPD);

- the Parental Leave Directive (Directive 96/34/EC) (the PLD) ;

- the Part Time Workers Directive (Directive 98/2) (the PTWD);

- the ARD and WTD (mentioned above at 1.54);

- the Fixed-Term Contracts Directive (Directive 99/70) (the FTCD);

- the Equal Treatment Framework Directive (Directive 2000/78) (the ETFD).

**1.62** It will be seen from the above list that EU law has had a major influence on the development of many aspects of domestic labour law. A detailed consideration of this aspect of the subject is contained in Chapter 2.

## Further reading

Deakin, S, & Morris, G, *Labour Law* (3rd ed, 2001) Butterworths (chapters 1 & 2). 102–126.

Smith, I, & Thomas, G, *Industrial Law* (8th ed, 2003) Butterworths (chapter 1).

*Articles*

Earnshaw, J, & Hardy, S, (2001) 'Assessing an Arbitral Route for Unfair Dismissal', *Industrial Law Journal*, Vol. 30, No. 3, September, pp. 289–304.

McKay, S, (2001) 'Dispute resolution: Shifting the focus from tribunals to the workplace', *Industrial Law Journal*, Vol 30, No 3, September, pp. 331–333.

Craig, V, (2001) 'Employment Tribunals and the Human Rights Act: Part 1', *Employment Law Bulletin*, No 44 (August), pp. 2–4.

Craig, V, (2001) 'Employment Tribunals and the Human Rights Act: Part 2', *Employment Law Bulletin*, No 45 (October), pp. 2–4.

www.dti.gov.uk/er

www.acas.org.uk

www.eoc.org.uk

www.cre.org.uk

www.drc.org.uk

## Self-test questions

1.  What are the major employment law institutions in the UK? What powers do they have?

2.  Evaluate the role played by the EOC, CRE and DRC in employment law? What reforms lie ahead for these bodies?

3.  List the sources of employment law and explain how each influences its development.

4.  'ACAS offers more effective alternative methods to employment tribunals in terms of dispute resolution, but employers and employees alike still prefer a tribunal hearing.' Discuss.

# CHAPTER TWO

# The European Dimension

## Summary

This chapter considers the role and influence of European social law and policy on UK labour law. Furthermore, it examines the origins of EU input, its development and its content, as well as its overall impact on UK law and practice. In addition, the EU's pervasive influence is examined and its application evaluated. EU remedies and state liability, such as Francovich actions, are explained. The interface of EU law with human rights is also considered.

The key points in this chapter are:

- EU labour law is the result of a long historical path in which the point of departure was the Treaty of Rome;

- the Treaty of Rome established in its modest Articles 117–118, that the pursuit of economic objectives would carry as an automatic consequence an improvement in the quality of life and of work for workers;

- European legislation on social rights is now the great artifice of community social law;

- the importance of jurisprudence of the Court of Justice as social law enforcer; and

- the European Social Model now covers a wide range of both living and working issues, such as social protection, health, education and environmental issues, public services, as well as

> all aspects of employment rights, social dialogue, direct partici-
> pation, training and non-discrimination issues.

## Origins of the EU dimension

**2.1**  The European Economic Community (EEC) was formed as a result of the Spaak Report and established under the Treaty of Rome in 1957. The Treaty of Rome, as the foundational Treaty of the EU, sought to be the vehicle for economic integration. As the Treaty noted, its aim was to 'lay the foundations of an ever closer union among the peoples of Europe'. The Treaty of Rome observed the Monnet and Schumann view that economic integration will spill-over into political and social union.

### Foundation Treaty

**2.2**   Whilst the Treaty of Rome did not initially expound much social integration, it did have a Title on Social Policy, contained originally in Article 117 (now the heavily amended Article 136). Article 117 sought to 'promote improved working conditions and standards of living of workers'. The Spaak report relied for direction on social policy upon the Ohlin Report of ILO experts of 1956 which argued for transnational harmonisation, favouring economic flexibility above social protection. However, Spaak remained concerned about market distortion, which social policy should act to eliminate.

**2.3**  Articles 136–141 (previously Articles 118–121) provide that the Community may perform social action, by setting down directives adopted by special majority, in the fields of workers' health and safety, working conditions, the integration of those excluded from the labour market, of information and consultation of workers and equality for men and women. Matters relating to pay, the right of association, the right to strike and the right to impose lock-outs are still excluded from the provisions of Article 137. In contrast, Article 136, which refers to 'the Community and the Member States, having in mind fundamental social rights such as those set out in the European Charter of 1961 and in the 1989 Community Charter of Fundamental Social Rights', provides for extensive collective rights, including the rights of association and to strike. On the other hand, in *Kortner (C-175/73)* the Court has recognized freedom of association to be a fundamental right and in *Albany (C-67/96)* the Advocate-General suggested that the collective right to take action was a fundamental right.

## Free movement of workers

**2.4**  The modest origins of European labour law, which impacts upon all the EU Member States, arises from the Foundation Treaty's provisions on free movement of workers, guaranteed by Articles 39–42, which establish the principle that workers should enjoy the right to freedom of movement including the abolition of any discrimination based on nationality, as regards employment remuneration and any other conditions of work or employment. However, central to all the rights guaranteed under the fundamental freedom of movement is the key term 'worker', which is not defined by the Treaty or any other European legislation. Consequently, the European Court of Justice has interpreted this salient term: *Hoekstra (75/63)* defined the term 'worker' to also include job-seekers; *Levin (53/81)* and *Kempf (139/85)* accepted part-time workers; *Steymann (196/87)* noted that workers need not necessarily receive formal wages; and, *Bettray (344/87)* determined limits to the term 'worker' by requiring workers to be engaged in 'economic activities' or employment of a 'genuine nature'. Notwithstanding these cases, the ECJ accepted that the term 'worker' generally refers to an employed person.

**2.5**  The rights given under the Treaty and Directives 68/360 and 64/221, as well as Regulation 1612/68 include :

● right to exit, enter and reside (*C-2902/89 Antonissen* allows jobseekers reasonable time to reside in order to job search, however, *C-41/74 Van Duyn*, disallows entry on public policy or national security grounds. But such restrictions must be proportionate (see *C-36/75 Rutili, C-115 & 116/81 Adoui and Cornuaille,* and *C-30/77 Bouchereau*));

- right to equal treatment (both Articles 12 and 39 of the Treaty and Regulation 1612/68, in terms of housing, social and tax advantages, access to training and trade union membership (see *C-39/86 Lair* and *C-197/86 Brown* (education – tuition fees); *C-316/85 Lebon* (social advantages); *C-379/87 Groener* (linguistic knowledge));

- right to remain (Regulation 1251/70);

- rights relating to workers' families (Regulation 1612/68, including spouses, children (see *C-267/83 Diatta, C-131/85 Gul, C-59/85 Reed* and *C-370/90 Singh*)).

**2.6** Articles 43–55 provide similar rights and protections for self-employed persons under the right to establishment.

## Social Action Programmes

**2.7** The EU Commission, DG V (Employment and Social Affairs) is the EU institution which is responsible for setting out the Community Social Action Programmes (SAPs). These are its social priorities. SAPs seek to ensure that the social objectives are a constant concern of all EU policies. From 1974 to now, SAPs have identified key legislative developments on: employment protection; the working environment, equality between men and women, employee participation and employment creation. The Community's first SAP was in 1974, which proposed more substantive social policy than those in the original Treaty of Rome. The SAP was hailed as a 'human face' for the Community.

## Social policy and 'social dumping'

**2.8** With the enactment of the Treaty on European Union, the desire to combat unemployment, a high level of employment and social protection prevailed seeking to raise the standard of living and solidarity amongst Member States, including additional activities under new Article 3. These additional activities included 'a policy in the social sphere'. Here marked the evolution of EC social policy. Both the EU Commission's Green and White Papers on social policy attempted to clarify the EU's social competences. Later these were set in Articles 136–139 of the Amsterdam Treaty.

**2.9** The highly controversial '*Hoover Affair*', involving the decision by Hoover to close its factory in Dijon in France and move to Glasgow, UK, culminating in 600 job losses and the recruitment of some 400 fixed-term contract employees, clearly defines social dumping. In the Hoover case, the motive was clear – cheaper Scottish labour, given the UK's deregulatory style of employment regulation which causes social dumping. Whilst the concept of social dumping is easy to understand, the term itself is quite obscure. Social dumping in effect describes the behaviour designed to give a competitive advantage to companies due to low labour standards rather than productivity. Consequently, employers that move businesses to a location where there are lower labour standards are said to be engaged in social dumping. In addition, Member States who deregulate, in an attempt to capitalise from such practices, are equally guilty of such a charge.

**2.10** Due to the prospect of social dumping within the EU, the EU Commission has committed itself to 'legislating for higher labour standards and employee rights across the EU in the social field', in order to ensure that social dumping is avoided. Yet the OECD denies that social dumping is widespread in European countries.

## Social Europe?

**2.11** The social objectives of the EU are broadly centred on the aspirations of social protection. COM(95) 466 defined social protection and its objectives as 'the collective transfer systems designed to protect people against social risks'. To that end, the EU Commission, whilst accepting the enormity in the variance between national systems, requires that all Member States provide specific laws relating to the protection of workers. The social objectives of the EU are set out in both the European Employment Strategy and the Social Action Programmes.

**2.12** The new social policy agenda seeks to work towards core European objectives and increased co-ordination of social policies (COM(2000) 379). It was the Treaty of Amsterdam which moved social policy to the centre of EU policy. The strategic objectives 2000–2005 (*Shaping the New Europe*, COM(2000) 154) include :

- promoting new forms of European governance;
- a stable Europe with a stronger voice in the world;
- a new economic and social agenda; and
- better quality of life.

**2.13**  Taking up the subsequent Social Policy Agenda (COM(2000) 370) the EU Commission seeks to further policies aimed at building a competitive and inclusive knowledge-based economy promoting social cohesion and full employment. Subsequently, the European Employment Strategy emerged as the new Social Policy Agenda. More significantly, since the Lisbon Summit, an open method of co-ordination in terms of social policy agenda emerges.

## Social policy after Maastricht

**2.14**  The first substantive revision of the original Treaty, the Treaty of Rome 1957, took place in 1987 under the auspices of the 1986 Single European Act. Firstly, the Act recognized and formalized the EU's relationship with the European Council (established in 1974 and composed of the Heads of State of each government member), providing for two meetings per year. More importantly, the Court of First Instance was created; the co-operation procedure for legislation was passed; the creation of the Single Market by 1992 was agreed; and, qualified majority voting was recognized as the norm.

**2.15**  The Treaty on European Union (TEU), more commonly known as the Maastricht Treaty, was agreed in 1992. The Maastricht Summit had two main aims: to sustain the pace of change captured by the earlier Single European Act; and to create the European Union, continuing to change the direction away from economic integration fully (under the EEC) and political union (under the EC) and towards social Europe (under the auspices of the EU). Consequently, the newly formed EU under the Treaty on European Union increased the Community's powers in the social sphere. The Community was supposed to not only work towards raising living standards but also to ensure a high level of social protection. The Social Fund's remit was widened and a whole new section was inserted on education and vocational training. The involvement of the European Parliament in the legislative process was again increased, by extending the co-operation procedure further and the introduction of the co-decision procedure. The TEU overall broadened the aims of the EU to include monetary union and social and environmental protection. The Court of Auditors and the creation of a European Central Bank were formally recognised.

**2.16**  Under the TEU three pillars were created : Pillar I (the EC); Pillar II (Common Foreign and Security Policy); and, Pillar III (Justice and Home Affairs). Pillars II and III do not, unlike Pillar I, provide legally binding acts. As a consequence, the European Court of Justice has no role in Pillars II and III. Above all, under the TEU, all EU Member States' nationals became EU citizens under this distinctly newly created organisation – the EU.

## The UK opt-out!

**2.17**  In an EU social policy context, the adoption of the Treaty meant that two sets of rules applied in the social area: the EC Treaty covering all (then) 15 Member States and the Agreement set out in the 'Protocol (No 14) on social policy' from which the UK opted out. The Agreement set out in Protocol No 14, which was annexed to the TEU, contained two significant innovations: a major boost for the role of management and labour; extension of qualified majority voting in the Council in the following areas: improvements in the working environment to protect employees, working conditions, information and consultation of workers, equal opportunities for men and women in the labour market and equal treatment at work, and occupational integration of people excluded from the labour market. On the basis of the Agreement, the 14 Member States adopted four directives: Council Directive 94/45 on the introduction of European works councils, Council Directive 96/34 on the framework agreement on parental leave (a proposal on parental leave had been blocked in the Council for several years), Council Directive 97/80 on the burden of proof in cases of discrimination based on sex and Council Directive 97/81 concerning the Framework Agreement on part-time work. The UK eventually opted into the Social Protocol on 7 June 1997.

## EU social policy post-Amsterdam

**2.18** The Treaty of Amsterdam (1998), which came into effect in May 1999, is essentially a consolidating Treaty. Its main purpose was to improve both law-making, decision-making and policy formulating processes. Consequently, greater openness in decision-making was brought about. The Treaty also transfers a number of areas formerly contained in Pillar III to Pillar I, including free movement of persons. As a result of such a transfer, much of the original Treaty was renumbered. Pillar III was also renamed Police and Judicial Cooperation. In addition to this, Article 136 (former Article 117) has been altered, thus now including references to the European Social Charter of Turin and the Community Charter of the Fundamental Rights of Workers. The Amsterdam Treaty also provide that the Council can act by unanimity, as before, but now in co-decision with the European Parliament on matters such as:

- implementing decisions relating to the European Social Fund;

- provisions for facilitating the exercise of citizen's right to move and reside freely within the territory of the Member States;

- social security for Community migrant workers.

**2.19** In particular, new additions to the Treaty included a new non-discrimination provision, which provided the authority to create legislation on gender, race, ethnic origin, religion or belief, disability, age and sexual orientation. The usage of the co-decision procedure was expanded.

## Nice Treaty 2002

**2.20** Romano Prodi, the EU President, described the aim of the Nice Summit in December 2000 as 'the reunification of Europe'. The outcome of the Summit was the Nice Treaty. This was eventually ratified in December 2002. This Treaty facilitates the enlargement of the EU. Since it was anticipated that 10 or more new member States would in the future join the EU, including former Eastern European countries, institutional changes were proposed as follows:

- the number of Commissioners would increase to 26 (though larger Member States would lose their second Commissioner as a result, by 2005);

- qualified majority voting would be extended within the Council (a decline in unanimity is expected);

- the reweighting of votes in the Council in favour of the larger Member States would take place.

**2.21** In addition to this institutional business vis à vis enlargement matters, the European Council agreed that the EU's Charter of Fundamental Rights should be viewed as a political document and therefore not necessarily legally binding in each member State. The UK has tended to treat it as not legally binding. The EU now stands as the EU25, including new Member Accession States: the Czech Republic, Cyprus, Estonia, Hungary, Latvia, Lithuania, Malta, Poland, Slovak Republic and Slovenia.

## Constitutional Treaty 2004

**2.22** On 18 June 2004, the new EU of 25 agreed a new Constitutional Treaty. This new Treaty will consolidate previous Treaties and encompass enlargement to 25 EU Member States. The institutional changes enacted were:

- a new Commission, comprising a college of 18 Commissioners from 2014;

- a new Presidency term of 18 months;

- the extension of qualified majority voting; and

- a new Charter of Rights, including a social (solidarity) chapter.

At time of writing, this is a recent development and the detail and the national implementation methods and/or drafts which will embrace this new Treaty are not yet fully known. The UK Prime Minister has announced a referendum on its implementation.

## EU social policy – its development

**2.23**  The EU Commission's White Paper on Social Policy (COM(94) 333) proposed the creation of the 'European Social Model', founded on individual rights, free collective bargaining, the market economy, equality of opportunity, social welfare, democracy and solidarity (para. 3). The ensuing Treaty of Amsterdam (1998) created the Employment Chapter – Title VIII. This Title was fast-tracked following an initiative by the Commission in 1997 (COM(97) 497), sought to converge both labour market policy and employment levels within the EU. Subsequently, Member States were requested to draw up National Employment Action Plans (NAPs) by June 1998. The Title sought to promote the practice that NAPs be focused on employability, entrepreneurship, adaptability and equal opportunities (the 'four pillars' of the Luxembourg Jobs Summit, 1997 (COM(99)442)). The NAPs were discussed at the Cardiff Summit in 1998. The Employment Title is a remarkable achievement demonstrating a commitment amongst all Member States.

### Social dialogue

**2.24**  Under 118B (now Article 139) social dialogue was formalised, albeit voluntary and informal. This later developed into the role of the social partners. In fact, it was the former EU Commission President, Jacques Delors, who championed the concept of social dialogue. Yet Article 118B enabled the EU Commission in the first instance to promote social dialogue. Since the Treaty of Amsterdam, new Articles 138–139 ensure that social dialogue is an integral part of EU policy and its legal competence. It is often referred to as 'bargaining in the shadow of the law'. Such a methodology is often criticized for being outside the usual institutional law-making processes.

**2.25**  Social dialogue occurs where the two sides of industry, namely the employers and the workers, develop a dialogue which focuses upon a consensus on social policy objectives and policies. In 1991, the social partners, the ETUC, UNICE and CEEP, reached a landmark agreement establishing a consultative, quasi-legislative role, whereby they should be consulted prior to the passing on any social policy. This agreement later became the ratified Concordat of the Social Partners of 1993 (COM(93) 600). Originally, Article 118B of the Treaty of Rome recognized 'relations based on agreement'. Now Article 138 promotes such consultation of 'management and labour'. Subsequently, the EU Commission must consult with the social partners and is obliged under Articles 136–145 to involve the social partners in a two-stage consultation process, the pre-legislative, as well as their opinion before concluding its proposal.

**2.26** However, this social dialogue amongst the recognized social partners was challenged in 1996 by UEAPME (*Union Europeenne de l'Artisant et des Petits et Moyennes Entreprises*), a group representing small and medium sized businesses, arguing about the representativeness of the self-selected, designated social partners. UEAPME agued that their exclusion from consultation and negotiation created an unfair, unrepresentative closed shop. The Court ruled that UEAPME did not have a general right to be consulted. Consequently, the Council and the Commission must verify the representativeness of labour and management of the signatories to any agreement affecting labour and management. Since this ruling UEAPME has become an umbrella organization of UNICE. Clearly, the social partners have a fundamental role to play in the development of social policy and labour law in the EU.

## European Social Model (ESM)

**2.27** The Essen Council, convened 9–10 December 1994, confirmed the EU's commitment to the promotion of employment objectives. This followed on from the contradictory proposals of the Commission's Green (COM(93) 551) and White (COM(94) 333) Papers on the future of European Social policy setting out conflicting arguments for and against the development of a European Social Model.

Following on from Essen, five emerging themes were identified:

- promoting employment;
- reorganizing work;
- combating social exclusion;
- mainstreaming gender equality;

• consolidation, compliance and enforcement of social legislation.

**2.28** These co-ordinated priorities became known as the 'European Employment Strategy' (EES). Whilst these priorities, the so-called EES, were in the first instance without Treaty powers and are therefore a non-binding legal instrument, they were later formalized in Title VIII (Articles 125–130) of the Amsterdam Treaty. Under the EES, each Member State is responsible for ensuring the transposition of EU directives and activity in key areas of action in their respective individual national employment policy.

## EU labour law – its content

**2.29** The first pieces of EU labour law were the Directives on Equal Pay (75/117) and Equal Treatment (76/207). These were followed by collective redundancies (75/129) and business transfers (77/187) which emphasised the two-pronged aspirations of the evolving early social Europe project, that of equality and workers' rights to job security. In the 1980s, these aspirations sought to include health and safety under the 1989 Framework Directive.

**2.30** Mainly EU social legislative initiatives have further promoted equality of treatment: Directive 76/207/EEC on equal treatment with regard to access to employment, vocational training, promotion, and working conditions, aimed at eliminating all discrimination, both direct and indirect, in the world of work and providing an opportunity for positive measures and Directive 79/7/EEC on the progressive implementation of equal treatment with regard to statutory social security schemes. For example, during the 1980s, Directive 86/378/EEC sought to implement equal treatment in occupational schemes of social security, which was later amended by Directive 96/97/EC in light of the Barber decision (C-268/88 (1990) ECR I-1889). In addition, during that period, Directive 86/613/EEC on equal treatment for men and women carrying out a self-employed activity, including agriculture, was adopted.

**2.31** More recently, the Treaty of Amsterdam explicitly introduced equality between men and women as one of the tasks (Article 2) and activities (Article 3) of the Community. Article 13 also allows the Council, acting unanimously on a proposal from the Commission, to take action to combat any form of discrimination, including that based on sex. The principle of equal treatment is defined by Article 2(1) as 'there shall be no discrimination whatsoever on grounds of sex either directly or indirectly by reference in particular to marital or family status'. In the EU Charter of Fundamental Rights, Article 23 states that 'Equality between men and women must be ensured in all areas, including employment, work and pay. The principle of equality shall not prevent the maintenance or adoption of measures providing for specific advantages in favour of the under-represented sex'.

**2.32**  Gender equality, at EU level, became a mainstream phenomenon in 1995. The Fourth Action Programme (COM(95) 381) promoted that more should be done in this important legal area, since actual inequalities in employment persisted. Article 2 of Council Decision 95/593 defined 'mainstreaming' as the principle of integrating equal opportunities for women and men. Furthermore, the Commission (COM(94) 333) initiated the publication of an annual 'Equality Report', in order to review and monitor developments at both Member State and EU level on equality policies.

**2.33**  The success of these initiatives led to gender equality becoming a priority task of the Community (COM(96) 67). Council Decision 95/593, which was to form the basis of this new, high level, commitment to promoting equality in all areas, included :

- reconciling working and family life;
- promoting a gender balance in all EU decision-making;
- making conditions more conducive to exercising equality rights; and
- promoting equal opportunities for men and women in education, training and the labour market.

**2.34**  In 1998 Articles 2 and 3(2) of the revised Treaty reinforced the EU's new commitment to gender equality and extended the provisions beyond the labour market. Council Directives 2000/43 (race equality) and 2000/78 (age, disability and sexual orientation) are a result of such a legal change in legal competences under the Treaty.

## The UK and the impact of EU labour law

**2.35** Historically, the Agreement on Social Policy (SPA) was enacted in order to enable the UK Government's opt-out from the processes which formalised the role of the social partners in decision-making at Community level. As noted above, in 1997 the newly elected UK Government ended the UK's opt-out under the Agreement on Social Policy. Later, the Amsterdam Treaty (1998) further strengthened the provisions formerly contained in Article 118B (now Articles 138–139) by providing an obligation on the part of the Commission to consult the social partners before making any labour law proposals (COM(96) 488). Overall, the SPA originally allowed 11 out of 12 (excluding the UK) Member States to utilise the EU institutions in an innovative way to establish a clearly defined legal basis for Community labour law. It also provided for the beginning of the development of the role of the social partners in creating an EU-wide collective agreement on social affairs and employment strategy.

**2.36** From 1990–97, the SPA formed a two-speed Europe. Latterly, post-Amsterdam, in EU Social Policy development terms, the SPA marked a paradoxical significant beginning in the broadening of the scope of Community competence in the social field. For instance, it extended the usage of qualified majority voting. In addition, the SPA envisaged a greater role for the social partners in being consulted and negotiating collective agreements on labour law.

## Using EU labour law

**2.37** Much of what EU legislators propose seeks, to some extent, to harmonise all existing EU measures and practices. However, positive harmonization (ie the establishment of minimum standards) was recognised by the Social Action Programmes the First Social Action Programme being an admission of such aims. Historically, ex Article 100 was therefore the appropriate legal base in providing direct affect. The need for a broad equivalence in labour standards emerges under the EU's banner of promoting a need for a 'level playing field' of competition. It should be noted that the ECJ in 1988 (*C-324/86 Foreningen af Arbejdsledere Danmark v Daddy's Dance Hall A/S*) defined 'harmonisation' as 'not intending to establish a uniform level of protection throughout the Community, but by extending the protection guaranteed to workers independently by the laws of the individual Member States'. Essentially, 'harmonisation' seeks to identify a common problem in Europe. However, it is the variance in EU Member States' employment relations and systems of labour law which prevents full harmonization.

**2.38**   The EU is founded, like all Member States' legal systems, on the Rule of Law. To that end, Article 220 of the Treaty observes that the role of the European Court of Justice (ECJ) is 'to ensure that, in the interpretation and application of the Treaty, the law is observed'. Articles 220–245 of the Treaty explain the composition, structure, procedure and function of the Court. The Court is located in Luxembourg. Since 1989, the ECJ has been assisted by the Court of First Instance (CFI). The CFI was belatedly created in order to relieve the ECJ of its excessively growing caseload.

**2.39**   The Court is currently composed of 15 judges. The ECJ is also assisted by 8 Advocates General (AGs), whose role is to assist the judges by presenting a non-binding written opinion which provides advice prior to the Court's deliberations and ruling. Procedurally, the Court has 2 stages: the written; followed by the oral hearing, the emphasis being on the written stage. The matters brought before the Court are divided into either preliminary rulings or direct actions. Preliminary rulings are requests by Member States' national courts which asks the ECJ either to interpret Community law or rule on the validity of EU secondary legislation. Direct actions are those brought by the Commission against the various Member States which have failed to fulfil their obligations under Community law or individuals seeking to challenge the validity of certain EU legislation.

**2.40**   Overall, the ECJ has a specific role to ensure that EU law is observed. This broad general function allows the Court to adopt a purposive, or as it is known more commonly, a teleological approach to interpreting community law. As noted in the *CILFIT* case *(C-283/81)*, such an approach allows the ECJ to 'fill the gaps' left by Community law. Such judicial activism has been both praised and criticised over the years. But it cannot be denied that the ECJ has created a 'new legal order' (see *C-26/62, Van Gend*).

**2.41**   The EU's doctrine of direct effect was established by the European Court of Justice to provide rights and obligations to individuals, enforceable in national courts. This principle was established in *Van Gend en Loos (C-26/62)*. This case involved Dutch importers challenging the imposition of a duty, having imported chemicals from Germany. The ECJ affirming its 'new legal order' observed that EU law conferred rights and obligations on individuals, as well as Member States, without the need for implementing legislation. Consequently, EU law was given direct effect, which means that both Member sates and individuals are granted rights and obligations and that such rights and obligations are enforceable by individuals through their national courts.

**2.42**   Subsequently, the so-called Van Gend criteria emerged, suggesting when direct effect applied: the provision to comply must be clear and sufficiently precise (which could include only part of a provision – see *Defrenne v Sabena (C-43/75)*); the right relied upon must be unconditional (see *Van Duyn C-41/74*); and, not subject to any other implementing measure either at Community or national level (see *Reyners v Belgium (C-2/74)*). Following Van Gend, the doctrine of direct effect applied to Treaty articles (Article 25), Regulations (Article 249), Decisions (see *Franz Grad (C-9/70)*), international agreements (see *Kupferberg (C-104/81)*)and Directives (but only where the date for implementation has passed (*Ratti C-148/78*).

**2.43**   The Doctrines of direct effect and direct applicability have given rise to an important question – what bodies are to be considered part of the State for the purposes of legal action under Community law? Consequently, the term 'emanations of the State' emerges. The European Court of Justice has been seen to adopt a rather liberal approach to the term 'State'. For example, a health authority in *Marshall (C-152/84)*, local government in *Fratelli Constanzo (C-103/88)*, and a Police Chief in *Johnston (C-222/84)*.

**2.44**   However, the landmark case of *Foster v British Gas plc (C-188/89)* pushed wider the parameters. The ECJ ruled that a Directive could be relied upon against organisations or bodies which were subject to the authority or control of the State, or had special powers beyond those which result from the normal rules applicable. Such organisations and bodies are deemed to be 'emanations of State'.

**2.45**   Article 249 provides 'that a directive shall be binding, as to the result to be achieved, upon each member State to which it is addressed'. Directives are therefore not directly applicable, they require implementation before taking effect. Within the EU, such implementation is undertaken by the EU Member States. The *Von Colson case (C-14/83)* reminds EU Member States of their duty under Article 10 of the Treaty to 'ensure the fulfillment of the obligations ...'. Consequently, not only do national governments have to transpose Directives into national law, but national courts are obliged to interpret and apply them in a manner which is consistent with the purpose and wording of the Directive concerned.

**2.46**   Due to the European Court of Justice's refusal to permit the horizontal direct effect of Directives, the principle of indirect effect has emerged. Indirect effect is also known as the 'interpretive obligation'. It was the *Von Colson* ruling *(C-14/83)* which was instrumental in creating a principle of indirect effect. Clearly, whilst Directives do not have direct effect, EU Member States have a duty to implement Directives. Yet post-Colson, Member States' courts also hold a duty to interpret national legislation in light of Community Directives. However, this principle is subject to 3 limitations:

- where to interpret national legislation in the light of a Directive, which would conflict with other general principles of EU law (see *Kolpinghuis Nijmegen (C-80/86)*);

- only measures enacted prior to the Directive may be interpreted in this manner (see *Marleasing, C-106/89*);

- it does not apply where criminal proceedings could result (see *Arcaro (C-168/95)*.

**2.47**   Where EU law places obligations on EU Member States only, such as through Directives, in such circumstances it may be possible for an individual to enforce those rights against the State. This concept is known as vertical direct effect: *Marshall (No 1) v Southampton and South West Hampshire Area Health Authority (C-152/84)*, in which Miss Helen Marshall wished to enforce her rights under the Equal Treatment Directive (Directive 76/297). The ECJ held that Miss Marshall could rely on the Directive against the State, the health authority being an emanation of State, the State being her employer. Hence, vertical direct effect permitted her to apply the rights and obligations under the Directive against her employer. Since Community law forms part of each EU Member State's domestic legal system, rights and obligations from EU law are normally enforced before the national courts. National courts can however utilise the preliminary reference procedure in order to seek the advice of the European Court of Justice. It has been left to the Member States' discretion to designate which national courts will hear actions founded on Community law, as well as the procedures to be adopted. As the ECJ ruled in *Comet* (*C-45/76*): 'It is for the domestic law of each Member State to designate the courts having jurisdiction and the procedural conditions governing actions at law intended to ensure the protection of the rights which subjects derive from the direct effects of Community law'.

**2.48**  Article 234 of the EC Treaty provides the European Court of Justice with the jurisdiction to give preliminary rulings on the interpretation of the Treaty and the validity of secondary legislation, when requested to do so by the national courts of the EU Member States. The purpose of a preliminary ruling is to ensure the uniform application and interpretation of Community law by national courts. Whilst the ECJ does not bind itself, it having no rule of precedent, it does ensure its own consistency (see *C-28–30/62, Da Costa*): a referring national court will be bound by the ECJ's ruling. Above all, the preliminary ruling procedures provide an important link between the national courts and the ECJ. The availability of such procedures also allows EU Member States' courts to familiarise themselves with EU law. Article 234 provides that 'any court or tribunal of a Member State may request a reference'. A national court will only make a reference where it considers that its decision rests upon a point of Community law. Notably, it is the court that decides to make the reference, not the parties to the case under scrutiny.

**2.49**  Whilst the right to refer is discretionary, it becomes an obligation where there is no remedy in national law. However, following the *CILFIT* (*C-283/81*) ruling it will not be necessary to refer the case to the ECJ where :

● the question of EC law is irrelevant to the case being heard by the national court;

- the question of EC law has already been interpreted by the ECJ in a previous ruling;

- the correct interpretation is so obvious as to leave no scope for doubt (acte clair).

The actual referral procedure requires the national court to formulate a question or questions to be addressed by the ECJ.

## Francovich actions and State liability

**2.50**　The principle of State liability was introduced by the European Court of Justice under the *Francovich* ruling (*C-6 & 9/90*). This ruling allowed for damages to be awarded against a State where that Member State had failed to correctly implement the aims of a Directive. Consequently, damages flowed from the State due to the State's breach which had caused the ensuing losses.

**2.51**　This principle has since been refined in subsequent rulings. For instance, in *Brasserie du Pecheur and Factortame (No. 3) (C-46 & 49/93)* serious breach as a concept was included. Serious breaches are considered those breaches which were intended (see *Dillenkofer, C-178, 179, 188–190/94*). Following *Brasserie du Pecheur*, a threefold test applies:

1.　the law infringed must be intended to confer rights on individuals;

2.　the breach must be sufficiently serious;

3.　there must be a causal link established between the breach and the individual's damage being claimed.

**2.52**　The concept pf State damages has developed under this principle. In *Rewe-Zentralfinanz (C-33/76)* the European Court of Justice was careful to ensure that appropriate remedies (ie compensation) should be available with regard to breaches of Community laws and rules. The ECJ ruled that it relied upon the national courts to ensure such remedies were available. Therefore, remedies available for similar breaches of national law should also be available for breaches of EC law. The remedy should therefore be an effective remedy. This was defined in *Von Colson (C-14/83)* where the ECJ explained that Article 10 of the Treaty (ex Article 5) provided that EU Member States' national courts should have remedies which act as a deterrent and be adequate to remedy the damage sustained, to be effective.

**2.53** The ECJ later developed this principle based on proportionality in *Johnston v Chief Constable of the RUC (C-222/84)* highlighting the need for effective judicial protection for those who have sustained losses as a result of a breach of EU law. It was eventually *Marshall v Southampton and South West Hampshire Area Health Authority (No 2) (C-271/91)* which declared that not only did the remedy have to be comparable with that available for a similar national breach, but where such an effective remedy was not available then EU Member States should devise a new suitable remedy in those circumstances.

**2.54** Such a legal situation seeks to promote uniformity amongst Community remedies. However, there is one exception to the rule, *Francovich* claims (see *C-6 & 9/90, Francovich*). State damages, ie where a Member State has failed to correctly implement the aims of a Directive, compensation is available from the State due to the State's breach which caused the ensuing losses of those concerned. This right ensures that Member States do not benefit from their own breaches of Community law. In *Brasserie du Pecheur (C-46/93)* (see also *Factortame (No. 3), C-49/93*) serious breaches are included.

Serious breaches are considered as those breaches which were intended (see *Dillenkofer, C-178, 179, 188–190/94*).

## Human rights and labour law

**2.55** The objective of the member governments of the Council of Europe, under whose auspices the text of the European Convention of Human Rights (ECHR) was concluded in November 1950, was to secure the universal and effective recognition and observance of rights that had been proclaimed in the Universal Declaration of Human Rights on 10 December 1948 by the General Assembly of the United Nations. They 'resolved, as the Governments of European countries which are like-minded and have a common heritage of political traditions, ideals, freedom and the rule of law, to take the first step for the collective enforcement of certain of the rights stated in the Universal Declaration'. The rights chosen were civil and political in character. Economic and social rights were left aside until later.

**2.56** The Articles of the ECHR not only proclaimed fundamental rights but also laid down limitations and balancing safeguards. A European Commission of Human Rights and a European Court of Human Rights (the 'Strasbourg Court') were set up. States could choose to accept the competence of the Human Rights Commission to examine petitions from individuals claiming that they were victims of a violation of their human rights. The rights proclaimed in the convention and the procedures for their enforcement have had a substantial impact on the relationship between the individual and the State. A human rights perspective has had to be introduced into the decision-making of public authorities for whose acts States may, ultimately, be held accountable before an international tribunal.

## *1950 ECHR*

**2.57** The 1950 European Convention on Human Rights (ECHR) established protection for basic human rights to: life, non-degrading treatment and slavery, liberty, punishment in accordance with law, fair hearing, privacy, freedom of conscience and expression, association and non-discrimination. In Opinion 2/94 (Accession to the ECHR) the EU proposed that the 1950 ECHR should be incorporated into Community law. The European Court of Justice in *Rutili v Ministre de l'Interieur* (*C-36/75*) expressly confirmed that the Convention's rights are protected in Community law.

**2.58** The 1989 Charter of Fundamental Social Rights of Workers was a result of a Working Party of the Commission on Social Rights. Due to the UK opt-out of social policy at that time, 11 out of 12 of the then EU Member States approved the Charter, the end result of the Working Party. Consequently, the UK opt-out until 1997 ensured that the Charter could not be integrated into the Treaty and therefore its legal status was that of a political declaration, ie status confirmed in its Preamble and later by the European Court of Justice in the Albany case

(C-67/96, para. 137, per A-G Jacobs). The Charter itself was presented at the Strasbourg Summit in 1989 and provided for a core set of social rights :

- free movement (Articles 1–3);

- remuneration (Articles 4–6);

- improved living and working conditions (Articles 7–9);

- social protection (Article 10);

- freedom of association (Articles 11–14);

- vocational training (Article 15);

- equal treatment between men and women (Article 16);

- information, consultation and participation (Articles 17–18);

- health and safety (Articles 19);

- protection of children and adolescents (Articles 20–23);

- elderly persons (Articles 24–25);

- disabled persons (Article 26);

- Member States action (implementation) (Articles 27–30).


**2.59** Its focus was that of 'workers' rather than citizens. However, the 1989 Charter had similar intent to that of the 1972 Paris Declaration of the Council (COM (91) 511). The overall impact of the Charter was that it formed a legislative agenda which was useful in the refocussing of labour law issues across the EU. However, in particular it should be noted that notwithstanding its restrictive nature, the Charter did result in Directives on : Information (91/533); Collective Redundancies (92/56); Pregnant Women (92/85); Working Time (93/104); Young People (94/33); and Posted Workers (96/71). The Charter endorsed both individual employment rights, as well as collective rights. In any event, the Charter proved to be the impetus required for the development of social rights in the context of the social dimension, not the internal market. Above all, labour and worker's rights were given special relevance under this Charter

## Charter of Fundamental Rights (2000)

**2.60**  The EU's Charter of Fundamental Rights was approved at the December 2000 Nice Summit and was ratified in late 2002. However, it remains a non-binding document (Chapter VII, Articles 51–54). Its origins go back to the 1975 Tindemans Report (COM(75) 481) which sought to promote citizenship. Whilst the Social Charter 1989 guaranteed fundamental social rights for workers, there were no references to social citizenship. The Comite des Sages of 1996 which pre-empted the Charter broke the deadlock and advanced the notion of social citizenship the underlying idea of the Charter being to mould the embryonic EU citizenship into social citizenship. The ILO's 1998 Declaration on Fundamental Rights at Work also promoted social rights and therefore influenced EU thinking prior to the Charter.

**2.61**  The Charter itself is divided into 3 parts; Preamble, 6 chapters comprising over 50 rights, freedoms and principles; and its scope. The Preamble reasserts the EU's proclamation of 'an ever closer union' with fundamental rights. The rights themselves are headed under 6 titles: dignity, freedoms, equality, solidarity, citizens rights and, justice.

**2.62**  The Solidarity Chapter covers EU employment and social law. Chapter IV confers employment rights and social entitlements, including:

- Article 27 – information and consultation;
- Article 28 – collective bargaining and action;
- Article 30 – protection from unfair dismissal;
- Article 31 – fair and just working conditions;
- Article 32 – prohibition of child labour and protection of young people;
- Article 33 – family and professional life;
- Article 34 – social security and assistance.

**2.63**  Although this Chapter does not provide an exhaustive list of comprehensive fundamental social rights, this discussion does provide a higher profile for social citizenship. Yet the rights to work, remuneration and housing remain omitted. Again, this Charter provides evidence of the emerging soft law approach to EU labour law and social policy.

## The influence and impact of EU law on labour law

**2.64** The Convention on the Future of Europe will have a major impact on the institutional framework and governance mechanisms of the Union. Issues of legitimacy and political authority are at the core of the reform process. The Convention is charged with four main tasks:

- division of competences: to clarify when and where competence lies, whether at the Community level, national or sub-national level (e.g. regional);

- institutional reform: should the EU have a 'federal' structure with the European Commission acting as government and the European Parliament as legislature, is a Europe of nation states with a stronger role for the Council more effective, or neither of these (whatever the choice the current 'Community method' has to change);

- simplification of the Treaties: presently, the legal basis of the EU rests on four treaties and assorted other constitutional acts. These should be integrated into a single text in a manner, which makes them accessible to EU citizens;

- democratisation: throughout Europe national parliaments are losing power to their governments, while for those in EU countries the effect is greater due to the increasingly important role of the European Parliament as co-legislator.

### The Future of an Enlarged EU

**2.65** The Treaty of Nice was ratified in December 2002, having been agreed in December 2000. It was intended to facilitate the enlargement of the EU. The Summit held on 16 April 2003, sought to confirm the commitment of the new acceding signatories to EU membership. The term 'enlargement' is used to describe the widening of membership to the EU. The six founding nations (Belgium, France, Germany, Italy,

Luxembourg and the Netherlands) established the EEC under the Treaty of Rome in 1957. The UK, Ireland and Denmark joined in 1973. Greece joined in 1981. Portugal and Spain acceded in 1986 and Austria, Finland and Sweden in 1995. The new EU25 Member States include, as already noted above, the Czech Republic, Cyprus, Estonia, Hungary, Latvia, Lithuania, Malta, Poland, Slovak Republic and Slovenia.

## Further reading

Allen, R, & Crasnow, R, *Employment Law and Human Rights* (2002) Oxford.

Barnard, C, *EC Employment law* (2 ed. 2000), Oxford.

Barnard, C, *Substantive Law of the EU* (2004) Oxford.

Bercusson, B, *European Labour law* (1996) Butterworths.

Deakin, S, & Morris, G, *Labour law* (3 ed. 2001) Butterworths pp. 102–126.

### Articles

Bercusson, B, 'The European Social Model comes to Britain', *Industrial Law Journal*, 2002, Vol. 31 (3), pp. 209–244.

Dashwood, A, 'The Constitution of the EU After Nice :law-making procedures', *European Law Review*, 2001, Vol. 26, pp. 215–238.

Ewing, K, 'The EU Charter of Fundamental Rights: a waste of time or wasted opportunity?', Institute of Employment Rights: London, 2002.

## Self-test questions

1.  What recourse do UK citizens have for Governmental failure to adequately implement EU labour laws?

2.  To what extent does EU labour law protect workers, whereas UK law has or does not? Give examples from various Directives.

3.  "The European Court of Justice has become the most effective social law making institution, post-Amsterdam." Discuss with reference to recent decisions of the Court.

4.   How has the European Convention on Human Rights (1950)
     impacted upon employment law since 1998?

# CHAPTER THREE

# Contract of Employment

## Summary

This chapter introduces the employment relationship which is central to Labour Law. It is based on the notion of a 'contract of employment', which, like all contracts, contains both express and implied terms. The key points in this chapter are:

- general aspects of express and implied terms;
- specific terms;
- restrictive covenants; and
- the duty of trust and confidence.

It also considers how terms may be varied and concludes with a discussion of illegal contracts.

## Parties to the contract

*Employees*

**3.1** The following points should be noted here:

(1) many statutory rights are given to employees and it is therefore important to identify who is an employee;

(2)    the generality of the statutory definitions has led to a substantial body of case law in which the Courts have set out the tests for identifying an employee and the approach to be used;

(3)    it is arguable that the scope of employment law should be widened and that ERA 1996, s 23 should be used to extend employment protection to all workers.

**3.2**  Many of the statutory rights discussed in this book are available only to 'employees', though there are some significant rights which are available to 'workers', a concept defined in the Employment Rights Act 1999, s 230(3) and considered later at paras. 3.5 and 3.33. An employee is said to be employed under a 'contract of service' or a 'contract of employment'. This relationship is to be distinguished from that of independent contractor or self-employed person, who works under a 'contract for services'. The distinction between these two different types of relationship lies in the nature of the obligation undertaken. Both may be engaged to achieve a particular result, but the independent contractor may have far greater latitude than the employee in the way he or she achieves that result, for example in hours of work and use of sub-contractors; this relationship is considered below at para. 3.16.

**3.3**  The Employment Rights Act 1996 (ERA 1996), s 230(1) defines an 'employee' as 'an individual who has entered into or works under … a contract of employment.' 'Contract of employment' means 'a contract of service or apprenticeship, whether express or implied, and (if it is express) whether it is oral or in writing': see s 230(2). There is no definition of 'self-employed person', 'independent contractor' or 'contract for services' in the Act.

**3.4**  The generality (or vagueness) of these statutory definitions has led to the courts laying down tests to enable a distinction to be made between employees and self-employed and contracts of service and contracts for services. Many of the older cases used what was called the 'control' test, and some used the 'organisation' or 'integration' test. The test currently used is the 'multiple' test, which may take different forms. The fundamental problem is to identify correctly those who should fall within the embrace of Employment Law and to exclude those who have sufficient economic independence to make it unnecessary to protect them. It is arguable that the tests to be considered below too readily treat people as self-employed persons.

## Employees: the tests

**3.5**   *Ready Mixed Concrete (South East) Ltd v Minister of Pensions and National Insurance* (1968) was the first case to formulate the 'multiple' test. In it MacKenna J set out the conditions to be fulfilled for a contract of employment to exist. He said: 'A contract of service exists if the following three conditions are fulfilled:

(i)   The servant agrees that in consideration of a wage or other remuneration he will provide his own work and skill in the performance of some service for his master.

(ii)   He agrees expressly or impliedly that in the performance of that service he will be subject to the other's control in sufficient degree to make that other master.

(iii)   The other provisions of the contract are consistent with its being a contract of service.'

**3.6**   The judge reached his conclusion by asking whether the person in question was in business on his own account. A significant number of factors in the case suggested that the person concerned was an employee, but the judge concluded that he was self-employed treating as the determinative factor what he called 'the ownership of the instrumentalities', ie the tools of the trade. It will also be noticed that he used the old-fashioned terms 'master' and 'servant'. Today, the parties are called 'employer' and 'employee'.

**3.7**   This case was followed soon after by *Market Investigations Ltd v Minister of Social Security* (1969). Cooke J's approach was similar to that of MacKenna J, but he refined the third part of that judge's test. He said that the fundamental test was: 'Is the person who has engaged himself to perform these services performing them as a person in business on his own account?' He went on:

> No exhaustive list has been compiled and perhaps no exhaustive list can
> be compiled of considerations which are relevant in determining that

question, nor can strict rules be laid down as to the relative weight which the various considerations should carry in particular cases. The most that can be said is that control will no doubt always have to be considered, although it can no longer be regarded as the sole determining factor; and that factors, which may be of importance, are such matters as whether the man performing the services provides his own equipment, whether he hires his own helpers, what degree of financial risk he takes, what degree of responsibility for investment and management he has, and whether and how far he has an opportunity of profiting from sound management in the performance of his task.

**3.8** See also *Lee Ting Sang v Chung Chi-Keung* (1990) to a mason working mainly for a sub-contractor who was paid either a piece rate or a daily rate for his work, depending upon the nature of the work. The most recent case in which the Court of Appeal has considered this issue is *Express and Echo Publications Ltd v Tanton* (1999). The facts of the case are similar to those of *Ready Mixed Concrete*. They involved a driver who was made redundant from his employment and who was later re-engaged under a contract which the company intended, and the driver agreed, should be a contract for services. Clause 3.3 of the agreement provided that should the driver be 'unable or unwilling to perform the services personally he shall arrange at his own expense entirely for another suitable person to perform the services.' The driver applied to the employment tribunal for a declaration that his status was that of employee. The tribunal determined that he was an employee and the Employment Appeal Tribunal (EAT) dismissed the company's appeal. The Court of Appeal, however, allowed the company's appeal, saying that as a matter of law where a person is not required to perform the contract personally the relationship is not one of employee and employer. Thus, clause 3.3 was wholly inconsistent with the contract being one of service. Peter Gibson, LJ, with whom the other members of the Court agreed, said: '... (I)t is necessary for a contract of employment to contain an obligation on the part of the employee to provide his services personally. Without such an irreducible minimum of obligation, it cannot be said that the contract is one of service ...'

**3.9** In the later case of *MacFarlane v Glasgow City Council* (2001) the EAT distinguished *Tanton's* case. The case involved qualified gymnastic instructors working at sports centres operated by the Council. If an instructor could not take a class, she would arrange for a replacement from a register of coaches maintained by the council. The replacements were paid by the Council and not by the applicant. Lindsay J, President of the EAT, said that *Tanton* was distinguishable on the grounds, amongst others, that the applicant could not simply choose not to work in person and that she was not free to provide any substitute, but only someone from the Council's own register. Further the Council paid the substitute direct. Of *Tanton* the EAT said: 'The individual there, at his own choice, need never turn up for work. He could, moreover, profit from his absence if he could find a cheaper substitute. He could choose the substitute and then in effect he would be the master.'

**3.10**    The approach set out above is not without its drawbacks, since the way the question is posed will tend to dictate the answer given. If one asks the question whether a given individual is in business on his or her own account, it is quite likely that the answer will be different from what it would have been had the question been whether the individual was economically dependent on the provider of labour. This is not, however, an argument which has commended itself to those making the decisions whose impact has been discussed above.

## Employees: application of the tests

**3.11**    The process of deciding whether a person carries on business on his or her own account has been described by Mummery J in *Hall v Lorimer* (1992) in the following terms:

> '[I]t is necessary to consider many different aspects of that person's work activity. This is not a mechanical exercise of running through items on a checklist to see whether they are present in, or absent from, a given situation. The object of the exercise is to paint a picture from the accumulation of detail. The overall effect can only be appreciated by standing back from the detailed picture which has been painted, by viewing it from a distance and by making an informed, considered, qualitative appreciation of the whole. It is a matter of evaluation of the overall effect of the detail, which is not necessarily the same as the sum total of the individual details. Not all details are of equal weight or

importance in any given situation. The details may also vary in importance from one situation to another ... The process involves painting a picture in each individual case.'

**3.12** The case was a tax case, but the judge accepted that the question whether or not there is a contract of employment is to be determined by reference to the general law of employment, as applied to all the facts of the particular case. The EAT's decision was upheld by the Court of Appeal.

**3.13** A recurrent question relates to the weight to be attached to a declaration by the parties that the person in question is to be treated as an independent contractor. MacKenna J, in the *Ready Mixed Concrete* case, stated it to be a question of law, irrespective of what the parties have declared it to be, though he went on to say that in cases of doubt, a declaration might help in resolving the doubt one way or the other. Subsequently, however, the Court of Appeal has taken the view that the label should be disregarded, even in cases of doubt: see *Ferguson v John Dawson and Partners (Contractors) Ltd* (1976)and *Young & Woods Ltd v West* (1980); contrast *Massey v Crown Life Insurance Co* (1978). It is arguable that this might be an appropriate area in which to apply ERA 1996, s 203(1), since an agreement to provide work as a self-employed person is arguably an agreement which 'purports ... to exclude or limit the operation of any provision of' the 1996 Act.

## Employees: factors pointing towards employment

**3.14** The following factors are the most important to evaluate in painting a picture of a person's work activity:

1.  the contractual provisions;

2.  the degree of control exercised by the 'employer';

3.  the obligation of the 'employer' to provide work;

4.  the obligation on the person to do the work;

5.  the provision of tools, equipment, instruments and the like;

6.  the arrangements made for tax, National Insurance contributions, sick pay and VAT;

7.   the opportunity to work for other employers;

8.   other contractual provisions, such as fees, expenses, and holiday pay;

9.   whether the relationship by which the person is a self-employed independent contractor is genuine or whether it is designed to avoid the employment protection legislation.

**3.15** So far as the statutory provisions to be considered in this book are concerned, there is a clear divide between employees and self-employed: the former enjoy the benefit of the rights not to be unfairly dismissed and to receive a redundancy payment, whereas the latter do not. It may be noted, however, that, when the issue concerns health and safety rather than employment protection, particularly when a person has sustained injuries, the courts tend to treat as employees persons who might not be regarded otherwise as employees. This may be done in two ways: either by classifying the injured person as an employee, so that he or she is covered by the employer's common law duties, or by treating section 3 of the Health and Safety at Work Act 1974 as extending the employer's obligations so as to embrace the employees of sub-contractors. Examples of the first approach are to be found in *Ferguson v John Dawson and Partners (Contractors) Ltd* (1976) and *Lane v Shire Roofing Company (Oxford) Ltd* (1995). In both cases, persons who were effectively working 'on the lump' and who suffered serious personal injuries were classified as employees and were awarded large sums of damages, to which they would not have been entitled had they been classified as self-employed persons, since they would have been outside the employer's common law duty of care. Examples of the second approach are to be found in a series of cases involving injuries to employees of sub-contractors working on an 'employer's' site. In *R v Rhone-Poulenc Rorer Ltd* (1996), for example, three people were carrying out repairs at factory premises belonging to the company, two of whom were employees of a sub-contractor and one an employee of the company. One of the sub-contractor's employees fell and died. The Court of Appeal upheld the company's conviction under section 3 of the 1974 Act, saying that the proper discharge of an employer's obligations under that provision might well make it necessary to take the same precautions for the safety of a sub-contractor's employees as for that employer's own employees, if the sub-contractor's employees were under the employer's direction and control. The decision of the

House of Lords in *R v Associated Octel Co Ltd* (1996) makes it clear, however, that for the purposes of section 3 it is necessary to determine whether the activity in question is part of the employer's undertaking.

## Employees: homeworkers, casual workers and temporary workers

**3.16** It is not possible to consider all the various types of employment which have been considered in judicial decisions and reference should be made to the relevant reference works, for example, Upex, *The Law on Termination of Employment* (6th ed. 2001), pp. 15–26. The following categories have been considered:

1. directors;

2. partners;

3. part-time workers;

4. musicians;

5. sub-postmasters;

6. temporary workers;

7. church ministers and priests;

8. apprentices;

9. barristers' clerks; and

10. office-holders.

**3.17** There have been significant developments in judicial thinking in relation to two groups over the last few years: (1) homeworkers and casual workers and (2) so-called 'temporary workers'. Those who work for a person but do the work away from the premises are outworkers, and, if they do the work in their own domestic environment, are called homeworkers. Whether such persons are employees will depend upon the facts of any given case, as the cases have stressed. In *Airfix Footwear Ltd v Cope* (1978), for example, the decision that the homeworker in question was an employee was due to the fact that she had been working for Airfix Footwear five days a week for seven years.

In *Nethermere (St Neots) Ltd v Taverna and Gardiner* (1984) both the homeworkers involved worked under flexible arrangements; they took as much work as they wanted and did not work when they wanted. They were held to be employees. The Court of Appeal stressed that the question is essentially one of fact and that an appellate court should be slow to interfere with the decision of the employment tribunal.

**3.18** In *O'Kelly v Trusthouse Forte plc* (1983), which involved the question whether 'regular casuals' called in to work at banquets were employees, the decision of the employment tribunal was that they were not. The determinant factor was that there was no mutuality of obligation as they were effectively on 'standby' unless and until they were asked to come in and assist with a particular banquet. The Court of Appeal said that, as the tribunal had correctly weighed up all the factors involved in the case, there were no grounds for interfering with their decision. See also *Mailway (Southern) Ltd v Willsher* (1978).

**3.19** The status of casual employee has received attention from both the Court of Appeal and House of Lords in recent years. In *Clark v Oxfordshire Health Authority* (1998) the issue was whether a nurse retained by a health authority on a casual basis to fill temporary vacancies in hospitals was an employee. She worked for the authority's 'nurse bank'; she had no fixed or regular hours of work but was offered work as and when a vacancy occurred at one of the authority's hospitals. When she did not work, she had no entitlement to pay, or to holiday pay or sick leave. She worked on this basis for some three years, during which there were various gaps. The only issue decided by the employment tribunal, and thus the subject of appeal, was whether there was a 'global contract of employment' between the parties. This was described by Sir Christopher Slade in the case under discussion as 'a continuing overriding arrangement which governed the whole of (the parties') relationship and itself amounted to a contract of employment ...' If a global contract of employment existed, the gaps in employment during the time she was on the nurse bank would have counted towards her length of employment and she would have had sufficient continuity; if there was not, each gap would have broken continuity and she would not accumulate sufficient continuity: continuity of employment is discussed in Chapter 7. Following its previous decisions in *Nethermere (St. Neots) Ltd v Taverna and Gardiner*, above, and

*Hellyer Brothers Ltd v McLeod* (1987) the Court of Appeal said that a contract of employment cannot exist in the absence of mutual obligations subsisting over the entire duration of the relevant period. They said that, although the mutual obligations required to found a global contract of employment need not necessarily consist of obligations to provide and perform work, some mutuality of obligation is required. In the present case, there was no mutuality of obligation: the authority was under no obligation to offer work nor was she under any obligation to accept it. She had no entitlement to any pay when she did not work and no entitlement to holiday pay or sick leave. There was thus no global contract of employment. The Court of Appeal remitted the case, however, to the employment tribunal to consider other issues, such as whether there existed a specific engagement which could amount to a contract of employment and provide the basis for an unfair dismissal claim.

**3.20** The issue of casual staff was again considered by the House of Lords, in *Carmichael v National Power plc* (1999). The case involved tour guides who were taken on by means of an exchange of letters on a 'casual as required basis' to act as guides taking parties on tours of power stations operated by the predecessor of the respondent company. As in the *Clark* case, they were not obliged to take work and the company did not guarantee that work would be available. They were paid only for the hours they worked. The employment tribunal and the EAT held that they were not employees but the Court of Appeal allowed their appeal on the ground that the exchange of letters gave rise to a contract of employment. The majority of the Court of Appeal avoided that issue of absence of mutuality by implying terms relating to the performance of the guides' duties. The House of Lords rejected this approach and allowed the company's appeal. Lord Irvine of Lairg LC said that had the appeal turned exclusively on the construction of the exchange of letters he would have had no hesitation in holding as a matter of construction that there was no obligation on the company to provide work or the guides to accept it. He said that it was clear that the parties did not intend the letters to 'constitute an exclusive memorial of their relationship' and that, in looking at the documents, the surrounding circumstances and how the parties conducted themselves, the tribunal was correct to conclude that they did not intend that their relationship should be regulated by contract.

**3.21** The significance of both the above cases is that those who have informal arrangements with their 'employers' are unlikely to be held to have a contract of employment and that the point on which their argument is likely to founder is absence of mutuality of obligation. Even if it is held that a particular engagement does give rise to a contract of employment, the gaps between the engagements may lead to the consequence that each time an engagement ends there is a break in continuity of employment, so that at the start of the next engagement the employee has to start accumulating continuity again. The termination of an engagement would only give rise to an unfair dismissal claim in such circumstances if the engagement had lasted more than a year, so as to give the person concerned sufficient qualifying employment to present a complaint.

**3.22** Similar questions arise when considering whether part-time workers are employees as arose when considering the status of homeworkers and casual workers. It may be that a person may work for five different employers on five different days of the week, doing a full day's work for each employer. If that is so, then, if the factors set out above point to employment, such a person's status is properly to be regarded as that of an employee. Equally, however, the very fact that such a person does work for five different 'employers' on five different days of the week must also raise the question whether he or she is more properly to be regarded as self-employed. As with casual workers and homeworkers, this question is very much a question of fact. All that can be said is that it should not be too readily assumed that the status of those who work for a number of different 'employers' is that of an employee. All the factors relevant to their work should be considered.

**3.23** 'Temporary' workers are those whose services are supplied by an intermediary (the labour supplier) for the benefit of a third party (the hirer) for a limited period of time. Two relationships are involved – that between the worker and the agency and that between the worker and the hirer. In *Construction Industry Training Board v Labour Force Ltd* (1970) the Divisional Court expressed the view that the contractual relationship between the supplier/agency and the worker was not one of service but one *sui generis*. A similar decision was arrived at in *Wickens v Champion Employment* (1984), where temporaries were employed by an agency under a contract of service. Nevertheless, the court held that the other provisions of the contract were inconsistent with a contract of employment. The question in that case was whether the general terms of engagement of the agency's temporary workers gave rise to an employment relationship. In *McMeechan v Secretary of State for Employment* (1997), on the other hand, the employee's claim, as reformulated in the Court of Appeal, was that he was entitled to be treated as an employee of the agency in respect of a single engagement with a particular client in respect of which the money he was claiming on the agency's insolvency had been earned. The Court of Appeal held that he was, saying that there was no reason why a temporary worker might not be the employee of the agency in respect of each assignment actually worked. They added that whether or not employment status should, or should not, be allocated in any particular was a question of fact to be decided according to the particular circumstances of each case.

**3.24** In the later case of *Johnson Underwood Ltd v Montgomery* (2001) the tribunal decided that the applicant became an employee of the agency, following the *McMeechan* case. It considered all aspects of the relationship between her and the agency, including mutuality of obligation and control, and concluded that, on balance, those factors pointing to the existence of an employment contract outweighed those against. Included in the list of factors pointing against a contract of employment was the finding that there was 'little or no control, direction or supervision'; the tribunal also took the view, following *McMeechan*, that the absence of mutuality of obligation was irrelevant. The Court of Appeal held that it had erred in reaching this decision. They said that mutuality of obligation and control are the irreducible minimum legal requirements for the existence of a contract of employment and that the tribunal should have followed the guidance of McKenna J in the *Ready Mixed Concrete* case: see para. 3.5 above.

**3.25** In general, it is unlikely that a worker placed by an agency will become an employee of the hirer, though application of the tests set out above may lead to the conclusion that an employment relationship has arisen. Recent examples of this general proposition are *Costain Building & Civil Engineering Ltd v Smith and Chanton Group plc* (2000) and *Hewlett Packard Ltd v O'Murphy* (2002). In the *Costain* case, an engineer was supplied by an agency to Costain. There was an agreement between the agency and Costain for the supply of services by the engineer and the agreement stated that he would be under the strict supervision of Costain. There was no agreement between him and Costain, however, and he did not receive any disciplinary or grievance documentation, he did not expect to receive sick pay or holiday pay, and there was no clause providing for notice of termination. Because of the engineer's conduct, Costain informed the agency that they did not want him to continue to work on the site. He claimed that he had been unfairly dismissed by Costain contrary to ERA 1996, s 100(1)(b). The EAT held that he did not become an employee of Costain and that therefore he could not complain of unfair dismissal. It followed that his appointment as a health and safety representative was ineffective. They rejected the argument that the appointment of the engineer as a representative had the effect of altering his status.

**3.26** Recent decisions of the Court of Appeal have suggested that, given the appropriate factual scenario, a temporary worker may become the employee of the end user, ie the organisation which requests the employment agency to supply staff: see *Franks v Reuters Ltd* (2003) and *Dacas v Brook Street Bureau (UK) Ltd* (2004). Factors likely to lead to this conclusion are the length of time the employee has been with the end user and the degree of day-to-day control exercised by it. The *Dacas* decision is significant. See also *Motorola Ltd v Davidson and Melville Craig Group Ltd* (2001).

## Employees: approach of the appellate courts

**3.27** The final question which requires consideration here is the approach of the appellate courts to the question whether a person is an employee or not. This depends upon whether or not the construction of a written contract or document is involved. If, exceptionally, the relationship is dependent solely upon the true construction of a written document, the question will be one of law, upon which an appeal will lie: see *Davies v Presbyterian Church of Wales* (1986), *Lee Ting Sang v Chung Chi-Keung* (1990), and *McMeechan v Secretary of State for Employment* (1997). For a discussion of the historical basis for this rule see Lord Hoffman's speech in *Carmichael v National Power plc* (1999) (at pp. 1232–3). In other cases, it has generally been regarded as a mixed question of fact and law. In *O'Kelly v Trusthouse Forte plc* (1983), the Court of Appeal affirmed that a question of law is involved. A majority, however, also held that the answer to the question whether a person is an employee or not involves questions of degree and fact which it is for the employment tribunal to determine. An appellate tribunal may not interfere with the employment tribunal's decision unless the employment tribunal has misdirected itself in law or its decision is one which no tribunal, properly directing itself on the relevant facts, could have reached. The effect is to place a heavy burden on an applicant who disagrees with a tribunal's decision and to restrict the scope for appeals to the EAT and the Court of Appeal.

**3.28** In *Lee Ting Sang v Chung Chi-Keung* (1990), Lord Griffiths, who delivered the opinion of the Privy Council, pointed out that the decision whether or not a person is employed under a contract of employment will depend upon the evaluation of many facts and there will be many borderline cases in which similarly instructed minds may come to different conclusions. He said that in such situations an appeal court must not interfere. In *Hall v Lorimer* (1992), Mummery J applied *Lee Ting Sang's* case and stated:'The appellate court will not interfere with the conclusion of the fact finding tribunal where the decision ... comes within what has been described as the 'band of possible reasonable decisions.' The appellate court realises that there are borderline or grey areas in which tribunals, properly instructed on the law and facts, can legitimately and reasonably arrive at different conclusions ...'

**3.29** More recently, the Court of Appeal appears to have modified the approach to dealing with appeals set out above. In *Express & Echo Publications Ltd v Tanton* (1999), Peter Gibson LJ said that he accepted that the correct approach to the determination of the question whether or not an applicant is an employee is as follows:

(1) The tribunal should establish what were the terms of the agreement between the parties. That is a question of fact.

(2) The tribunal should then consider whether any of the terms of the contract are inherently inconsistent with the existence of a contract of employment. That is plainly a question of law, and although this court, as indeed the Employment Appeal Tribunal before us, has no power to interfere with findings of fact (an appeal only lies on a point of law), if there were a term of the contract inherently inconsistent with a contract of employment and that has not been recognised by the tribunal's chairman, that

would be a point of law on which this court, like the Employment Appeal Tribunal before us, would be entitled to interfere with the conclusion of the chairman.

(3)   If there are no such inherently inconsistent terms, the tribunal should determine whether the contract is a contract of service or a contract for services, having regard to all the terms. That is a mixed question of law and fact.

**3.30**   In that case, the Court of Appeal treated as an error of law falling within the second part of the approach set out above the decision of the chairman of the employment tribunal that the relevant clause of the contract was one of many factors to be taken into account and did not preclude the relationship of employer and employee coming into existence. The Court of Appeal's view in *Tanton* appears to be at variance with the approach taken by that Court in *O'Kelly v Trusthouse Forte plc* and subsequent cases in its suggestion that the approach of a tribunal to individual terms rather than to the whole contract may be characterised as an error of law. In other words, the second stage of the three-stage approach accepted by Peter Gibson LJ appears to be an additional and arguable supernumerary gloss on the previous approach.

## Employees: future developments

**3.31**   It is worth noting that the Employment Relations Act 1999 (ErelA 1999), s 23 contains a provision which gives the Secretary of State power by order to extend employment protection rights to groups who currently do not enjoy them, including individuals expressly excluded from the rights. The order made may confer the rights on individuals who are of a 'specified description'; it may also provide that individuals are to be treated as parties to workers' contracts or contracts of employment and make provision as to who are to be regarded as the employers of individuals. The order may also modify the operation of any rights as conferred on individuals by the order. It is not clear what steps are intended to be taken under this provision. It may be that specific groups who are currently treated as excluded from the legislation will be included within the order, for example clergy. Equally, there is no reason why the order should not be a general provision extending the relevant legislation to workers instead of employees, for example. In the latter case, the effect would be considerable and would, at least to some extent, reduce the problems involved in making a distinction between employees and self-employed persons.

**3.32**  In this context, it is worth observing that much of the legislation enacted in recent years has been expressly applied to a 'worker'. Before 1997, the only legislation to refer expressly to a worker was the Wages Act 1986, subsequently consolidated into the ERA 1996, Pt. II. It may be noted, however, that the definition of 'employment' to be found in the Sex Discrimination Act 1975 (SDA 1975) and the Race Relations Act 1976 (RRA 1976) is wide enough to embrace self-employed persons and thus goes wider than the definition of employee in the ERA 1996: see SDA 1975 s 82(1) and RRA 1976, s 78(1).

## Statutory definition of 'worker'

**3.33**  The ERA 1996, s230(3) defines 'worker' as 'an individual who has entered into or works under ... –

(a)    a contract of employment; or

(b)    any other contract, whether express or implied and (if it is express) whether oral or in writing, whereby the individual undertakes to do or perform personally any work or services for another party to the contract whose status is not by virtue of the contract that of a client or customer of any profession or business undertaking carried on by the individual ...'

**3.34**  Clearly the definition embraces all employees; it also seems to be wide enough to embrace self-employed persons who offer consultancy services and thus are effectively sole traders. One of the apparent oddities of the legislation is that many of the recently introduced rights, for example under the Working Time Regulations (SI 1998/1833, as amended by the Working Time Regulations 1999 (SI 1999/3372)) or the National Minimum Wage Act 1998, apply to 'workers' but if such persons are dismissed for a reason connected with the Regulations or the Act they may only complain of unfair dismissal if they are employees. This seems to be anomalous.

*Employer*

**3.35**  Whilst in most cases there may be no problems in identifying who the employer is, nevertheless there may be cases where this proves to be a problem. The most obvious situation is where there appears to have been a 'relevant transfer' and where it is possible that the Transfer of Undertakings (Protection of Employment) Regulations (TUPE) apply. This matter is considered in Chapter 9. An example of the problem arising outside a TUPE context is to be found in *Andrews v King* (1991) ICR 846. The case involved the assessment to tax of a farm worker who organised a number of men together for picking or grading potatoes as and when they were required by potato merchants. The farm worker, Andrews, was assessed to tax on the basis that he was a self-employed gang-master who employed the members of the gang. He was therefore assessed to tax as a self-employed person and served with PAYE determinations of tax payable by an employer. The Vice-Chancellor held that he was not carrying on business on his own account and that all the members of the gang, including Andrews, were employed by the potato merchants.

**3.36**  The other matter which may be relevant here is employment by 'associated employers'. This is usually of more importance for calculating continuity of employment, but may also arise when it is necessary to decide who is a person's employer. An employee taken into the employment of a new employer associated with the previous employer, may count the period of previous employment as employment with the associated employer: see ERA 1996, s 218(6). 'Associated employer' is defined in ERA 1996 s 231. The definition has two limbs. Under the first limb, two employers are to be treated as associated where 'one is a company of which the other (directly or indirectly) has control'; under the second limb, they will be treated as associated where 'both are companies of which a third person (directly or indirectly) has control'. In both cases, it should be noted that the controlling employer need not be a company and may, therefore, be a sole trader or a partnership. The Court of Appeal has held the definition to be exhaustive, which means that local authorities cannot be associated employers: see *Merton London Borough Council v Gardiner* (1981) and *Southwood Hostel Management Committee v Taylor* (1979).

**3.37**  The problem which has most frequently arisen in the context of this definition concerns the meaning of 'control'. In *Secretary of State for*

*Employment v Newbold and Joint Liquidators of David Armstrong (Catering Services) Ltd* (1981) the EAT said that control means control by the majority of votes attaching to shares, exercised in general meetings; it is not how or by whom the enterprise is actually run. It is clear, however, that, where a number of companies is involved, one person must have a majority share in all the relevant companies for them to be treated as associated. In *Russell v Elmdon Freight Terminal Ltd* (1989), for example, one person held 55 per cent of the shares of the first company and 50 per cent of the shares of the second, and a second person held no shares in the first and 49 per cent of the shares in the second. There was thus no one person who had voting control over both companies. The EAT stressed that, where two companies are involved, there must be one or more persons who have voting control over both companies. See also *South West Launderettes Ltd v Laidler* (1986), *Secretary of State for Employment v Chapman* (1989), and *Tice v Cartwright* (1999).

## Other relationships

**3.38** As has been seen, the coverage of Employment Law embraces 'employees' and, in some contexts and for some purposes, 'workers'. There are, however, other relationships by which one person performs services for another. The most obvious of these is that of the self-employed provider of services. Such people have different names or titles depending on the sector in which they work. They may be called 'independent contractors', 'consultants' or 'freelances'. It is important to ensure that, whatever title they are given, the substance of the relationship is clear. Put another way, it is no use giving a title which suggests self-employment to someone who is self-evidently an employee. An error of categorisation may be costly, particularly for an employer who finds that the Inland Revenue takes a different view. In every case of this kind, it is important to look at the substance rather than the label which has been attached to the relationship. Whilst it is well settled that tribunals will use the multiple test to determine whether a particular person is an employee or not, it is by no means axiomatic that this is the best test to use. As has already been pointed out, the form in which a question is asked will dictate the answer given. In view of the significant changes in working practices in recent decades, it is time to re-assess this test. A better test would be a test based on the economic dependence of the person doing the work. This is the approach taken by French law and is worthy of serious consideration.

## Sources of contractual obligations

**3.39**  The following principles in relation to sources of a contract of employment should be noted:

(1)   the main sources of an employment contract are express terms and implied terms;

(2)   express terms are to be found in the contract itself and/or documents expressly or impliedly incorporated into the contract, such as collective agreements or employers' handbooks;

(3)   in cases where interpretation or construction of the contractual documentation is necessary, the court or tribunal will apply the ordinary rules of construction for contracts, including the *contra proferentem* rule;

(4)   in cases where there is no employment contract, the existence of a written statement of terms and conditions under section 1 of the Employment Rights Act 1996 will assist the determination of what terms were agreed;

(6)   an express term may in appropriate cases be qualified by an implied term, such as the term not to behave in a way such as to undermine the relationship of trust and confidence between employer and employee;

(7)   implied terms will arise where the court or tribunal regards the implication of a term as necessary to give the contract business efficacy or reflect what the parties would have agreed had they addressed their minds to the issue;

(8)   terms may be implied from custom and practice, but such terms are of diminishing importance.

**3.40**  The main source of contractual obligations is the express terms of the contract. This process is assisted by the provisions of ERA 1996, s 1, which requires employers to give their employees written particulars of many of the more important terms of their contracts. Terms may be expressly incorporated by a reference in the contract to another document such as a collective agreement, but not all such terms are appropriate for incorporation; other documents may also be impliedly incorporated. A corollary of reducing a contract to writing is that the express terms (both in the contract and any incorporated document) should be clear and accurate so as to avoid the risk of a court interpreting the contract in a different way from what was originally intended. The construction of express terms is considered below.

**3.41** Even if the employer complies with the requirements of section 1 and gives a written statement or decides to give an employee a full written contract of employment, there are likely to be areas in the contract which are not covered by express terms. In that case the court or tribunal will have to consider resorting to implied terms to fill the apparent gap. An example is in the context of mobility. If the contract contains no express term, and there is a dispute between the employer and the employee as to whether he or she may be required to move elsewhere, the court or tribunal will have to decide whether a mobility term should be implied. It is, however, a general feature of implied terms that the term implied will be no wider than is necessary. An employer who wants a wide term will need to insert an express clause into the contract. It is also noticeable that in recent years, implied terms have been used to qualify the apparent width of express term, as in *United Bank Ltd v Akhtar* (1989).

**3.42** Finally, there is the possibility that custom and practice may be used either to interpret the contract or to fill a gap in the express terms of the contract. In contemporary conditions, the scope for custom and practice is considerably diminished.

## Statutory Written Statements

**3.43** The main statutory requirements are contained in ERA 1996, ss 1–7. In effect, the main terms of the contract should be set out in the written statement, covering such matters as pay, hours of work, holidays and holiday, sick pay, notice entitlement and the like. It is not necessary to set out details relating to pensions and pension schemes if the employee's pension rights depend upon the terms of a pension scheme set up under a provision contained in or taking effect under a statute and the provision requires the relevant body or authority to give a new employee information concerning his or her pension rights: see s 1(5).

**3.44** The statement may be given in instalments but the following particulars must all appear in a single document:

- the name of the employer and employee;

- the date of the start of employment with the employer;

- the date of the start of continuous employment; and

- the details relating to pay, hours of work, holiday entitlement, the employee's job title and the employee's place of work: see ss 1(2) and 2(4).

**3.45** The written statement must be given within two months (8 weeks) of the start of the employment; in the case of employees who are required within two months of the start of their employment to begin work outside the UK for more than one month, the statutory statement must be given them no later than the time of their departure from the UK to start the work. Furthermore, since 6 April 2003, and the coming into force of the Employment Act 2002 (s 37), employers should provide employees with copies of their actual contracts of employment. The employer may refer to some other 'reasonably accessible' document for particulars of the employee's entitlement because of absence caused by sickness or injury and pensions and pension schemes applicable to him or her. A reasonably accessible document is one which the employee has reasonable opportunities of reading in the course of employment or which is made reasonably accessible to him or her in some other way. For particulars of the notice provisions to which the employee is subject the statement may refer to the law or the provisions of a collective agreement which is reasonably accessible to him or her.

**3.46** There are specific provisions governing disciplinary and grievance procedures, which are set out in ERA 1996, s 3, as amended by the Employment Act 2002 (EA 2002). They do not apply to rules, disciplinary decisions, grievances or procedures relaying to health or safety at work. As required by section 3 the statement must include a note:

(1) stating whether there is in force a contracting-out certificate stating that the employment is contracted-out employment;

(2) specifying any disciplinary rules applicable to the employee or referring the employee to a document containing the rules which is reasonably accessible to him or her;

(3) specifying any procedure applicable to the taking of disciplinary decisions relating to the employee, or to a decision to dismiss him or her, or referring him or her to the provisions of a reasonably accessible document;

(4) specifying a person to whom the employee can apply if dissatisfied with any disciplinary decision or decision to dismiss;

(5) specifying a person to whom the employee can apply for the purpose of asking for a grievance relating to his or her employment to be dealt with and the manner in which the application should be made;

(6) where there are further steps consequent on an application under (4) or (5) above, explain those steps or refer to the provisions of a reasonably accessible document which explains them.

The term 'reasonably accessible' is defined in section 6 and set out above.

**3.47** In *W A Goold (Pearmak) Ltd v McConnell* (1995) the EAT used the existence of the statutory provisions relating to the provision of a note by employers relating to their grievance procedures as a basis for implying a term that an employer will 'reasonably and promptly afford a reasonable opportunity to their employees to obtain redress of any grievance they may have'.

**3.48** ERA 1996, s 4 deals with changes in the terms and conditions covered by section 1. Any such changes must be notified to the employee by means of a written statement within one month. It should be noted, however, that this is a procedural requirement: it does not authorise an employer to change an employee's contractual terms simply by giving a notice of change. There must be a variation which is effective in law: see para. 3.186. As with the original statement under section 1, the statement of change under section 4 may refer to other reasonably accessible documents for the same matters as those which may be referred to by the original statement. Similarly, in the case of changes in the notice provisions to which the employee is subject, the statement of change may refer to the law or the provisions of a collective agreement which is reasonably accessible to him or her. The term 'reasonably accessible' is defined in section 6 and set out above.

## Legal effect of written statements

**3.49**   Despite confusions of terminology, particularly in the case law, it is clear that a written statement given by virtue of the requirements set out in ERA 1996, s 1 is not itself a contract of employment. It is, of course, evidence of the contract of employment and in many cases will probably be the best evidence available. The fact, however, that it is not the contract of employment means that it is open to an employee to argue in subsequent court or tribunal proceedings that the particulars contained in the statement did not represent what was agreed between the parties. In *System Floors (UK) Ltd v Daniel* (1982), approved by the Court of Appeal in *Robertson v British Gas Corporation* (1983), Browne-Wilkinson J said:

> ... [The statutory statement] provides very strong prima facie evidence of what were the terms of the contract between the parties, but does not constitute a written contract between the parties. Nor are the statements of the terms finally conclusive: at most, they place a heavy burden on the employer to show that the actual terms of contract are different from those which he has set out in the statutory statement.

**3.50**   The earlier decision of the Court of Appeal in *Gascol Conversions Ltd v Mercer* (1974) appears to suggest that a written statement is conclusive. Subsequent cases have distinguished *Gascol*, however, on the basis that in that case the employee signed the written particulars as constituting the new terms of his contract of employment, not merely the receipt for new particulars of employment. In such a case, therefore, care needs to be taken, since, if the written statement is converted into a written contract, the parties should make sure that the terms contained in it are correct. Otherwise, it will not be possible for them to change it without the agreement of both parties.

**3.51**  ERA 1996, s 11 provides for enforcement of the employee's right to be given a written statement. That is in addition to the employee's ordinary rights to sue the employer for breach of contract before the ordinary courts or, where appropriate, the employment tribunal. Section 11 enables the employee to make a reference to the tribunal for it to decide what particulars ought to have been included, in cases where either no statement has been given or the statement does not comply with what is required. Where a statement has been given but there is a dispute as to what particulars ought to have been included or referred to in it, the employer or the employee may refer the matter to the tribunal. Section 12 gives the tribunal the power to determine what particulars ought to have been included, or whether any particulars which were included should be confirmed, amended or substituted.

**3.52**  It is clear from the decided cases that the powers given by what is now section 12 are restricted and that the tribunal's role is effectively confined to declaring what the parties agreed to, on the basis of the evidence before it: see, for example, *Cuthbertson v AML Distributors Ltd* (1975) and *Construction Industry Training Board v Leighton* (1978). Thus, if there is a complaint that the written statement does not contain a term that was actually agreed, the tribunal's powers under section 12 are adequate to deal with it. If, however, the employee's complaint is that particulars of a term were not included in the situation where there had not in fact been any agreement, it is doubtful whether the tribunal has any power to deal with the matter. Despite suggestions by Stephenson LJ in *Mears v Safecar Security Ltd* (1982), the decision of another division of the Court of Appeal in *Eagland v British Telecommunications plc* (1993) makes it clear that the tribunal has no power to include in its determination terms which have not been agreed. Parker LJ observed at p. 652:

> The wording of the section makes it perfectly plain ... that there may be no such terms (*sc.* relating to pension, sick pay, holiday pay or disciplinary rules) and there is nothing in any section of the Act which empowers or

requires the tribunal to impose upon the parties terms which had not been agreed when the statute recognises that it may be the case that no such terms have been agreed.

**3.53** Leggatt LJ said, at p.654:

> If an essential term, such as a written statement must contain, has not been agreed, there will be no agreement. If it has, it is the duty of the employment tribunal, where necessary, to identify the term as having been agreed, whether expressly, by necessary implication, or by inference from all the circumstances, including in particular the conduct of the parties, without recourse to invention.

This firmly expressed decision of the Court of Appeal shows how limited are the powers of the employment tribunal under section 12.

**3.54** The Employment Act 2002 has introduced a limited penalty which may be imposed on employers who fail to give a statement under ERA 1996, s 1 or 4. In the case of proceedings to which EA 2002, s 38 and Sch.5 apply (for example, sex discrimination claims of complaints of unfair dismissal), where the tribunal finds in favour of the employee, and the employer was in breach of its duty under s 1 or 4, the tribunal must make a minimum award of compensation in respect of the failure: see s 38(2) − (4).

## Works Rules

**3.55** If an employer draws up works or company rules, it is possible that they may become terms of the employees' contracts. If all or any of the rules do become part of the employees' contracts, the consequence will be that they cannot be altered unilaterally by the employer, but only with the agreement of the employees, and the employees can insist on working those rules and refuse to operate any other rules. If, on the other hand, they are not contractual, they may be changed unilaterally by the employer and an employee who refuses to operate the rule in its changed form will be refusing to obey any lawful and reasonable order. Few cases have considered the position of works rules, but guidance may be obtained from cases involving other types of provision which are considered below. This issue is also important in relation to variation of contracts: an employer who unilaterally alters a provision or withdraws a facility will not be in breach of contract if the provision or facility is not contractual.

**3.56** To determine whether a particular benefit or provision is contractual or not, much depends upon the intention of the parties. The question is whether it is reasonable to infer from the circumstances that the parties intended the provision to have contractual force. So, for example, if the contract specifies that a disciplinary procedure is to be incorporated into the employees' contracts, it will be incorporated; if it is stated not to be of contractual effect, it will not be incorporated. For an example of an incorporated disciplinary procedure, see *Dietmann v London Borough of Brent* (1988). In *Robertson v British Gas Corporation* (1983), the Court of Appeal held that an incentive bonus scheme had been incorporated into employees' contracts and could not, therefore, be unilaterally determined by the employer, despite the fact that no bonus scheme was in force at the time. On the other hand, in *Quinn v Calder Industrial Materials Ltd* (1996) the unilateral abandonment of a policy governing enhanced redundancy payments was held not to be in breach of the employees' contracts. This case is more fully discussed at para. 3.73, below. A similar decision was reached in *Secretary of State for Employment v ASLEF (No. 2)* (1972), where the Court of Appeal refused to hold that detailed works rules set out in a staff handbook were contractual; they were held to be collateral instructions to the employees as to how they were to carry out their work. It is clear, therefore, that not all works rules have contractual effect.

**3.57** Similar considerations apply in the case of bonus schemes or share option schemes; if they are stated not to be contractual but capable of discontinuance at the employer's discretion, the employer will not be in breach of contract in exercising the discretion to discontinue. In *Cadoux v Central Regional Council* (1986), for example, the question was whether the employer was entitled to withdraw a non-contributory life assurance scheme. The employee's contract stipulated that his post was 'subject to the Conditions of Service laid down by the National Joint Council for Local Authorities Administrative, Professional, Technical and Clerical Services (Scottish Council) and as supplemented by the Authorities' Rules and as amended from time to time.' The Court held that this last phrase was sufficient to incorporate into the employment contract all the provisions of the Rules but went on to say that, as a matter of construction, the Rules were made unilaterally by the employers and could not be regarded as rules which were the subject of agreement between the employers and the unions. That being so, the Court concluded that the employers were entitled to vary, alter or cancel any of the provisions in the Rules and were entitled, therefore, to withdraw the scheme.

**3.58** It is also possible that, in the case of a non-contractual provision, the employer will be at liberty to introduce a change which lies within the managerial prerogative. In that case, the employee will be bound to comply with it, if it amounts to a lawful and reasonable instruction. An example of a proposed change falling within the managerial prerogative is *Cresswell v Inland Revenue Board* (1984). There, the employees tried to argue that the Inland Revenue was in breach of their terms of service in requiring them to operate the proposed computerisation of the PAYE system. Walton J. held that, although the proposed introduction of computerisation changed the way the employees performed their duties, they were still administering the PAYE system and performing the duties of tax officers. See para. 3.191, where this case is more fully discussed. Similarly, in *Dryden v Greater Glasgow Health Board* (1992), the employee claimed to have been constructively dismissed when she resigned after the introduction by the employer of a no-smoking policy. The EAT held that this was within the employer's managerial prerogative, so that there was no breach of contract on the part of the employer.

## Express Terms

**3.59** The following points in relation to express terms should be noted:

(1) express terms are the principal sources of contractual obligations and the starting-point for a consideration of the respective rights and obligations of the parties is the contract or written statement of particulars;

(2) express terms may be written or oral or partly written and partly oral;

(3) the best evidence of an express term is an express term contained in a written contract of employment, but, in the absence of such a written contract, the statutory written statement given to an employee under the Employment Rights Act 1996, s 1 is likely to provide the best evidence, though it is not conclusive as to the terms agreed;

(4) the express terms of the contract may also be found in documents expressly or impliedly incorporated into the contract, such as collective agreements or employers' handbooks;

(5) if the contract contains an express term covering a particular matter such as mobility, there will be no scope for the implication of a term in relation to that matter;

(6) an express term may in appropriate cases be qualified by an implied term, such as the term not to behave in a way such as to undermine the relationship of trust and confidence between employer and employee;

(7) where interpretation or construction of the contractual documentation is necessary, the court or tribunal will apply the ordinary rules of construction for contracts, including the *contra proferentem* rule.

(8) an apparently wide clause, such as a flexibility clause, will not always give the employer as free a hand as its terms suggest;

(9) clauses which are apparently unreasonable may be subject to the Unfair Contract Terms Act 1977.

## Incorporation of terms from other documents: collective agreements

**3.60** As a general rule, if a contract expressly refers to some other document, that document will be incorporated into the contract: see, for example, *National Coal Board v Galley* (1958), where the contract was expressed to be 'subject to the collective agreement for the time being in force' and it was held that the collective agreement was incorporated. Other documents may be incorporated expressly, impliedly or by custom and practice.

**3.61** The main principles governing the incorporation of collective agreements are as follows:

(1) a collective agreement may be expressly incorporated into a contract of employment and thus become enforceable as between employer and employee, even though as between the collective parties, the employer and the trade unions, it is expressed to be binding in honour only and is thus not enforceable as between them;

(2) even if a collective agreement is expressly incorporated into an individual employee's contract, the terms of the agreement will only be enforceable by an individual if they are apt for enforcement, such as terms fixing rates of pay and hours of work, but not terms setting up machinery for resolving disputes between the union and the employer;

(3) the terms of a collective agreement which has been incorporated into an individual employee's contract will remain enforceable despite the lapse of the agreement;

(4) a collective agreement which is not expressly incorporated may be incorporated by implication or by custom and practice, but only if its terms are appropriate for incorporation.

**3.62** A convenient starting-point for a discussion of this issue is the decision of the Court of Appeal in *Robertson v British Gas Corporation* (1983), which involved the question whether an incentive bonus scheme in a collective agreement had been incorporated into an employee's contract. The Court of Appeal held that the scheme was incorporated into employees' contracts by virtue of their letters of appointment. Since the scheme gave no power to the employers to terminate it, the Court held that, when they tried to do so, they committed a breach of contract. Kerr LJ said, at p. 358:

> It is true that collective agreements ... create no legally enforceable obligation between the trade union and the employer. Either side can withdraw. But their terms are in this case incorporated into the individual contracts of employment, and it is only if and when those terms are varied collectively by agreement that the individual contracts of employment will also be varied. If the collective scheme is not varied by agreement, but by some unilateral abrogation or withdrawal or

variation to which the other side does not agree, then ... the individual contracts of employment remain unaffected.

**3.63** The Court therefore held the employees to be entitled to the bonus payments to which they were contractually entitled. This case also makes it clear that the terms of a collective agreement which are incorporated into individual employees' contracts will survive the lapse of the collective agreement from which they originated.

**3.64** The Court of Appeal followed this decision in *Marley v Forward Trust Group Ltd* (1986) in which the employee's contract of employment incorporated the employers' personnel manual which included the terms of a collective agreement made between the employers and the union. The agreement was expressed to be binding in honour only and included a provision that, if a redundancy situation arose, an employee who accepted redeployment would have six months in which to assess its suitability without prejudicing his rights to redundancy compensation. This happened to the employee who, after two months, informed his employers that his new position was unsuitable and that he wished to exercise his 'redundancy option'. The employers took the view that the employee had been transferred under a mobility clause in his contract and not because of a redundancy situation. They therefore treated him as having resigned. The Court of Appeal held that the terms of the collective agreement had been incorporated into the individual employee's contract (even though the agreement itself was unenforceable) and that the employers could not rely upon the mobility clause when redeploying the employee.

**3.65** The above two cases are examples of the well-established principle that a document referred to in the contract will be expressly incorporated into it and show the operation of the principle in relation to collective agreements. A further example is to be found in *Cadoux v Central Regional Council* (1986), which was considered above at para. 3.57.

**3.66** The *Alexander* litigation concerned terms in two separate collective agreements governing the procedure to be adopted in the event of a redundancy situation and whether those terms had become part of the employees' contracts. Both terms were to the effect that redundancy selection would be on the basis of 'last in first out'. In the first part of the *Alexander* litigation, *Alexander v Standard Telephones & Cables Ltd* (1990), the employees sought injunctions to restrain the employers from proceeding with the redundancies without applying this principle. The Court refused to grant an injunction. Aldous J. said that the terms incorporated must be terms intended to govern the relationship between the employer and individual employees, and not the relationship between the employer and the trade union. He held that the employees had an arguable case that the provisions in the collective agreement providing for 'last in first out' in the event of a redundancy were part of their contracts of employment, although he refused them an injunction.

**3.67**  In *Alexander v Standard Telephones & Cables Ltd (No. 2)* (1991), which was the trial of the action, the employees sought damages for breach of contract for the loss of their employment up to their respective retirement ages. Hobhouse J. held that the seniority provisions in the collective agreements were not expressly or impliedly incorporated into the individual contracts of employment and the employees therefore had no contractual right not to be made redundant without LIFO being applied. So far as *express* incorporation was concerned, the judge held that as a matter of construction the agreement was not incorporated. The section 1 statement referred to 'the basic terms and conditions' and he held that it covered only those topics which are required by what is now the ERA 1996 to be dealt with in such a statement, and not redundancy matters. He also pointed out that 'even express general words of incorporation do not remove the need to consider whether all the contents of the incorporated document are apt to be terms of the actual contract of employment'. As regards *implied* or *inferred* incorporation, he said, at p. 293:

> Where it is not a case of express incorporation, but a matter of inferring the contractual intent, the character of the document (ie the collective agreement) and the relevant part of it and whether it is apt to form part of the individual contract is central to whether or not the inference should be drawn.

**3.68**  He held that the relevant clauses were not apt for incorporation and remained part of the joint consultation scheme within a procedure agreement. Examining these clauses in the context in which they arose, particularly in view of the fact that none of the other clauses of the collective agreement were apt for incorporation, he said that it would require 'some cogent indication' in the clause 'that it was to have a different character and to be incorporated into the individual contracts of employment': see p. 293.

**3.69**

This case may be contrasted with *Kaur v MG Rover Group Ltd* (2004), Judge Alton (sitting in the High Court) held that a provision in a collective agreement stating that there would be no compulsory redundancies was incorporated into the employee's employment contract so that the employer's right to dismiss the employee with notice for any reason had to be read subject to his contractual right not to be dismissed for redundancy. He held that the job security provision was apt for incorporation. The cases considered above tend to suggest that terms in a collective agreement which are not obviously normative, for example, those governing a redundancy procedure, must be specifically incorporated if they are to be incorporated at all and must be apt for incorporation. Terms which are normative, such as terms governing pay or working hours, are unlikely to pose such problems of incorporation. For a further example of a collective agreement held not to be apt for incorporation, see *Griffiths v Buckinghamshire County Council* (1994), which related to the provisions of an early retirement and voluntary redundancy scheme. The judge held these to be primarily concerned with procedural matters such as consultation requirements and recommendations. Although the cases discussed tend to suggest that the courts are reluctant to allow certain types of term to be enforceable, there is no reason in principle why this should not be so. It does not seem unreasonable to suggest that an employer who has agreed a procedure with the unions should be held to it.

**3.70**  An analogous question arises in relation to the incorporation of a collective agreement entered into by the employer after the start of the employee's employment. In *Hamilton v Futura Floors Ltd* (1990), the employers became members of the relevant employers' association after the employee started employment with them. Lord Kirkwood in the Court of Session (Outer House) in Scotland said that the fact that the employers joined the employers' association did not have the effect of altering, by necessary implication, the terms and conditions of the employee's contract, so that the provisions of the relevant collective agreement could be regarded as incorporated. He said that the terms of the association did not contain any reference to the agreement nor did it seek to impose any obligation on members of the association to introduce any particular term or condition into their employees' contracts. He also said that there was no evidence of a custom or trade by which the provisions of the agreement would be assumed to be incorporated.

**3.71** The incorporation of collective agreements may be relevant in considering whether an employer has power to vary an employee's contract of employment. This aspect of collective agreements is considered later in this chapter: see para. 3.202.

## Incorporation of terms from other documents: documents other than collective agreements

**3.72** Documents other than collective agreements may also be incorporated into the contract. A common example is disciplinary procedures. *Dietmann v London Borough of Brent* (1987), for example, involved the construction of a disciplinary procedure incorporated into an employee's contract, and is considered more fully below: see para. 3.80. See also *Jones v Gwent County Council* (1992), in which the employee successfully sought an injunction against her employers to restrain them from dismissing her unless proper grounds for her dismissal existed and a proper procedure was carried out in accordance with her contract of employment.

**3.73** *Quinn v Calder Industrial Materials Ltd* (1996) involved the unilateral abandonment of a policy governing enhanced redundancy payments and the question was whether this action was in breach of the employees' contracts. The policy was in a document containing guidelines on enhanced payments issued to companies in the group of which the employers were a part. The employers did not communicate the terms of the scheme to the employees or trade unions, although they became generally known. On the occasions when the need to make redundancies arose, the employers applied the guidelines and made enhanced payments. Payments were not made automatically, however, but required the managers to obtain instructions as to whether to pay the enhanced payments. The EAT said that the way the payments were introduced and handled did not warrant the inference that the employers intended to become contractually bound by the scheme. The relevant factors which were taken into account by the EAT in reaching this decision were the period of time over which the policy was applied, the way in which the policy became known to the employees and the fact that, when payments were made, the process was not automatic but required a decision on each occasion. The EAT applied the dictum of Browne-Wilkinson J in *Duke v Reliance Systems Ltd* (1982) (at p. 452):

> A policy adopted by management unilaterally cannot become a term of the employees' contracts unless it is at least shown that the policy has been drawn to the attention of the employees or has been acted followed without exception for a substantial period.

**3.74** In following this dictum, Lord Coulsfield pointed out that these factors are likely to be among the most important circumstances, 'but they have to be taken into account along with all the other circumstances of the case'. A similar decision was reached in *Secretary of State for Employment v ASLEF (No. 2)* (1972), where the Court of Appeal refused to hold that detailed works rules set out in a staff handbook were contractual; they were held to be collateral instructions to the employees as to how they were to carry out their work.

## Construction of express terms

**3.75** The general principles governing construction of written documents are as follows:

(1) an offer which, upon acceptance, is relied upon as altering the legal relationship between the parties, must be construed objectively. Evidence to show what the offeror intended to be the meaning of the term is not admissible for that purpose;

(2) evidence of the action of the parties to a contract is not admissible for the purpose of determining the proper construction of it, but such evidence will be admissible to prove the making of a new contract, whether by addition of a new term or variation of an existing term;

(3)     when the agreed term has been proved, whether it is in writing or oral, the court in construing the term must have regard to the circumstances with reference to which the words were used and must have regard to the object, appearing from those circumstances, which the person using them had in view; and evidence of mutually known facts may be admitted to identify the meaning of a descriptive term;

(4)     if one interpretation of the agreed term completely frustrates the object of the transaction, so as to render the contract futile, that may be a strong argument for an alternative interpretation, if that can be reasonably found; and if one interpretation is unreasonable it may properly cause the court to search for some other possible meaning of the contract;

(5)     an agreement cannot be construed in the light of the subsequent action of the parties;

(6)     if the words used in the contract are ambiguous they will be construed in the way least favourable to the party relying upon them;

(7)     there is a general rule of construction that, in the absence of clear language to the contrary it is not to be assumed that parties to a contract intended that one party could deprive the other of rights and benefits under the contract by relying on his or her own breach of contract.

**3.76** In *Hooper v British Railways Board* (1988), for example, the question was whether the terms of a negotiated agreement were modified by the later actions of the employers and the trade unions. The original term involved a contractual right to full pay of a member of staff declared fit for work by his or her own doctor but who failed to meet the medical standards required by the railway medical officer. The term as drafted obliged the employers to pay such employees until resumption of work in their own post or in other suitable work. The question was whether the term operated so as to entitle an employee to be kept on full pay until he or she was redeployed or reached retirement age; in other words whether the term imposed no limitation on the right or whether it was only to be of short-term duration.

**3.77** The employers tried to argue that the term had been modified as a result of a later document in which they put forward their view that the original term was intended to provide for payment only for situations of a short-term duration. The Court of Appeal rejected this argument, applying the principle that an agreement cannot be construed in the light of the subsequent actions of the parties. They therefore upheld the employee's argument that the contractual right had not been modified. The employers were thus held to an interpretation of the term which they felt was not what had been agreed with the unions.

**3.78**  A similar view was taken in *Lee v GEC Plessey Telecommunications* (1993), considered in more detail at para. 3.203, where the judge said that the employers' practice of issuing General Instructions and Notices did not have the effect of varying the employees' contracts. Much the same approach was taken by the EAT in *Johnson v Peabody Trust* (1996) in dealing with the question of redundancy in the context of an employee who was employed as a roofer but who was subject to a flexibility clause requiring him 'where possible ... to carry out multi-trade operations'. The EAT said that the 'work of a particular kind', within the meaning of what is now ERA 1996, s 139(1)(b) (formerly section 81(2)(b) of the 1978 Act), was the work of a roofer and that the obligation to do work on multi-trade operations was 'very much a subsidiary obligation introduced to operate a degree of flexibility within the workforce in times of increasing economic difficulty': see p. 389.

**3.79**  In *White v Reflecting Roadstuds Ltd* (1991), considered more fully at para. 3.211, the EAT refused to construe a flexibility clause as being subject to an implied term that the employer would act reasonably when implementing the clause. They did add, however, that if there were no reasonable or sufficient grounds for the view that the employee should be required to move there would be a breach of the flexibility clause: see p. 742. A similar view was expressed in *McClory v The Post Office* (1993) in which the court held that there is an implied term that an employer cannot exercise its power under a contractual provision on unreasonable grounds. It is important to bear in mind, therefore, that, even if an express clause is of apparently wide ambit, the court will either construe it narrowly or construe it subject to the implied term that the employer will not do anything to damage the relationship of trust and confidence between the parties. Flexibility clauses and clauses giving an employer the right to vary are considered in more detail at para. 3.202.

**3.80** Incorporated documents also give rise to problems of interpretation. In *Dietmann v London Borough of Brent* (1988), the document in question was a disciplinary procedure. The relevant clause read:

> Any breach of the disciplinary rules will render you liable to disciplinary action, which will normally include immediate suspension followed by dismissal, or instant dismissal, for offences of gross misconduct unless there are mitigating circumstances.

The employer's argument was as follows: (1) a breach of the disciplinary rules will lead to disciplinary action; (2) disciplinary action will normally include immediate suspension followed by dismissal; (3) for offences of gross misconduct, instant dismissal not preceded by suspension and without the need for a formal disciplinary meeting was permissible. The employee's argument was: (a) any breach will lead to disciplinary action; (b) if the alleged breach amounts to gross misconduct then this will normally mean immediate suspension pending the outcome of the disciplinary hearing; (c) in a case of gross misconduct the hearing may recommend (i) instant dismissal or (ii) dismissal on proper notice. The Court of Appeal followed the employee's argument. See also *Honeyford v City of Bradford Metropolitan Council* (1986) and *McGoldrick v London Borough of Brent* (1987), which both involved the interpretation of a disciplinary procedure.

## Specific express terms

**3.81** Express terms relating to the following matters are considered here:

- mobility;
- working time;
- pay;
- benefits in kind;
- holidays;
- 'garden leave';
- notice and pay in lieu of notice.

## MOBILITY

**3.82** It is advisable to include an express mobility term in the employment contract; otherwise, a term will fall to be implied. Clearly, employers who want to save arguments later will be well advised to include an express clause. If a term is implied, there is the risk that the term will have a disproportionate effect which could have been avoided. In any case, ERA 1996, s 1(4)(h) requires the written statement to specify the place of work or 'where the employee is required or permitted to work at various places, an indication of that and of the address of the employer'. The provisions of section 1(4)(k) should also be noted. These come into operation for employees required to work outside the United Kingdom for more than one month. These statutory provisions are considered at para. 3.43 above.

**3.83** The Court of Appeal decision in *Meade-Hill v British Council* (1995) has led to suggestions that mobility clauses may be indirectly discriminatory and contrary to the provisions of the Sex Discrimination Act 1975. This is debatable, particularly as the Court of Appeal remitted to the county court for it to consider whether the term was justified. The observations of Millett LJ, at p. 862, suggest that this should not be too difficult for an employer. As has already been mentioned, even a wide express clause does not entitle the employer to behave unreasonably in relying on it to require mobility from an employee. See, for example, *United Bank Ltd v Akhtar* (1989), which is discussed at para. 3.122. In the light of that case, a mobility clause should provide for reasonable notice and financial assistance to be provided to employees affected. For examples of cases involving express terms, reference should be made to *United Kingdom Atomic Energy Authority v Claydon* (1974) and *Rank Xerox Ltd v Churchill* (1988). In the first case, the relevant clause read: 'The (employers) reserve the right to require any member of their staff to work at any of their establishments in Great Britain or in posts overseas'. In the *Rank Xerox* case, the relevant clause read: 'The company may require you to transfer to another location'. The EAT held that the words of the term were perfectly clear and simple and did not need to be qualified by words such as 'within a reasonable daily travelling distance of your home'. If the clause is ambiguous, it will be construed against the person seeking to rely upon it, ie in practice the employer. In the absence of an express mobility clause, a mobility term may fall to be implied, but it is likely that it will be of more restricted scope than could have been provided for by an express mobility clause. This matter is discussed at para. 3.135 below.

## WORKING TIME

**3.84** The arrangements for working time will depend upon the nature of the employer's work. For example, the employer may operate a shift system for production staff and flexitime arrangements for administration staff; field sales staff and managers may have fixed hours. Although theoretically the employer might demand of the employee long working hours, it is possible that this might be subject to an implied restriction, arising from the decision of the Court of Appeal in *Johnstone v Bloomsbury Health Authority* (1991), which is considered more fully at para. 3.125. The effect of the Working Time Regulations 1998 (SI 1998/1833) should be noted. The Regulations were introduced to implement Council Directive 93/104/EC, but not before the UK Government had brought an (unsuccessful) action against the European Commission arguing that the legal basis upon which the Directive adopted was incorrect: see *United Kingdom v Commission of the European Union* (1997).

**3.85** The Regulations apply to workers (as defined by reg. 2(1)) and specify that working time, including overtime, should not exceed an average of 48 hours for each seven days in any 'reference period'. A reference period is usually a period of 17 weeks, though in certain circumstances it may be as long as 26 or, in some cases, 52 weeks: see regs. 4(1), (3) and (5) and 23. 'Working time' is defined in reg. 2(1); the main definition is 'any period during which (the worker) is working, at his employer's disposal and carrying out his activity or duties.' Whilst time spent commuting to work is clearly not covered by this definition, there are issues as to whether time spent on call or similar waiting time is. See *Sindicato de Médicos de Asistencia Pública (SIMAP) v Consellería de Sanidad y Consumo de la Generalidad Valenciana* (Case C-303/98) (2001). The maximum weekly working time does not apply to workers whose agreement in writing has been previously obtained by their employer: see reg. 4(1). The agreement is terminable by seven days' notice in writing: reg. 5(2)(b).

**3.86** There are also provisions relating to night work, daily and weekly rest periods and rest breaks: regs. 6 and 10–12. The Regulations do not apply to those in 'domestic service' and workers in relation to whom 'on account of the specific characteristics of the activity in which he is engaged, the duration of his working time is not measured or predetermined or can be determined by the worker himself ...' See reg. 20(1) which then goes on to give as an example 'managing executives or other persons with autonomous decision-taking powers'. In the early days of the Regulations, employers tried to designate those groups of workers who were covered by this regulation, but the fact is that such attempts are pointless since it is up to the courts or tribunals to decide who falls within this category. Although the Directive (and Regulations) originally exempted various sectors, such as the transport and maritime sectors and junior doctors, these exemptions have been removed or narrowed down by subsequent amending Directives: see EC Directive 2000/34, transposed into domestic law by the Working Time (Amendment) Regulations 2003 (SI 2003/1684).

## PAY AND BENEFITS IN KIND

**3.87** Employees are usually either salaried or hourly paid and they are paid weekly or monthly (or at four weekly intervals). The rate of pay may either be negotiated with the individual employee concerned or determined according to a collective agreement. In the latter case, the contract should cross-refer to the relevant agreement. The terms relating to pay may also make provision for profit-sharing, performance-related pay, bonuses, commission and the like. The effect of the National Minimum Wage Act 1998 should be borne in mind.

**3.88** An employee may be entitled to an increase in salary or to a bonus, but only if the relevant clause(s) in the contract can be construed as conferring that entitlement. In this connection, the cases of *Clark v BET plc* (1997) and *Clark v Nomura International plc* (2000) are relevant. In *Clark v BET plc*, the relevant clause stated as follows:

> The executive's salary shall be reviewed annually and be increased by such amount if any as the board shall in its absolute discretion decide. In making their decision the board shall consider a comparative group of

companies similar to that used in section 4 of the report 'Review of Executive Remuneration' dated 14 December 1993 produced by William M. Mercer Ltd.

**3.89**  Timothy Walker J took the view that this clause was to be construed as obliging the employers to provide an annual upward adjustment in salary but leaving the amount (if any) of the increase to the absolute discretion of the board. In *Clark v Nomura International plc* the employee's contract provided for a 'discretionary bonus scheme which is not guaranteed in any way and is dependent on individual performance and after the first 12 months your remaining in our employment on the date of payment.' He was a senior proprietary equities trader who in the relevant period was responsible for profits for his employers of around £6.5 million. He was dismissed with three months' notice but, although he was still in employment at the date of payment of the bonus, he did not receive it. He made a claim for damages alleging that the employers' failure to pay him any bonus amounted to a breach of contract. The judge upheld his claim. According to Burton J, an employer exercising a discretion which on the face of the contract of employment is unfettered or absolute, will be in breach of contract if no reasonable employer would have exercised the discretion in that way. See also *Brand v Compro Computer Services Ltd* (2004) and contrast *Peninsula Business Services Ltd v Sweeney* (2004).

**3.90**  It is common for employers to provide benefits in kind or 'fringe benefits' to their staff. Some, such as pensions or season ticket loans, may be provided to all staff who have been in the employer's employment long enough to qualify; some will be provided on the basis of the needs of the employee, for example company cars for salesmen; some will be provided on the basis of status, for example company cars, membership of a private medical expenses scheme and the like. In all cases, it is essential to make clear whether the benefit is discretionary or contractual. If it is contractual and the employee's employment is terminated in breach of the contract, the loss of the benefit will be included in the calculation of damages to be awarded to the employee: see, for example, *Shove v Downs Surgical plc* (1984). Even if the benefit is contractual, the employer may wish to retain some discretion, for example over the choice of company car or pension scheme. Benefits to which employees are contractually entitled are liable to be taxed. There are special provisions relating to the taxation of company cars.

**3.91** Other benefits which an employer may wish to offer all or some of the employees are:

- health insurance (eg membership of BUPA);
- free or subsidised canteen;
- free or subsidised uniform or safety clothing;
- season ticket loan scheme;
- participation in a share option scheme.

**3.92** In the case of an option scheme, the employer may wish to exclude the employee from benefit in certain circumstances, for example, cessation of employment or dismissal. In *Micklefield v SAC Technology Ltd* (1990), the relevant clause read:

> If any option holder ceases to be an executive for any reason he shall not be entitled, and by applying for an option an executive shall be deemed irrevocably to have waived any entitlement by way of compensation for loss of office or otherwise howsoever to any sum or other benefit to compensate him for the loss of any rights under the scheme.

For the purposes of the decision it was assumed that the employee was wrongfully dismissed and the question was whether he was entitled to recover damages for loss of the option to purchase shares. It was held that the clause was an exemption clause which exempted the employers from part of the liability for their wrong. The judge went on to say that, if he was wrong in that conclusion, nevertheless as a matter of construction the clause had the effect of excluding the principle that a person cannot take advantage of their own wrong. He also held that the Unfair Contract Terms Act 1977 did not apply to invalidate the clause, since Schedule 1, paragraph 1(e) excludes any contract 'so far as it relates to the creation or transfer of securities or of any right or interest in securities'. See also *Levett v Biotrace International plc* (1999). In *Mallone v BPB Industries Ltd* (2002), the Court of Appeal made clear that where a scheme gives the directors of a company the discretion to cancel options, that discretion must be exercised properly and rationally.

HOLIDAYS

**3.93**  Until the advent of the Working Time Regulations (WTR) there was very limited statutory regulation of holiday rights and in practice an employee's entitlement to holiday depended upon the terms of the employment contract. Now regs. 13 and 16 entitle workers to four weeks' annual paid leave in each leave year (as defined by reg. 13(2)). There are detailed provisions dealing with the dates on which leave may be taken, which entail either party giving notice within prescribed time limits and containing prescribed information. An employer wishing to escape these provisions may do so by having a 'relevant agreement', in practice a collective agreement or employment contract: see the definition in reg. 2(1). Leave may not be bought out unless the worker's employment is terminated: see reg. 13(9). It should be noted that ERA 1996, s 1(4)(d)(i) requires the written statement given to employees to contain particulars of terms and conditions relating to holidays, including public holidays, and holiday pay. The particulars must be sufficient to enable the employee's holiday entitlement, including any entitlement to accrued holiday pay on the termination of employment, to be precisely calculated. These particulars must be given in the written statement itself; it is not permissible to refer to another document which is reasonably accessible to the employee.

**3.94**  This provision was considered by the Court of Appeal in *Morley v Heritage plc* (1993). The employee tried to argue that, on termination of his employment, he was entitled to accrued holiday pay in lieu of the unused holiday entitlement by virtue of a term which has to be implied to satisfy the requirements of s 1. The Court of Appeal said that s 1(4)(d)(i) merely recognises that a contract can include a provision relating to accrued holiday pay and that, if it does, the written statement should contain particulars of it. The Court also said that it was unnecessary, having regard to the terms of the particular contract and the status of the particular employee, to imply a term entitling the employee to accrued holiday pay to give the contract business efficacy. This suggests that there may be cases in which it may be possible to imply a term. See also *Thames Water Utilities v Reynolds* (1996) in which the issue was whether a clause entitling an employee to accrued holiday pay should be construed as entitling him to holiday calculated on the basis of calendar days or working days.

## 'GARDEN LEAVE' CLAUSES

**3.95** A 'garden leave' clause is a clause found in employment contracts by which the employer reserves the right to require the employee not to perform his or her duties as an employee but agrees that he or she will continue to be paid. Such clauses have so far given rise to relatively little case law and such case law as there is has tended to be concerned the principles upon which injunctions are granted.

**3.96** The first case to consider a garden leave clause was *Provident Financial Group plc v Hayward* (1989). The employee's contract as financial director provided that, during the continuance of his employment, he would not 'undertake any other business or profession or be or become an employee or agent of any other person or persons or assist or have any financial interest in any other business or profession.' Another clause provided that the company was under no obligation to provide him with work but could suspend him from performance of his duties or exclude him from any premises of the company, but his salary was not to cease to be payable by reason only of the suspension or exclusion. During 1988 Mr Hayward tendered his resignation and continued working until 5 September when the employers decided that they did not want him to work out his notice. They were prepared to pay in full until the agreed termination date (31 December), provided that he did not work for anyone else. From 5 September, therefore, Mr Hayward was on 'garden leave.' On 13 October, he wrote to his employers announcing his intention to start work on the following Monday with another company. His employers were concerned about confidential information and applied for an injunction to stop him from doing so. The Court of Appeal upheld the judge's decision not to grant an injunction but their reasons for doing so had nothing to do with the validity or otherwise of the 'garden leave' clause. They really concerned the principles on which injunctions are granted. Although the Court of Appeal did not need to decide on the validity of the clause in question, Dillon LJ did comment on the fact that 'garden leave' clauses are capable of abuse, particularly as employers tend to have somewhat exaggerated views of what will or may affect their businesses. He also said that an employee is concerned to work and to exercise his or her skills. See also *Crédit Suisse Asset Management Ltd v Armstrong* (1996).

**3.97** In the light of these decisions there are uncertainties surrounding garden leave clauses, since an excessively long period of notice linked with garden leave might be held to be in restraint of trade and thus void and unenforceable. A number of questions have yet to be fully considered:

(1)    can a garden leave clause be used to prevent an employee from working either at all or during the notice period?

(2)    if so, does it conflict with the 'right to work'?

(3)    are there/should there be any limits on the period of garden leave? and

(4)    in what circumstances will such a clause be enforceable by injunction?

It may be that the method of termination may affect the employer's chances of enforcing restraints against an ex-employee: see *General Billposting Co Ltd v Atkinson* (1909) and *Rex Stewart Jeffries Parker Ginsberg Ltd v Parker* (1988). It is clear from these cases that an employer who dismisses an employee in breach of contract will not be able to rely upon any restraints in the contract of employment. See further paras. 3.99, 3.100 and 3.104 below.

It is unlikely that in the absence of an express garden leave provision the court would be prepared to imply such a provision: see *William Hill Organisation Ltd v Tucker* (1999) ICR 291, at p. 301.

## NOTICE

**3.98**    At common law, the parties are free to choose whatever notice provision they like, though an employer who sought to impose an excessively long notice period on an employee might be prevented from doing so by the doctrine of restraint of trade. If the contract of employment does not specify a notice period a reasonable period of notice will be implied. In most cases where there are no express notice provisions, the situation is likely to be governed by ERA 1996, s 86, which gives a statutory right to a minimum period of notice. Employees continuously employed for one month or more but less than two years are entitled to at least one week's notice. After two years' employment, they are entitled to one week's notice for each year of continuous employment, but, if they have been employed for more than 12 years, their statutory entitlement will not exceed 12 weeks. Section 86(2) obliges an employee continuously employed for one month or more to give at least one week's notice. The notice must be definite and explicit and must specify the date of termination or give sufficient facts from which the date of termination can be ascertained: *Morton Sundour Fabrics Ltd v Shaw* (1967) and *Walker v Cotswold Chine Home School* (1977). Once a notice has been given, it cannot be withdrawn unilaterally, but only with the agreement of the other party: see *Riordan v War Office* (1959) and *Harris and Russell Ltd v Slingsby* (1973). Although an attempt to provide for a shorter period will be ineffective, section 86(3) provides that either side may waive his or her right to notice or accept a payment in lieu of notice. It is open to an employee and employer to agree upon longer periods of notice than those set out in section 86.

**3.99** In the absence of an express clause the employee might seek to argue that he or she was impliedly entitled to a longer period of notice than the one week provided for by section 86(2). The length of notice afforded by an implied term is unlikely to be as long as that which may be provided for by an express term and is unlikely to exceed a year, even for the most senior of employees; in most other cases, it is unlikely that it would exceed six months. In addition to terms governing notice, employment contracts sometimes contain a clause providing for the employee to receive pay in lieu of notice to avoid the risk of any post-termination restraints being held to be unenforceable. An example of such a clause, sometimes called an 'agreed damages clause' is to be found in *Rex Stewart Jeffries Parker Ginsberg Ltd v Parker* (1988). The employee's contract provided that his employment could be 'determined by the giving in writing of six calendar months' notice on either side or the payment of six months' salary in lieu thereof.' He was given one week's notice and six months' salary in lieu of notice. He claimed that this amounted to a breach of contract but the Court of Appeal rejected this argument. Had it succeeded, he would have been able to claim that he was no longer bound by a non-solicitation clause. This is because of the principle stated in *General Billposting Co Ltd v Atkinson* (1909), that an employer who wrongfully dismisses an employee cannot enforce a restrictive covenant against him or her. The method of termination of an employee's contract of employment may, therefore, affect the employer's chances of enforcing a restraint against an ex-employee.

**3.100** There are suggestions in the later case of *Rock Refrigeration Ltd v Jones and Seward Refrigeration Ltd* (1996) that this principle is of less wide application than had previously been thought. In that case the Court of Appeal refused to strike down as unreasonable restrictive covenants expressed to operate upon termination of the contract 'howsoever arising' or 'howsoever occasioned' in the circumstances that the employee resigned from the company to join a competitor. A majority of the Court said that the *General Billposting* principle would apply if the employers wrongfully dismissed the employee, but said that it did not apply to the circumstances which had arisen. Phillips LJ went further and suggested that the rule 'accords neither with current legal principle nor with the requirements of business efficacy'. His view was that the parties should be at liberty to agree to a restraint which continues to operate even if one of them repudiates the contract. This would appear to give generous latitude to contract-breakers.

**3.101** At common law, the parties are free to insert an agreed damages clause into the contract, provided that the clause is not in the nature of a penalty. In that case, the amount stipulated will not be recoverable and the plaintiff will have to prove what damages he or she can. See *Dunlop Pneumatic Tyre Co Ltd* v *New Garage and Motor Co Ltd* (1915), where the principles governing penalty clauses are set out. There Lord Dunedin summed up the law in the following propositions, at pp. 86–88:

> (1) Though the parties to a contract who use the words 'penalty' or 'liquidated damages' may prima facie be supposed to mean what they say, yet the expression is not conclusive. The court must find out whether the payment stipulated is in truth a penalty or liquidated damages ...
> (2) The essence of a penalty is a payment of money stipulated as *in terrorem* of the offending party; the essence of liquidated damages is a genuine pre-estimate of damage.
> (3) The question whether a sum stipulated is a penalty or liquidated damages is a question of construction to be decided upon the terms and inherent circumstances of each particular contract, judged of at the time of the making of the contract, not as at the time of the breach.
> (4) To assist this task of construction various tests have been suggested which, if applicable to the case under consideration, may prove helpful or even conclusive. Such are:

(a)    It will be held to be a penalty if the sum stipulated for is extravagant and unconscionable in amount in comparison with the greatest loss which could conceivably be proved to have followed from the breach.

(b)    It will be held to be a penalty if the breach consists only in not paying a sum of money, and the sum stipulated is a sum greater than the sum which ought to have been paid ...

(c)    there is a presumption (but no more) that it is penalty when a single lump sum is made payable by way of compensation, on the occurrence of one or more or all of several events, some of which may occasion serious and others but trifling damage.

on the other hand:

(d)    It is no obstacle to the sum stipulated being a genuine pre-estimate of damage, that the consequences of the breach are such as to make precise pre-estimation almost an impossibility. On the contrary, that is just the situation when it is probable that pre-estimated damage was the true bargain between the parties.

**3.102**    A more recent example of the application of this principle is to be found in *Neil v Strathclyde Borough Council* (1984) IRLR 14, which involved a clause by which the employee agreed to refund to her employers a proportion of their outlays in respect of a period of leave of absence during which she took a training course if she left their service within two years of completion of the course. She tried to argue that the provision was a penalty and therefore unenforceable, but the Sheriff Principal upheld the employers' claim against her, applying the principles set out above.

## Restrictive covenants

**3.103**    For a restrictive covenant to be enforceable, it must protect the employer's legitimate business interests, either trade secrets or goodwill and trade connections. It is not possible to prevent competition as such. A restrictive covenant in a contract of employment will be prima facie void, but will be enforceable if it is reasonable:

> ... reasonable, that is, in reference to the interests of the parties concerned and reasonable in reference to the interests of the public, so framed and so guarded as to afford adequate protection to the party in whose favour [they are] imposed, while at the same time ... in no way injurious to the public.

See Lord MacNaghten in *Nordenfelt v Maxim Nordenfelt Guns and Ammunition Co Ltd* (1894).

**3.104** The covenants most likely to be enforced are those which are reasonably necessary to protect the employer's trade secrets and trade connection. It is possible that employees and suppliers may also be legitimate interests, but they would need to be clearly defined. An employee who accepts employment in which he or she would be likely to damage these interests may be restrained. If, therefore, an employee would be likely to use the employer's trade secrets in new employment, he or she may be restrained. He or she may also be restrained from soliciting the ex-employer's customers or from setting up his or her own business or accepting a position with one of the ex-employer's competitors, if that is likely to damage the employer's trade connection by a misuse of his or her acquaintance with the employer's customers or clients. The factors to be taken into account include:

(1)   the area of restraint;

(2)   the period of restraint;

(3)   the nature of the interest sought to be protected; and

(4)   the subject-matter of the restraint.

As a general rule, an employer who breaches the contract of employment, for example by wrongfully dismissing the employee, will not be allowed to enforce any restrictive covenants contained in the contract. This was established by the House of Lords in *General Billposting Ltd v Atkinson* (1909), and reiterated by the majority of the Court of Appeal in *Rock Refrigeration Ltd v Jones and Seward Refrigeration Ltd* (1996). See also *Rex Stewart Jeffries Parker Ginsberg Ltd v Parker* (1988).

**3.105** The following points should also be noted here:

1.  It is for the judge to decide, on the basis of the appropriate evidence, whether in the particular of the case a restraint is reasonable or not. This means that a decision in one case that a particular restraint is reasonable (for example, two years in the case of a milk roundsman) does not mean that in all subsequent cases involving the same type of employment a judge is bound by that decision: see *Dairy Crest Ltd v Pigott* (1989). The Court of Appeal said that the judge was wrong in considering that he was bound by principle to hold that in the case of a milk roundsman a two-year restraint was not unreasonable.

2.  If there is a change of employer, in circumstances such that the Transfer of Undertakings (Protection of Employment) Regulations 1981 apply, the transferee employer may be able to enforce a restrictive covenant entered into between the transferor employer and the employee. But a transferee employer will not be able to enforce a restrictive covenant introduced into the transferring employees' contracts as a result of the transfer. See *Morris Angel & Son Ltd v Hollande* (1993) and *Credit Suisse First Boston (Europe) Ltd v Lister* (1999).

3.  In appropriate cases, 'severance' may be possible.

4.  The fact that a restrictive covenant is not restricted to the United Kingdom will not necessarily make it unreasonable: see *Scully UK Ltd v Lee* (1998).

## Non-solicitation covenants

**3.106** These covenants are intended to prevent ex-employees from soliciting the business of clients or customers of their former employer in competition with their former employer for a period of time after the employment ends. It must be shown that the employee's contact with the customers is sufficiently direct or influential as to give rise to the real possibility of misuse of the employee's knowledge of the customers. A covenant not to solicit customers may be enforced so as to prevent the solicitation of those who were customers not only at the date of termination of the employment but at any other time during the period of employment (even if they had ceased to be customers before its termination); it will not be reasonable to restrain solicitation of persons who might become the employer's customers after termination, for example by a clause restraining an employee from soliciting anyone in the relevant trade in the area in which he or she used to operate for the employer. In *The Marley Tile Co Ltd v Johnson* (1982), the court refused to restrain the solicitation of those who were customers of the employer within the 12 months preceding the termination of the employee's employment, on the grounds that the number of customers involved (said to be some 2,500) was so large that he could not possibly have known of or come into contact with more than a small percentage of them. In *Office Angels Ltd v Rainer-Thomas* (1991), the covenant in question prohibited the employees from setting up or being employed in or otherwise engaged in the trade or business of an employment agency within 1,000 metres of the branch where they had previously worked for a period of six months after the termination of their employment. The employees involved worked in one of the employers' four branches in the City of London, at Bow Lane. After leaving the employers, they set up in an employment agency operating from premises within 1,000 metres of Bow Lane. The Court of Appeal refused to enforce the restrictive covenant. They noted that the effect of the restriction was to preclude the employees from opening an office anywhere within an area of about 1.2 square miles, including most of the City of London. They said that an area restriction was not appropriate because it would do little to protect the employers' connection with their clients. Client orders were placed over the telephone and it was of no concern to them where the office was located. They took the view that this was not an appropriate form of covenant for the protection of the employers' connection with its clients and was wider than was necessary, though they acknowledged that they were entitled to protect their goodwill.

**3.107**  A second type of non-solicitation covenant which is much less common is a covenant restricting the solicitation or employment of former colleagues. This type of covenant, which is sometimes called a 'non-poaching' covenant, was considered by the Court of Appeal in *Hanover Insurance Brokers v Schapiro* (1994). The Court refused to enforce the particular covenant. Although such covenants are not inherently unenforceable, it is clear that the courts are wary of enforcing them. Two cases in which non-poaching clauses have been upheld are *Ingham v ABC Contract Services Ltd* (unreported) and *Alliance Paper Group plc v Prestwich* (1996). To stand any chance of being enforced, they will have to be narrowly drawn and applicable only to employees who were colleagues of the ex-employees at the same time; probably, too, they will need to be applicable only to particular types of employees. In *Massey* (1999), the judge refused to uphold a non-solicitation covenant involving employees of a company on the two grounds that (a) the covenant prohibited solicitation of any employee without reference to his or her importance in the business or technical knowledge or experience and (b) that it applied to any employee who joined the company during the prohibited period including those whose employment began after the employee sought to be restrained had ceased to be an employee.

## Non-competition covenants

**3.108** These types of covenants are used to protect employers where the employee has a close relationship with clients (as in *Marion White Ltd v Francis* (1972)) or has knowledge of the employer's trade secrets or confidential information (as in *Commercial Plastics Ltd v Vincent* (1964)). In both cases, the restraint must be restricted to activities connected with the goodwill or trade secrets the employer is trying to protect; duration and area limitations are particularly impor-tant. An example is *Littlewoods Organisation Ltd v Harris* (1997), in which the Court of Appeal construed a clause which, on its face, prevented an ex-employee from working for a rival organisation or any of its subsidiaries throughout the world, so as to prevent him from working for the rival in the United Kingdom. Lord Denning M R said: '... I think that limiting words ought to be read into the clause so as to limit it to the part of the business for which the (employers) are reasonably entitled to protection.' (See also *Lansing Linde Ltd v Kerr* (1991) and *Turner v Commonwealth & British Minerals Ltd* (2000)) Another example of a covenant involving an attempt by an employer to protect trade secrets is to be found in the case of *FSS Travel and Leisure Systems Ltd v Johnson* (1998), in which the relevant clause read as follows:

> For a period of one year after termination of your employment hereunder (howsoever caused) you shall not:

either alone or jointly as a manager or agent for any person directly or indirectly carry on or be engaged or concerned in any business in the United Kingdom which competes with the business of the FSS Group in which you shall have been personally concerned at the date of such termination.

**3.109**  At first instance the judge held that the company had trade secrets which it was entitled to protect but that the duration of the restraint was not reasonable. The Court of Appeal dismissed the appeal, although they held that the judge had erred in holding that the employers had trade secrets which they were entitled to protect. They said that the critical question in deciding whether an employer has trade secrets which are legitimately protected by means of a restrictive covenant is whether there are trade secrets which can fairly be regarded as the employer's property, as distinct from the skill, experience, know-how and general knowledge which can fairly be regarded as the property of the employee to use without restraint for his or her own benefit or in the services of a competitor. In each case, it is a question of examining closely the detailed evidence relating to the employer's claim for secrecy and deciding, as a matter of fact, on which side of the boundary line it falls. In the present case, the evidence adduced by the employers was not sufficiently specific, precise or cogent to identify and establish a separate body of objective knowledge qualifying for protection as a trade secret by means of a restrictive covenant. Subsequently, in *SBJ Stephenson Ltd v Mandy* (2000), Bell J. reiterated that the true distinction to be made is between 'objective knowledge' which is the property of the employer and 'subjective knowledge' which is the employee's own property, following Lord Shaw's dictum in *Herbert Morris Ltd v Saxelby* (1916), at p. 714.

## Implied terms

**3.110**  The following points should be noted:

(1)    even if the employer complies with the requirements of ERA 1996, s 1 and gives a written statement or decides to give an employee a full written contract of employment, there are likely to be areas in the contract which are not covered by express terms and where the court or tribunal will have to consider resorting to implied terms to fill the apparent gap;

(2)    a term will only be implied where there is no express term governing the matter over which there is dispute;

(3)    if a term is implied the term will be no wider than is necessary to give efficacy to the contract;

(4)    an express term may in some cases be qualified by an implied term;

(5)    there is a difference between terms such as mobility/flexibility terms which have to be determined according to the particular contract, and 'status' or 'legal incidents' terms which, where used, establish rules for contracts of employment as a class;

(6)    if a term is not implied on the basis of the tests set out below, it may be possible to imply a term based upon custom and practice, if the custom is reasonable, certain and notorious.

**3.111**  Although there are specific terms which are implied into the employment contract and which give rise to specific obligations, it is worth drawing attention to the observation of Edmund-Davies LJ in *Wilson v Racher* (1974) (at p.430):

> Reported decisions provide useful, but only general guides, each case turning upon its own facts. Many of the decisions which are customarily cited in these cases date from the last century and may be wholly out of accord with current social conditions. What would today be regarded as almost an attitude of Czar-serf, which is to be found in some of the older cases where a dismissed employee failed to recover damages, would, I venture to think, be decided differently today. We have by now come to realise that a contract of service imposes upon the parties a duty of mutual respect.

**3.112**  It is important, therefore, to bear in mind that the decision of the court in a particular case may well turn on its own facts and that a single action in one context may amount to a breach which is sufficiently serious to justify summary dismissal, whereas in another context it would not. A good example of this is the decisions in *Pepper v Webb* (1969) and *Wilson v Racher*, above. In both cases the employee used bad language to the employer, but in the first case the use of bad language was coupled with a history of disobedience and the use of bad language coupled with disobedience of an order was the 'final straw'; in the second the employer provoked the employee into using the bad language. In the first case, the wrongful dismissal claim failed, whereas in the second it succeeded. At common law, a breach by either party of an implied term may give the other party the right to terminate the contract without notice. Thus, a breach of an implied term by the employer may give the employee the right to resign and argue that the breach was so significant as to amount to a repudiation and to entitle him or her to treat the contract as at an end. In the context of the statutory right not to be unfairly dismissed this is usually called a constructive dismissal. In other contexts, it is probably best called a wrongful repudiation or simply a breach of contract: see Chapter 5.

**3.113** If the *employee* is in breach of an implied term, again the question is whether the breach by the employee amounts to a repudiation of the contract. In *Laws v London Chronicle (Indicator Newspapers) Ltd* (1959), Lord Evershed MR said:

> ... [T]he question must be – if summary dismissal is claimed to be justifiable – whether the conduct complained of is such as to show the servant to have disregarded the essential conditions of the contract of service.

The facts of each case must be looked at to see whether what has happened amounts to a repudiation of his or her contract by the employee (or, indeed, the employer). Thus, in one context a single act may warrant instant dismissal (as, for example, in *Sinclair v Neighbour* (1967) ), whereas in another the case may involve a history of acts similar to the act which causes the dismissal and effectively constitutes the 'final straw': see *Pepper v Webb* (1969), which involved unsatisfactory work, and *Clouston v Corry* (1906), which involved drunkenness. Much therefore depends upon the type of reason involved and the context in which it arises. In *Jupiter General Insurance Co Ltd v Shroff* (1937), the Privy Council emphasised that 'the test to be applied must vary with the nature of the business and the position held by the employee, and that decisions in other cases are of little value.' They also pointed out that in such cases 'one must apply the standards of men, and not those of angels, and remember that men are apt to show temper when reprimanded.'

**3.114** It should also be borne in mind that attitudes change as social conditions change, a fact commented upon by Edmund-Davies LJ in *Wilson v Racher*, above. A good example of the need to be responsive to change is the EAT's decision in *Denco Ltd v Joinson* (1991), which involved deliberate misuse of a computer during employment. The *Denco* case also makes clear that the categories of implied terms are not closed and that it will often fall to a court of tribunal to consider whether a term should be implied and, if appropriate, what its ambit should be. Examples of this are to be found in the cases of *W A Goold (Pearmak) Ltd v McConnell* (1995), *Spring v Guardian Assurance plc* (1994) and *Aspden v Webbs Poultry & Meat Group (Holdings) Ltd* (1996). In the first case, the EAT used the existence of the statutory provisions relating to the provision of a note by employers relating to their grievance procedures as a basis for implying a term that an employer will 'reasonably and promptly afford a reasonable opportunity to their employees to obtain redress of any grievance they may have'. The employers' failure to provide and implement a grievance procedure was held by the EAT to amount to a breach of contract sufficiently serious to entitle the employee to resign and complain that he had been unfairly constructively dismissed.

**3.115** In *Spring v Guardian Assurance plc*, Lords Slynn of Hadley and Woolf said, *obiter*, that it was an implied term of the employee's contract of employment that an employer will ensure that reasonable care is taken in the compiling and giving of a reference to a prospective employer. The main issue in the case was whether the employers were negligent or not, but the approach of two of their Lordships shows the development of a contractual liability in this area. It is possible that a similar line of reasoning may emerge in relation to the employer's common law duty to provide a safe system of work for the employees. For example, in *Walker v Northumberland County Council* (1995), the employers were held to be in breach of their duty of care to an employee in respect of a second mental breakdown he suffered whilst working for them. Although their liability arose in tort, there seems to be no reason why the claim should not also be framed in contract, relying upon the existence of an implied term. This is echoed in the case of *Johnstone v Bloomsbury Health Authority* (1991), which is also considered more fully at para. 3.125.

**3.116** *Aspden v Webbs Poultry & Meat Group (Holdings) Ltd* involved an employee whose contract contained an express term allowing the employers to dismiss by reason of prolonged incapacity. At the time of entering into the contract (in early 1986), the employee was a member of a health insurance scheme which he had joined in early 1985. The scheme provided for an employee to receive three quarters of his last payable annual salary, starting 26 weeks after the start of the incapacity and ending with his death, retirement date or the date on which he ceased to be an eligible employee (which included dismissal on any ground). He was dismissed while on sick leave and claimed damages for wrongful dismissal. Sedley J. held that a term should be implied into the contract that, in circumstances where the employee's entitlement to benefit under the employers' health insurance scheme was dependent upon the continuance of the employment relationship, the employers would not terminate the contract while the employee was incapacitated for work. He implied the term on the footing that both parties knew, or would have realised had they considered it, that the written terms were not comprehensive and that they required qualification. The contract was not drafted with the insurance scheme in mind, nor was its aptness in the light of the scheme considered or negotiated. The judge therefore held that the employers were in breach of contract in dismissing him while he was unable to work.

**3.117**  *Ali v Christian Salvesen Food Services Ltd* (1997), on the other hand, is an example of a case in which the Court of Appeal refused to imply a term. The issue was whether there should be implied into an 'annualised hours' agreement a term entitling employees whose employment was terminated by the employer before the end of the pay year to be paid the standard hourly rate for hours actually worked in excess of 40 per week. The Court of Appeal refused to imply such a term. It is an example of an established doctrine that 'where the parties have entered into a carefully written contract containing detailed terms agreed between them', the court will be reluctant to imply a term: see *Jones v St. John's College, Oxford* (1870). Reference may also be made to *Stubbes v Trower, Still & Keeling* (1987), where the Court of Appeal refused to imply a term into the contract of an articled clerk in a firm of solicitors that at the start of articles he would either have passed the whole of the final examination or be awaiting the result of it.

**3.118**  It is important to be aware of the tendency of courts and tribunals to make express terms in the employment contract subject to the qualification that the employer will not rely upon an express term in such a way as to breach the implied duty not to undermine the relationship of trust and confidence between employer and employee: see para. 3.122.

## Basis for the implication of terms

**3.119** The two tests used historically for the implication of terms are the 'business efficacy' test and the 'officious bystander' test. The first derives from *The Moorcock* (1889) and the second from *Shirlaw v Southern Foundries (1926) Ltd* (1939). A third basis for the implication of terms was developed by Viscount Simonds in *Lister v Romford Ice & Cold Storage Co Ltd* (1957). He said in that case that the existence of an implied term depended on general considerations relating to the nature of contracts of employment. This is sometimes called the 'status' test. This type of implied term was referred to by Lord Reid in *Sterling Engineering Co Ltd v Patchett* (1955) as 'a term inherent in the nature of the contract which the law will imply in every case unless the parties agree to vary or exclude it'.

**3.120** The implication of terms was considered by the House of Lords in *Liverpool City Council v Irwin* (1977). Lord Wilberforce said:

> Where there is, on the face of it, a complete bilateral contract, the courts are sometimes willing to add terms to it, as implied terms: this is very common in mercantile contracts where there is an established usage: in that case the courts are spelling out what both parties know and would, if asked, unhesitatingly agree to be part of the bargain. In other cases, where there is an apparently complete bargain, the courts are willing to add a term on the ground that without it the contract will not work – this is the case, if not of *The Moorcock* ... itself on its facts, at least of the doctrine of *The Moorcock* as usually applied. This is ... a strict test.

**3.121** Lord Wilberforce went on to disagree with Lord Denning's view about the implication of reasonable terms and said that the test was a test 'of necessity'. An example of this strict approach is to be found in *Stubbes v Trower, Still & Keeling* (1987), where the Court of Appeal refused to imply a term into the contract of an articled clerk in a firm of solicitors that at the start of articles he would either have passed the whole of the final examination or be awaiting the result of it. Similarly, in *Nelson v BBC* (1977), the Court of Appeal refused to imply a restriction to a term by virtue of which the employee could be required to work when and where the Corporation demanded. The employee worked in the Caribbean service and, when they closed it down, the BBC sought to argue that he was only employed in that service and that he was therefore redundant. The Court of Appeal said that it was impossible to imply a restriction of this sort. In recent years, the court and tribunals have been more willing to imply terms which appear to them to be reasonable in all the circumstances, rather than relying upon the supposed intention of the parties or a notion such as business efficacy. An important example of this more objective approach is to be found in the Court of Appeal's decision in *Courtaulds Northern Spinning Ltd v Sibson* (1988). The facts were that the employee worked as a lorry driver at the same depot from the start of his employment in 1973. His contract had no express mobility term. All the drivers belonged to the same union, but in 1985 he resigned from the union. To avert strike action, the employer required him to rejoin the union or transfer to another depot. He resigned and claimed that he had been constructively dismissed. The Court of Appeal held that, in order to give the contract business efficacy a term had to be implied in the contract, as being a term which the parties, acting reasonably, would probably have agreed if they had considered the matter, that the employer could, for any reason, direct the employee to work at any place within reasonable daily reach of the employee's home. The employers had therefore acted within their contractual rights and the employee had not been constructively dismissed. The Court rejected the employment tribunal's qualification of the implied term that the employer's request to the employee should be reasonable or 'for genuine operational reasons' as being potentially uncertain and difficult in operation but agreed that the employee could reasonably have demanded that the mobility requirement should be reasonable daily travelling distance. This view of the basis for implying terms appears to be in conflict with Lord Wilberforce's views, as expressed above, and should, therefore, be viewed with some caution, as it was by the EAT in *Aparau v Iceland Frozen Foods plc* (1996) when considering whether to imply a mobility term. In *Aparau* the EAT was reluctant to hold that any mobility term should be implied into the employee's contract beyond a term as to the place of her employment. They went on to say, however, that, if they were wrong and some term as to mobility fell to be implied, there was no basis for implying a term that the employee could be transferred against her will.

## Relationship between express terms and implied terms

**3.122**  The traditional common law view of the operation of an express term is that if the employer relies upon it, however unreasonably, the employee cannot complain. Thus, if the contract contains an unrestricted express mobility clause and the employer activates it with little or no warning, the traditional view is that the employee must comply with what he or she has agreed. Judicial decisions over the last 15 years or so have suggested, however, a tendency to qualify this position. *United Bank Ltd v Akhtar (1999)* concerned the exercise of a mobility clause by employers and its effect upon the employee's right to resign and claim constructive dismissal. The terms of the mobility clause were:

> The bank may from time to time require an employee to be transferred temporarily or permanently to any place of business which the bank may have in the UK for which a relocation allowance or other allowances may be payable at the discretion of the bank.

**3.123**  The employee was a junior clerk in the Leeds branch of the bank and was given six days' notice that he was to be transferred to the Birmingham branch. He asked his manager for a postponement of the transfer for three months because of personal difficulties relating to his wife's ill-health and the impending sale of his house. His request was refused. He wrote another letter asking for 24 days' leave which was due to him in order to sort out his affairs and start work afterwards. His pay was stopped. He complained that he had been constructively dismissed. The EAT upheld the employment tribunal's decision that he had. They said that the tribunal was entitled to imply into the employee's contract a term that reasonable notice should be given in the exercise of the bank's powers to require mobility of its employees and that the employers' discretion under the mobility clause was one which they were bound to exercise in such a way as not to make it impossible for him to comply with his contractual obligation to move. They also upheld the tribunal's decision that the employers' conduct in relation to the employee's transfer amounted to a fundamental breach of the implied term that employers must not, without reasonable and proper cause, behave in a manner calculated or likely to destroy or seriously damage the relationship of trust and confidence between employer and employee. This decision suggests a tendency to erect certain implied terms, such as the implied term of mutual trust and confidence, into terms which effectively override the powers given to an employer by the express terms of the contract.

**3.124** A similar approach may be detected in later cases. In *White v Reflecting Roadstuds Ltd* (1991), for example, considered more fully at para. 3.211, the EAT refused to construe a flexibility clause as being subject to an implied term that the employer would act reasonably when implementing the clause. They did add, however, that if there were no reasonable or sufficient grounds for the view that the employee should be required to move there would be a breach of the flexibility clause: see p. 742. In *McLory v The Post Office* (1993) the court held that there is an implied term that an employer cannot exercise its power under a contractual provision on unreasonable grounds. See also *BPCC Purnell Ltd v Webb* (EAT 129/90), considered at para. 3.210, below.

**3.125** Another term which may fall into this category is the employer's obligation to ensure the employee's health and safety: see *Johnstone v Bloomsbury Health Authority* (1991), which concerned the legal challenge to the lengthy hours worked by junior hospital doctors. The relevant clause in their employment contracts stipulated that their hours of duty should consist of a standard working week of 40 hours and an additional availability on call up to an average of 48 hours per week over a specified period. The employee in question worked some weeks in excess of 88 hours and, as a result of working those hours with inadequate sleep, became ill. He brought an action asking for a declaration that he should not be required to work in excess of 72 hours a week and damages for personal injuries and loss allegedly suffered as a result of the employers' breach of their duty to take reasonable steps to ensure his safety. The case reached the Court of Appeal on an interlocutory point and the Court was not therefore called upon to reach a considered conclusion on the issues involved. A majority of the Court of Appeal (Leggatt LJ dissenting) held that the result of the inter-action of the employee's express obligations and his employers' implied obligation to take care for his safety, they were not entitled to require him to work for so many hours in excess of his standard working week as would foreseeably injure his health. Leggatt LJ's view was that reliance upon an express term cannot breach an implied term: see p. 282. There is a difference between the judgements of the two judges who were in the majority, however. Stuart Smith LJ was prepared to make the express term subject to the requirement of health and safety, and thus appears to have mixed the employers' duties in contract and tort. Sir Nicolas Browne-Wilkinson V-C did not go that far, saying that 'where there is a contractual relationship between the parties their respective rights and duties have to be analysed wholly in contractual terms and not as a mixture of duties in contract and tort': see p. 283. He said:

> Therefore, if there is a term of the contract which is in general terms (eg a general duty to take reasonable care not to injure the employee's health) and another term which is precise and detailed (eg an obligation to work on particular tasks notwithstanding that they may involve an obvious health risk expressly referred to in the contract) the ambit of the employer's duty of care for the employee's health will be narrower than it would be if there were no such express term ... The express and the implied terms of the contract have to be capable of co-existence without conflict.

**3.126** Subject to these possible exceptions, the general rule is that there is no room for the implication of a term where the matter is already covered by an express term. The implied duty of trust and confidence and, possibly, the duty to take care of the employee's health and safety, however, are emerging as terms which the courts and tribunals regard as qualifying the powers given to employers by express terms. For a recent example of a case in which the Court has qualified the operation of an express term by the use of an implied term, see *Jenvey v Australian Broadcasting Corporation* (2003). In that case, Elias J implied a term the effect of which was to prohibit the employer from dismissing the employee for any reason other than redundancy once it had decided to terminate the contract for that reason.

## Terms implied by custom and practice

**3.127** A term may be implied on the basis of custom and practice, if it is reasonable, certain and well-known. So, for example, in *Sagar v*

*Ridehalgh & Son Ltd* (1931) the court accepted that it was part of the custom and practice of the Lancashire cotton industry that employers might make deductions from weavers' wages for bad work so that this became part of the individual weaver's contract. In *Marshall v English Electric Co Ltd* (1945) the established practice of using suspension as a disciplinary measure was held to be incorporated into the employees' contracts. It is not clear whether the custom needs to be known to and accepted by the employee, but it seems likely that the court or tribunal would treat a custom as applicable to an individual in cases where it is well known within the industry or where it is so well established that the employee must be taken to have accepted employment subject to it. In *Sagar v Ridehalgh & Son Ltd* (1931) Lawrence LJ said, at p. 336:

> ... [I]t is clear that the [employee] accepted employment in the [employer's] mill on the same terms as the other weavers employed at that mill ... Although I entirely agree with the [trial judge] in finding it difficult to believe that the [employee] did not know of the existence of the practice at the mill, I think that it is immaterial whether he knew or not, as I am satisfied that he accepted employment on the same terms as to deductions for bad work as the other weavers at the mill.

**3.128** Even if the employee may be taken to have accepted the custom, the other requirements for incorporation need to be present also. A custom which is unreasonable may lead to the view that the employee would be unlikely to have accepted it and the mere fact that a practice has happened once before is not sufficient to lead to its incorporation. Such terms are less important than formerly because of the move towards increased formalisation of terms of employment and statutory regulation.

## Employees' obligations: good conduct

**3.129** Although it is clear that an employee is under a duty not to commit acts of misconduct, the ambit of the duty is of necessity vague. As Lord James of Hereford observed in *Clouston & Co Ltd v Corry* (1906) (at p. 129):

> There is no fixed rule of law defining the degree of misconduct which will justify dismissal. Of course there may be misconduct in a servant

which will not justify the determination of the contract of service by one of the parties to it against the will of the other. On the other hand, misconduct inconsistent with the fulfilment of the express of implied conditions of service will justify dismissal ... In such a case the question whether the misconduct proved establishes the right to dismiss the servant must depend upon facts – and is a question of fact.

**3.130** In *Sinclair v Neighbour* (1967), for example, the employee, who was a manager of a betting shop, borrowed money from the till in the betting shop in the knowledge that permission would have been refused had he asked. The employer dismissed the employee summarily on learning of what had happened. The Court of Appeal held that the employee's dismissal was justified since, even though his conduct might not have been dishonest, it was nevertheless of such a grave and weighty character as to undermine the relationship of confidence which should exist between an employer and employee. This case is an example of a single relatively minor act justifying instant dismissal, since money was involved and, even if the employee was not dishonest, his behaviour undermined the employment relationship. Employees are under no general duty to disclose their own misconduct nor are they obliged to disclose misconduct of fellow-employees: see *Bell v Lever Bros Ltd* (1932) and *Nottingham University v Fishel* (2000). In this last case, the court held that the employee was not obliged to disclose to his employers that he was doing outside work in breach of his contract, nor was he obliged to apply for consent, although his contract required him to do so. On the other hand, the terms and nature of a particular employment may be such, however, that there is a contractual duty to disclose the conduct of other employees, even if that disclosure will inevitably lead to disclosure of the employee's own conduct: see *Sybron Corporation v Rochem Ltd* (1983). One aspect of the duty of good conduct is obedience to reasonable instructions which is considered in the next section.

## Employees' obligations: obedience to instructions

**3.131** An employee is under an obligation to obey lawful and reasonable instructions given by the employer. This is a fairly wide obligation, which in effect enshrines the employer's managerial preroga-tive. It extends beyond the normal situation of obedience to instruc-tions given in the workplace to such issues as mobility and the need to adapt to changes in working practice, as in *Cresswell v Board of Inland Revenue* (1984), considered more fully at para. 3.191. There, the employees tried to argue that the Inland Revenue was in breach of their terms of service in requiring them to operate the proposed computerisation of the PAYE system. Walton J. held that, although the proposed introduction of computerisation changed the way the employees performed their duties, they were still administering the PAYE system and performing the duties of tax officers. He said, however, that this was subject to the proviso that the employer must provide any necessary training or re-training for them. If, however, the nature of the work alters so radically that it is outside their contractual obligations, it will not be reasonable to expect the employees to adapt.

**3.132** In *Laws v London Chronicle (Indicator Newspapers) Ltd* (1959), the facts were that the employee disobeyed an instruction given to her by the managing director not to leave a meeting after a row had developed between him and her superior. She was summarily dis-missed. The Court of Appeal upheld her wrongful dismissal claim. Lord Evershed MR said, at p. 701:

> I think it is not right to say that one act of disobedience, to justify dismissal, must be of a grave and serious character. I do, however, think ... that one act of disobedience or misconduct can justify dismissal only if it is of a nature which goes to show (in effect) that the servant is repudiating the contract, or one of its essential conditions; and for that reason, therefore, ... the disobedience must at least have the quality that it is 'wilful': it does (in other words) connote a deliberate flouting of the essential contractual conditions.

**3.133** In *Pepper v Webb* (above), on the other hand, the employee's wrongful dismissal claim failed. His disobedience of the order which led to his summary dismissal was the 'last straw' in a series of incidents and, although the single act of disobedience might not of itself have warranted summary dismissal, the cumulative effect of the previous incidents, taken together with the final act of disobedience and the use of bad language, was such as to warrant summary dismissal. If the employer's instruction is unlawful or unreasonable, the employee is not obliged to obey it. Thus, for example, in *Ottoman Bank Ltd v Chakarian* (1930), it was held that an Armenian was within his rights for refusing to obey an order to stay in Constantinople, where he had previously been sentenced to death. Similarly, in *Bliss v South East Thames Regional Health Authority* (1987), the Court of Appeal held that an employee was entitled to refuse to comply with the employer's requirement to submit to a medical examination, taking the view that that requirement was a breach of the implied term of mutual trust and confidence.

**3.134** Allied to obedience to reasonable instructions is compliance with mobility requirements. This is best dealt with by means of an express term in the employee's contract, as in *United Kingdom Atomic Energy Authority v Claydon* (1974), which contained a wide clause reserving to the employers 'the right to require any member of their staff to work at any of their establishments in Great Britain or in posts overseas'. See also *Nelson v BBC* (1977).

**3.135** If a mobility term falls to be implied the court or tribunal is likely to imply a term of restricted ambit, as happened in *O'Brien v Associated Fire Alarms Ltd* (1968). In that case, which involved an employee of a company with a country-wide operation who lived in Liverpool and generally worked within commutable distance of his home, the Court of Appeal implied a term that he should work within daily travelling distance of his home and no more. They rejected the employers' argument that there was an implied term in his contract that he would work anywhere in the north west and that he could be compelled to work 120 miles away in Barrow-in Furness. In *Jones v Associated Tunnelling Co Ltd* (1981) Browne-Wilkinson J said, at p. 480:

> The term to be implied must depend on the circumstances of each case. The authorities show that it may be relevant to consider the nature of the employer's business, whether or not the employee has in fact been moved during the employment, what the employee was told when he was employed, and whether there is any provisions made to cover the employee's expenses when working away from daily reach of his home ... [A]ll the circumstances have to be considered ...

As in the *O'Brien* case, the EAT implied a term that the employee could be required to work within reasonable daily reach of his home.

**3.136**   On the other hand, in *Stevenson v Teesside Bridge and Engineering Ltd* (1971), the court implied a wider term, that he could be required to work at any site where he might be required to work as steel erector. The implication of this term depended on the nature of the work involved, the fact that before being taken on the employee stated that he was prepared to work away from home and the provisions of his contract which envisaged the necessity of travelling and staying away from home. If the tribunal does imply a term relating to mobility, the term is likely to be subject to the implied qualification that reasonable notice must be given. This is particularly likely following the decision of the EAT in *United Bank Ltd v Akhtar* (1989). In *Prestwick Circuits Ltd v McAndrew* (1990) the employee was required to transfer to another site some fifteen miles away but was only given four days' notice of the transfer; he subsequently resigned. The employment tribunal decided that the employers' implied right to transfer the employee was subject to the implied qualification that reasonable notice of any transfer would be given to him and that the employers had breached this right. They therefore concluded that the employee had been constructively dismissed. The Court of Session upheld this decision. This decision represents an emerging trend, which shows that courts and tribunals are prepared to imply a term that an employer will not exercise its power under a contractual provision on unreasonable grounds.

**3.137**   In *Jones v Associated Tunnelling Co Ltd* (above) the EAT said (at p. 480) of mobility clauses:

> ... [A] contract of employment cannot simply be silent on the place of work: if there is no express term, there must be either some rule of law that in *all* contracts of employment the employer is (or alternatively is not) entitled to transfer the employee from his original place of work or some term regulating the matter must be implied into each contract ... In order to give the contract business efficacy, it is necessary to imply *some* term into each contract of employment.

**3.138**   In the later case of *Aparau v Iceland Frozen Foods plc* (1996), the EAT distinguished *Jones's* case on the grounds that in the context of an employer with a chain of stores it is not necessary to imply a term entitling the employer to move employees around, whereas in the context of an employer who carries out specialist tunnelling work (as in *Jones's* case) some term must be implied because the nature of the work is such that it cannot be expected to continue indefinitely at the same place. They conceded that it is necessary to have a term relating to the place of work, but refused to go any further and imply a term entitling the employer to move the employee around against her will.

## Employees' obligations: exercise of care and skill

**3.139**  It is an implied term in a contract of employment that the employee is reasonably competent to do the job: see *Harmer v Cornelius* (1858). Thus, a serious act of incompetence may justify the employer in terminating the contract summarily at common law. Similarly, the employee impliedly agrees to take reasonable care in the performance of his or her duties under the contract. Although the employer will usually be vicariously liable for the employee's act of negligence, theoretically the employer may sue the employee for an indemnity for breach of the duty of care, as in *Lister v Romford Ice & Cold Storage Co Ltd* (1957). In appropriate circumstances, carelessness may justify summary dismissal at common law, though clearly it would have to satisfy the general principle that it was so serious as to amount to a repudiation on the employee's part of his or her contractual obligations: see *Power v British India Steam Navigation Co Ltd* (1930) and *Jupiter General Insurance Co Ltd v Shroff* (1937). In this last case, an act of negligence by a manager was held to amount to serious misconduct justifying the summary dismissal. So too in *Baster v London and County Printing Works* (1899) a single act of forgetfulness by an employee which caused damage to a valuable machine used in the employer's printing business was held to justify summary dismissal.

**3.140**  Negligence is sometimes given the epithet 'gross' but in *Wilson v Brett* (1843), Rolfe B. said that he 'could see no difference between negligence and gross negligence – that it was the same thing, with the addition of a vituperative epithet'. Similarly, in *Dietmann v Brent London Borough Council* (1987) (at p. 748), Hodgson J characterised this usage as unhelpful.

## Employees' obligations: loyalty and fidelity

**3.141**  The following points should be noted:

(1)    an employer may rely upon the implied duty of loyalty and fidelity as an alternative to an express restrictive covenant or in the absence of such a covenant;

(2)    the implied term may be used against an employee during the currency of the employment or after it has ended;

(3)    enforcement is likely to be by means of an injunction.

**3.142**  As an alternative to relying upon an express restrictive covenant (or in the absence of such a clause in the contract of employment), an employer may seek to rely upon the implied duty of loyalty and fidelity. The employer's argument will be that the ex-employee's contract contained an implied term obliging him or her to respect confidential information relating to the employer's trade secrets and trade connections acquired during the course of the employment. In an appropriate case an ex-employee who commits a breach of the implied duty of loyalty and fidelity may be restrained from committing or continuing to commit the breach. As the cases show, however, the implied duty is of fairly limited ambit. It is advisable for employers who are concerned about protecting their trade secrets and trade connection to make sure that their employees' contracts contain express restraints which can then be sought to be enforced after termination. A further point to note is that the contractual doctrine of repudiation may operate so as to effect the situation. In *Thomas Marshall (Exports) Ltd v Guinle* (1978), for example, the employee was subject to various express restraints, which, to differing extents, affected him both during and after his employment. He purported to resign when his service contract still had four and a half years to run. Sir Robert Megarry V-C held that this repudiatory act did not automatically terminate the contract and that, although the court could not force him to work, it could restrain him from committing other breaches of his obligations during the continuance of his contract. The Vice-Chancellor then went on to restrain him from dealing with the company's customers and suppliers and from using confidential information belonging to the company, on the basis of the employee's breach of the implied duty of loyalty and fidelity. The clause expressly restraining him during his employment covered only the *disclosure*, not the *use* of confidential information, but the implied term was held to cover both. *Guinle's* case shows the interaction of the implied duty and express restraints; it also suggests that the courts are more prepared to use the implied duty against employees during their employment and express restraints against them once their employment has ended. In an appropriate case, however, the implied duty may be invoked against an ex-employee. If it is, it should be noted that it will not be subject to any limitation of time; on the other hand, it is essential that an express restraint be limited in time since it will otherwise be held to be unreasonable.

**3.143** The implied duty of loyalty and fidelity may be invoked against an employee during the course of his or her employment. The duty covers:

(1) acceptance of bribes, inducements or other payments from a third party;

(2) the use of information for the employee's own benefit which is obtained during the performance of the contract;

(3) the disclosure to third parties of confidential information relating to the employer's undertaking;

(4) competition with the employer's business, or conduct likely to damage the employer's business.

**3.144** An example of the first type of situation is *Boston Deep Sea Fishing & Ice Co v Ansell* (1888), in which the managing director of a company contracted for the construction of some fishing boats and took a commission from the shipbuilders on the contract, without the knowledge of the company. He also owned shares in an ice-making and fish-carrying company which paid bonuses to shareholders who used its services. He was held to have acted in breach of contract in relation to the receipt of the commission and bonuses. The payments were also held to be recoverable by the employer. See also *Reading v Attorney-General* (1951), in which the House of Lords held to be recoverable bribes which an Army sergeant had received. It should be noted in this last case that the money was recoverable by the employer (the Crown) despite the fact that it was earned by a criminal act and that the employer had suffered no loss. In effect, the payment was recoverable because of his abuse of his position.

**3.145** It is well established that there is a duty lying on the employee not to disclose confidential information, but the courts have had difficulty in establishing what amounts to confidential information in any particular case. A distinction must be made between an individual employee's general knowledge or individual skill, which he or she may legitimately put to use in the future, and a trade secret which the employer is entitled to protect. In *Printers and Finishers Ltd v Holloway* (1964), at pp. 735–6, Cross J. said:

> The mere fact that the confidential information is not embodied in a document but is carried away by the employee in his head is not of itself a reason against the granting of an injunction to prevent its use or disclosure by him. If the information in question can fairly be regarded as a separate part of the employee's stock of knowledge which a man of ordinary honesty and intelligence would recognise to be the property of his old employer and not his own to do as he likes with, then the court, if it thinks that there is a danger of the information being used to the detriment of the old employer, will do what it can to prevent that result by granting an injunction. Thus an ex-employee will be restrained from using or disclosing a chemical formula or a list of customers which he has committed to memory.

**3.146** Although the confidential information need not be of a complicated nature (as in *Cranleigh Precision Engineering Ltd v Bryant* (1965)), the question is whether, in any particular case, the information is confidential. In *Thomas Marshall (Exports) Ltd v Guinle*, Sir Robert Megarry, V-C. suggested, *obiter*, a test containing four elements:

> First ... the information must be information the release of which the owner believes would be injurious to him or of advantage to his rivals or others. Second ... the owner must believe that the information is confidential or secret, ie that it is not already in the public domain ... Third, the owner's belief under the previous two heads must be reasonable. Fourth ... the information must be judged in the light of the usage and practices of the particular industry or trade concerned. It may be that information which does not satisfy all these requirements may be entitled to protection as confidential information or trade secrets; but I think that any information which does not satisfy them must be of a type which is entitled to protection.

**3.147** The Court of Appeal considered this issue fully in *Faccenda Chicken Ltd v Fowler* (1986) (see also *Balston Ltd v Headline Filters Ltd*

(1987) and *Berkeley Administration Inc v McClelland* (1990), where the information sought to be protected was information derived from financial projections in an appendix to the employers' own business plan.) They upheld the existence of an implied duty in relation to the use and disclosure of information, but in effect confined it to trade secrets or their equivalents, ie information which has a sufficiently high degree of confidentiality to warrant protection after the employment has ended by means of an implied term. At first instance, Goulding J. identified three classes of information which an employee might acquire in the course of employment (pp. 598–600):

> First there is information which, because of its trivial character or its easy accessibility from public sources of information, cannot be regarded by reasonable persons or by the law as confidential at all. The servant is at liberty to impart it during his service or afterwards to anyone he pleases, even his master's competitor ... Secondly, there is information which the servant must treat as confidential (either because he is expressly told it is confidential, or because from its character it obviously is so) but which once learned necessarily remains in the servant's head and becomes part of his own skill and knowledge applied in the course of his master's business. So long as the employment continues, he cannot otherwise use or disclose such information without infidelity and therefore breach of contract. But when he is no longer in the same service, the law allows him to use his full skill and knowledge for his own benefit in competition with his former master; and ... there seems to be no established distinction between the use of such information where its possessor trades as a principal, and where he enters the employment of a new master, even though the latter case involves disclosure and not mere personal use of the information. If an employer wants to protect information of this kind, he can do so by an express stipulation restraining the servant from competing with him (within reasonable limits of time and space) after the termination of his employment ... Thirdly, however, there are, to my mind, specific trade secrets so confidential that, even though they may necessarily have been learned by heart and even though the servant may have left the service, they cannot lawfully be used for anyone's benefit but the master's.

**3.148**  Neill, L.J., giving the judgment of the Court of Appeal, said that the court must consider all the circumstances of a case, taking into account the following factors:

(a)   The nature of the employment. Thus employment in a capacity where 'confidential' material is habitually handled may impose a high obligation of confidentiality because the employee can be expected to realise its sensitive nature to a greater extent than if he were employed in a capacity where such material reaches him only occasionally or incidentally.

(b)   The nature of the information itself ... [T]he information will only be protected if it can be properly classed as a trade secret or as material which, while not properly to be regarded as a trade secret, is in all the circumstances of such a highly confidential nature as to require the same protection as a trade secret ...

(c)   Whether the employer impressed upon the employee the confidentiality of the information ... [T]hough an employer cannot prevent the use or disclosure merely by telling the employee that certain information is confidential, the attitude of the employer towards the information provides evidence which may assist in determining whether or not the information can properly be regarded as a trade secret ...

(d)   Whether the relevant information can be easily isolated from other information which the employee is free to use or disclose ... [W]e would not regard the separability of the information in question as being conclusive, but the fact that the alleged 'confidential' information is part of a package and that the remainder of the package is not confidential is likely to throw light on whether the information in question is really a trade secret.

**3.149** In the *Faccenda* case, the information in issue was sales information which the employers were very anxious to keep confidential; there were no express restrictive covenants in the employees' contracts. The Court of Appeal concluded that the information fell into Goulding J.'s second category and not the third category but did not rule out the possibility that information relating to an employer's commercial interests could be protected in certain circumstances. On the facts in the instant case, the employers had not done enough, however, to be able to protect their business information. A similar conclusion was reached in *Wallace Bogan & Co v Cove* (1997), where the Court of Appeal refused to imply a term into the contracts of solicitors whose effect would be to restrain them from canvassing or doing business with clients of their former employers. The Court's view was that the way for employers to protect themselves in a case of this kind was for them to extract a restrictive covenant from the employees concerned. See also the Court of Appeal's decision in *Brooks v Olyslager OMS (UK) Ltd* (1998), and *A T Poeton (Gloucester Plating) Ltd v Horton* (2000), which involved the disclosure by a former employer of information relating to his former employers' financial position.

**3.150** In *Lancashire Fires Ltd v SA Lyons & Co Ltd* (1997), on the other hand, the Court of Appeal said that for information to a trade secret falling within Goulding J.'s third category (see above), it is not necessary for the employer to point out to the employee the precise limits of what is sought to be protected as confidential. In the instant case, the employee acquired information about the processes involved in producing artificial coals and logs for use in gas fires. Carnwath J. at first instance said that the information did not fall within the third category, but the Court of Appeal reversed his decision on that point.

**3.151** As was mentioned earlier, the implied duty also covers competition during the continuance of the employee's contract. It is important to define the ambit of this aspect of the duty, since the way an employee uses his or her spare time may be seriously affected by an overly wide interpretation of it. In general, employees are free to spend their spare time as they please and, if they engage in 'moonlighting', they are free to do so provided their activities do not affect the employer's business. In *Hivac v Park Royal Scientific Instruments Ltd* (1946), the facts were that two highly skilled employees who had access to all their employer's manufacturing data and who were engaged in the assembly of miniature valves for use in hearing aids, performed similar work for a competing company on Sundays. They were held to be in breach of the implied duty. Lord Greene MR said:

> It would be deplorable if ... a workman could ... knowingly, deliberately and secretly set himself to do in his spare time something which would inflict great harm on his employer's business.

**3.152** This decision should be contrasted with the decision in *Nova Plastics Ltd v Froggatt* (1982), in which the employee was an odd-job man who worked for a rival business in his spare time. The EAT held that, even though the other business was in competition, the work which the employee did for the other company was not work which contributed seriously to any competition with the primary employer.

He was not, therefore, in breach of the duty of fidelity. It is important to keep in mind the restricted ambit of the implied duty. It does not apply to employees who do work in their spare time which has no relationship with the work of their primary employer; nor does it extend to the situation where an employee's spare time work (or other activities) has an effect on his or her work for the primary employer. Inadequate performance or sub-standard work is not covered by the implied duty of loyalty and fidelity. An employer who wishes to rely upon the implied term *after* the employment relationship has ceased will probably only be able to do so where the breach is actually committed before the employment ceased: see *Robb v Green* (1895), *Worsley and Co Ltd v Cooper* (1939) and *Wessex Dairies Ltd v Smith* (1935). In addition, the courts are more likely to restrain the use of tangible, rather than intangible, information.

**3.153**   It is clear that the ex-employee will be restrained from using a list of the ex-employer's customers copied out before leaving the employment (as in *Robb v Green*) and from deliberately soliciting the employer's customers, before leaving, to transfer their custom after his or her departure: see *Wessex Dairies Ltd v Smith*. (See also *Adamson v B. & L. Cleaning Services Ltd* (1995)) But if there is no written list, the court will be reluctant to restrain the ex-employee who solicits those customers whose names he or she can remember, unless there is evidence to suggest that he or she has deliberately committed an entire list to memory: see *Hart v Colley* (1890) and *Baker v Gibbons* (1972). In this last situation, the case may be difficult to prove, as happened in *Baker v Gibbons*. A further requirement in cases of this kind is that the employee must not be allowed to acquire an unfair advantage. This rule particularly applies where he or she deliberately obtains, memorises or copies lists of customers in breach of the implied duty. An example of this type of situation is *Robb v Green* (1895), in which an employee was restrained from using after his employment had ended a list of his employers' customers which he had copied out before his departure.

**3.154**   More recently, in *Roger Bullivant Ltd v Ellis* (1987), the Court of Appeal said that 'it is of the highest importance that the principle of *Robb v Green* ... which ... is one of no more than fair and honourable dealing, should be steadfastly maintained'. When he left his employment, the employee took with him a card index showing the names and addresses of his employer's customers. The Court of Appeal said that in such circumstances it was appropriate to grant an injunction, but that the injunction should be limited to the period during which the unfair advantage might be expected to continue. This was limited to 12 months, as there was an express restraint limited to this period. Nourse L.J. said:

> Having made deliberate and unlawful use of the [employer's] property, [the employee] cannot complain if he finds that the eye of the law is unable to distinguish between those whom, had he so chosen, he could have lawfully contacted and those whom he could not.

**3.155** The final point to note here is that the public interest may require the disclosure of confidential information to those who have a 'proper interest' to receive it. In *Gartside v Outram* (1856), Wood V.C. said: 'There is no confidence as to the disclosure of iniquity.' In *Initial Services Ltd v Putterill* (1968), the Court of Appeal held that an exception to the implied duty arises where the information relates to iniquity or misconduct on the part of the employer which is of such a nature that it ought in the public interest to be disclosed to someone who has a proper interest in receiving it. This was followed in *Re a Company's Application* (1989), in which an injunction was granted to restrain the disclosure of confidential information but was expressed not to cover disclosure to the appropriate regulatory body (FIMBRA) which had the power to investigate whether the employers were complying with the regulatory scheme, or information concerning fiscal matters to the Inland Revenue.

**3.156** The remedies most likely to be sought by the employer are an injunction against the ex-employee to restrain him or her from continuing to disclose or use the trade secrets or confidential information, and damages for breaches of contract already committed. The employer may also seek injunctions and/or damages against third parties to whom the trade secrets or confidential information have been passed.

## Employer's obligations: provision of work

**3.157** The general rule at common law is that an employer is not obliged to provide work for the employee to do but only to pay the wages due under the contract. The classic statement of this rule is that of Asquith J in *Collier v Sunday Referee Publishing Co Ltd* (1940) (at p. 650):

> It is true that a contract of employment does not necessarily, or perhaps normally, oblige the master to provide the servant with work. Provided I pay my cook her wages, she cannot complain if I choose to take any or all of my meals out.

**3.158**  So, for example, in *Turner v Sawdon & Co* (1901), which involved a salesman on a fixed-term contract who was given no work to do but whose salary was still paid, the Court of Appeal held that there was no obligation on the employers to provide him with work. A.L. Smith MR said :

> It is within the province of the master to say that he will go on paying the wages, but is under no obligation to provide work.

It was argued that a failure to give the employee employment would mean that he could not keep his hand in and would become a less efficient salesman. AL Smith MR said of this argument:

> To read in an obligation of that sort would be to convert the retainer at fixed wages into a contract to keep the servant in the service of his employer in such a manner as to enable the former to become au fait with his work. In my opinion, no such obligation arises under this contract ...

Thus, application of the general rule means that an employer who pays the employee but gives him or her no work to do will not be in breach of contract.

**3.159**  There are, however, exceptions to the general rule which have arisen in cases where the law has recognised that in certain types of contract it is essential to the contract that the employee is given the opportunity to work. So, for example, it will be a breach of contract to fail to provide work for an employee paid on a piecework or commission basis, as in *Devonald v Rosser & Sons* (1906) and *Turner v Goldsmith* (1891). In this last case, the Court of Appeal said that an agent paid on a commission basis was entitled to be sent a reasonable amount of work to enable him to earn his commission. See also *Bauman v Hulton Press Ltd* (1952).

**3.160** Another group of exceptions arises in cases where the nature of the work is such that the opportunity for publicity is as important as the remuneration paid to the employee. This applies to actors, singers and the like. Thus, for example, in *Marbé v George Edwardes (Daly's Theatre) Ltd* (1928), a well-known actress was engaged by the managers of a theatre to play a particular part in a play. There was also a collateral agreement by which the managers undertook to advertise her name in a prominent position. On the day of the dress rehearsal they refused to allow her to appear in the part. The Court of Appeal held that the contract imposed an express obligation upon the managers to allow her to appear in the part as agreed. They also held that damages for breach of that obligation might include compensation for loss of reputation. A similar decision was reached by the House of Lords in *Clayton and Waller Ltd v Oliver* (1930), which expressly approved *Marbé's* case. These cases concern the loss of opportunity for an actor or actress to enhance his or her reputation and arise in circumstances where the contract specifically contemplated such an enhancement of reputation. They show also that the obligation may be to provide work of a particular kind or standard (for example, a particular role or part), rather than any work. This exception was extended to authors in *Tolnay v Criterion Film Productions Ltd* (1936), but the Court of Appeal refused to extend it to a company director: see *Re Golomb* (1931).

**3.161** Although there are no decided cases dealing with other classes of employees whose career depends upon their receiving publicity through the media, such as broadcasters, journalists and the like, it is arguable that in their case too the enhancement of their reputation is contemplated by their contract. In this context it is worth noting the words of Goddard J in *Tolnay v Criterion Film Productions Ltd*, above, at p. 1626:

> All persons who have to make a living by attracting the public to their works, be they ... painters or ... literary men ... or ... pianists, must live by getting known to the public.

**3.162** In the light of this dictum, it must be likely that in appropriate cases, the reasoning of the cases discussed above would apply. In *Provident Financial Group plc v Hayward* (1989), Dillon LJ said:

> The employee has a concern to work and a concern to exercise his skills. That has been recognised in some circumstances concerned with artists and singers who depend upon publicity, but it applies equally, I apprehend, to skilled workmen and even to chartered accountants.

**3.163** It may be that there is a further exception in the case of employees engaged to fill a particular office, particularly if it is of a professional nature. For example, in *Collier v Sunday Referee Publishing Co Ltd* (1940), from which Asquith J's dictum was quoted above, the employee concerned was employed as the chief sub-editor of a newspaper. The owners sold the newspaper, thus putting it out of their power to continue to employ him. Asquith J held that when they sold the newspaper they destroyed the position to which they had appointed him and thereby committed a breach of contract. Although this may remain a correct proposition of law, it should be remembered that the position would now be likely to be governed by the Transfer of Undertakings (Protection of Employment) Regulations 1981 (as amended). A further possible area of exception arises in relation to cases where the employee arguably has an implied right to work. The possibility of such a right existing was canvassed in a robust judgement by Lord Denning MR in *Langston v Amalgamated Union of Engineering Workers* (1974). The case arose under long-repealed provisions of the Industrial Relations Act 1971. For the employee to succeed in his claim, he had to show that the union had induced a breach of contract in circumstances where the employers were continuing to pay his salary. He thus had to show that he had a contractual right to be provided with work. Lord Denning commented upon the age of the previous cases and said that the courts had repeatedly said that a person had the right to work. He went on, at p. 190:

> To my mind, therefore, it is arguable that in these days a man has, by reason of an implication in the contract, a right to work. That is, he has a right to have the opportunity of doing his work when it is there to be done ...

**3.164** The other members of the Court were less emphatic than the Master of the Rolls. It should be noted, however, that this was an interlocutory decision, where the Court merely had to be satisfied that the employee *arguably* had the right. Further, even if such a right does or may exist, its existence only enjoys the status of an implied term. A further problem concerns the definition of the right. It is not clear whether the right as formulated by the Court of Appeal in *Langston's* case is a right to be given work so as to maintain the employee's job satisfaction or whether it is a right for him or her to keep his or her hand in and remain au fait with developments. In either of the latter cases, the resignation by the employee as a result of a failure to provide work might amount to a constructive dismissal, as was argued in *Breach v Epsylon Industries Ltd* (1976). This case also is of limited utility, however, since the EAT remitted the case to the employment tribunal to consider whether there was an implied obligation to provide work suitable for a chief engineer. The EAT did suggest, however, at p. 322, that the case fell within an exception 'which, as it were, is a blend of thought between *Collier v Sunday Referee Publishing Co Ltd* and the other cases where exceptions have been found, moderated by the changed climate of opinion ...'.

**3.165** That is not the end of the matter, however. There is the question of whether the implied right to work can survive in cases where there is an express 'garden leave' clause. The nature of such a clause is that the employer expressly reserves the right to require the employee not to work but agrees to continue to pay the wages due under the contract during that time. The clause may also contain the limitation that it may only be invoked during a period of notice given by either party. This sort of clause was considered in *Provident Financial Group plc v Hayward* (1989). In this case, it gave power to the employer to suspend the employee from work 'at any time or from time to time'. Although the Court of Appeal upheld the judge's refusal to grant an injunction, on the grounds that the judge below had correctly exercised his discretion, there is nothing in the judgements of the Court to suggest that the clause itself was unenforceable. Taylor LJ said, at p. 169: 'As a matter of principle I consider the court does have power to grant injunctive relief such as is claimed in the present case.' Dillon LJ recognised (at p. 165) that garden leave clauses are capable of abuse, but the general tenor of the judgements of the Court of Appeal in the *Provident Financial* case is to suggest that the court would be unlikely to exercise its discretion to grant an injunction in a case where it considered that the employer was trying to insist on an excessively long period of garden leave. See also para. 3.95, where garden leave clauses are discussed.

## Employers' obligations: remuneration

**3.166** The obligation lying upon the employer to pay the employee the wages which are due is at the heart of the employment contract. Normally, the contract will contain express provisions dealing with the remuneration due, and it is a statutory requirement that details of the scale, rate or method of calculation of the remuneration should be given to the employee in writing: see ERA 1996 s 1(4)(a) and (b). Employees also have a statutory right, under ERA 1996 s 8, to receive an itemised pay statement upon payment of wages or salary. In the event of there being no express term governing pay, the court of tribunal would imply a term, no doubt to the effect that the employee should receive 'the going rate for the job'. Alternatively, the employee would be able to recover on the basis of *quantum meruit*, as in *Way v Latilla* (1937), where there was an understanding that the employer would look after the employee's interests. See also *Powell v Braun* (1954).

**3.167** An area which has given rise to problems is the question of whether an employee is impliedly entitled to be paid sick pay in cases where there is no express term in the contract of employment. Although Pilcher J accepted in *Orman v Saville Sportswear Ltd* (1960) that there is a rebuttable presumption that wages will continue to be paid during the employee's sickness, the Court of Appeal in *Mears v Safecar Security Ltd* (1982) disapproved that approach and said that the court or tribunal must look at all the facts and circumstances of the relationship between the parties, including their subsequent acts under the contract. In view of the facts that it was well known that the employer's practice was not to pay wages during sickness, that he did not ask about sick pay before taking on the job and that he took sick leave without pay for seven out of the 14 months his employment lasted and never asked for sick pay, the Court decided that nothing was payable. If sick pay is payable by virtue of an implied term, the question then arises as to how long it is payable for. In *Howman & Son v Blyth* (1983) the EAT said that the tribunal should imply a reasonable term as to its duration having regard to the normal practice in the industry concerned. In the case in question, they looked to the working rule agreement for the industry involved.

## Employers' obligations: safety and care

**3.168** This term embraces a number of different facets of the employment relationship, ranging from the common law duty to care for the employee's health and safety to a duty to take care in the compilation of references for the employee. The decision of the House of Lords in *Wilsons & Clyde Coal Co Ltd v English* (1938) established that the employer owes a duty to an employee to provide competent and safe fellow-employees, to provide adequate materials and to provide a safe system of working. It may be a corollary of the first aspect of this duty that an employer is under a duty to take steps to terminate the employment of a potentially dangerous employee. Although the duty is generally regarded as arising in the law of tort, it gives rise to a contractual obligation on the part of the employer to act reasonably in matters of safety. This means that an employee who resigns because of the employer's failure in this respect may claim to have been constructively dismissed. So, for example, in *British Aircraft Corporation Ltd v Austin* (1978) the employer's failure to investigate the employee's complaint about the protective eyewear provided was held by the EAT to amount to conduct entitling him to resign without notice. In such a case, however, the breach by the employer must be sufficiently serious as to amount to a repudiation of the contract: see *Graham Oxley Tool Steels Ltd v Firth* (1980).

**3.169** There are suggestions in *Johnstone v Bloomsbury Health Authority* (1991) that the express terms in an employee's contract may be qualified by the implied duty of care owed by the employer. In the case in question, the employee's contract stipulated that his hours of duty should consist of a standard 40-hour week and an additional availability on call up to an average of 48 hours a week over a specified period. A majority of the Court of Appeal said that the employers were not entitled to require the employee to work so many hours in excess of his standard working week as would foreseeably injure his health. Stuart-Smith LJ suggested that the employers' power under this contractual provision had to be exercised in the light of their implied duty of care, but Sir Nicolas Browne-Wilkinson V-C merely said that they had the right, subject to their ordinary duty not to injure the employee, to call upon him to work those hours up to the stipulated maximum.

**3.170**  In *Reid v Rush & Tompkins Group plc* (1990) the facts were that an employee suffered a road accident whilst working for his employers in Ethiopia but, as a result of the law in that country, he received no compensation for his injuries. He therefore tried to argue that there was an implied term in his contract either that his employers would take out appropriate insurance cover indemnifying him against the risk of death or injury whilst driving in the course of his employment or that, before he left for Ethiopia, his employers would give him all necessary advice relating to work conditions there, including any special risks such as a road accident involving an uninsured driver (as happened) and would advise him to obtain appropriate cover himself. The Court of Appeal considered the various bases upon which terms may be implied and, in the light of them, refused to imply any such term. Another aspect of the duty to take care is that the employer may be under an obligation to indemnify the employee against expenses necessarily incurred in the course of employment (including the cost of defending legal proceedings): see *Burrows v Rhodes* (1899), *Re Famatina Development Corporation Ltd* (1914) and *Gregory v Ford* (1951).

**3.171**  Finally, there is the duty of the employer to take care in giving references in respect of an ex-employee. It is clear from *Hedley Byrne & Co Ltd v Heller & Partners Ltd* (1964) that the employer will be liable to the new employer in negligence, but the question is whether it is possible to incur liability to the ex-employee. In *Spring v Guardian Assurance plc* (1994) the House of Lords by a majority held that an employer has a duty of this sort. Lord Slynn of Hadley and Lord Woolf also took the view that the ex-employee's contract contained an implied term that his employers would take reasonable care in the compiling and giving of the reference. Lord Woolf based this view on the decision of the House of Lords in *Scally v Southern Health and Social Services Board* (1991), which stated (at p. 647):

> recognises that, just as in the earlier authorities the courts were prepared to imply by necessary implication a term imposing a duty on an employer to exercise due care for the physical well-being of his

employees, so in the appropriate circumstances would the court imply a like duty as to his economic well-being, the duty as to his economic well-being giving rise to an action for damages if breached.

**3.172** Clearly, there is scope for further development of the implied term in this area. One area to comment upon is the developing case law in relation to stress claims. Such claims may be founded in tort – thus being a species of negligence claim – or they may be based upon the implied term to care for the employee's health and safety. The first case of any significance in this area was *Walker v Northumberland County Council* (1995). Subsequently, the principles underpinning these types of claims were reviewed by the Court of Appeal, in *Hatton v Sutherland* (2002). Although the Court of Appeal in this last case categorised the *Walker* claim as being based on the implied term and treated the claim in the instant case as falling within that category, the summary of principles set out by the Court in paragraph 43 of its judgement tends to suggest an approach based more upon tort than contract. The Court of Appeal reviewed these principles in *Pratley v Surrey County Council* (2003). In *Barber v Somerset County Council* (2004), the House of Lords said that the guidance given by the Court of Appeal in *Hatton v Sutherland* was a valuable contribution to the development of the law but should not be read as having anything like statutory force. They said that every case depends on its own facts.

## Employers' obligations: reasonable notice

**3.173** There may be circumstances in which it is necessary to imply a term into an employee's contract as to the amount of notice he or she is entitled to receive or obliged to give. In most cases, if the parties have not agreed upon a notice period, the effect of section 86 of the Employment Rights Act 1996 will be to insert a statutory term relating to notice. This comes into play in the case of employees who have been continuously employed for one month or more. In the case of employment up to two years, the employee's entitlement is to one week's notice; after that, it increases by one week for each year of employment up to 12, which is the maximum statutory amount of notice. Under the statute, the employee is only obliged to give one week's notice of termination. In cases where there is no express term and either party wishes to argue that the other is obliged to give more notice than that provided for by the statutory provisions, it will be necessary to contend for the implication of a term relating to notice. In *Richardson v Koefod* (1969), Lord Denning MR said: 'In the absence of express stipulation, the rule is that every contract of service is determinable by reasonable notice. The length of the notice depends upon the circumstances of the case.'

**3.174** It is not possible to set out any rules as to the amount of notice to be implied into any contract. Much depends upon the facts of each case and all the circumstances must be looked at, including:

- the type of employment;

- any local, trade or professional customs;

- the intervals at which remuneration is paid; and

- the period in relation to which remuneration is stated.

**3.175** A consideration of the case law on this subject, much of it dating from the 19th century, suggests that the notice to which an employee is impliedly entitled will lengthen with seniority, but that only in exceptional cases will a term of notice longer than six months be implied. The cases tend to deal with the amount of notice to which an employee is *entitled* rather than *obliged to give*. Arguably, perhaps, an employee entitled to three months' notice may also be obliged to give the same notice, but the cases say little about this. The fact remains, of course, that, as with other contractual terms, the parties should deal with the matter expressly rather than rely upon the unpredictable operation of an implied term.

## Mutual trust and confidence

**3.176** Reference was made at the beginning of this chapter to Edmund-Davies LJ's observation in *Wilson v Racher* (1974) that 'a contract of service imposes upon the parties a duty of mutual respect'. This case was decided when the law relating to unfair dismissal was in its infancy. Since the decision of the Court of Appeal in *Western Excavating (ECC) Ltd v Sharp* (1978), however, which emphasised that a constructive dismissal will only take place where the employer is in breach of an express or implied term in the contract and the breach if so serious as to amount to a repudiation of the contract, this implied duty has been considerably refined and developed, particularly as far as the employer's behaviour is concerned. Subsequent case law has shown that the duty is flexible and will tend to vary with the circumstances of any particular case.

**3.177**   In the context of constructive dismissal cases, the implied term has been variously formulated as a term obliging the employer to maintain the relationship of trust between the parties, or as a term obliging the employer not to treat the employees arbitrarily, capriciously and not in accordance with good industrial relations practice. So, for example, in *Woods v W M Car Services (Peterborough) Ltd* (1981), Browne-Wilkinson J ruled:

> ... [I]t is clearly established that there is implied in a contract of employment a term that the employers will not, without reasonable and proper cause, conduct themselves in a manner calculated or likely to destroy or seriously damage the relationship of confidence and trust between employer and employee ... To constitute a breach of this implied term it is not necessary to show that the employer intended any repudiation of the contract: the tribunal's function is to look at the employer's conduct as a whole and determine whether it is such that its effect, judged reasonably and sensibly, is such that the employee cannot be expected to put up with it ...

**3.178**   The case went to the Court of Appeal, which upheld the EAT's decision: see (1982). The same judge later followed this dictum in applying the implied term to an employer's exercise of its powers under a pension scheme, in *Imperial Group Pension Trust Ltd v Imperial Tobacco Ltd* (1991). The rules of the pension scheme enabled the committee of management of the scheme to amend it 'with the consent in writing of the company'. The question arose whether the exercise by the company of its power to grant or withhold consent was qualified by an obligation to act in good faith. Sir Nicolas Brown-Wilkinson V-C held that the power was subject to an implied obligation that it would not be exercised so as seriously to damage the relationship of confidence between employer and employee and that, if the company exercised its power in breach of that obligation, the exercise of the power would be invalid.

**3.179** The scope of the term was examined by Lord Steyn in *Mahmud v Bank of Credit and Commerce International SA* (1997). He approved the formulation of the term as set out by Browne-Wilkinson J above. Subsequently, the Court of Appeal made it clear that tribunals should follow that formulation and not use language which may detract from the correct test or suggest that a different test has been applied: see *Transco plc v O'Brien* (2002). In this last case, the Court of Appeal held that the employer had been in breach of the implied term in failing to offer an employee a new contract when offering them to all other permanent employees, despite the employer's mistaken belief (arrived at in good faith) that he was not a permanent employee. As Hart J observed in *University of Nottingham v Eyett* (1999), the terms in which the duty have been expressed have been 'in the negative form of prohibiting conduct calculated or likely to produce destructive or damaging consequences, rather than as positively enjoining conduct which will avoid such consequences'. This analysis may be said to underpin the cases considered in this section.

**3.180** The case of *University of Nottingham v Eyett* (1999) suggests that the implied duty of mutual trust and confidence in a contract of employment does not extend so far as to include a positive obligation on the employer. In the case in question, the employer failed to warn an employee who was proposing to exercise important rights in connection with the contract of employment that the way he was proposing to exercise them might not be the most financially advantageous. Hart J. said that, although the duty of mutual trust and confidence may in principle impose positive obligations, recognition of a duty to alert an employee to the possibility that he was making a financial mistake would have far-reaching consequences for the employment relationship and would not sit well with other default obligations implied by law in the employment context. The House of Lords in *Eastwood v Magnox* (2004) extends the terms to post-employment and removes the statutory cap of compensation for these types of cases. However, in *Dunnachie v Kingston-upon-Hull CC* (2004) their Lordships held that s. 123(1) (the making of a compensatory award for unfair dismissal claims) does not allow for the recovery of non-pecuniary loss.

**3.181** The EAT has treated as a breach of the implied term a failure to deal with a female employee's complaint of alleged sexual harassment and a failure by the employer to provide a grievance procedure for the employees: see *Bracebridge Engineering Ltd v Darby* (1990) and *W A Goold (Pearmak) Ltd v McConnell* (1995). In this last case the EAT used the existence of the statutory provisions relating to the provision of a note by employers relating to their grievance procedures as a basis for implying a term that an employer will 'reasonably and promptly afford a reasonable opportunity to their employees to obtain redress of any grievance they may have'. In *TSB Bank plc v Harris* (2000) the EAT upheld the tribunal's decision that the employers were in fundamental breach of the implied term of trust and confidence by revealing in a reference to a prospective employer complaints against the employee of which she was unaware, thereby blocking her progress in the financial services sector. They rejected the argument that the employers were not in breach of the implied term because they were only doing what was required of them under regulations governing the financial services industry. They said that the obligation of the employers to their regulators is not the measure of their obligation to their employees. In *Euro-Die (UK) Ltd v Skidmore* (EAT 1158/98) the EAT held that an employer's failure to assure an employee that his continuity of employment would be protected following a transfer of the business amounted to a fundamental breach of the term of trust and confidence. The consequence was that the employee was treated as constructively dismissed and the transferee was liable for the unfair dismissal. A similar conclusion was reached in *Visa International Service Association v Paul* (2004), in relation to a failure by the employer to notify an employee absent on maternity leave of a vacancy for which she would have applied had she been aware of it.

**3.182**  On the other hand, the EAT has refused to treat the introduction of a non-smoking policy as a breach of the implied term, in *Dryden v Greater Glasgow Health Board* (1992), taking the view that the employer's action was within the scope of its managerial prerogative. See also *Sita (GB) Ltd v Burton* (1998). Cases involving an alleged breach of the implied term are not of course confined to the context of unfair dismissal complaints. See, for example, *Bliss v South East Thames Regional Health Authority* (1987). In that case, during a dispute between the authority and a consultant surgeon, the authority required the surgeon to undergo a psychiatric examination when there was no mental or pathological illness and suspended him when he refused. In the context of the surgeon's claim for breach of contract, the Court of Appeal held that this behaviour amounted to a breach of the implied term which was so fundamental as to constitute a repudiation of the contract. The Court followed Browne-Wilkinson J's formulation of the term used in the *Woods* case, above.

**3.183** The EAT has in fact gone further and used the implied term to impose limitations on the managerial prerogative given by express terms, as in the case of *United Bank Ltd v Akhtar* (1989) and *Johnstone v Bloomsbury Health Authority* (1991), considered at paras. 3.122 – 3.125. The cases so far considered in this section have involved breaches by the *employer* of the implied duty of mutual trust and confidence, largely because it is in the context of an unfair dismissal or breach of contract claim that the issue arises. It is not confined, however, to employers, as is shown by the case of *British Telecommunications plc v Ticehurst* (1992). The case involved deductions from the employee's wages made as a result of her participation in industrial action. She claimed that the deductions had been made in breach of contract. The Court of Appeal held that, as the employee was in breach of the implied term, the employers were justified in withholding part of her wages. They formulated the term as 'an implied term to serve the employer faithfully within the requirements of the contract': see Ralph Gibson LJ at p. 398, with whom the other two Lords Justices agreed. In doing so, he adopted the formulation of Buckley LJ in *Secretary of State for Employment v ASLEF (No. 2)* (1972).

**3.184** At the beginning of this section, mention was made of the flexible and variable nature of the implied term of mutual trust and confidence, which has been adapted to circumstances such as a failure to deal with a complaint of sexual harassment or to institute a grievance procedure. The question of whether to extend the scope of employers' obligations is regularly canvassed before courts and tribunals and it is clear that, over the years since the introduction of the concept of constructive dismissal, they have developed this implied term. This can be seen in a case such as *Imperial Group Pension Trust Ltd v Imperial Tobacco Ltd* (1991), above, at p. 3.178, and in *Scally v Southern Health and Social Services Board* (1991), where the House of Lords held that an employer had an implied obligation to take reasonable steps to publicise to an employee his rights under a pension scheme. The Court of Appeal followed *Scally* when considering whether an employer had fulfilled the duty to inform an employee of proposed changes to his pension rights and the availability of an option to transfer his accrued rights with a special enhancement to a new pension scheme. They said that attaching letters detailing the changes and options to his pay slips was sufficient: see *Ibekwe v London General Transport Services Ltd* (2003). There is no duty, however, to take care for the employee's general well-being by warning the employee of the detrimental effect of his proposed resignation on his rights under a contractual permanent health insurance scheme: see *Crossley v Faithful and Gould Holdings Ltd* (2004). This case illustrates the point made earlier that the duty of trust and confidence does not involve positive steps such as that required in the case in question.

**3.185** In this context, the decision in *McClory v The Post Office* (1993) should also be noted. There, the court said that there is an implied term that an employer cannot exercise its power under a contractual provision (an express power to suspend) on unreasonable grounds.

## Variation of contract

**3.186** The main principles governing variations of an employment contract are as follows:

(1)    for a variation of an employment contract to be effective the proposed change must be notified to the employee and the employee must consent to it;

(2)    the employee's consent may be express or inferred and, if express, need not be in writing;

(3)    consent may be inferred from other contractual material, such as a collective agreement, a flexibility clause or a clause in the employment contract giving the employer a power of unilateral variation;

(4)    a unilateral notification by one party to the other of a change in the contract will not amount to a variation in the absence of agreement;

(5)    the imposition of a unilateral change by the employer will constitute a repudiatory breach of contract giving the employee the right to resign and claim breach of contract or to claim a constructive dismissal giving rise to liability on the part of the employer for unfair dismissal or a redundancy payment;

(6)   an employer who is unable to obtain the employee's agreement to a proposed change and chooses not to impose the change unilaterally may in the alternative dismiss the employee with notice and offer re-employment under a contract containing the changed terms but risks claims for unfair dismissal and redundancy;

(7)   a variation of contract in the context of a transfer of an undertaking falling within the Transfer of Undertakings (Protection of Employment) Regulations 1981 (as amended) may be affected by those Regulations.

## The main legal principles

**3.187**   The two main issues which arise in the context of a variation are (1) whether the proposed variation relates to a contractual or non-contractual provision; and (2) whether the employee consented to it. Both may raise difficult questions. In the first case, questions will arise as to whether the particular provision has become part of the contract or not. If not, it is open to the employer to make a unilateral variation by, for example, discontinuing or abandoning or altering the particular provision, for example a bonus scheme or enhanced redundancy payment scheme. A further question here will be whether the proposed change falls within the employer's managerial prerogative. If the proposed variation requires consent, the question will then be whether it has been given. It is a fundamental principle of contract law that, as it takes the agreement of both parties to enter into the contract, so it takes the agreement of both to vary it: see *Robinson v Page* (1826), *Goss v Lord Nugent* (1833), *British and Beningtons Ltd v North Western Cachar Tea Co Ltd* (1923) and *Royal Exchange Assurance v Hope* (1928).

**3.188**   If the proposed variation does not require consent, it may be imposed unilaterally by the employer. If, however, the variation requires consent and the employer imposes it unilaterally, that act will constitute a repudiatory breach of contract giving the employee the right to resign. He or she will then be able to make a claim for breach of contract based upon the employer's breach; it will also be possible to complain of unfair dismissal or claim a redundancy payment, arguing that the resignation caused by the breach amounts to a constructive dismissal. If the variation involves a reduction in the employee's wages, he or she may also make a claim under Part II of the Employment Rights Act 1996 (formerly the Wages Act 1986).

**3.189** As an alternative to imposing the claim unilaterally, the employer may dismiss the employee with notice and offer re-employment under a contract containing the changed terms and conditions. The risk in following that strategy is that the employer will then be exposed to complaints of unfair dismissal and claims for redundancy payments, though it does not follow that the unfair dismissal complaints will necessarily succeed. These principles are considered in more detail in the sections which follow. Finally, at the end of the chapter, variations of contract in the context of transfers of undertakings will be considered: see para. 3.222.

## Requirements for an effective variation: contractual and non-contractual provisions

**3.190** The first question to consider here is whether the proposed variation is one which requires consent at all. Obviously, if it is a variation of a contractual term, then consent is essential. If, however, the employer is proposing to vary a non-contractual benefit or provision or to introduce a change which lies within the managerial prerogative and amounts to a lawful and reasonable instruction, there will be no need for the employee's consent. In the first situation, he or she can do nothing about the proposed change, simply because it is non-contractual; in the second, the change will fall within the employee's implied duty to obey the employer's orders. If the proposed change amounts to a contractual variation, the employer must give the employee notice of it: see para. 3.193, below. To determine whether a particular benefit or provision is contractual or not, much depends upon the intention of the parties. The question is whether it is reasonable to infer from the circumstances that the parties intended the provision to have contractual force. So, for example, if the contract specifies that a disciplinary procedure is to be incorporated into the employees' contracts, it will be incorporated; if it is stated not to be of contractual effect, it will not be incorporated. For an example of an incorporated disciplinary procedure, see *Dietmann v Brent London*

*Borough Council* (1988). In *Robertson v British Gas Corporation* (1983) the Court of Appeal held that an incentive bonus scheme had been incorporated into employees' contracts and could not, therefore, be unilaterally determined by the employer. In that case, the employee's letter of appointment to a new grade stated: 'Incentive bonus scheme conditions will apply to meter reading and collection work'. The statutory statement given to the employee stated: 'Any payment which may, from time to time, become due in respect of ... incentive bonuses ... will be calculated in accordance with the rules of the scheme in force at the time.' The Court of Appeal said that the words used in the letter clearly and expressly imported into the employee's contract an obligation to pay the bonus. Ackner LJ went on to say that he did not consider there to be an inconsistency between the words of the letter and those of the statement, but that, if that view was wrong, the letter took precedence over the statement, which provided strong prima facie evidence of the terms of the contract but did not constitute the contract: see pp. 356–7. He added that the employer's statement given years after the contract was made could not be used as admissible evidence for the interpretation of the contract itself. This case is also considered in the context of the requirement of consent: see para. 3.202, below. This decision should be contrasted with *Quinn v Calder Industrial Materials Ltd*, considered more fully at para. 3.73, in which the EAT held that the unilateral abandonment of a policy governing enhanced redundancy payments was held not to be in breach of the employees' contracts. See also to similar effect *Secretary of State for Employment v ASLEF (No. 2)* (1972), where the Court of Appeal refused to hold that detailed works rules set out in a staff handbook were contractual; they were held to be collateral instructions to the employees as to how they were to carry out their work. Similar considerations apply in the case of bonus schemes or share option schemes; if they are stated not to be contractual but capable of discontinuance at the employer's discretion, the employer will not be in breach of contract in exercising the discretion to discontinue. An example is *Cadoux v Central Regional Council* (1986), the question was whether the employer was entitled to withdraw a non-contributory life assurance scheme.

## Changes within the managerial prerogative

**3.191**  An example of a proposed change falling within the managerial prerogative is *Cresswell v Board of Inland Revenue* (1984). There, the employees tried to argue that the Inland Revenue was in breach of their terms of service in requiring them to operate the proposed computerisation of the PAYE system. Walton J. held that, although the proposed introduction of computerisation changed the way the employees performed their duties, they were still administering the PAYE system and performing the duties of tax officers. He said that an employee is expected to adapt to new methods and techniques in performing his or her duties provided that the employer arranges for training in the new skills and that the nature of the work does not alter so radically that it is outside the contractual obligations of the employee. He emphasised that it is a question of fact and degree whether the introduction of new methods and techniques alters the work that an employee has agreed to perform so much that it is no longer the work that the employee agreed to perform under the terms of his or her contract. His conclusion therefore was that the Inland Revenue could vary the duties of the tax officers as proposed.

**3.192**  More recently, in *Dryden v Greater Glasgow Health Board* (1992), the issue arose as to whether the introduction by an employer of a ban on smoking amounted to a significant breach in an employee's contract entitling her to resign and claim constructive dismissal. The EAT held that the introduction of the new policy fell into the category of a works rule and therefore did not amount to a repudiatory breach. Lord Coulsfield said, at pp. 471–2:

> There can ... be no doubt that an employer is entitled to make rules for the conduct of employees in their place of work, as he is entitled to give lawful orders, within the scope of the contract ... Where a rule is introduced for a legitimate purpose, the fact that it bears hardly on a particular employee does not ... justify an inference that the employer has acted in such a way as to repudiate the contract with that employee.

It is, however, possible for an employer to act in such a way that, albeit that the action is within the managerial prerogative or is expressly permitted by a contractual term, the implied term of mutual trust and confidence is breached: see *United Bank Ltd v Akhtar* (1989), discussed at para. 3.122.

## Requirements for an effective variation: notice of the proposed change

**3.193** Once it is clear that the proposed change is a contractual variation, the next question is whether the employee has been given notice of the variation, since an employee can hardly be said to have agreed to something of which he or she was not informed. In *Cowey v Liberian Operations Ltd* (1966), the issue was whether the employee was bound by a variation that reduced his notice entitlement from three months to one month. The method used to change the term was an office memorandum passed round and initialled by the staff, including the employee in question. He took the view, in the light of discussions he had had with a superior at the time of his appointment, that it did not apply to him; but he initialled it and passed it on. The judge held that the method used to vary the contract was ineffective. A relevant factor was that the employee's attention was not drawn to the fact that the change was intended to apply to him.

### The requirement of agreement: introduction

**3.194** A variation will not be effective unless both parties agree. In the context of a variation of an employment contract, the main question is likely to be whether the *employee* consented to the proposed variation. The following types of consent are possible:

(a)  express consent;

(b)  tacit or inferred consent;

(c)  consent arising by virtue of
     –  a provision in a collective agreement;
     –  a flexibility clause in the employment contract;
     –  a provision in the contract giving the employer power to vary the contract unilaterally.

## The requirement of agreement: express consent

**3.195** Although in many cases it will be clear whether or not the employee has agreed, as, for example, in *Burdett-Coutts v Hertfordshire County Council* (1984), questions may arise as to whether the employee's action amounts to express consent. In that case, Kenneth Jones J refused to accept that employees faced with a unilateral change in their pay who stayed on and accepted the lower pay whilst making it clear that they were not prepared to accept the new terms should be treated as having accepted the unilateral variation. He therefore held them to be entitled to recover the wages which they should have been paid under their original contract. This case is considered further below, at para. 3.201. Similarly, in *Miller v Hamworthy Engineering Ltd* (1986), the question was whether the evidence established an agreement between the employer and the trade union entitling the employer to make deductions from his wages by putting the employee on a three-day week. The Court of Appeal held that the documentary evidence did not establish that negotiations between the employers and the employee's trade union had resulted in a variation of his contract entitling them to reduce his salary. The Court said that references to short-time working and work-sharing in the employee's written terms and conditions and in a redundancy agreement entered into between the unions and the employers did not point to an agreement that was capable of varying the existing contractual terms between the employee and the employers. See also *Gibbons v Associated British Ports* (1985). In that case, the trade union terminated the applicable collective agreement. The employers argued that the termination of the agreement removed from the employee's contract the existing rate of remuneration to which he was entitled and allowed them to substitute a lower rate. The High Court rejected that argument and said that the employers were in breach of contract in unilaterally varying the contract, whose terms remained unaffected by the termination of the collective agreement.

## The requirement of agreement: tacit or inferred consent

**3.196** Questions as to whether there has been tacit or inferred consent may arise in the following cases:

- where the employee makes no response to a variation which amounts to a repudiation but continues to work and accept wages;

- where the employee consents to a variation in circumstances where he or she is faced with the alternative of dismissal;

- where the employee is given notice of a change in the contractual terms continues to work subject to the new terms but under protest.

**3.197** In the absence of express agreement on the employee's part to a variation, he or she may be held to have consented impliedly, but the cases make it clear that a court or tribunal will be slow to infer consent. One type of situation which may give rise to an argument that consent is to be inferred if it is not express is that which arose in *Cowey v Liberian Operations Ltd* (above), where the employee initialled an internal office memorandum announcing changes to the employees' contracts. Because no steps were taken to explain to him that the document affected him and what those changes were, and because the changes conflicted with what he had been told on his appointment by a superior, the court was not prepared even to infer consent from the fact that he had initialled the office memorandum. In *Jones v Associated Tunnelling Co Ltd* (1981), the EAT said:

> If ... there is no evidence of any oral discussion varying the original terms, the fact that a statement of terms and conditions containing different terms has been issued cannot be compelling evidence of an express oral variation. The most that can be said is that by continuing to work without objection after receiving such further statement, the employee may have impliedly agreed to the variation recorded in the second statement or be estopped from denying it ... [T]o imply an agreement to vary or to raise an estoppel against an employee on the grounds that he has not objected to a false record by the employer of the terms actually agreed is a course which should be adopted with great caution. If the variation related to a matter which has immediate practical application (eg the rate of pay) and the employee continues to work without objection after effect has been given to the variation (eg his pay packet has been reduced) then obviously he may well be taken to have impliedly agreed. But where ... the variation has no immediate practical effect the position is not the same ... We would not

be inclined to imply any assent to a variation from mere failure by the employee to object to the unilateral variation by the employer of the terms of employment contained in a statutory statement.

**3.198** It is more likely that the employee will be taken to have consented impliedly where the employer proposes a change to the contract which amounts to a repudiation and the employee makes no response. In *Western Excavating (ECC) Ltd v Sharp* (1978), Lord Denning MR said, at p. 226:

> [The employee] must make up his mind soon after the conduct of which he complains: for, if he continues for any length of time without leaving, he will lose his right to treat himself as discharged. He will be regarded as having elected to affirm the contract.

**3.199** Thus an employee who continues to work and to accept reduced wages without making any protest is likely to be taken to have affirmed the contract. In *W E Cox Toner (International) Ltd v Crook* (1981), for example, the employee delayed for seven months after repudiatory conduct on the part of his employers. For the first six months, the employee made objections to the repudiatory conduct and it was arguable that during this time he had not affirmed the contract. His solicitors then wrote to his employers saying that he would resign unless the allegations constituting the repudiatory conduct were withdrawn. He resigned a month later. The EAT decided that, in view of the fact that six months had already elapsed, he should be held to have affirmed the contract by continuing to work after this ultimatum. Browne-Wilkinson J pointed out, however, at p. 828, that 'mere delay by itself (unaccompanied by any express or implied affirmation of the contract) does not constitute affirmation of the contract; but if it is prolonged it may be evidence of an implied affirmation ...' Thus, in the case in question, the employee was held to have affirmed the contract by staying on only one month after the ultimatum, but it is clear that the EAT arrived at this conclusion because of what had happened in the preceding six months. Had the employee stayed on for six months without making any protest, it is highly likely that he would have been taken to have affirmed the contract earlier than the expiry of the six months. A court or tribunal will be reluctant to infer that an employee has consented to a variation of his or her contract in circumstances where he or she was faced with the alternative of dismissal. In *Sheet Metal Components Ltd v Plumridge* (1974), Sir John Donaldson said, at p. 376:

> It is without doubt the law that there is no dismissal where both parties to a contract of employment freely and voluntarily agree to vary its terms ... However, the courts have rightly been slow to find that there has been a consensual variation where an employee has been faced with the alternative of dismissal and where the variation has been adverse to his interests.

**3.200**   In that case, the employees were told that they were to be transferred to the employers' parent company some distance away and they reluctantly agreed. After two months they left. The employment tribunal decided that they had no option to move since, had they refused, they would have been dismissed and that their conditional acceptance of the move did not amount to a consensual variation of their contracts. The NIRC upheld that decision. This decision does not mean, however, that an employee who agrees under threat of dismissal to a change in the terms of his or her contract will never be held to have consented to the variation. Consistently with the principles already considered, the time must come when he or she will be taken to have consented impliedly. In the *Plumridge* case, the employees worked for two months before resigning. Had they remained for six months or more, it is likely that it would have been inferred that they had given their consent to the change. A further possibility is that the employee given notice of a change to the contractual terms continues to work subject to the new terms but under protest. This is what happened in *Rigby v Ferodo Ltd* (1988), considered below. The basic principle was set out by Browne-Wilkinson J in *W E Cox Toner (International) Ltd v Crook* (1981). He said, at pp. 828–9:

> [I]f the innocent party further performs the contract to a limited extent but at the same time makes it clear that he is reserving his rights to accept the repudiation or is only continuing so as to allow the guilty party to remedy the breach, such further performance does not prejudice his right subsequently to accept the repudiation ...

**3.201**   Two possibilities arise from this statement of principle: (1) that the employee continues to work under protest or (2) that, after a period of working under protest, he or she resigns. An example of the latter situation is to be found in the *Cox Toner* case itself. The employee continued to work for six months under protest after a repudiatory act on the part of his employers and then, having delivered an ultimatum, continued to work for another month. This last act caused the EAT to hold that he had affirmed the contract. Had he left at the end of the six months, the conclusion of the EAT would have been that his actions had not prejudiced his right to accept the repudiation and claim constructive dismissal. An example of the first situation is to be found in *Burdett-Coutts v Hertfordshire County Council* (1984), where the employers unilaterally imposed a reduction in the employees' wages; the employees continued to work under protest and started proceedings for breach of contract. The judge upheld their claim and granted a declaration that the employers were not entitled to impose the variation; he also ordered the employers to pay the arrears of pay. This was a decision at first instance, but is impliedly supported by the later decision of the House of Lords in *Rigby v Ferodo Ltd* (above). The facts in that case were that the employer imposed upon the employee a five per cent. reduction in his wages because of severe financial pressures. The employee continued to work under protest for the employer at the reduced rate of pay but sued for the difference between the wages to which he was entitled under his contract and the wages actually paid to him. The House of Lords held that he had not accepted a variation in the terms of his contract and upheld his claim. They rejected the argument that the behaviour of the employers brought the contract to an automatic end and that the employee's only remedy was to sue for damages for the period of notice to which he was entitled under that contract (12 weeks). They also refused to hold that there was some sort of implied acceptance on his part of the employers' repudiation.

## The requirement of agreement: consent by virtue of a contractual provision

**3.202** In addition to the possibility of consent being inferred, there is the possibility that consent will be treated as arising by virtue of one of the following mechanisms:

(a)     a provision in a collective agreement; or

(b)   a flexibility clause or similar provision in the employment con-
      tract giving the employer power to vary the contract unilaterally.

These mechanisms are in effect methods by which an employer may
argue that the employee has abrogated his or her power to refuse to
accept a proposed change in the contractual terms. In the case of a
collective agreement questions will arise as to whether the agreement
itself or the relevant provisions were incorporated into individual
employees' contracts. This issue was discussed in Chapter 2. An
example of a case in which a collective agreement was incorporated is
*Robertson v British Gas Corporation* (1983), in which the Court of Appeal
held that an incentive bonus scheme was incorporated into employees'
contracts by virtue of their letters of appointment. Since the scheme
gave no power to the employers to terminate it, the Court held that,
when they tried to do so, they committed a breach of contract. Kerr LJ
said, at p. 358:

> It is true that collective agreements ... create no legally enforceable
> obligation between the trade union and the employer. Either side can
> withdraw. But their terms are in this case incorporated into the
> individual contracts of employment, and it is only if and when those
> terms are varied collectively by agreement that the individual contracts
> of employment will also be varied. If the collective scheme is not varied
> by agreement, but by some unilateral abrogation or withdrawal or
> variation to which the other side does not agree, then ... the individual
> contracts of employment remain unaffected.

**3.203**   The Court therefore held the employees to be entitled to the
bonus payments to which they were contractually entitled. A similar
conclusion was reached in *Miller v Hamworthy Engineering Ltd* (1986),
which was considered at para. 3.195, above, and *Gibbons v Associated
British Ports* (1985), considered at para. 3.195, above. In the latter case,
the court held that the terms of a lapsed collective agreement
remained part of an individual employee's contract and could only be
varied with the agreement of the employee and not unilaterally, as the
employers tried to do. *Lee v GEC Plessey Telecommunications* (1993)
involved the withdrawal of an enhanced redundancy payment scheme.
The scheme which was in dispute in this case was introduced as the
result of the conclusion of a collective agreement providing for a
specified level of enhanced payments. After it had been concluded, the

employers issued statutory statements in 1985 expressly incorporating 'general instructions and notices' and provisions of relevant collective agreements into individual contracts. The employers conceded that the collectively agreed terms became incorporated into the individual employees' contracts. A subsequent statement of terms and conditions issued in 1990 made no reference to the incorporation of general instructions and notices, or the provisions of collective agreements into individual contracts. Later, the employers by means of a general instruction purported to withdraw the scheme. The two arguments advanced on behalf of the employers before Connell J which are relevant for present purposes were: (1) the introduction of the enhanced terms into individual contracts in 1985 was unsupported by consideration and the terms were not therefore binding; and (2) the employers had reserved to themselves the power to alter individual contracts of employment unilaterally, via general instructions. So far as the first argument was concerned, the employees argued that the consideration for an improvement in terms and conditions in the context of a pay claim is (a) the employees continuing to work and (b) not continuing with their pay claim so that the employer avoids industrial action and benefits from the services of a known employee. Connell J accepted this argument, saying at p. 389:

> Where, in the context of pay negotiations, increased remuneration is paid and employees continue to work as before, there is plainly consideration for the increase by reason of the settlement of the pay claim and the continuation of the same employee in the same employment.

**3.204** Otherwise, as the employees' counsel argued, a pay increase would be liable to be withdrawn unilaterally by the employer at any time on the basis that there was no consideration for the increased payment. In relation to the second argument, Connell J said that the terms (which were conceded by the employers to have become incorporated into individual contracts) remained part of the contracts unless and until specifically removed, either by agreement or by virtue of a specific right found within the contract. He refused, however, to find that there was any agreement as to their removal, saying, at p. 390: 'I do not find there (ie in the 1985 statutory statement) clearly set out the right to effect unilateral adverse variations to the contract for which the (employers) contend.' Further, the 1990 statutory statement contained no reference to the incorporation of collective agreements or general instructions and notices. At that point, therefore, there was certainly no right to effect a unilateral variation by means of a general instruction.

**3.205** *Lee's* case bears a superficial resemblance to the more recent case of *Quinn v Calder Industrial Materials Ltd* (1996), considered above at para. 3.73, in that both cases involved the withdrawal of an enhanced redundancy payment scheme. The difference between the two cases, however, is that in *Lee* the question was whether the terms of the collective agreement had been incorporated and could be unilaterally revoked, whereas *Quinn* involved a policy unilaterally introduced by the management and the question was whether it had even become incorporated into individual contracts by dint of the fact that it had been acted upon over a period of time. A similar conclusion to that arrived at *Lee* and *Robertson* was reached in *Davies v Hotpoint Ltd* (1994), which involved a provision in a collective agreement incorporated into the employees' contracts. It said: 'Where approved short time is worked as an alternative to redundancy ... the guarantee shall be reduced accordingly.' The issue was whether the employers could reduce the employees' guaranteed wages unilaterally during a period of short time working introduced without the approval of the trade unions. The EAT held that they could not, taking the view that the correct construction of the quoted provision was that the approval of the unions on behalf of the employees was required before the employers were entitled to reduce the employees' wages. The EAT said (at p. 540) that the use of the term 'approved' indicated 'as a matter of ordinary English, a requirement of the consent or agreement of someone other than the person making the decision to be approved'. They said that the term would be redundant if it meant 'approved by the employer'.

**3.206** In *Airlie v City of Edinburgh District Council* (1996), by way of contrast, the EAT had to construe the provisions of an incentive bonus scheme, which were unilaterally varied by the employers without the agreement of the trade unions or the employees. The scheme was contained in a code of practice set out in an appendix to a collective agreement. The EAT upheld the employment tribunal's decision that the code was incorporated into the individual employees' contracts, by virtue of a provision expressly incorporating the collective agreement which itself expressly incorporated the code. They also said that an individual contract may be varied if it includes a provision allowing unilateral variation of its terms, whether such a provision is included directly or by the incorporation of other agreements. Construing the code as a whole, the EAT said that, although there was no express provision giving the employers a power to alter the bonus scheme in a wholesale and comprehensive way, there was a number of provisions which indicated that the employers had the right to control its operation and to make adjustments to it. In view of the code's emphasis of the employers' right to manage and the fact that they were entitled to terminate the whole scheme, the EAT concluded that the proper construction of the provisions was that, after a review of the scheme had been embarked upon, changes could be put into effect without agreement as to the terms. A consideration of the relevant clause of the scheme (para. 16) raises the question whether the conclusion arrived at by the EAT is correct and suggests that it would have been open to them to have arrived at the opposite conclusion.

**3.207** It is clear from the cases which have been examined in this section that provisions incorporated from collective agreements are unlikely to contain a clause providing for consent to any future changes in the employees' contracts, not least because a trade union would be unlikely to agree to such a provision. Thus, in both *Lee* and *Robertson* the court's conclusion was that the benefit provided for in the contract could not be withdrawn unilaterally; similarly, in *Davies v Hotpoint Ltd*, the EAT said that a unilateral change in the employees' wages could not be effected by the employers. Although the EAT's conclusion in *Airlie* was that the correct construction of the provisions of an incentive bonus scheme taken as a whole permitted the employers to make adjustments to the scheme, despite the absence of an express power to alter the scheme in a wholesale and comprehensive way, a close reading of the provisions of the scheme leads to the view that the EAT's conclusion in this case is arguably wrong.

**3.208** As will be seen from a consideration of the relevant decisions, difficult questions of construction are often involved in these cases, whether or not a collective agreement is involved. The cases considered so far have involved provisions incorporated into individual employees' contracts from collective agreements, but the same problems of construction arise in relation to contractual provisions which are not imported from collective agreements. *Cadoux v Central Regional Council* (1986), for example, involved the withdrawal of a non-contributory life assurance scheme. Although the Court of Session held that the provisions relating to the scheme were incorporated into the individual employee's contract, it held that the correct construction of the Rules (which included a rule concerning the scheme) was that any of the rules, including that relating to the scheme, could be varied, altered or cancelled by the employers. That case also shows that not all provisions which are incorporated into employees' contracts require agreement if they are to be changed. The point about the case, however, is that the relevant contractual provisions did not give the express power to the employer unilaterally to vary the contract; the power arose by virtue of the fact that the rules in question were made unilaterally by the employer and were, therefore, held to be capable of being changed unilaterally.

**3.209**   An employer may reserve the right to make changes in the employee's contract either by reserving an express power to make variations or by inserting a flexibility clause. In both cases, the court or tribunal is likely to construe the clause against the employer, applying the *contra proferentem* rule, and, particularly in the case of a clause permitting variation, to construe it narrowly. Thus, if the clause states that it will only be invoked in an emergency or in certain circumstances, the court will look to see if the events contemplated by the clause have taken place. An example of an express clause permitting variations in an employment contract is:

> The [employer] reserves the right to make alterations to the contract of employment. Such changes will be notified to you either individually, by an amendment to this handbook or by announcement on Branch Notice Boards.

See *United Association for the Protection of Trade Ltd v Killairn* (EAT 787/84). In that case, the employment tribunal construed the clause as giving the employers a free hand to re-write the contract and to introduce new terms of a substantial or fundamental character. The EAT rejected this view as erroneous and said that the power of unilateral variation was limited to changes of a minor and non-fundamental character. A similar view was taken in *Lee v GEC Plessey Telecommunications*, above, where the judge said that the employers' practice of issuing General Instructions and Notices did not have the effect of varying the employees' contracts.

**3.210** An example of a flexibility clause is to be seen in *BPCC Purnell Ltd v Webb* (EAT 129/90), where the relevant clause provided:

> Subject only to the Company providing the necessary training there will be total flexibility between all pre-press departments and between NGA Chapels covering specified NGA occupations.

The employee resigned and claimed that he had been constructively dismissed as a result of the company's decision to move him to another department and its subsequent decision that he should work day hours only. The move to another department would have involved the loss of a shift premium because of a change to a different shift system; the subsequent decision would have involved a further loss of pay. The employment tribunal's view of the flexibility clause was that it entitled the company to move the employee to a different department involving different work subject to an implied term that he would not be transferred to a place where his health made it impossible to continue work. They also took the view, however, that the flexibility clause did not entitle the company to change the employee's hours substantially or to reduce his pay and that since both decisions would have involved a loss of pay, the company was in breach of contract. The EAT refused to accept this view, holding that it was not possible to infer the limitations suggested by the tribunal. They went on to say, however, that the cumulative effect of the two decisions was such as to involve a breach of the implied term that employers will not, without reasonable and proper cause, conduct themselves in a manner calculated or likely to destroy or seriously damage the relationship of trusts and confidence between employer and employee.

**3.211** This decision may be contrasted with that of *White v Reflecting Roadstuds Ltd* (1991), in which the relevant clause was:

> The company reserves the right, when determined by requirements of operational efficiency, to transfer employees to alternative work and it is a condition of employment that they are willing to do so when requested.

The issue in the case was whether the employer's decision to move the employee from one department to another amounted to a breach of his contract which was sufficiently serious as to amount to a repudiation entitling him to resign and claim constructive dismissal within section 95(1)(c). The tribunal decided that this express clause should be qualified by an implied term requiring the employers to act reasonably when deciding to move an employee. They also said that the employers were in breach of contract in causing loss of income to the employee when acting within the scope of the flexibility clause. The EAT rejected this and said that the tribunal had erred and that it was not necessary to give the contract business efficacy to imply the terms. The employee's constructive dismissal claim therefore failed. The EAT distinguished *United Bank Ltd v Akhtar* (1989), on the grounds that the implied term used to qualify an express mobility term was to the effect that the employer should not exercise the discretion conferred by the contract in such a way as to prevent the employee from carrying out his or her part of the contract. In *Prestwick Circuits Ltd v McAndrew* (1990), the Court of Session implied a mobility term into an employee's contract but said that it was subject to the implied qualification that the employee should be given reasonable notice of any transfer.

**3.212**  A comparison of *Akhtar* and *McAndrew*, on the one hand, with *White* and *Webb*, on the other, tends to suggest that the court or tribunal may be more prepared to qualify an express mobility term than a flexibility term, though it must be regarded as unlikely that the EAT in *White* would have treated a substantial change which caused considerable financial loss to the employee as being permitted by the express term, a view confirmed by the attitude of the EAT in *Webb*. What is clear is that, in both types of case, it is unlikely that an employer will be allowed to act in a wholly unfettered way, despite the apparent width of a flexibility or mobility clause, and that the express power will be qualified, where appropriate, by the implication of a term such as that used in *Webb*.

## Effect of a unilateral variation

**3.213**  On the assumptions (a) that the employer has no power to impose a unilateral variation and (b) that the employee's consent has not been given, the following possibilities arise as a result of an attempt by an employer to impose a variation unilaterally:

(a) the employee may resign and make a claim for breach of contract;

(b) the employee may resign and make a complaint of unfair dismissal or a claim for a redundancy payment based on a 'constructive dismissal';

(c) the employee may make a claim under Part II of the Employment Rights Act 1996 alleging that the unilateral variation amounts to an unlawful deduction of 'wages';

(d) the employee may continue to work for the employer and claim damages for breach of contract or a declaration that the contract has been breached;

(e) the employee may seek an injunction against the employer to restrain the employer from implementing the variation, though it is unlikely that the Court will grant an application.

**3.214** In the first situation, where the employee wishes to claim breach of contract, the claim will be that the employer's act amounted to a wrongful repudiation of the contract entitling the employee to claim damages for breach of contract. The breach may be actual or anticipatory. An example of an anticipatory breach is threatened changes to a pattern of shift working or a threat to take an employee off one type of work and transfer him or her to another, as in *BPCC Purnell Ltd v Webb* (EAT 129/90). Another example of an anticipatory breach is to be found in *Harrison v Norwest Holst Group Administration Ltd* (1985), which also makes it clear that the employee must also accept a repudiation unequivocally. In the second situation, the first step in a claim will be to persuade the employment tribunal that the resignation in fact amounted to a constructive dismissal within section 95(1)(c) or 136(1)(c) of the Employment Rights Act 1996: see Chapter 7. The third possibility – of a claim under Part II of the Employment Rights Act 1996 (formerly the Wages Act 1986) – may arise if the variation amounts to the unilateral withdrawal by the employer of a benefit which falls within the definition of 'wages' in section 27 of that Act. Thus, the withdrawal of an incentive bonus scheme or the unilateral introduction of short-time working with a consequent reduction in pay may trigger such a claim: see, for example, *Davies v Hotpoint Ltd* (1994) and *Airlie v City of Edinburgh District Council* (1996), considered at paras. 3.205 and 3.206, above, and *International Packaging Corporation (UK) Ltd v Balfour* (2003). In the fourth situation, the employee may choose not to resign but to continue to work under protest and either claim a declaration that the employer has acted unlawfully or claim damages for breach of contract. Examples of the former type of claim are to be found in *Burdett-Coutts v Hertfordshire County Council* (1984), and *Lee v GEC Plessey Telecommunications* (1993); examples of the latter in *Rigby v Ferodo Ltd* (1988). In the latter type of case, it is unlikely that the damages should be limited to the employee's notice period, unless the employer has clearly given him or her notice of termination of employment. Otherwise, the breach will be effectively a continuing breach and the employee's loss of wages will accrue from day to day. So, for example, in *Miller v Hamworthy Engineering Ltd* (1986), the employee was awarded the difference between the amount of salary he would have received had he worked a five-day week and the amount he in fact received during the period of short-time working, which was held by the Court of Appeal to have been introduced in breach of contract. In *Gibbons v Associated British Ports* (1985), the employee was awarded both.

## Alternatives to unilateral variation

**3.215**  An employer who decides not to vary the contract unilaterally, possibly because the consent of all the employees is not forthcoming, is left with little choice but to dismiss them and offer re-engagement on new terms. Clearly this course of action exposes the employer to various claims arising from dismissal, of which the most likely are claims for breach of contract (wrongful dismissal) and unfair dismissal. A claim for a redundancy payment is also possible though less likely. For a more detailed discussion of these possible claims reference should be made to Chapters 6 and 7. What follows is an outline of the general considerations to be taken into account. An employer who clearly dismisses the employee but offers re-engagement on new terms will not risk claims for damages or an injunction provided that the correct notice of dismissal is given. In other words, a breach of contract action will not be possible. It is essential, however, that the communication to the employee makes clear that the contract is being terminated. In *Burdett-Coutts v Hertfordshire County Council* (1984), for example, the employer's letter gave 12 weeks' notice of the change in the employees' terms and conditions. Kenneth Jones J refused to treat this as a notice of termination of employment and said that it was merely notice of a change in their terms and conditions. A similar argument was advanced in *Rigby v Ferodo Ltd* (1988), but Lord Oliver of Aylmerton said that on the facts of the case the contention could not be sustained, observing, as had the trial judge, that 'the deliberate implementation of a policy preferred over others in order to keep the whole workforce in work cannot sensibly be construed as evincing an intention to terminate the contract of service': see p. 33.

**3.216** For the purposes of the statutory rights, there must be a dismissal, whether actual or constructive, before the employee may make a claim. The question is whether the unilateral imposition of new terms and conditions without an express dismissal amounts to a dismissal within the meaning of the statutory language. Applying the facts of a case such as *Burdett-Coutts v Hertfordshire County Council*, above, to the statutory provisions, the conclusion which would be likely to follow would be that there was no dismissal and that all an aggrieved employee could do would be to make a claim for damages for breach of contract or for unlawfully deducted wages, but that, since there had been no dismissal within the meaning of section 95 or 136 of the Employment Rights Act 1996, no claim under the unfair dismissal or redundancy payments provisions of the Act would be possible. If, however, the decision of the EAT in *Alcan Extrusions v Yates* (1996) is correct, then an employee affected by a unilateral variation could stay on and continue to work for the employer under protest but could also complain of unfair dismissal or, if appropriate, claim a redundancy payment. In that case, the facts were that a group of employers unilaterally imposed a variation on the employees, in circumstances which amounted to a repudiation of the contract. The employees chose not to resign but to continue to work the new terms under protest; they also complained of unfair dismissal. The EAT upheld the tribunal's decision that there had been a dismissal, taking the view that, where an employer unilaterally imposes radically different terms of employment, there is a dismissal if, on an objective construction of the relevant letters on the part of the employer, there is a withdrawal or removal of the old contract. They refused to accept that the imposition of changes in breach of the employees' contracts must always be characterised as a potential repudiatory breach giving the employee the choice of resigning and claiming constructive dismissal or remaining with the employer. It went on to say that whether the imposition of radically different terms has the effect of withdrawing and terminating the original contract is a question of fact for the tribunal to decide. They based themselves on a previous decision of the EAT in *Hogg v Dover College* (1990).

**3.217** Although it is possible to imagine cases where one could say that the employer had terminated the old contract by departing radically from it, in most cases one would have thought that the correct analysis would be that the imposition of different terms amounted to a repudiatory breach by the employers and that it would require clear language to hold that the employer was in fact terminating the old contract and substituting a new contract. In view of the decision of the House of Lords in *Rigby v Ferodo Ltd* (1988) and the remarks of Lord Oliver of Aylmerton, it must be questioned whether this decision is correct. It may be noted that, although the EAT quoted from Lord Oliver's opinion, it made no attempt to deal with the case or to distinguish it. The fact that a dismissal – whether actual or constructive – has been established does not necessarily mean that the dismissal is unfair. It is likely that the reason for the dismissal will be treated as 'some other substantial reason' within section 98(1)(b) of the Employment Rights Act 1996 and the main question will be whether the employer acted reasonably or unreasonably in treating that reason as a sufficient reason for dismissing the employee, within section 98(4): see para. 3.219, below. A number of cases have considered the question whether and in what circumstances a dismissal caused by a change of contractual terms or operational changes will be fair, but cases such as *Hollister v National Farmers' Union* (1979) suggest that, provided that the employment tribunal has found that there was a substantial reason justifying dismissal, it is not necessary for the employers to show that the proposed changes are essential. All that needs to be shown is a sound commercial reason for making the changes. See also *RS. Components Ltd v Irwin* (1973), which concerned the introduction into the employee's contract of a restraint of trade clause and *Horrigan v Lewisham London Borough Council* (1978), where the EAT regarded as fair the dismissal of an employee who refused to work regular overtime in circumstances where the effect of his refusal was to cause substantial disruption to the Council's services to the public. Similarly, in *St. John of*

*God (Care Services) Ltd v Brooks* (1992), in which the employees were dismissed for refusing to accept new, and less favourable, terms of employment, the employment tribunal held the dismissals to be unfair on the basis that the crucial question was whether the terms offered were those which a reasonable employer would offer. The EAT allowed the employers' appeal and said that to look only at the offer would necessarily exclude from consideration everything that happened between the time when the offer was made and the dismissal and would be contrary to the wording of section 98(4), which points to the dismissal.' ... (W)hether it was fair or unfair must be judged in the light of the situation when it occurred and not when an earlier step was taken': see p. 722.

**3.218** In *Catamaran Cruisers Ltd v Williams* (1994) stressed that, in deciding whether a dismissal of an employee for refusing to accept a contractual change is fair, the tribunal should not only look at the advantage or disadvantage of the new contract from the employee's perspective but should also consider and take into account the benefit to the employer in imposing the changes. To some extent, this is a balancing exercise, though it is clear from this case, as well as from the others already cited, that an employer who can satisfy the tribunal of the need for the changes is likely to be held to have been dismissed fairly. See also *Chubb Fire Security Ltd v Harper* (1983), which involved an employee's refusal to accept a new contract as a sales representative in a new territory and under different pay arrangements, as he foresaw a sizeable drop in his income; again, the dismissal was held to be fair.

**3.219** What these decisions suggest is that a dismissal for a refusal to accept new terms and conditions will not be of itself unfair. They are not to be taken, however, as authorities for the notion that an employer need not observe a fair procedure in arriving at the decision to dismiss. Thus, an employer who wishes to avoid the risk of an adverse tribunal decision should ensure that advance warning of the changes is given, together with a suitable lead-in period, that consultation with trade unions takes place, where appropriate, and that alternatives to dismissal have been considered, such as alternative jobs or locations, and that steps have been taken to accommodate an employee's reasonable grounds for refusing to agree to the change.

**3.220** If the employee makes a claim for a redundancy payment, the main issues are likely to be (i) whether an employee who is subject to a flexibility clause can be said to be redundant and (ii) whether an employee who refuses new terms and conditions of employment will be held to have unreasonably refused a suitable offer and thus be disentitled by section 141 of the 1996 Act from receiving a redundancy payment. So far as the first issue is concerned, it is clear from the recent case of *Johnson v Peabody Trust* (1996) that in looking to see whether an employee is redundant within the definition in section 139(1) an employment tribunal should look at the employee's contract in a common-sense manner to see what the basic task is that the employee was employed to do. In that case, the employee was employed as a roofer but was also subject to a flexibility clause stating: 'Where possible, tradespersons will be expected to carry out multi-trade operations'. By the time he was made redundant he was spending more time on multi-trade operations than on roofing. The EAT upheld the tribunal's decision that he was redundant and pointed out that otherwise an employer would never be able to establish that an employee subject to a flexibility clause was redundant unless it was possible to establish that there was a redundancy situation in every single trade encompassed by the flexibility clause. See also *Birds Eye Walls Ltd v Austin* (EAT 581/86), in which a similar conclusion was reached.

**3.221** Cases such as the above are consistent with the general tenor of cases involving changes by employers of their employees' terms and conditions of employment. In *Lesney Products & Co Ltd v Nolan* (1981) Lord Denning stressed that 'it is important that nothing should be done to impair the ability of employers to reorganise their workforce and their terms and conditions of work so as to improve efficiency'. Similarly, in *Johnson v Nottinghamshire Combined Police Authority* (1974), he said, at p. 176:

> [A]n employer is entitled to reorganise his business so as to improve its efficiency and, in doing so, to propose to his staff a change in the terms and conditions of their employment: and to dispense with their services if they do not agree. Such a change does not automatically give the staff a right to a redundancy payment. It only does so if the change in the terms and conditions is due to a redundancy situation.

**3.222** So far as the second issue mentioned in para. 3.220 is concerned, it is unlikely that an employee offered new terms and conditions involving a reduction in pay will be held to have been made a suitable offer of alternative employment and still less likely that his or her refusal would be considered reasonable. See *Taylor v Kent County Council* (1969).

## Variations in the context of a transfer of an undertaking

**3.223** The question which arises in the context of variations of contract concerns the extent, if any, to which the rules considered in this chapter are affected by the Transfer of Undertakings (Protection of Employment) Regulations 1981 (as amended). The Regulations are considered in detail in Chapter 9, to which reference should be made. In the present context, the regulations which require examination are regulation 5 and, to a lesser extent, regulation 8. As the law stands, two propositions may be stated:

1.    an employee who is transferred from a transferor employer to a transferee employer without being dismissed and, on transfer, agrees to a variation of his or her terms and conditions of employment will not be bound by the agreed variation

2.    an employee who is dismissed by the transferor employer with the termination payments to which he or she is entitled and is then re-employed by the transferee employer on different terms and conditions will be bound by the new terms and conditions.

**3.224** The authority for the first proposition is *Crédit Suisse First Boston (Europe) Ltd v Lister* (1998), in which the Court of Appeal held that a variation of the employee's contract was made unenforceable by virtue of reg. 5(1). The facts were that CSFB bought part of an undertaking owned by BZW (the transferor) and entered into negotiations with the transferring employees, including L. He agreed, *inter alia*, to a restrictive covenant governing working for a competitor. When CSFB tried to enforce this, the Court of Appeal held that reg. 5(1) made the agreement unenforceable on the grounds that he was not entitled to waive his rights under his contract with BZW even though under his new contract viewed as a whole he was better off than under his contract with BZW. The Court said that, since the transferor employer could not have prevented the employee from working for a competitor after the termination of his employment, the transferee could not do so either. It was irrelevant that the new contract also gave the employee a compensating benefit in return for agreeing to the imposition of the restriction. Clarke L.J. quoted with approval the statement of Moore-Bick J. (at first instance): '... the agreement is ineffective in so far as it purports to impose on the employee an obligation to which he was not previously subject. To that extent it is disadvantageous to him and it is no answer to say that in the instant case it also gave him a compensating benefit which more than made up for it.' This follows the decision of the ECJ in *Foreningen af Arbedsledere I Danmark v Daddy's Dance Hall* (1988). See also *Viggósdóttir v Íslandspóstur hf* (2002) and *Martin v South Bank University* (2003). This rule does not apply, however, to non-binding employment practices: see *Ralton v Havering College of Further & Higher Education* (2001). Nor does it apply to changes taking place some time after the transfer and unconnected with the transfer: *Norris v Brown and Root Ealing Technical Services Ltd* (EAT 386/00).

**3.225** The authority for the second proposition is the House of Lords decision in *Wilson v St. Helens Borough Council* and *Meade v British Fuels Ltd* (1998). Thus, if an employee is dismissed by the transferor and re-engaged by the transferee, he or she will not be able to insist on the observance by the transferee of his or her previous terms or conditions and will be bound by the terms and conditions agreed with the transferee. It should be noted, however, that this decision only deals with the issue of new terms and conditions following a *dismissal* and not with agreed changes where there is no dismissal. Clearly, in such a case there will be issues of liability arising by virtue of reg. 5, which are considered in Chapter 9.

## Illegal contracts of employment

**3.226** A contract of employment is illegal either if it is prohibited by statute or if its objects are forbidden by the common law on the grounds of public policy. The most significant impact which the doctrine of illegality has had upon this area of the law is in relation to contracts which involve the commission of a fraud on the Inland Revenue, and which may be made void at common law as being contrary to public policy. An example is *Miller v Karlinski* (1945), where the employee was employed under a contract which provided that he should receive a salary of £10 per week and should also recover from the employer the amount of income tax payable on that salary, by including it in an account for travelling expenses. Du Parcq L.J. said, at p. 86: 'I find it impossible to say that, where a man agrees to work and to be paid according to a scheme devised ... so as to defraud the revenue, the whole agreement is not an illegal agreement which the courts will not enforce.' A similar view was taken by the Court of Appeal in *Napier v National Business Agency Ltd* (1951).

**3.227** Illegal contracts fall into two distinct categories. In the first category are contracts which are illegal *per se*, or which cannot be performed by one or both of the parties otherwise than illegally, for example where employer and employee agree to defraud the Revenue. In such cases the state of knowledge of the parties is irrelevant and their ignorance of the illegality will not save them from the consequences: see *Miller v Karlinski* (1945), *Corby v Morrison* (1980) and *Newland v Simons & Willer (Hairdressers) Ltd* (1981). In these cases, as Lord Coulsfield explained in *Salvesen v Simons* (1994), the principle is that 'if a party knew what was being done, it is irrelevant that he did not know that it was illegal'. In this last case, the arrangement between the employee and his employer was that part of his wages should be paid as a management fee to a business operated by him and his wife in partnership. The EAT held that this arrangement involved a misrepresentation to the Inland Revenue in that there was no proper basis for the payment of a management fee to the partnership, since the payment was not for services provided but was a diversion of the employee's remuneration; to that extent it was a fraud on the Revenue. The employee's contract was therefore unenforceable. On the other hand, if the payments in question are irregular the employee's contract will not necessarily be rendered illegal: see *Annandale Engineering v Samson* (1994). It should be noted, however, that an arrangement will not necessarily be illegal if it is entered into in good faith and is a proper method of reducing tax, which is open and above board and either has been or will be disclosed to the Inland Revenue: see *Lightfoot v D. & J. Sporting Ltd* (1996).

**3.228** In the second category are contracts which are ex facie legal but illegally performed, for example where the employer defrauds the Revenue by failure to deduct tax from the employee's wages, or where performance of the contract by the employee involves acts for sexually immoral purposes, as in Coral Leisure Group Ltd v Barnet (1981), the facts of which were briefly that the employee's contract involved him in obtaining prostitutes for customers of his employers. In such cases, the employee's state of mind will be decisive. In Newland v Simons and Willer (Hairdressers) Ltd (1981) May J. said:

> ... [W]here both employer and employee knowingly commit an illegality by way of a fraud on the revenue in the payment and receipt of remuneration ..., which is an essential part of such a contract, ... there can be doubt that this does turn it into a contract that is prohibited by statute or common law, and consequently the employee is precluded from enforcing any rights [he or] she might otherwise have against [the] employer.

**3.229**  In *Coral Leisure Group Ltd v Barnet* (1981) Browne-Wilkinson J. drew a distinction between '(a) cases in which there is a contractual obligation to do an act which is unlawful and (b) cases where the contractual obligations are capable of being performed lawfully and were initially intended so to be performed, but which have in fact been performed by unlawful means.' In the former case, if it is possible to sever or separate the tainted contractual obligations from the untainted, the whole contract will not be unenforceable. In the latter case, the fact that the employee in the course of his or her employment has committed an unlawful or immoral act will not by itself prevent him or her from enforcing the contract unless the contract is entered into for the purpose of doing the unlawful or immoral act or the contract itself (as opposed to the mode of its performance) is prohibited by law. See also the later Court of Appeal decision in *Hewcastle Catering Ltd v Ahmed* (1992) and *Colen v Cebrian (UIK) Ltd* (2004). In this last case, the Court of Appeal said that a contract which is perfectly lawful at its inception and was intended to be lawfully performed does not automatically become lawful and unenforceable by any act of illegal performance.

**3.230**  The effect of applying these common law principles of illegality to employees' statutory rights has often been disproportionate to the wrong done by them, since if the tribunal finds that there has been illegality it will be bound to conclude that the employee's statutory rights are unenforceable: see *Tomlinson v Dick Evans 'U' Drive Ltd* (1978).

In *Corby v Morrison* (1980), for example, the illegality arose from the fact that the employee was paid an extra £5 a week without any deduction being made in respect of income tax or social security liability. The EAT held that the contract was illegal per se, and added, obiter, that if the contract had been one which was ex facie legal and knowledge had become relevant, the test was subjective, not objective. An example of a contract ex facie legal is *Newland v Simons & Willer (Hairdressers) Ltd*, where the EAT emphasised that the actual state of the employee's knowledge was what mattered and it was not enough that she ought to have known but in fact did not know, whether through stupidity, misunderstanding or inexperience.

**3.231** As can be seen from this discussion of the case law, most of the cases in which illegality has been contended for have been cases which involved a method of payment of wages to an employee involving a fraud on the Inland Revenue. Another type of case which should be considered, however, is one where the employee enters employment whilst an illegal immigrant. Few cases have considered this question and those that have have done so fairly cursorily. In *Sharma v Hindu Temple* (EAT 253/90) the facts were that the employee was employed by the temple at a time when he had no visa relating to his stay in the United Kingdom or employment here. The employment tribunal dismissed his complaint on the ground of illegality. The EAT held that the tribunal had made insufficient findings of fact, particularly as to whether the employee was knowingly in breach of the conditions of his leave to enter the country, and remitted the case for a rehearing. In the course of the judgment, Wood J. quoted from the judgment of Devlin J. in *St. John Shipping Corporation v Joseph Rank Ltd* (1957):

> [A] contract which is entered into with the object of committing an illegal act is unenforceable. The application of this principle depends upon proof of the intent, at the time when the contract was made, to break the law; if the intent is mutual the contract is not enforceable at all, and, if unilateral, it is unenforceable at the suit of the party who is proved to have it.

**3.232** Wood J. went on to say that if the employee was held knowingly to be in breach of the condition of his leave, the contract would be illegal in its formation. This approach was followed by the EAT in the later case of *Bamgbose v The Royal Star and Garter Home*: EAT

841/95. It follows from the present state of the law that, if an employee is employed under a contract of employment tainted with illegality, no week of employment under that contract will count in computing continuous employment: see Chapter 7, for a discussion of continuity of employment. The illegality or otherwise of a contract does not, however, affect the employment tribunal's jurisdiction to hear a case, but only concerns the parties' right to enforce the contract: see *Wilkinson v Lugg* (1990).

## Further reading

Deakin, S, & Morris, G, *Labour Law* (3rd ed, 2001) Butterworths (chapters 3 & 4), pp. 102–126.

Smith, I, & Thomas, G, *Industrial Law* (8th ed, 2003) Butterworths (chapter 3).

## *Article*

Lindsay, J, (2001) 'The Implied Term of Trust and Confidence', *Industrial Law Journal*, Vol. 30, pp. 1–18.

Mogridge (1981) 'Illegal Employment Contracts: Loss of Statutory Protection', *Industrial Law Journal*, Vol. 10, pp. 23 et seq.

## Self-test questions

1.    Keith was registered with the Sorted Employment Agency. For seven years he has been assigned to Bullet Ltd; to work as a cleaner. Under the terms of his contract with the Agency he agreed to co-operate with the client company to whom he was assigned and to obey all reasonable orders. He was obliged to submit time sheets to the Agency at the end of every week to indicate the number of hours he had worked for Bullet Ltd during the preceding week and he was subject to any disciplinary measures the Agency might deem to be necessary. Two years ago Bullet Ltd redeployed Keith as a member of their catering staff 'as

required' which resulted in his wages, still paid through Sorted Employment Agency, being increased.

Keith wishes to know if he has an employer and who it may be?

2. Explain the House of Lords decision in *Johnson v Unisys* (2001) and its implications for the implied term of mutual trust and confidence.

3. 'Implied terms are dangerous in the hands of employers'. Discuss.

4. Put the case for or against – Illegal contracts should be enforceable, where they protect employees from bad employers.

# CHAPTER FOUR

# Discrimination and Equal Pay

## Summary

This chapter assesses the prohibited grounds: gender and transsexualism; race; disability; sexual orientation; religion or belief. The key points examined are:

- sex and race discrimination: direct; indirect; victimisation; segregation (race only);

- disability discrimination;

- transsexualism;

- sexual orientation and religion or belief: the Employment Equality Regulations; and

- equal pay.

## Introduction – the prohibited grounds of discrimination: sex and transsexualism; race; disability; sexual orientation; religion or belief

**4.1** In Great Britain, there are a number of grounds on which discrimination is prohibited. They are sex (including sexual orientation and a change of sex, ie transsexualism), race, disability, and religion or belief. Until recently, there were only three statutes covering discrimination: the Sex Discrimination Act 1975 ('the SDA 1975'), together with the Equal Pay Act 1970 ('the EqPA 1970') comprising the legislation on sex discrimination (and discrimination on the ground of marital status), and the Race Relations Act 1976 ('the RRA 1976') covering discrimination on the ground of race (from July 2003 this has been widened to include race and ethnic or national origins). Discrimination on the ground of disability was made unlawful (at least, in the field of employment) by the Disability Discrimination Act 1995 (DDA 1995 1995), the employment provisions of which came into force on 2 December 1996. We will be considering these statutes from the labour law perspective, although it should be remembered that the scope of the SDA 1975, RRA 1976 and DDA 1995 1995 is wider: these statutes also cover, for example, education and the provision of goods, services and facilities.

**4.2** Discrimination against transsexuals, which is discussed below, was initially rendered unlawful through a ruling of the European Court of Justice ('the ECJ') in the case of *P v S and Cornwall County Council* (1996), but was put on a statutory footing from 1 May 1999 by the Sex Discrimination (Gender Reassignment) Regulations 1999 (SI 1999/1102), which amended the SDA 1975. Discrimination on the ground of sexual orientation and religion or belief was made unlawful in December 2003 by regulations implementing provisions of the Equal Treatment Framework Directive 2000 (Directive 2000/78/EC) ('the ETFD'). These grounds of discrimination are discussed below.

**4.3** There is no legislation making age discrimination unlawful, but the ETFD requires Member States to introduce such legislation by 2006. Therefore, it is likely that Great Britain will introduce such legislation by October 2006.

## Sex and Race Discrimination

**4.4** There are distinct types of discrimination under both the SDA 1975 and the RRA 1976, bearing similar definitions: direct discrimination; indirect discrimination; harassment; victimisation; and (under the RRA 1976 only) segregation. It is important to stress the fact that direct discrimination cannot be justified under the SDA 1975 or the RRA 1976, whereas indirect discrimination may be. The SDA 1975 and the RRA 1976 will be discussed together in this chapter, as many of the concepts and definitions used in these statutes are similar.

**4.5** In terms of race discrimination, there have been two previous statutes, both of them largely ineffective, the Race Relations Act 1965 and the Race Relations Act 1968. The former, which was not applicable in the employment field, established the Race Relations Board, with powers of investigation and conciliation, while the latter prohibited discrimination in employment but was not really effective: there was no individual right of complaint to a tribunal. Complaints first had to be made to the Race Relations Board, which was the only body allowed to take proceedings concerning such complaints. In terms of eliminating race discrimination, these statutes failed.

## Marital Status

**4.6** The SDA 1975 makes unlawful discrimination against married persons in respect of employment (SDA 1975, s 3(1)); for a rare, recent case on this see *Chief Constable of Bedfordshire Constabulary v Graham* (2002), EAT). However, under EU law, discrimination is prohibited against a person on grounds of 'marital or family status' (Equal Treatment Directive (Directive 76/207, Art 2(1)), which is wide enough to cover single as well as married persons.

## Scope of the SDA 1975 and RRA 1976

**4.7** The territorial scope of both statutes is Great Britain (SDA 1975, s 10; RRA 1976 s 8). The statutes do not apply where a person is employed wholly outside Great Britain. It should be noted that the SDA 1975 applies to men as well as women (SDA 1975, s. 2). Both statutes apply to: job applicants, employees and those working under 'a contract personally to execute any work or labour', ie independent contractors (SDA 1975, ss 6 and 82; RRA 1976, ss 4 and 78); agency workers (sometimes called 'contract workers'), who are protected from discrimination by both employment agencies and principals: SDA 1975 ss 9 and 15; RRA 1976, ss 7 and 14, and see, for example Harrods Ltd v Remick (1998)). Former employees may claim for post-termination discrimination (see SDA 1975, s 20A; RRA 1976, s 27A). The range of possible respondents is wide and includes: employers; trade unions (SDA 1975, s 12; RRA 1976, s 11); qualification bodies for trades or professions (such as the Law Society) (SDA 1975, s 13; RRA 1976, s 12).

## The prohibited grounds: sex, race, colour, nationality, ethnic or national origin

**4.8** As has been mentioned above the SDA 1975 extends to discrimination on grounds of sex and marital status (ie it protects married persons). The RRA 1976 prohibits discrimination against a person on grounds of colour, race, nationality and ethnic or national origin. The difficulty is determining what these terms mean.

**4.9** In the well-known RRA 1976 case of *Mandla v Dowell Lee* (1983), HL, concerning a Sikh boy who was refused entrance to a private school because he could not comply with the school's uniform requirements as he wore a turban, the House of Lords defined 'ethnic group'. To be regarded as an ethnic group, the group had to regard itself, and be regarded by others, as a distinct community by virtue of certain characteristics. Two were essential: a long, shared history, and a cultural tradition of its own. Other relevant characteristics include either a common geographical origin or descent from a small number of common ancestors; a common language, literature or religion; and/or a sense of being a minority (or oppressed or dominant) group. The House of Lords held, applying these tests, that Sikhs were indeed a distinct racial group.

**4.10** Using these criteria, the courts have held that Jews (*Seide v Gillette Industries* (1980) and gypsies (*Commission for Racial Equality v Dutton* (1989)) are ethnic groups but Rastafarians are not (*Crown Suppliers Property Services Agency v Dawkins* (1993).

**4.11** Nationality is not the same as national origins, so the English, Scots and Welsh have different national origins, but the same nationality, ie British (*Northern Joint Police Board v Power* (1997)).

## The Race Directive (Directive 2000/43/EC)

**4.12** The Race Directive, which was issued to combat discrimination across a number of grounds, was implemented by the Race Relations Act 1976 (Amendment) Regulations 2003. Unfortunately, the scope of the Directive and that of the RRA 1976 is not the same: the Directive concerns discrimination on the ground of race, or ethnic or national origin, while the RRA 1976 extends to discrimination on the grounds of colour or nationality. Therefore, although the 2003 Regulations amend the RRA 1976 in a number of respects, these amendments do not apply to discrimination on the grounds of colour or nationality, which is unsatisfactory and makes the application of the RRA 1976 even more complex.

## The Burden of Proof

**4.13** It may be very difficult for a complainant under the SDA 1975 or the RRA 1976 to prove his or her case. The Burden of Proof Directive (Directive 97/80/EC) was intended to address this problem by changing the burden of proof in sex discrimination cases (it is sometimes erroneously stated that the Directive reverses the burden of proof, which it does not). The Sex Discrimination (Indirect Discrimination and Burden of Proof) Regulations 2001 implement the Directive by inserting a new section in the SDA 1975, s 63A. This means that if the complainant proves facts from which the ET could conclude, in the absence of an adequate explanation, that the respondent committed an act of discrimination against them, the ET will uphold the complaint, unless the respondent proves that he or she did not commit it. The same burden of proof provision applies in the RRA 1976 (s 54A). Although this might appear to be a significant change in the law, courts and tribunals had reached a similar position, ie they would take adverse inferences once the complainant had established a prima facie case (see *King v Great Britain China Centre* (1991), CA.

## Direct discrimination

**4.14** Direct discrimination is defined in the SDA 1975 and RRA 1976 as less favourable treatment on the ground of sex, marital status, or gender reassignment (SDA 1975, s 1(1)(a), 3(1)(a), and 2A(1)(a)), or on racial grounds (RRA 1976, s 1(1)(a)). (Gender reassignment is considered under the section on transsexualism below.) (For the purposes of the employment parts of the RRA 1976, ie Part II, the definition of indirect discrimination differs from that for the other parts of the statute.) This is the most overt and explicit form of discrimination.

## Direct discrimination and motive

**4.15**  The motive of the discriminator is irrelevant. In *James v Eastleigh Borough Council* (1990), which is not an employment case, the respondent council operated a concession to old age pensioners wishing to use its swimming pool, who were allowed entry free of charge. Others had to pay 35p. Both Mr and Mrs James were 61. However, Mrs James gained free entry, since the state pensionable age was 60 for women, while Mr James did not, because the pensionable age for men was 65. The council had no intention to discriminate in this case (in fact, just the opposite!) but the House of Lords held that the test in direct discrimination is objective: the 'but for' test was applied, ie but for the complainant's sex, would they have been treated less favourably. The answer here was 'no', so there had been direct discrimination. The intention or motive of the discriminator was irrelevant to that issue. The case also establishes that the application of a discriminatory criterion constitutes direct discrimination.

**4.16**  The employer's motive in *Ministry of Defence v Jeremiah* (1979) was also held to be irrelevant. In that case, the employer required men to work in a colour-bursting shop producing munitions, which was dirty work, but the women employees were not required to do so on the ground that it was necessary to shower after this work, which would ruin the women's hair-do. The men were paid an extra sum for this uncongenial work. They claimed that this was sex discrimination. The Court of Appeal held that a discriminator cannot buy the right to discriminate and that this was direct discrimination.

## Comparators

**4.17**  Less favourable treatment requires a comparison to be carried out. The complainant must be treated less favourably than the way the employer treats *or would treat* a man (under the SDA 1975) or a person not of the same race (under the RRA 1976) (author's emphasis). This means that an actual or a hypothetical comparator may be used. This requirement of finding an appropriate comparator has caused particular problems when considering pregnancy-related discrimination claims (see below).

## Detriment

**4.18** Less favourable treatment alone is insufficient to found a claim: the complainant must go on to show that they have suffered a detriment (which means being put at a disadvantage): SDA 1975, s 6(2)(b); RRA 1976, s 4(2)(c). Often, it is not difficult to find that the complainant has been put at a disadavantage, eg by not being appointed to the post applied for, by not getting the promotion or transfer, etc. One particular problem with finding a detriment is whether the test is objective or subjective, ie should the individual's views be considered, or should the test be whether a reasonable worker would consider that they had suffered a detriment? In *Shamoon v Chief Constable of the Royal Ulster Constabulary* (2003), the House of Lords held that the latter was the correct approach. Further, it was not necessary to find an economic or physical disadvantage to find a detriment: the detriment in *Shamoon* arose when a police inspector was relieved of the duty of conducting annual appraisals with junior officers.

## Dress Codes

**4.19** A number of cases have involved the application of rules concerning dress codes on employees. Clearly, if such codes are to be imposed on male and female employees, they would have to be different, to take into account the difference in sex and in compliance with convention. However, generally the courts have found that, provided such codes are applied in an even-handed way, ie such dress codes are not contrary to the SDA 1975 (although some interesting human rights points are raised on this issue). In *Smith v Safeway plc* (1996), a male delicatessen assistant wore his long hair in a ponytail. The dress code required men to wear their hair shorter, whereas women were allowed to have long hair provided it was tied back. The

Court of Appeal held that there was no sex discrimination in this case. Such codes were not discriminatory provided they merely imposed general rules (with relevant changes to account for the difference in sex) enforcing a conventional or smart appearance: the question was whether, taken as a whole, there was less favourable treatment (see also *Schmidt v Austicks Bookshop* (1978), and *McConomy v Croft Inns Ltd* (1992).

## Harassment

**4.20** Sexual and racial harassment constitutes direct discrimination, being a form of detriment based on the prohibited grounds. The Race Directive contains provisions relating to harassment, and changes have been made to the RRA 1976 by the Race Relations Act 1976 (Amendment) Regulations 2003 (SI 2003/1626) which insert a definition of harassment into the RRA 1976. The SDA 1975 has not yet been amended so as to insert express reference to harassment (as is required by the Equal Treatment Amendment Directive (Directive 2003/73/EC).

## Racial Harassment

**4.21** The Race Relations Act 1976 (Amendment) Regulations 2003 insert a new section 3A(1) into the RRA 1976. Harassment occurs where, on the grounds of race or ethnic or national origins, a person engages in unwanted conduct which has the purpose or effect of (a) violating a person's dignity, or (b) creating an intimidating, hostile, degrading, humiliating or offensive environment for her or him. There are both objective and subjective elements to the definition because conduct is to be regarded as having that effect 'only if, having regard to all the circumstances, including in particular the perception of that other person, it should reasonably be considered as having that effect.' The new definition applies only to harassment on grounds of race or ethnic or national origin.

## Sexual harassment

**4.22** There is currently no express provision in the SDA 1975 concerning sexual harassment, although such complaints are brought under ss 1(1)(a) and 6(2)(b), the latter concerning subjecting a person to a detriment. As sexual harassment is a form of direct discrimination, being less favourable treatment on the ground of sex, it is necessary to establish that (a) the treatment was on this ground (see *Porcelli v Strathclyde Regional Council* (1984) and (b) that the complainant has suffered a detriment judged from the recipient's perspective (see *Shamoon* (above) and *Wileman v Minilec Engineering* (1988). A single act of harassment, if it is sufficiently serious, may amount to harassment (see *Bracebridge Engineering Ltd v Darby* (1990) for an example of an outrageous act of discrimination). However, a series of incidents, no one of which taken on its own amounting to harassment, may be sufficient: see *Reed v Stedman* (1999).

## Employers' liability for harassment

**4.23**  Employers may be liable for acts of harassment committed by employees in the course of their employment (SDA 1975, s 41; RRA 1976, s 32). The test to determine whether an act was done 'in the course of employment' is not that used in the law of tort. In *Jones v Tower Boot Co Ltd* (1997), the Court of Appeal held that the statutory test was distinct from the common law one, ie the words 'in the course of employment'. This concept has been stretched to include acts of sexual harassment taking place outside working hours and away from the employer's premises in a social setting (drinks after work): see *Chief Constable of Lincolnshire Police v Stubbs* (1999) in which the EAT held that this was an 'extension' of employment. This would seem to stretch the scope of employers' liability under the statute in a way which leaves them vulnerable.

**4.24**  The employer has a defence to liability for acts of harassment by employees, which is that it has taken reasonably practicable steps to prevent the acts (SDA 1975, s 41(3); RRA 1976, s 32(3)). This may be satisfied by employers having in place an equal opportunities policy, ensuring that all staff are aware of it and have been given some instructions or guidance on it (see *Balgobin v Tower Hamlets London Borough Council* (1987)).

## Pregnancy

**4.25**  Discrimination against a woman on ground of pregnancy is clearly discrimination on the ground of her sex (see the ECJ's ruling in

*Dekker v Stichting Vormingscentrum voor Jong Volwassenen (VJV-Centrum) Plus* (1991), where the ECJ held that it was direct discrimination) but this area has caused some problems in the past because the SDA 1975 requires a comparator, actual or hypothetical, of the opposite to be identified. Further, the relevant circumstances of the complainant and the comparator had to be 'the same or not materially different' (SDA 1975, 5(3)). The courts and tribunals initially took the approach that a pregnant woman who was, for example, off work because of a pregancy-related reason and who was then dismissed for her absence should be compared with a male employee who was off work with illness for a similar period (*Hayes v Malleable Working Men's Club and Institute* (1985).

**4.26** This approach was held to be incorrect by the ECJ ruling in *Webb v EMO Air Cargo (UK) Ltd* (1993). In Webb a female employee who was about to go on maternity leave was replaced by a woman taken on to cover the temporary absence of the pregnant employee, although the employer intended to keep the replacement on after the woman returned from maternity leave. When the replacement discovered that she too was pregnant, she was dismissed as she would not be able to provide the cover required, ie the employer argued, nothing to do with sex. The ECJ ruled that this was contrary to EC law. A pregnant woman should not be compared to a man who was off work through sickness: pregnancy is not an illness, and comparisons with illness are inappropriate. As pregnancy is gender-related, it is direct sex discrimination to dismiss a woman because she is pregnant (see also the House of Lord's decision in in *Webb v EMO Air Cargo (UK) Ltd (No 2)* (1995).

**4.27** The ECJ has ruled that the period of pregnancy and maternity leave constitutes a protected period and dismissal of a woman for a pregnancy-related reason, including an illness related to childbirth, during this period will be unlawful sex discrimination (*Brown v Rentokil* (1998). In Brown, the ECJ ruled that dismissal for absence caused by a pregnancy-related illness after this protected period has ended would only be unlawful if a man who was absent for a similar period through illness would not have been dismissed. However, the period of absence during the protected period itself should not be taken into account. Finally, it should be remembered that the SDA 1975, s 99, provides that it is automatically unfair to dismiss a woman for a reason related to pregnancy (no qualifying period of continuous employment is required).

## Indirect discrimination

**4.28** Indirect discrimination is the application of an apparently gender-neutral or race-neutral requirement which places persons of one sex or persons of one colour, racial group, ethnic or national origins, at a disadvantage, and which cannot be objectively justified. Essentially, the indirect discrimination provisions concern disparate impact. The relevant provisions concerning the employment field are contained in the SDA 1975, s 1(2)(b) and the RRA 1976, s 1(1A). the SDA 1975, s 1(2)(b) provides that:

a person discriminates against a woman if–
(b) he applies to her a provision, criterion or practice which he applies or would apply equally to a man but–
    (i) which is such that it would be to the detriment of a considerably larger proportion of women than of men, and
    (ii) which he cannot show to be justifiable irrespective of the sex of the person to whom it is applied, and
    (iii) which is to her detriment.

**4.29** Section 1(1A) of the RRA 1976 (which applies to the employment field) is now drafted in rather different terms to the indirect discrimination provision in the SDA 1975, as a result of the need to comply with the obligations imposed by the Race Directive. The RRA 1976 now requires the complainant to establish that the provision, criterion or practice puts those of one racial group 'at a particular disadvantage' compared with others. Therefore, it would appear that there is no need to deal with proportions, it being enough merely to establish the disadvantage to a racial group (although this provision does not apply to discrimination on grounds of colour or nationality).

## Provision, criterion or practice

**4.30** It should be noted that these provisions under the two statutes as originally drafted referred to a 'requirement or condition' rather than the current drafting which refers to a 'provision, criterion or practice'. This was introduced to comply with the UK's obligations under the Burden of Proof Directive, which is applicable only in the employment field. It would seem that the new drafting is wider than the old 'requirement or condition' wording, which, as will be seen from the following discussion, sometimes led to a rather restrictive analysis (see below). The new wording is likely to be broad enough to encompass, for example, job specifications that are divided into 'essential' and 'desirable' qualities or qualifications: the latter would probably not have been caught by the 'requirement or condition' provision, whereas the new wording would do so.

**4.31** There are numerous cases under the old wording concerning what has been held to be a 'requirement or condition'. In *Price v Civil Service Commission (No 2)* (1983), for example, it was an age requirement for a Civil Service post (the successful applicant had to be between 17 and 28). The complainant, who was 32, succeeded in her claim that this was indirect sex discrimination as it disadvantaged women, who would be more likely to be over this age as they often took time out of their career for childbirth and child-rearing.

**4.32** The limitations of the 'requirement or condition' wording may be illustrated by the decision in *Perera v Civil Service Commission (No 2)* (1983), in which the Court of Appeal held that only an absolute bar would constitute a requirement or condition under the RRA 1976. This was followed in *Meer v Tower Hamlets LBC* (1988), brought under the RRA 1976, where the requirement was that the applicant had previous experience working for the local authority, which the applicant contended screened him out as he was of Indian origin. As it was not an absolute bar (described as a 'must' in some of the cases) it did not constitute a requirement or condition. The new wording of RRA 1976, s 1A should avoid these pitfalls.

## Ability to comply

**4.33** Another important change is that the old wording of SDA 1975, s 1 required the woman to establish that the requirement or condition was a detriment 'because she could not comply with it'. The new wording (relating to the employment field only) contained in s 1(2)(b)(iii) omits this phrase: if the 'provision, criterion or practice' is to her detriment, it is prima facie sex discrimination.

*Considerably larger proportion – establishing adverse impact – SDA 1975, s 1(2)(b)(i); RRA 1976, s 1(1A)*

**4.34**  Indirect discrimination claims under both statutes require disparate, adverse impact to be established. Under the old wording of the SDA 1975, the indirect discrimination provision in the SDA 1975 called for a finding as to whether 'the proportion of women who can comply with' a particular requirement or condition was 'considerably smaller than the proportion of men who can comply with it' (under the new wording, the provision, etc., must be to the detriment of a considerably larger proportion of women than men, although this will probably alter the analysis and approach very little). This meant that complainants had to select the correct 'pool' of comparators (see Jones v University of Manchester (1993), CA – a case where the complainant failed because she had selected the wrong pool), and compare the ratio of male to female in it to establish that a 'considerably smaller' proportion of women could comply with the requirement.

**4.35**  It will be seen from this that many ET hearings were and are taken up with a close scrutiny of relevant statistics. The problem is that there are no fixed guidelines as to what constitutes a 'considerably smaller' or, now, a 'considerably larger' proportion. An example of the difficulties encountered by complainants facing this vague wording may be seen in *London Underground Ltd v Edwards (No 2)* (1998), CA. When the employer introduced new shift patterns for train drivers, Ms Edwards could not comply with them because of child-care responsibilities. The proportions established that 100% of male train drivers could comply with the new shift patterns compared to 95% of female drivers (but the male drivers numbered 2033, and the female drivers only 21). The Court of Appeal held that there was indirect sex discrimination which the employer had to justify.

*Justification*

**4.36**  Under the SDA 1975, it is a defence to an indirect discrimination claim if the employer can establish that the provision, criterion or practice is justifiable, irrespective of the sex of the person to whom it is applied (SDA 1975, s 1(2)(b)(ii)). However, under the amended RRA 1976, the defence requires the employer to show that the provision, criterion or practice is 'a proportionate means of achieving a legitimate aim' (NB this defence applies to discrimination on the ground of race or ethnic or national origins (RRA 1976, s 1(1A)(c). This defence appears to mirror that set out by the ECJ in *Bilka-Kaufhaus v Weber von Hartz* (1987), concerning objective justification to be established under Article 141 of the Treaty. The ECJ ruled that the provision in question applied by the employer must:

(a)     correspond to a real need on the part of the employer;

(b)     be appropriate to that end; and

(c)     be necessary for that objective.


**4.37**     The objective approach in Bilka was followed in *Hampson v Dept of Education and Science* (1989) where the Court of Appeal rejected the employer's justification defence that the complainant's qualifications as a teacher in Hong Kong were not comparable to those required in the UK. The Court held that an objective balance needs to be struck between the discriminatory effect of the provision and the employer's legitimate business needs (the decision was reversed in the House of Lords but not on the justification ground) (see also the ECJ's ruling in *R v Secretary of State for Employment, ex p Seymour-Smith and Perez* (1999) and the House of Lords decision in *R v Secretary of State for Employement, ex p Seymour-Smith and Perez (No 2)* (2000) where the House of Lords held that the qualification period for unfair dismissal rights of part-timers, which was then two years, was objectively justifiable).


## Genuine occupational qualification

**4.38**     Where sex or race is a genuine occupational qualification (GOQ) for the job, less favourable treatment will be allowed (SDA 1975, s 7; RRA 1976, s 5). This exception comprises a fairly narrow range of reasons, eg, under SDA 1975, s 7(2):

> (a)where the essential nature of the job calls for a man for reasons of physiology (excluding physical strength or

stamina) or, in dramatic performances or other entertainment, for reasons of authenticity, so that the essential nature of the job would be materially different if carried out by a woman;

(b)the job needs to be held by a man to preserve decency or privacy because:

(i)it is likely to involve physical contact with men in circumstances where they might reasonably object to its being carried out by a woman, or

(ii)the holder of the job is likely to do his work in circumstances where men might reasonably object to the presence of a woman because they are in a state of undress or are using sanitary facilities.

(c)The job is likely to involve the holder of the job doing his work, or living, in a private home and needs to be held by a man because objection might reasonably be taken to allowing a woman—

(i)the degree of physical or social contact with a person living in the home, or

(iii)the knowledge of intimate details of such a person's life, which is likely, because of the nature or circumstances of the job, or of the home, to be allowed to, or available to, the holder of the job.

**4.39** The number of GOQs permitted under the RRA 1976, s 5 is fewer. The GOQs are to secure authenticity in (i) dramatic performances; (ii) as an artist's or photographer's model; (iii) work in a place where food or drink is provided for payment (sometimes called 'the Italian waiters' exception); and (iv) where the holder of the job is to provide personal services to persons of a particular racial group. See: *Tottenham Green Under Fives' Centre v Marshall (No 2)* (1991) and *Lambeth London Borough Council v Commission For Racial Equality* (1990). Implementing Race Directive obligations, a new s 4A was inserted into the RRA 1976, extending the GOQ to situations where the nature of or the context in which the employment is carried out makes being of a particular race or of particular ethnic or national origins a genuine and determining occupational requirement, and it is proportionate to apply that requirement.

## Transferred discrimination – RRA 1976

**4.40** It is possible for a person to claim under the RRA 1976 on the ground that they have been treated less favourably because of another person's race, colour, nationality, etc. In *Showboat Entertainment Centre Ltd v Owens* (1984) an employee was dismissed for refusing to carry out the instruction to exclude young blacks from an amusement arcade. He was successful in his claim that he had been discriminated against contrary to the RRA 1976 on the basis of another's colour (see also *Zarczynska v Levy* (1978) where a woman was dismissed for serving a black customer, against her employer's instructions; and *Weathersfield Ltd v Sargent* (1999) where a female employee was dismissed for failing to comply with her employer's instructions not to allow Asians to rent vehicles). Such instructions to discriminate are unlawful under the RRA 1976, s 30, but only the CRE may take enforcement action (see the similar provision in SDA 1975, s 39, which only the EOC may enforce (s 72)).

## Victimisation

**4.41** Victimisation is a form of direct discrimination, ie it is less favourable treatment of a person by reason that they have brought proceedings, given evidence or information, or alleged a contravention of the SDA 1975, RRA 1976 or EqPA 1970, ('the protected acts') or where the discriminator knows or suspects that that the person victimised intends to do any of those things, or suspects the person has done, or intends to do, any of them (SDA 1975, s 4; RRA 1976, s 2).

**4.42** The allegation by the person victimised must be true and made in good faith. The alleged motive of the discriminator is not relevant – indeed, it may be unconscious or sub-conscious (*Nagarajan v London Regional Transport* (1999), HL: a case where the complainant was not appointed to a position because he had made claims against the employer before under the RRA 1976). The House of Lords held that the protected act need not be the only reason for the treatment, it is sufficient if it is a substantial reason. In *Constable of West Yorkshire Police v Khan* (2001) IRLR 830, HL, the House of Lords held that the correct comparison was with someone who had not performed a protected act. Victimisation is established if the person has been treated less favourably by reason that he has performed such an act. In *Khan*, their

Lordships held that it was the existence of proceedings brought by Mr Khan which meant that they could not supply the reference he requested for the purpose of a job application he had made to another police force, as this might prejudice those proceedings. The decision in *Khan* seems difficult to reconcile with the House of Lords in *Nagarajan*.

## Segregation

**4.43** It is unlawful under the RRA 1976 to segregate from other persons on racial grounds (RRA 1976, s 1(2)). This is less favourable treatment, ie direct discrimination. There is no equivalent to this provision in the SDA 1975. The concept of segregation does not loom large in the race discrimination field, and the only case on it (*Pel Ltd v Modgill* (1980), EAT) was unsuccessful, since the employer had not deliberately separated Asian employees on racial grounds, they had simply grouped themselves together in a particular part of the workplace, rather than there having been a deliberate and conscious policy on the part of the employer.

## Enforcement and Remedies

**4.44** An individual may make an application to an employment tribunal within three months of the alleged act of discrimination, although the tribunal may extend this where it considers it is just and equitable to do so (SDA 1975, s 76; RRA 1976, s 68). The EOC and the CRE have powers to assist applicants where the case raises matters of principle or it is unreasonable to expect the applicant to deal with the case without support (SDA 1975, s 75; RRA 1976, s 66).

**4.45** If the complaint is upheld, the tribunal may order (i) a declaration of the rights of the parties; (ii) compensation (which is unlimited); (iii) a recommendation that the employer takes action within a specified period to obviate or reduce the effect of the discrimination (SDA 1975, s 65(1); RRA 1976, s 56(1)(a)). On recommendations, see *British Gas plc v Sharma* (1991); *North West Thames Regional Health Authority v Noone* (1988).

**4.46** Compensation for injury to feelings may be awarded, and often comprises a major part of the compensation (SDA 1975, s 66(4); RRA

1976, s 57(4)). The statutory cap on compensation in discrimination was removed in 1993 following the ECJ's ruling in *Marshall v Southampton & South-West Hampshire Area Health Authority (No 2)* (1993) in which the statutory limits were held to be in breach of the Community law requirement that domestic remedies were adequate for a breach of Community law. The Sex Discrimination and Equal Pay (Remedies) Regulations 1993 (SI 1993/2798) removed the statutory cap on compensation for sex discrimination, and the RRA 1976 was amended by the Race Relations (Remedies) Act 1994, which abolished the statutory limit on compensation in race discrimination cases.

**4.47** The Court of Appeal gave guidance to tribunals on compensation awards in *Vento v Constable of West Yorkshire Police (No 2)* (2003), and *Ministry of Defence v Cannock* (1994) indicates the size of awards that can be made by tribunals.

## The Equal Opportunities Commission (EOC) and the Commission for Racial Equality (CRE)

**4.48** These two Commissions have been discussed in chapter 1, but it is worth pointing out that their statutory duties include working towards the elimination of discrimination and promoting equality of opportunities. They also have a statutory duty to keep the discrimination statutes under review. They may also make formal investigations into areas of employment with a view to investigating and working towards the elimination of discrimination (SDA 1975, s 57; RRA 1976, s 48). They may also issue non-discrimination notices following a formal investigation. They also have powers to support complainants in the courts and tribunals in cases raising matters of principle. Finally, only the EOC and the CRE may take action concerning discriminatory advertisements (SDA 1975, s 38; RRA 1976, s 29).

## Disability Discrimination

**4.49** Legislation concerning discrimination on the ground of disability has been on the statute books for some time. However, the Disabled Persons (Employment) Act 1944 required a person with sufficient degree of disability to register so that the quota system could operate, ie employers with 20 or more employees were required to employ a quota (3%) of disabled persons. This scheme was not successful because there were no civil remedies for breach of the provisions; employers evaded the quota scheme by securing blanket permits allowing them to employ able-bodied employees (their argument was that there were no suitably qualified disabled persons for the job); and only about one third of those disabled registered under the scheme. The Act was replaced by the Disability Discrimination Act 1995 (the DDA 1995).

## The Disability Discrimination Act 1995·

**4.50** The DDA 1995 covers discrimination against disabled persons in employment (Part II of the Act) and in relation to the provision of goods, services and facilities (Part III), although this discussion considers the former. Part II of the DDA 1995 was brought into force on 1 December 1996. In 1996, in addition to the main statute, two sets of regulations were brought into force (the Disability Discrimination (Meaning of Disability) Regulations 1996 (SI 1996 No 1455), and the Disability Discrimination (Employment) Regulations 1996 (SI 1996 No 1456)). The Secretary of State has also issued guidance, pursuant to powers under DDA 1995, s 3: 'Guidance on matters to be taken into account in determining questions relating to the definition of disability' ('the Guidance'). The Secretary of State has also issued a Code of Practice giving practical guidance on matters relating to the elimination of disability discrimination in employment, encouraging good employment practices in relation to the disabled, and on reasonable adjustments. The EAT has stated that ETs should make express reference to the Code in their decisions (see *Ridout v TC Group* (1998); *Goodwin v The Patent Office* (1999)). The Court of Appeal has held that, when determining whether there has been less favourable treatment, the relevant provisions of the Code should be taken into account (*Clark v Novacold Ltd* (1999)).

**4.51** There is a Disability Rights Commission (DRC), which replaced the National Disabilities Council originally set up under the DDA 1995, with powers similar to those of the EOC and the CRE. In particular, it has supported a number of disability claimants in the courts and tribunals. Following amendments to the DDA 1995 (see below), from

1 October 2004, the DRC will have enforcement powers concerning instructions and pressure to discriminate, and discriminatory advertisements.

## Comparison of the DDA 1995 with the SDA 1975 and RRA 1976

**4.52** As originally drafted, the DDA 1995 differed in some important respects from the two earlier discrimination statutes, the SDA 1975 and the RRA 1976. Some of these differences have disappeared as a result of amendments to the DDA 1995 which come into force from October 2004 (see below). However, in the unamended version of the DDA 1995, the main differences were: (i) there was no explicit distinction between direct and indirect forms of discrimination; (ii) the DDA 1995 used a different comparison for identifying discrimination; (iii) the justification defence was broader under the DDA 1995; (iv) unlike the SDA 1975 and the RRA 1976, the DDA 1995 imposes a positive duty upon employers to make reasonable adjustments to accommodate disabled persons; and (v) the DDA 1995 contained a small employer's exemption. The amendments referred to below substantially alter the DDA 1995 in respect of the differences identified in (i), (iii) and (v) above.

## Amendment to the DDA 1995 – the Equal Treatment Framework Directive (ETFD)

**4.53** The ETFD (Directive 2000/78/EC) contained provisions relating to disability discrimination as a result of which the DDA 1995 had to be amended by 2006. This has been done by the Disability Discrimination Act 1995 (Amendment) Regulations 2003 (SI 2003/1673) ('the Amendment Regulations'). The amendments come into force on 1 October 2004. The main changes brought about by these amendments concern the introduction of an indirect discrimination provision and changes to the justification defence (see below). (NB The following discussion concerns case-law decided prior to the coming into force of the amendments made to the DDA 1995 in the Amendment Regulations.)

## Scope of the DDA 1995

**4.54** As is the case in the SDA 1975 and the RRA 1976, the DDA 1995 applies to employees, ie those working under a contract of employment or apprenticeship, and those who work under 'a contract personally to do any work' (DDA 1995, s 68). It includes employees and contract workers (new ss 4 and 4B). The employment provisions of the DDA 1995 apply to work in an establishment in Great Britain. From 1 October 2004, employees currently not covered by the Act, eg police officers, fire-fighters, partnerships, barristers and prison officers will be within the scope of the Act's employment provisions (armed forces members will continue to be excluded) (DDA 1995, ss 6A, 7A, 64, 64A).

### Post-termination discrimination

**4.55** The DDA 1995, s 4(2), as originally drafted, did not cover discrimination against former employees: it concerned discrimination by employers against a person 'whom he employs'. From 1 October 2004, coverage is now extended to ex-employees (see the Amendment Regulations, reg 15, which insert a new s16A in DDA 1995). This position had already been reached in the case-law: see *Rhys-Harper v Relaxion Group plc* (2003), HL.

### Small employer's exemption

**4.56** When it was first introduced, the DDA 1995 contained an exemption for small employers: those with fewer than 20 employees were outside the scope of the DDA 1995. This exemption excluded the vast majority of employers. The limit was reduced in 1998, so that employers with fewer than 15 employees were excluded, although it is estimated that over 90% were still outside the DDA 1995. The Amendment Regulations remove this exemption altogether from 1 October 2004.

### Meaning of disability

**4.57** The relevant definitions relating to 'disability' and 'disabled person' are set out in DDA 1995, s 1 and Sch 1. The DDA 1995 takes

the 'medical model' of disability, ie essentially, medical evidence determines whether a person is disabled, rather than the 'social model', in
which a person may be seen as suffering discrimination because they
are perceived to be disabled. A person has a disability for the purposes
of the DDA 1995 if he or she has a physical or mental impairment
which has a substantial and long-term adverse effect on his ability to
carry out normal day-to-day activities. Section 2 includes in the
definition of a 'disabled person' a person who has had a disability. This
covers situations were someone with a past disability who is no longer
suffering any effects may still be discriminated against (see *Greenwood v
British Airways* (1999), where the applicant was refused promotion
because of his absenteeism record in the past, which was caused by his
previous depression). The key points to note about this definition are:

A person has a disability if he or she has–

• a physical or mental impairment, and

• that impairment has an adverse effect on his or her ability to
  carry out normal day-to-day activities, and

• that effect is substantial, and

• that effect is long-term.

**4.58**  Addictions, eg alcoholism, drug addiction and nicotine addiction,
are outside the scope of the definition, although where these addictions cause other problems, eg liver damage, they will come within the
definition (Sch 1, paragraph 1(2)(a); Disability Discrimination (Meaning
of Disability) Regulations 1996, regs 2 and 3(1). However, the question
is not what caused a condition but whether a particular condition
constitutes a disability: see *Power v Panasonic UK Ltd* (2003), EAT, where
alcoholism caused the applicant's depression.

**4.59**  Mental impairments include learning, psychiatric and psychologi-
cal impairments; if the impairment results from or consists of a mental
illness, it must be clinically well-recognised to come within the
definition (Sch 1, para 1(1)). However, psychopathic or anti-social
disorders (eg kleptomania, pryomania and paedophilia) are excluded
(reg. 4(1)). Spectacle wearers and hay-fever sufferers are also outside
the definition of disability.

**4.60** 'Normal day-to-day activities' (NB not necessarily those concerning the job the employee is or will be doing) must be affected ie:

(a)   mobility;

(b)   manual dexterity;

(c)   physical coordination;

(d)   continence;

(e)   ability to lift, carry or otherwise move everyday objects;

(f)   speech, hearing or eyesight;

(g)   memory or ability to concentrate, learn or understand; or

(h)   perception of the risk of physical danger (Sched 1, para 4(1)).

**4.61** The effect must be substantial and adverse. Whether an impairment has a substantial adverse effect upon a person is amplified by the Guidance, which indicates that factors relevant to this question will include: the time taken to carry out an activity; the way in which an activity is carried out; the cumulative effects of an impairment; and the effects of behaviour or environment (see the Guidance Part II, paras A2–A10). Some ETs were interpreting 'substantial' in the context of the DDA 1995 to mean very large, although this approach was corrected by the EAT in *Goodwin v The Patent Office* (1999), in which the ET had held that a paranoid schizophrenic was not disabled, despite clear evidence of the substantial effect his impairment had upon his ability to carry out day-to-day activities. The EAT held that he was disabled, and advised ETs to focus on the things the applicant in a DDA 1995 claim could not do, or could only do with difficulty, rather than on what he could do (see also *Leonard v Southern Derbyshire Chamber of Commerce* (2001), EAT).

**4.62** Recurring effects are included, ie where the impairment has ceased to have a substantial adverse effect on a person's abililty to carry out day to day activities, if that effect is likely to recur (Sch 1, para 2(2)). Severe disfigurements are also to be treated as having that effect (Sch 1, para 3). Progressive conditions such as cancer, multiple sclerosis and HIV infection which affects the person's abililty to carry out day to day activities is also to be taken as having a substantial adverse effect (even when it is not) if the condition is likely to result in such an impairment (Sch 1 para 8(1)). However, the applicant must establish that the effect is likely to become substantial (see *Mowat-Brown v University of Surrey* (2002), EAT. Applicants whose impairment results from the treatment for the condition, rather than the condition itself, are also covered (*Kirton v Tetrosyl Ltd* (2003), CA).

**4.63** The effect of medical treatment, prostheses or aids is to be disregarded when considering whether the impairment is likely to have a substantial adverse effect (Sch 1, para 6(1). This means that it is the 'deduced effects' that are considered. In *Kapadia v London Borough of Lambeth* (2000), the EAT held that the effects of an employee's clinical depression, which was attenuated by counselling, allowing him to continue work, should be judged as they would have been without the counselling. The evidence was that he would have had a breakdown without this counselling.

**4.64** It is a matter for the ET to determine what constitutes day-to-day activities and whether the effect is substantial (*Vicary v BT plc* (1999), EAT). 'Substantial' in this context means more than minor or trivial (see the Guidance and Code of Practice).

**4.65** The effect is a long-term adverse effect if the impairment lasts at least 12 months, or is likely to do so (or is likely to last for the rest of a person's life, in the case of a terminally ill person). Remissions and periods of good health are allowed for in the DDA 1995, eg conditions such as arthritis and MS, and recurring conditions which cease to have a substantial effect are nevertheless to be treated as long-term if they are likely to recur, but one recurrence must be (or be likely to be) at least 12 months after the first (Sch 1, para 2(1).

**4.66** A condition only occurring at work is to be taken into consideration when deciding whether it has a substantial adverse effect on an employee's ability to carry out normal day to day activities (*Cruickshank v VAW Motorcast Ltd* (2002), EAT: the applicant suffered from occupational asthma, which improved when he was not at work). Cruickshank is also authority for the principle that the impairment must be considered at the time of the alleged discrimination, and not only at the time of the hearing – this is particularly important for fluctuating conditions.

## Meaning of 'discrimination'

**4.67** There are three forms of discrimination under the DDA 1995: direct, discrimination by way of a failure to comply with the duty to make reasonable adjustments, indirect and discrimination by victimisation. One of the most interesting aspects of the DDA 1995 as originally drafted was that it contained a definition of direct discrimination (s 5) which was similar to that in the SDA 1975 and RRA 1976, ie less favourable treatment but, unlike those statutes, it was possible to justify such discrimination. From 1 October 2004 a new definition applies (s 3A): from that date, it will not be possible to justify direct discrimination (s 3A(4)and (5)). The amendments also clarify the position on comparators: s 3A(5) provides that the appropriate comparator in a direct discrimination case is a non-disabled person whose abilities are the same as (or not materially different from) the abilities of the disabled person.

## Knowledge of the disability

**4.68** It is irrelevant that the employer did not know the complainant was disabled: *H J Heinz & Co Ltd v Kenrick* (2000), EAT. The test is an objective one: was the person treated less favourably for a reason that relates to his disability? The employer's reason for so treating the person must be both material and substantial (see *Jones v Post Office* (2001), CA). For example, where the employee has been absent from work for a reason related to his disability, the comparison must be with a person who has not been absent (*Clark v Novacold Ltd* (1999), CA).

## Reasonable adjustments

**4.69** There is a duty on employers to make reasonable adjustments where (under the new provisions, s 4A) any provision, criterion or practice applied by the employer or any physical feature of premises occupied by the employer 'places the disabled person concerned at a substantial disadvantage in comparison with persons who are not disabled'. In such situations, it is the duty of the employer to take 'such steps as it is reasonable, in all the circumstances of the case, for him to have to take in order to prevent the provision, criterion or practice, or feature, having that effect.'

**4.70** Examples of reasonable adjustments are given in s 18B(2) and the Code, and may include: making adjustments to premises; allocating some of the disabled person's duties to another person; transferring the person to fill an existing vacancy; altering the person's working hours; or assigning the person to a different place of work. This is a non-exhaustive list, and the range of possible adjustments may be very wide indeed. For example, in *Archibald v Fife Council* (2004), HL, the House of Lords held (in a case on the previous provision on reasonable adjustment, ie s 6) that the duty might extend to transferring a female road-sweeper to a sedentary job at a higher grade without requiring her to compete with other applicants. However, the duty does not apply to the provision of a personal carer to attend to personal needs so as to enable a job applicant to work for the employer (*Kenny v Hampshire Constabulary* (1999), EAT.

**4.71** The duty applies only when the employer knows, or could reasonably be expected to know, either (i) in the case of job applicants, that the disabled person is either an applicant for the job or a potential applicant, or (ii) in any case, 'that that person has a disability and is likely to be affected' by being put at a substantial disadvantage in comparison with persons who are not disabled (s 4A): see *Ridout v TC Group* (1998), EAT; *Mid-Staffordshire General Hospitals NHS Trust v Cambridge* (2003). This provision means that job applicants will have to disclose their disability for the duty to be engaged, and existing employees will have to make such disclosure if their disability is not apparent.

**4.72** In determining what is reasonable in terms of adjustments, a number of factors may be taken into consideration, including: the extent to which a particular step would prevent the effect in relation to which the duty is imposed; the practicability of taking the step; and the financial and other costs incurred in taking it (s 18B).

## Justification

**4.73** The pre-amendment DDA 1995 allowed a justification defence for failure to make reasonable adjustments under s 5. The Amendment

Regulations have amended the DDA 1995 in this regard by repealing that provision and substituting a new s 3A (in force from 1 October 2004), which provides that, apart from direct discrimination (see s 3A(4)), discriminatory treatment may be justified where the reason for it is both 'material to the circumstances of the particular case and substantial'. However, the pre-amendment case-law will continue to be of importance. This establishes that the standard to be applied when considering the justification is the objective one, ie the ET must come to its own conclusion on the matter, ie on whether (under the new amended DDA 1995) reasonable adjustments could be made (the pre-amendment case-law concerns direct discrimination, ie less favourable treatment, as well as the duty to make reasonable adjustments). If it decides that there were reasonable adjustments that could be made, then it must consider whether the employer was reasonable in not carrying them out (see *Morse v Wiltshire CC* (1998), EAT). According to the Court of Appeal in *Jones v Post Office* (2001), the test is akin to that applied by ETs when considering whether a dismissal was unfair, ie the band of reasonable responses test is applied.

## Instructions and pressure to discriminate

**4.74**  It is unlawful for a person with authority over another (such as an employer) to instruct another person to commit an unlawful act of discrimination under Pts II or III of the DDA 1995, ie employment and the provision of goods, services and facilities, or to procure or attempt to procure such an act (s 16C).

## Advertisements

**4.75**  Publishing or causing discriminatory advertisements to be published is unlawful (s 16B). Only the DRC may bring proceedings for this contravention (s 17B).

## Aiding unlawful acts and liability of employers

**4.76**  It is a criminal offence to knowingly aid another person to do an unlawful act under the DDA 1995 (s 57), and employers and principals

197

are liable for acts done by employees or agents, unless they took reasonably practicable steps to prevent the employee or agent from doing that act (s 59). Only the DRC may bring proceedings for this contravention (s 17B).

## Harassment

**4.77** From 1 October 2004 harassment is expressly covered. A person subjects a disabled person to harassment 'where, for a reason which relates to the disabled person's disability, he engages in unwanted conduct which has the purpose or effect of (a) violating the disabled person's dignity, or (b) creating an intimidating, hostile, degrading, humiliating or offensive environment for him.' Conduct is to be regarded as having that effect 'only if, having regard to all the circumstances, including in particular the perception of the disabled person, it should reasonably be considered as having that effect' (s 3B).

## Victimisation

**4.78** As in the SDA 1975 and RRA 1976, it is unlawful to discriminate against a person by way of victimisation (s 55). The definition is similar to those in the other two statutes, ie less favourable treatment of a person who has engaged in the protected activities (or where the employer believes or suspects that the person has done so). These activities are: bringing proceedings under the DDA 1995; giving evidence or information in relation to proceedings under the DDA 1995; otherwise doing anything under the DDA 1995; and alleging that another person has contravened the DDA 1995 (this allegation must be made in good faith).

## Enforcement and remedies

**4.79** Complaints under the DDA 1995 are made to the ET within three months of the act complained of (s 17A). The ET may make a declaration, or an order for compensation (which is unlimited, and may include a sum for injury to feelings), or a recommendation to the respondent. Compensation can be very high in disability cases. For example, over £100,000 was awarded to the complainant in *British Sugar plc v Kirker* (1998), EAT.

## Burden of proof

**4.80** In line with amendments made to the SDA 1975 and the RRA 1976 as a result of Article 10 of the ETFD, a new provision is inserted into the DDA 1995 which establishes facts from which it may be presumed that discrimination has taken place, then the burden of proof is shifted to the employer to prove that there has been no discrimination (s 17A(1C), in force from 1 October 2004).

# Transsexualism

**4.81** Transsexuals are individuals who are born into one sex but believe that they should have been born into the other sex. In medical terms they are said to have gender identity disorder, and they often seek to reassign their gender by chemical and/or surgical means. The case of *P v S* (1996) concerned a male employee who was dismissed because he intended to undergo gender reassignment surgery. The SDA 1975, s 1, concerns discrimination 'on the ground of sex', and the terms used throughout the Act are 'man' and 'woman' (see s 5(2) for definitions of these terms). The Truro industrial tribunal (as they were then called) referred the case to the ECJ, which held that, taking a purposive interpretation of Article 5(1) of the Equal Treatment Directive (Directive No.76/207/EEC), which refers to discrimination 'on grounds of sex', and applying the equal treatment principle, it should be read to include discrimination that was based essentially on the sex of a person (the Advocate General's opinion interpreted Article 5(1) of the ETD as including discrimination based on grounds of a change of sex). The EAT held in the later transsexuals case of *Chessington World of Adventures Ltd v Reed* (1997) that the SDA 1975 could be read so as to be consistent with the ETD, although the SDA 1975 was amended on 1 May 1999 by regulations (discussed below).

**4.82** The SDA 1975 has now been amended by the Sex Discrimination (Gender Reassignment) Regulations 1999 (SI 1999/1102), which insert a new s 2A in the SDA 1975. The section renders unlawful less favourable treatment (indirect discrimination is not included in the amendment) on the ground that a person 'intends to undergo, is undergoing or has undergone gender reassignment.' Section 82 of the SDA 1975 defines gender reassignment as, 'a process which is undertaken under medical supervision for the purpose of reassigning a person's sex by changing physiological or other characteristics of sex, including any part of such process.' The protection only extends to employment and vocational training, ie Parts II (the employment field) and III (but only so far as they relate to vocational training), including ss 35A and 35B concerning discrimination by, or in relation to, barristers (or advocates in Scotland).

**4.83** Under s 2A(3)(a), a person who is absent due to undergoing gender reassignment treatment must not be treated less favourably than someone who is off work through sickness or injury, although under s 2A(3)(b) they may be compared to employees absent due to some other cause, and it is reasonable in all the circumstances to treat them no less favourably than those employees.

**4.84** The Court of Appeal held that, for the purposes of employment law, post-operative transsexuals should be treated as having their reassigned sex (*Chief Constable of West Yorkshire Police v A (No 2)* (2003) ICR 161). However, this principle does not mean that transsexuals should be regarded as having their reassigned gender for all purposes and at all stages of the process of gender reassignment: the Court of Appeal in *Croft v Royal Mail Group plc* (2003) held that a male-to-female pre-operative transsexual was not to be treated as of the sex to which they wished to reassign, so the complainant had not been treated less favourably when the employer refused to allow him to use the female lavatories. The employer had to exercise a judgement as to when a person in these circumstances was to be regarded as female for such a purpose.

**4.85** In *Ashton v Chief Constable of West Mercia* (2001), the EAT held that the dismissal of a transsexual who was undergoing gender reassignment and who was taking medication as part of her treatment which caused her to be depressed and affected her work, had not suffered or been discriminated against. She had been dismissed fairly on the capability ground. The fact that her poor performance was caused by the depression brought about by the treatment was not sufficient to establish discrimination: the 'necessary causative link' had not been established.

**4.86**   As in the case of discrimination against men and women under the SDA 1975, there are genuine occupational qualification exceptions applying to transsexuals (SDA 1975, ss 7A and 7B), eg where a job might involve carrying out 'intimate physical searches pursuant to statutory powers' (s 7B(2)(a)).

## Sexual Orientation; Religion or Belief

**4.87**   Despite the fact that there has been discrimination legislation at domestic level concerning sex and race since the middle of the 1970s, there has been a gap concerning other grounds of discrimination, ie sexual orientation, religion or belief and age (with disability not being addressed until 1995 under the DDA 1995). Impetus for change came once again from the EU with the introduction under the Amsterdam Treaty in 1997 of a new Article 13 to be incorporated in the Treaty of Rome. This empowered the Council of Ministers to take action to combat discrimination across a wide range: sex, racial or ethnic origin, religion or belief, disability, age or sexual orientation. The EU used this power to adopt the Equal Treatment Framework Directive (2000/78/EC), which required Member States to legislate against these forms of discrimination by 2003, with the exception of age and disability, for which the implementation date is 2006.

**4.88**   As a result of the Directive, two sets of regulations were adopted: the Employment Equality (Sexual Orientation) Regulations 2003 (SI 2003/1661) ('the SO Regs'), which came into force on 1 December 2003) and the Employment Equality (Religion or Belief) Regulations 2003 (SI 2003/1660) ('the R or B Regs'), which came into force on 2 December 2003.

### Sexual orientation

**4.89**   Until recently, there was no protection in Great Britain concerning discrimination on the ground of sexual orientation. The SDA

1975 renders unlawful discrimination 'on the ground of sex', whereas gay and lesbian complainants were bringing claims under the SDA 1975 on the ground of sexual orientation.

**4.90** The courts and tribunals took a restrictive view: the SDA 1975 requires a comparison between the complainant and an actual or hypothetical comparator of the opposite sex, so the complainant would succeed only where it could be established that an actual or hypothetical person of the opposite sex but with the same sexual orientation, ie homosexuality, would not have been treated less favourably. Where such a comparator would have been treated in the same way as the complainant, ie badly, there was no contravention of the SDA 1975. Thus, in *Pearce v Governing Body of Mayfield Secondary School* (2003) a case concerning homophobic abuse by pupils of a female teacher who was lesbian, the House of Lords held that this was not direct sex discrimination as a male homosexual teacher would have been subjected to such abuse (see also *Smith v Gardner Merchant Ltd* (1998)). The acts complained of in *Pearce* took place before the coming into force of the Human Rights Act 1998 on 2 October 1998, so no claim could be brought on the basis of an infringement of human rights (see below).

**4.91** The ECJ took a similar view in *Grant v South West Trains Ltd* (1998), in which a lesbian employee brought a challenge under Article 119 (current Article 141) of the EC Treaty against her employer's granting of travel concessions to spouses and live-in partners of the opposite sex but did not extend this to same-sex partners. The ECJ held that if a male homosexual would have been treated in the same way (which he would) there was no sex discrimination, since the Article did not cover sexuality but only discrimination on the ground of sex.

**4.92** The only redress available until recently (before the European Convention on Human Rights was incorporated into English law by the Human Rights Act 1998), at least for employees of public authorities, was not to be found in domestic courts under the SDA 1975 but in the European Court of Human Rights (ECHR) through claims based on the European Convention on Human Rights (ECHR), on the basis that the complainants' Article 8 right to privacy had been breached, and therefore their Article 14 right had been breached. These claims succeeded before the European Court of Human Rights in two cases concerning members of the armed services who were subjected to questioning concerning their sexual orientation: *Smith and Grady v UK* (1999) and *Lustig-Prean and Beckett v UK* (2000).


## The Employment Equality (Sexual Orientation) Regulations 2003

**4.93**  The SO Regs now extend protection to persons who face discrimination on the ground of their sexual orientation. Regulation 2 defines 'sexual orientation' as orientation towards persons of the same sex, the opposite sex, or both the same sex and the opposite sex. The legislation therefore covers homosexuals, heterosexuals and bi-sexuals, making it unlawful to discriminate against a person in any one these categories because of his or her sexual orientation.

**4.94**  However, it should be noted that it is unlawful to discriminate 'on grounds of sexual orientation', rather than on the ground of the applicant's sexual orientation. This definition is wide enough to cover those who are discriminated against because, for example, they support or fraternise with others of a particular sexual orientation, even though they are not discriminated against on the ground of their own orientation. It is also wide enough to cover discrimination against a person where the employer believes that they are of a particular orientation, although they may not be.

**4.95**  The forms of discrimination covered are: direct, indirect, harassment and victimisation.


## Direct discrimination – reg 3(1)(a)

**4.96**  The SO Regs adopt the familiar division of discrimination into direct and indirect forms. Direct discrimination occurs where a person is treated less favourably than another on grounds of sexual orientation.

## Indirect discrimination – reg 3(1)(b)

**4.97** Indirect discrimination occurs where a provision, criterion or practice which is applied generally to persons not of the same sexual orientation puts persons of a particular sexual orientation at a disadvantage. It is unlawful if it is not a proportionate means of achieving a legitimate aim (reg 3(1)(b)). The circumstances of the complainant and his/her comparator must be the same or not materially different (reg 3(2)).

## Harassment on grounds of sexual orientation – reg 5

**4.98** Harassment is defined as unwanted conduct which has either the purpose or the effect of violating another person's dignity or 'creating an intimidating, hostile, degrading, humiliating or offensive environment' for the other person. Conduct is to be regarded as having that effect only if it should reasonably be considered as having that effect taking into account the perception of the other person.

## Victimisation

**4.99** Victimisation is less favourable treatment by a person (A) of another person (B) by reason that B has brought proceedings against A or any other person, given evidence or information in connection with proceedings, done anything under or by reference to the SO Regs, or alleged that A or any other person has committed an act which contravenes or would contravene the SO Regs (reg 4). This does not apply if the allegation, evidence or information was false and not made or given in good faith (reg 4(2)).

## Scope of the SO Regs

**4.100** Protection is extended to: job applicants and employees, and ex-employees (regs 6 and 21); post-employment contract workers (reg 8); office-holders (including constables) (regs 10 and 11); barristers and advocates (regs 12 and 13); partnerships (reg 14); and civil servants and members of the armed forces (reg 36). A trade union (which includes any organisation of workers or of employers) is prohibited from discriminating against intending or actual members on grounds, inter alia, of sexual orientation (reg 15). Discrimination by employers is unlawful, as is discrimination by the following bodies: trade organisations (reg 15); bodies conferring professional and trade qualifications (reg 16); training providers (reg 17); employment agencies (reg 18); and further and higher education institutions (reg 20). Sexual orientation discrimination by trustees and managers of occupational pension schemes is also covered (reg 9A).

## Contract terms or terms in collective agreements

**4.101** A term of a contract or collective agreement or any rule made by a trade organisation will normally be either unenforceable or void if it purports to exclude or limit any provision of the regulations (Sch 4).

## Genuine occupational requirements – reg 7

**4.102** As in the SDA 1975 and the RRA 1976, there are genuine occupational requirement exceptions provided for in the SO Regs. These exceptions apply where: a particular sexual orientation is a genuine and determining occupational requirement, and it is proportionate to apply that requirement (reg 7); and where national security is at risk (reg 24). The exceptions include one concerning religious organisations with a doctrinal objection to particular sexual orientations (eg homosexuality, which is contrary to some religious doctrines) (reg 7(3). This provision was introduced after lobbying from various religious groups. Regulation 7, together with the exception in reg 25, discussed below, was the subject of judicial review proceedings (see *R (on application of Amicus, NATFHE, UNISON, NASUWT, Public & Commercial Services Union, NURMTW and NUT) v Secretary of State for Trade and Industry* (2004), as an improper implemenation of the Framework Directive and an infringement of the Article 8 right in the ECHR. The unions argued that these exceptions could be used to discriminate against homosexual teachers in faith schools. The High Court rejected the unions' arguments, holding that, taking a purposive interpretation, the SO Regs properly implement the Framework Directive. However, the High Court gave leave to appeal to the Court of Appeal.

**4.103** There is also a general exception in regulation 25 which provides that:

> Nothing in [the main part of the regulations] shall render unlawful anything which prevents or restricts access to a benefit by reference to marital status.

**4.104** This exemption would exclude, for example, retirement and occupational pension schemes providing pensions to surviving spouses. As the law currently stands, and as reflected in regulation 25, such pensions are not available to the same sex partners of homosexual employees. As discussed above, this provision was unsuccessfully challenged in the High Court (and see the TUC Press Release 'Unions challenge gay law in High Court' 16 March 2004). However, in June 2003 the Government issued proposals concerning 'civil partnerships', which would mean that gay couples legally registering such a partnership would secure equal rights with married couples, including next-of-kin-entitlements such as surviving-spouse pensions.

## Questionnaire procedure

**4.105** Employees who believe they may have been discriminated against or subjected to harassment contrary to the regulations may serve a questionnaire on their employers (reg 22 and schedules 2 and 3).

## Vicarious liability of employers

**4.106** As is usual under the discrimination legislation, employers are vicariously liable for the unlawful acts of their employees, unless they prove that they took reasonably practicable steps to prevent the employee committing such acts (reg 22).

## Aiding unlawful acts

**4.107** Anyone knowingly aiding another person to do an act rendered unlawful under the SO Regs is treated as doing the act themselves, unless they reasonably relied on a statement that such an act was not unlawful (reg 23).

## Employment tribunals – claims, burden of proof and remedies

**4.108**  A complainant under the SO Regs may lodge a claim with an employment tribunal within three months of the act complained of. The burden of proof is the same as in the SDA 1975 and RRA 1976, ie the complainant must establish facts from which the tribunal could conclude that an unlawful act of discrimination has taken place and the respondent must then prove that he did not commit any such act (reg 29). The usual remedies of a declaration, compensation and a recommendation may be made (regs 27 – 30). There is no statutory maximum on the amount of compensation a tribunal can order to be paid to a person who brings a successful claim (reg 30).

## ACAS Guides

**4.109**  ACAS have published two sets of guides on the SO Regs and the R or B Regs: 'Putting the Employment Equality (Sexual Orientation) Regs 2003 into practice for employers & staff' (4 November 2003); 'Guide to the Employment Equality (Religion or Belief Regulations 2003' (4 November 2003).

## Employment Equality (Religion and Belief) Regulations 2003

**4.110**  The Employment Equality (Religion and Belief) Regulations 2003 (SI 2003/1660) ('the R or B Regs') are drafted in similar terms to the SO Regs, with the relevant changes being made. The four forms of discrimination rendered unlawful are direct, indirect, harassment and victimisation, with similar definitions, mutatis mutandis, as those in the SO Regs. Thus, for direct discrimination the definition is less favourable treatment on the grounds of religion or belief, while indirect discrimination involves, (i) the application by A of a provision, criterion or practice which he applies or would apply to persons not of the same religion or belief as B, but (ii) which puts or would put persons of the same religion or belief as B at a particular disadvantage when compared with other persons, (iii) which puts B at that disadvantage, and (iv) which cannot be shown to be a proportionate means of achieving a legitimate aim (reg 3). The religion or belief must not be that of A (reg 3(2)).

**4.111** It should be noted that, in direct discrimination, the less favourable treatment must be on 'grounds of religion or belief', which does not necessarily have to be that of the complainant. For example, the definition could apply to an individual (X) who fraternises with or supports another person (Y), whether financially or in other ways, but who does not share Y's religion or belief, who is discriminated against because of that fraternisation or support of Y.

**4.112** The Regulations cover, inter alia, job applicants and employees, terms of employment, opportunities afforded for promotion, transfer, training, or any other benefit, and dismissal (reg 6).

**4.113** One major area of difficulty in the Regulations concerns exactly what is meant by 'religion or belief', which is defined as meaning, 'any religion, belief, religious belief, or similar philosophical belief' (reg 2). The explanatory notes accompanying the Regulations refer to belief systems or beliefs affecting world view or way of life, so it would seem that the legislation is wide enough to cover discrimination against atheists and humanists, as well as others holding beliefs that are not necessarily 'religious'. However, it is unlikely that they also cover any philosophical approach or system of analysis, such as political philosophy.

**4.114** There is an exception for a genuine occupational requirement (GOR), where, 'having regard to the nature of the employment or the context in which it is carried out being of a particular religion or belief is a genuine and determining occupational requirement', and it is proportionate to apply the requirement, and the person to whom it is applied does not meet it, or the employer is not satisfied that the person meets it (reg 7(2)). There is a specific GOR, in similar terms to that in reg 7(2), where an employer 'has an ethos based on religion or belief'.

**4.115** There are similar provisions in the R or B Regs as in the SO Regs relating to: vicarious liability (reg 22); aiding unlawful acts (reg 23); the questionnaire procedure (reg 33); and enforcement by way of a complaint to the employment tribunal, with the same burden of proof provision as in the SO Regs (regs 27 – 34), with the usual remedies available of a declaration, unlimited compensation, and a recommendation (reg 30).

## Equal Pay

**4.116**  Equal pay is essentially a form of sex discrimination, although a separate statute, the Equal Pay Act 1970, rather than the SDA 1975, deals with this matter (the EOC has called for the two statutes to be merged, but this has not happened to date). Equal pay legislation is necessary to eliminate sex discrimination from pay systems, and therefore to close the so-called 'gender pay gap', ie the difference in pay between men and women for equal work: women currently earn only 80% of men's pay for equal work (see the New Earnings Survey 2003). Equal pay is governed by domestic legislation and Community law. The idea that men and women should receive equal pay for work of equal value is enshrined in Article 141 (ex Art 19) of the EC Treaty (which states that 'men and women should receive equal pay for equal work'), which is a directly enforceable Treaty provision (see *Defrenne v Sabena (No 2)* (1976)) and comes within the non-discrimination principle, which is one of the fundamental principles of Community law. The Equal Pay Directive (Directive 75/117/EEC) ('EPD') provides more detailed provisions relating to pay and concerns the application of Article 141, and the Equal Treatment Directive (Directive 76/207/EEC) ('ETD') may also be relevant in interpreting equal pay law. Article 1 of the Equal Pay Directive provides that the principle of equal pay, 'means, for the same work or for work to which equal value is attributed, the elimination of all discrimination on grounds of sex with regard to all aspects and conditions of remuneration.'

### Scope of the EqPA 1970 compared with that of Article 141

**4.117**  The EqPA 1970 covers all contractual benefits, whereas Article 141 applies to 'remuneration' an employee receives from her employer, including contractual benefits, gratuitous benefits and any benefits which the employer is required to provide by statute. However, 'pay' has been given a very wide meaning under Article 141. The Article defines pay as 'the ordinary basic or minimum wage or salary and any other consideration, whether in cash or in kind, which the worker receives, directly or indirectly, in respect of his employment from his employer.' It has been held by the ECJ to include, for example: concessionary, non-contractual travel facilities (*Garland v British Rail Engineering Limited* (1982); statutory redundancy payment and benefits paid under private, occupational pension schemes (*Barber v Guardian Royal Exchange Assurance Group* (1990), because it arises 'by reason of the existence of the employment relationship'); unfair dismissal compensation (*R v Secretary of State for Employment ex parte Seymour Smith and Perez* (1999); and statutory sick pay (*Rinner-Kuhn v FWW Spezial-Gebaudereinigung GmbH & Co KG* (1989).

**4.118** The Equal Pay Act 1970 ('EqPA 1970'), which came into force at the same time as the SDA 1975 in 1975, is the domestic statute dealing with equal pay between men and women. The EqPA 1970 and the SDA 1975 together are supposed to form one homogeneous code of domestic legislation (*Shields v E Coomes (Holdings) Limited* (1978). However, the EqPA 1970 covers only contractual terms which, despite its title, extends to all contractual benefits, not only pay, whereas the SDA 1975 covers discrimination outside contractual rights and benefits, eg appointment to a job, promotion, and transfer, where these are non-contractual. The EqPA 1970 applies equally to men as well as women (EqPA 1970, s 1(13)), although the majority of cases under the Act concern claims brought by women (and the following discussion assumes a female applicant). The Act applies to employees, apprentices and those engaged under a 'contract personally to execute any work or labour' (EqPA 1970, s 1(6)(a)).

**4.119** The objective of the EqPA 1970 is not to secure fair wages (see the remarks of Lord Browne-Wilkinson in *Strathclyde Regional Council v Wallace* (1998) at 149): its objective is to eliminate gender-based pay discrimination, so differences in pay between men and women are allowed, provided they are due to factors other than sex, eg performance-related pay, pay to reward qualifications achieved, or, arguably, pay based on seniority (see the discussion of the genuine material factor defence below). Therefore it is a defence for the employer to show that the pay disparity is due to factors other than sex.

## The Equality Clause – s 1(1)

**4.120** If successful in a claim under the EqPA 1970, an equality clause is implied into the woman's contract of employment (s 1(1)).

However, the woman must establish that she is in the same employment (or working for an associated employer) as the selected comparator(s) of the opposite sex, who is/are engaged on one of the following three situations: (i) like work, (ii) work rated as equivalent, ie work which has been given an equivalent rating under a job evaluation study (JES), or (iii) work which is of equal value (EqPA 1970, s 1(2)(a), (b), (c): these requirements are discussed below). The equality clause operates where any term of the woman's contract is or becomes less favourable: the equality clause modifies the woman's contract of employment by raising the less favourable term in her contract so that it is not less favourable when compared to that of her male comparator.

**4.121** If there is no corresponding term in the woman's contact, it will be deemed to include one (EqPA 1970, s 1(2)). The *House of Lords in Hayward v Cammell Laird Shipbuilders Ltd* (1988) held that a term by term comparison is required under the EqPA 1970, ie the individual contractual terms in the claimant's contract must be considered alongside individual terms in her comparator's contract, rather than looking at the contracts overall (when looked at overall, Mrs Hawyard's terms were in fact more favourable than that of her male comparators). Upholding her equal value claim, their Lordships held that if there was any less favourable term in the woman's contract, the equality clause would operate to raise it so that it was not less favourable, ie there is upward equalisation.

## Comparators

**4.122** Unlike the SDA 1975, where a hypothetical person may be selected, the claimant must choose an actual comparator (although more than one is permissible) of the opposite sex who is engaged on like work, work rated as equivalent, or work of equal value (EqPA 1970, s 1(2)). The choice of comparator is left to the claimant, but selecting the wrong (ie inappropriate) comparator will prove fatal to the claim (see *Ainsworth v Glass Tubes and Components Limited* (1977): the EAT held that an industrial tribunal could not substitute for the applicant's choice of comparator another man whom it thought more appropriate).

**4.123**  More than one comparator may be selected, although the courts are alive to abuses of the equal value claims procedure process where the claimant might choose very many comparators, ie adopting a 'scatter-gun' approach (see *Leverton v Clwyd County Council* (1989)).

**4.124**  Case-law has established that permitted comparators may be predecessors or successors to the claimant, although evidential problems might arise if the time between when a predecessor left or a successor took up employment is too long. Thus, in *Macarthys Limited v Stone* (1980) the ECJ held that Article 141 (ex Art 119) did not require contemporaneous employment, and it therefore could apply in a case where a female manageress was paid less than a man who was employed on equal work some four months prior to her period of employment. The EqPA 1970 must be read in the light of this ECJ decision.

**4.125**  Successors may be selected as comparators. In *Diocese of Hallam Trustee v Connaughton* (1996) ICR 860, EAT, Ms. Connaughton selected as a comparator her male successor, who took up his post (on a higher salary) four months or so after she left her employment as Director of Music. The EAT allowed the comparison, but stated that such comparisons are likely to raise greater evidential problems than those involving a contemporary or immediate predecessor.

**4.126**  It is permissible for the claimant to select a comparator who is less than her equal, although if successful in her claim, her pay will be equalised upwards to his level, not above it. In *Evesham v North Hertfordshire Health Authority* and another (2000) – an equal value claim forming part of the aftermath of the long-running 'speech therapists' case' – the female claimant (a speech therapist) selected as her male comparator a clinical psychologist who was her junior in terms of years of service. She argued that, having successfully claimed equal pay with him, she should have been put on a point on the pay scale higher than his, since she had more years of service. This was rejected by the Court of Appeal, which held that the EqPA 1970, s 1(2)(c) only allowed her to receive the same pay as her comparator, not more. The Court held that the section requires equality of treatment, not more favourable than the term in her comparator's contract.

*Same employment – common terms and conditions – EqPA 1970, s 1(2) and (6)*

**4.127** The EqPA 1970 requires the claimant and her comparator to be in the 'same employment' (EqPA 1970, s 1(2) and (6)). Under s 1(6), they are in the same employment if comparator is employed by the same employer or an associated employer and either (i) the comparator is employed at the same establishment as the claimant, or (ii) he is employed at a different establishment of the employer (or an associated employer) but common terms and conditions of employment apply to both establishments.

**4.128** Under s 1(6)(c), two employers are to be treated as associated if one is a company controlled, either directly or indirectly, by the other employer (which need not be a company), or if both are companies of which a third person has control, either directly or indirectly.

**4.129** In *British Coal Corporation v Smith* (1996) HL, over 1,200 female canteen workers and cleaners working in a number of different establishments chose as their equal value comparators 150 male workers who were either surface mineworkers or in clerical posts. Their terms and conditions were governed by a national agreement, although there were some local variations, ie their terms and conditions were not exactly the same. The House of Lords held the terms of the comparators did not need to be identical as the claimants, they had only to be 'on a broad basis, substantially comparable'(at p 410). In this case, the comparators were held to be in the same employment (see also *Leverton v Clwyd County Council*, HL (1989)).

**4.130** A number of recent cases at domestic and ECJ level have clarified the scope of the comparison permitted under the EqPA 1970 or EU law. The ECJ has held that a claim under Article 141 will only succeed where the terms of the claimant and those of the comparator emanate from a single source. This is because it is only in such situations that the employer will be able to explain how the different pay rates arose and therefore establish a defence. In *Lawrence v Regent Office Care Ltd* (2002) the ECJ ruled that female employees employed by private companies who had successfully tendered for the catering and cleaning services in Yorkshire County Council schools could not use as comparators male employees employed directly by the same

Council who were carrying out equivalent work (despite the fact that the female workers had been employed by the County Council a few years earlier, and their jobs had been rated as of equal value in a job evaluation study, but they were now working for a private employer on lower rates of pay than the Council had paid them). The ECJ ruled that Article 141 could not be relied upon where the pay conditions cannot be attributed to a single source, ie there was no single body which is responsible for the pay inequality, and which could restore equal treatment.

**4.131** The ECJ gave the same ruling in *Allonby v Accrington & Rossendale College* (2004) where the applicant college lecturer who had been dismissed rejoined the college via an agency who placed her with the college. She was carrying out the same work (on lower pay) on a self-employed basis, and used as her comparator a male lecturer at the college. The ECJ ruled that such a comparison failed under Article 141, since pay could not be attributed to a 'single source': the college and the agency were separate sources.

**4.132** Collective agreements may constitute a single source. In *Morton v South Ayrshire Council* (2002) the Court of Session held that a female primary head teacher who claimed equal pay with a male comparator who worked for a different local authority as a secondary school head teacher had selected an appropriate comparator, on the basis that the source of their contractual terms was a national collective agreement applying to all teachers in Scotland. Thus, pay emanated from a single source, and came within the interpretation of Article 141 given in the ECJ's ruling in *Defrenne v Sabena* (1976), ie it was a source of pay having its origin in a collective labour agreement. Lord Johnston stated that, despite the fact that each local authority decided how salary scales agreed by the Scottish Joint Negotiating Committee were to be implemented, there was a sufficient connection in a 'loose and non-technical sense', so that the applicant and her comparator could be said to be in the same 'service' of education in Scotland.

**4.133** Contingent claims are also permitted under the EqPA 1970. In *Milligan v South Ayrshire Council* (2003), the Court of Session held that a male primary school headteacher, who was unable to make an equal pay claim using secondary school headteachers as comparators because all of the latter were also male, was allowed to make a contingent claim by comparing himself to a female primary school headteacher, and to have his claim stayed until resolution of his comparator's equal pay claim against a male secondary school headteacher. The Court of Session stated that the claimant, unless permitted to bring such a contingent claim, 'would suffer real prejudice in relation to back pay since he could lodge a claim only after the comparator's claim succeeded.' (per Lord Gill at p 156).

## Like work – EqPA 1970, ss 1(2)(a), (4)

**4.134** One of the situations in which a woman may bring an equal pay claim is where she is engaged on like work with her comparator. Section 1(4) defines 'like work' as work that is 'of the same or a broadly similar nature, and the differences (if any) between the things she does and the things they do are not of practical importance in relation to terms and conditions of employment'. When comparing the two jobs, 'regard shall be had to the frequency or otherwise with which any such differences occur in practice as well as to the nature and extent of the differences.'

**4.135** A tribunal will take a fairly broad brush approach when looking at whether work is similar, focusing on the type of work, and the skill and knowledge required to do it. For example, in *Capper Pass Limited v Lawton* (1976) a cook who prepared lunches for the company's directors (between 10 and 20) was held to be broadly similar to that of an assistant chef who worked in the canteen preparing meals for all the factory employees.

**4.136** The question is whether the differences (if any) between the two jobs are of practical importance. If the employer claims a difference between the jobs, it is for the employer to establish that difference is of practical importance in relation to terms and condi- tions. For example, in *Shields v E Coomes (Holdings) Limited* (1978), the employer claimed that male counter-staff at its betting shop were paid a higher hourly pay than female counter-workers because of risk of robbery, and the men were employed for security reasons. In fact, the men had never been called upon to perform any security function, and the Court of Appeal held that, as the men had never been required to deal with any disturbance or attempted violence, the jobs were essentially the same. However, a difference in the responsibilities between the woman and her comparator may be a difference of practical importance, as in *Eaton Limited v Nuttall* (1977), where an error by a female scheduler who dealt with items worth about £2.50 each, would have been less significant than those of male scheduler (the comparator) who dealt with items worth between £5 and £1,000. The time the work is carried out is not necessarily a difference of practical importance (*Dugdale v Kraft Foods* (1977), although the ECJ has held that a difference in qualifications, training and experience between the claimant and the comparator was a significant difference justifying a difference in pay (*Angestelltenbetriebsrat der Wiener Gebietskrankenkasse v Wiener Gebietskrankenkasse* (1999)).

## Work rated as equivalent – EqPA 1970, ss 1(2)(b), (4), and 5)

**4.137** Where work has been rated as equivalent under a job evaluation study (JES) under which the claimant's and the comparator's job have been rated as equivalent, an equality clause may be inserted under section 1(2). Claims under this provision depend upon the employer having carried out a JES, which is probably why so few claims are brought under this part of the EqPA 1970.

**4.138** Section 1(5) requires that the jobs of the comparator and the applicant have been given an equal value 'in terms of the demand made on a worker under various headings (for instance effort, skill, decision)', or where they would have been given equal values, but for the JES itself being discriminatory. There are a number of methods of job evaluation, although only the 'points assessment' and 'factor comparison' systems satisfy the requirements of s 1(5), since the JES must be analytical and objective (*Bromley and others v H & J Quick Limited* (1988). 'Analytical' means that the jobs of each worker covered by the JES must have been valued appropriately in terms of the demand made on the worker under various headings. 'Objectivity' means that the JES must be free from any subjective or discriminatory elements. Concerning the evaluation of the nature of the work done may lead to a finding that the JES does not satisfy the legislative requirements. The ECJ made this clear in *Rummler v Dato-Druck GmbH* (1987) (a case brought under Art. 1(2) of the Equal Pay Directive), where a JES gave undue weight to muscular effort (which disadvantaged female employees) without being balanced by applying other criteria 'in relation to which women had a particular aptitude.' The employment tribunal may adjust the results of the JES to take into account any direct discrimination in its application. Finally, the JES, once accepted as valid by the parties, can be relied upon by the claimant, even if it has not been implemented (*O'Brien v Sim-Chem Limited* (1980).

## Work of equal value – EqPA 1970, s 1(2)(c)

**4.139** A claimant may bring an equal value claim under s 1(2)(c) where her work does not come under either of the two other categories (an equal value claim may not be brought if her comparator is engaged on like work or work rated as equivalent). She must be engaged upon work of equal value in terms of the demand made on her.

**4.140** The EqPA 1970, as originally drafted, provided for equal pay claims in only two situations: where the man and the woman were engaged on like work or work rated as equivalent. Further, there was no requirement under the Act for the employer to conduct a JES, and one could not be conducted without the employer's consent. This meant that, if an employer refused to conduct a JES, a woman employee who was engaged on work of equal value to that of a man could not bring an equal pay claim. This was successfully challenged as being inconsistent with the principle of equal pay in Article 141 of the EC Treaty (ex Article 119) and the Equal Pay Directive (Commission v United Kingdom (1982), and the EqPA 1970 was subsequently amended by the Equal Pay (Amendment) Regulations 1983 (SI 1983/1794) to allow a claim for equal pay to be made where work is of equal value, which is now contained in EqPA 1970, s 1(2)(c).

**4.141** Examples of the headings under which jobs considered under the equal value provisions may be assessed are given in s 1(2), eg 'effort, skill, decision.' The claimant may choose her comparator, even if there is a male employee working in the same job as her and on the same pay (*Pickstone v Freemans plc* (1988).This prevents the employer blocking an equal value claim by having a 'token' male doing the same job as the woman. In *Pickstone*, a female warehouse operative chose as her comparator a male checker warehouse operative, although there was a male warehouse operative on the same pay as the claimant. The House of Lords, applying a purposive interpretation of s 1(2)(c) to ensure compliance with Article 119 (current Article 141) and the Equal Pay Directive, allowed the claim to proceed.

**4.142** The employment tribunal procedure for equal value claims is complicated. Essentially, once an equal value claim is presented to the tribunal, it may appoint an independent expert from an independent panel to write a report on the issue within 42 days, which is also sent to the parties (s 2A(1)). However, the report is not binding on the tribunal. If the ET decides not to appoint an expert, the parties may appoint their own expert. An employer may conduct a JES after the presentation of an equal pay claim but before the final hearing, provided it considers the jobs as they were at the time of the complaint (*Dibro Limited v Hore* (1990), EAT; EqPA 1970, s 2A(2)).

**4.143** Given the complexity of the equal value procedure, the Government has been considering ways of streamlining it (if not simplifying it) and the DTI issued a consultation document on this in March 2004: 'Towards Equal Pay: A Consultation Document on Proposals to Streamline Equal Value Tribunal Procedures'. This includes new, draft regulations on employment tribunal procedure (Employment Tribunals (Equal Value) Complementary Rules of Procedure), which are expected to come into force before the end of 2004.

## The Genuine Material Factor Defence – section 1(3)

**4.144** If a claimant establishes that she is paid less than her male comparator who is engaged on like work, work rated as equivalent, or work of equal value, the employer may raise the defence that the difference in pay is not due to sex discrimination, and is a material difference between the claimant's case and the comparator's. This is the genuine material factor defence (GMF) under s 1(3). If the employer succeeds in this defence, the equality clause will not be implied to modify the claimant's contract. Where the complaint is based on like work or work rated as equivalent, the defence must be a material difference between the woman's case and the man's; where it is an equal value claim, it may be a material difference.

**4.145** In the GMF defence, the employer must identify a factor which is (a) the genuine cause of the difference in pay; (b) is material; and (c) is not the difference if sex. The requirement of genuineness means that the reason put forward by the employer is not a sham or a pretence (*Strathclyde Regional Council v Wallace* (1998), HL. In Wallace, their Lordships held that a material factor must be 'significant and causally relevant'. The employers argued that the pay disparities came about through different promotion structures of teachers and financial constraints. The House of Lords held that an employer is not required to justify its pay system in every case where unequal pay is alleged. The need to establish objective justification only arises where the factor relied upon is indirectly discriminatory.

**4.146** A similar conclusion was reached in *Glasgow City Council v Marshal* (2000) IRLR 272, HL, where the employers argued that the pay structure had been arrived at by different collectively bargained agreements, which was not tainted with sex discrimination. The House of Lords held that, where a pay system was not tainted with sex discrimination, the EqPA 1970 had no application, and the equality clause would not operate. The employer was not required to go further and to provide an explanation of how the pay disparity had come about. Therefore, it is only where there is evidence of sex discrimination in the pay structure that the employer will be required to objectively justify the pay disparity.

**4.147** However, pay disparities clearly tainted with sex discrimination will not satisfy the GMF defence (see *Ratcliffe v North Yorkshire County Council* (1995) (the 'Yorkshire Dinner ladies case'): where the claimants' jobs had been rated as equivalent to those of their male comparators under a JES, the reduction of their wages in order to compete with private contractor in a CCT exercise was an adequate defence to meet the requirements of section 1(3).

**4.148** It is not possible to provide an exhaustive list of factors which may satisfy the GMF defence requirements. Case-law establishes that a number of grounds have been upheld. For example, the 'market forces' defence may succeed: in *Rainey v Greater Glasgow Health Board* (1987), the House of Lords held that the pay difference between employees in the NHS prosthetic fitting service, which was facing staff shortages, and those recruited from the private sector had been objectively justified, since market forces meant that in order to recruit from the private sector commercial rates of pay had to be offered.

**4.149**  However, any factor argued under the GMF defence must be based on objectively justified factors which are unrelated to any discrimination on grounds of sex. The ECJ in *Bilka-Kaufhaus GmbH v Weber von Hartz* (1987), ruled that objective justification will be established where the practice: (a) corresponds to a real need on the part of the employer; (b) is necessary to achieve the objective in question; and (c) is proportionate to that objective ('the principle of proportionality'). The employer must balance the discriminatory impact of the practice against the reasonable needs of its business (see also *Hampson v Department of Education and Science* (1990)).

**4.150**  In Community law, the ECJ has ruled that where pay systems lack transparency (ie where employees do not know what criteria it involves or how they are applied), this is a potential breach of the Equal Pay Directive. The employer in such a case had to prove that pay differences were not discriminatory (see the *Danfoss* case (1989)).

### 4.151  Examples of specific factors argued under the GMF defence are:

'Red circling' – ie a practice where an employee is placed on a lower grade but who has his salary protected (or 'red circled'), while other employees on the same grade are paid at a lower rate (see *Snoxell and another v Vauxhall Motors Limited* (1978) where the argument did not succeed as it was based on past sex discrimination). In any event, this defence will not be available if the circumstances giving rise to the red circling come to an end (*Benveniste v University of Southampton* (1989).

Collective bargaining – In *Enderby v Frenchay Health Authority and another* (1994) ECJ (the famous 'speech therapists' case') Dr Enderby and a number of other speech therapists claimed equal pay with male pharmacists and clinical psychologists. The employer argued that the pay disparity was the result of separate collective bargaining processes which were themselves indirectly discriminatory, on the basis that, although the speech therapy profession was predominantly female, pharmacists and clinical psychologists in the grades to which the claim related were overwhelmingly male. The ECJ ruled that a prima facie case of sex discrimination will be established where 'significant statistics' show that a job performed almost exclusively by women attracts an appreciably lower rate of pay than a job carried out predominantly by men. The ECJ also ruled that, although separate collective bargaining structures could provide justification, this was not sufficient to account for the pay disparity. Furthermore, the ECJ held that where only part of the pay disparity is justified, the defence would stand for such part of the difference as could be attributed to that reason.

Other examples of the GMF defence are London weighting, ie a pay system where employees working in more expensive areas of the country, such as London, are paid more than those living in less expensive areas (see *Navy, Army and Air Force Institutes v Varley* (1976), and performance-related pay.

## Enforcement and Remedies – Bringing a claim for equal pay

**4.152** All equal pay claims must be brought in the ET (EqPA 1970, 2(1), and the claimant may rely upon EC law in the ET as well as the domestic legislation. It is not only employees who may make an application under the EqPA 1970: under s 2(1A), employers may apply to the ET for a declaration where there is a dispute over the effect of an equality clause. The Secretary of State may also bring proceedings where it appears that the employer of any women is or has been in breach of a term modified or included by an equality clause, and it is not reasonable to expect the women themselves to bring proceedings (eg because they do not have a union to support their claim): s 2(2). The EOC is also empowered to seek a ruling from a tribunal as to whether an employer has infringed a term modified or included by an equality clause, to enable it to exercise its powers under SDA 1975, ss 71 and 72 to apply for an injunction to restrain persistent discrimination (s 73, SDA 1975).

**4.153** Since the equality clause provision works by modifying the claimant's contract of employment, she may also bring an equal pay claim in the county court or High Court in the form of an action for breach of contract. However, the ordinary courts have the power to refuse to hear equal pay claims in two situations: (1) where it appears to the court that a claim or counterclaim in respect of the operation of an equality clause could more conveniently be disposed of by an ET, the court can strike the claim out in its entirety; and (2) where a question regarding the effect of an equality clause is part of a wider dispute which is before the court, the court may on the application of one of the parties or of its own motion refer that question to an ET (or direct one of the parties to do so) and stay proceedings in the meantime (s 2(3)).

## Time limits

**4.154**  Equal pay claims must be brought within six months of leaving the employment to which the claim relates (s 2(4)). This time limit was challenged in *Preston and others v Wolverhampton Healthcare NHS Trust* ECJ (2000), ECJ being incompatible with EC law. The claimants were part-time teachers employed on fixed-term contracts who argued that the six months' limit applied to the entire employment relationship, rather than the particular fixed-term contracts. The ECJ held that the six months' rule was not incompatible with EC law, provided that the limitation period was no less favourable for actions based on Community law than for actions based on domestic law (see also *National Power plc v Young* (2001), CA, where the Court of Appeal held that the word 'employment' in s 2(4) does not refer to the particular job on which the woman bases her claim but rather to the contract of employment.

**4.155**  The EqPA 1970 originally provided that a claimant could claim remuneration or damages in respect of the two years prior to the institution of proceedings. This was challenged in *Levez v TH Jennings (Harlow Pools) Ltd* (1999), and the ECJ ruled that the two-year limitation on claiming arrears of remuneration in EqPA 1970, s 2(5) is precluded if the section infringes the Community law principle of 'equivalence'. This requires that a procedural rule must not discriminate as between Community law rights and national law rights (eg breach of contract claims have six-year limit for claiming arrears). In *Preston and others v Wolverhampton Healthcare NHS Trust* (2000) ECJ, the ECJ ruled that the limitation of two years was incompatible with EC law, since it was a restriction on the right to have a full and effective remedy for breach of Article 141 (ex Article 119) and the Equal Pay Directive. The House of Lords followed this ruling in *Preston and others v Wolverhampton Healthcare NHS Trust (No. 2)* (2001).

**4.156** The EqPA 1970 has been amended in the light of these ECJ rulings. Although the time limit for bringing claims is still six months, there are special rules in certain cases where the employee and the employer had a stable employment relationship (even though one or more individual contracts of employment had ended). These are: (i) where the employer deliberately concealed relevant facts from the employee, or, (ii) where the employee was under a disability (meaning a legal incapacity), the time limit for bringing claims is six months from the date the woman discovered the concealed facts in (i) above, or six months from the time the woman ceased to be under a disability in (ii) (s 2ZA). There is now a six year limit for claiming arrears of pay which is subject to similar rules on concealment and disability as discussed above, except that there is no time limit on claiming arrears, ie applicants may claim arrears back to the date of the contravention (s 2ZB).

## Equal Pay Questionnaire

**4.157** Obtaining information about the pay of potential comparators in order to bring an equal pay claim is often difficult. The recently introduced Equal Pay Questionnaire, based on questionnaires which have been used for some time under the SDA 1975, RRA 1976 and DDA 1995 should assist claimants who wish to bring such claims (see EqPA 1970, s 7(B) and the Equal Pay (Questions and Replies) Order 2003 (SI 2003/722). Under the questionnaire provisions, a claimant (or proposed claimant) may ask the employer for relevant information which will assist them in establishing their complaint (or whether there are grounds to bring a complaint). The employer has eight-weeks in which to respond. Although there is no statutory duty on employers to supply answers to the questionnaire, employment tribunals are entitled to draw inferences from a deliberate refusal to answer, or from a reply which is evasive or equivocal.

223

## Code of Practice on Equal Pay

**4.158**  The EOC, using powers given by SDA 1975, s 56A, has issued a Code of Practice on Equal Pay ('the Code') whose objective is 'to provide practical guidance and recommend good practice to those with responsibility for or interest in the pay arrangements within a particular organisation'. The Code is admissible in evidence in proceedings under the EqPA 1970 (SDA 1975, s 56A).

## Further reading

Deakin, S, & Morris, G, *Labour Law* (3rd ed, 2001) Butterworths (chapter 6).

Smith, I, & Thomas, G, *Industrial Law* (8th ed, 2003) Butterworths (chapter 5).

## Articles

Fredman, S, (2001) 'Equality: a new generation?', *Industrial Law Journal*, Vol. 30, No. 2, June, pp. 145–168.

Vickers, L, (2003) 'Freedom of Religion and the workplace: the draft employment equality (religion or belief) regulations 2003', *Industrial Law Journal*, Vol. 32, No. 1, March, pp. 23–36.

Oliver, H, (2004) 'Sexual orientation discrimination: perceptions, definitions and genuine occupational requirement', *Industrial Law Journal*, Vol. 33, No. 1, March, pp. 1–21.

## Self-test questions

1.  Prakash and Hari are Sikhs: Winston, aged 27, is black, of West Indian origin and came to the UK five years ago. Vacancies for jobs on the production line at Quick Snacks' factory are advertised in the local press. A written application and four passes at O' level are required for applicants. Prakash has difficulty writing English and asks a friend to complete the application form. Quick Snacks board of directors decides as a matter of policy to reject all Sikh applicants: employees in the

personnel office who process the application are duly informed of this and instructed to comply with the board's decision. Prakash and Hari's applications are rejected as is Winston's on the ground that he does not have the required O' level passes. Robert, a clerical worker in the personnel department informs the Commission for Racial Equality about the board's policy: when his manager discovers this, Robert is summarily dismissed.

Advise Prakash, Hari, Winston and Robert.

2.   Daxon PLC owns two stores and a warehouse in Barsetshire. The stores are approximately 30 miles apart and 50 miles from the warehouse. Two unions operate at Daxon, the TGFU which represents the manual workers and negotiates on their behalf, and NELGO which similarly represents the white-collar staff.

Eva, a part-time supervisor at one of the stores wishes to claim equal pay with Donald, a loader at the warehouse. Consider Eva's right to do so, and any defences which may be open to Daxon.

3.   When the computer system at one of Mixco's establishments crashed, Graham, an information technology (IT) consultant, was hired to repair it. When the system was back in operation after 6 months, Mixco hired Graham to undertake the IT for another of its establishments on a fixed-term contract of 6 months. When this contract expired, Mixco offered Graham a 12-month contract.

Advise Graham, who wishes to obtain a permanent position with Mixco, of his rights under the Directive on Fixed-Term Work.

4.   'EC labour law at long last comprehensively protects atypical workers'.

Examine this statement with reference to the Directive on Part-Time Work.

# CHAPTER FIVE

# Work Life Balance

## Summary

Work/life balance and 'family-friendly' policies frame and focus new EU initiatives to combat discrimination at work, seeking to enhance equal treatment. This chapter examines the provisions underlying these policies:

- parental leave;
- maternity rights;
- paternity leave;
- adoption leave;
- flexible working;
- time off to care for dependants; and
- the Part-Time Workers Directive.

## Work/Life Balance and 'Family-Friendly' Policies

**5.1** There have been a number of social policy developments at both EU and domestic level over the last few years which have the objective of allowing workers to achieve a better balance between work and family commitments. As with many developments in the social policy field, the impetus for the introduction of what have become known as 'family-friendly' polices in the UK came from the European Union.

**5.2** The concern to achieve a better work/life balance for workers is articulated, inter alia, in the Community Charter of the Fundamental Social Rights of Workers (known as 'the Social Charter'): see, for example, para 16 which provides that 'measures should also be developed enabling men and women to reconcile their occupational and family obligations.' These objectives are incorporated in the Agreement on Social Policy annexed as a Protocol to the Treaty on European Union (TEU), and also underpin the Social Partners' Framework Agreement on Parental Leave, which is stated to be 'an important means of reconciling work and family life and promoting equal opportunities and treatment between men and women' (Preamble to the Framework Agreement).

**5.3** Although the UK originally opted of the Social Charter during the Conservative Government's term of office, the Labour Government, elected in 1997, pledged to opt in to it, which was done in the Treaty of Amsterdam in 1997, when the Agreement on Social Policy was incorporated into the Treaty of Rome (the TEU and the Treaty of Rome were merged by the Treaty of Nice in 2001, which came into force in February 2003).

**5.4** Within the UK, the family-friendly policies (and legislation) flowing from these developments are those relating to: parental leave; maternity leave; paternity leave; adoption leave; and time off work to care for dependants in certain circumstances. The introduction of flexible working arrangements, discussed below, is also part of the family-friendly package of policies.

**5.5** The DTI published a Green Paper in December 2000 entitled, 'Work and Parents: Competitiveness and Choice', concerning the entitlements identified above, and a Work and Parents Taskforce was established in 2001 to consider ways of introducing 'family-friendly' and 'business-friendly' flexible working practices. The Government published a document entitled 'Balancing work and family life: enhancing choice and support for parents', in January 2003, which considers further developments to improve work/life balance for the future.

## Parental Leave

**5.6** The major impetus for the introduction of a right to parental leave came from the European Union. During the 1980s and early 1990s, the United Kingdom vetoed proposals from the Commission concerning parental leave (whether paid or unpaid). The other Member States adopted the procedure set out in the Social Policy Protocol under which they could adopt social policy legislation without the UK blocking such moves.

**5.7** The Protocol requires consultation with the Social Partners (UNICE, CCEP and the ETUC), representing management and labour, under Article 138 (ex Article 118a) of the Treaty of Rome before social policy proposals may be put forward. The Social Partners may themselves reach an agreement on social policy matters and request the Council to implement it (Art. 139 (ex Article 118b) of the Treaty of Rome). The Social Partners reached a framework agreement on parental leave under this procedure on 14 December 1995, which was implemented by the Parental Leave Directive (Directive 96/34/EC). Having been adopted under the Protocol on Social Policy, from which the UK had opted out, the Directive did not apply to the UK, although the Labour Government which came into power in 1997 accepted the Agreement on Social Policy and the Directive was subsequently extended to the UK by Directive 97/75/EC. The transposition date was 15 December 1999, which was the date the Maternity and Parental Leave Regulations (MPLR) implementing the Directive came into force.

**5.8** The Parental Leave Directive actually requires the implementation of two 'family-friendly' rights: (i) the right to leave to care for young children (up to 8 years of age, according to Clause 2(1) of the Directive); and (ii) the right to time off work to care for dependants in family emergencies. This section deals with the former right, while the latter is considered in a subsequent section.

**5.9** Under the MPLR, both male and female employees, whether full-time or part-time, are entitled to unpaid parental leave of up to 13 weeks (per parent, per child) if they have one year's continuous employment and have (or expect to have) responsibility for the child (MPLR, regs 2 and 13(1)(a)(b), 14(1)). An employee has responsibility for a child where he or she has 'parental responsibility' (as defined in the Children Act 1989, s 3) – a definition which is wide enough to include an adopted child – or where they have been registered as the parent on the child's birth certificate. There is a separate entitlement for each parent. The period of 13 weeks' leave must be taken in periods of a week or multiples of a week, except for parents of disabled children who may take leave of a day or multiples of a day (the limitations of this provision are discussed below), during the first five years of the child's life or, in the case of an adopted child, within five years of the placement for adoption or the child's eighteenth birthday, whichever is the earlier (MPLR, regs 14(1), 15, Sch 2, para 7). This maximum leave period is extended to 18 weeks in the case of employees with a child who is entitled to disability living allowance (MPLR, reg 14(1A)). The leave is 'for the purpose of caring for that child' (MPLR reg. 13(1)).

**5.10** When first brought into force, the MPLR gave a right to parental leave only where the child was born (or adopted) on or after 15 December 1999, although this restriction was removed after the Government was subjected to severe criticism from a number of quarters, including the TUC, on the ground that it was a breach of the Parental Leave Directive, arguing that parental leave should have been available to parents of children aged five at that date (see R v Secretary of State for Trade and Industry, ex parte TUC (2000); and the Maternity and Parental Leave (Amendment) Regulations 2001, SI 2001/4010). The right to parental leave now applies to employees whose children were under five on 15 December 1999.

**5.11** Employers and employees may make their own agreements on how to implement the parental leave right by adopting individual, collective or workforce agreements. This would allow them to agree, for example, that parental leave could be taken in units of less than one week, eg one day, which may be more convenient for the employee. In the absence of such an agreement, the default provisions of Schedule 2 apply.

**5.12** Employers may require employees to provide evidence of their entitlement, including evidence of responsibility for the child and the child's date of birth (MPLR, Sch 2, paras 1(a) and 2). Failure to comply with these requirements means that the employee loses their entitlement to leave.

## Notice requirements

**5.13** Employees must give at least 21 days' notice of their intention to take parental leave (MPLR, Sch 2, para 1). In the case of employees giving this notice before the expected week of childbirth or placement for adoption, the employer must allow the leave. Apart from those two situations, the employer may postpone it for up to six months where he 'considers that the operation of is business would be unduly disrupted' if the employee took the leave, giving the employee seven days' notice in writing of the postponement (MPLR, Sch 2, para 6). An employee may complain to an employment tribunal that the employer has unreasonably postponed a period of parental leave or prevented or attempted him from taking it (ERA 1996, s 80).

## Terms and conditions of employment while on parental leave

**5.14** Under regulation 17, the employee is entitled to certain terms and conditions of employment which apply during the period of parental leave, apart from the right to pay. These are: the implied term of trust and confidence; notice of termination of the contract; compensation upon redundancy; and the disciplinary and grievance procedures. During leave, the employee is bound by: the implied obligation of good faith and any terms relating to: notice of termination; disclosure of confidential information; the acceptance of gifts of other benefits; or participation in any business.

## Right to return after parental leave

**5.15** Employees returning after parental leave of four weeks or less are entitled to return to the job they were doing before going on leave. Employees taking longer periods of leave are entitled to return to the job they were doing before going on leave or, where that is not reasonably practicable, to a suitable and appropriate job (MPLR, reg 18). Upon return, the employee's rights to remuneration, seniority, pension rights and other similar rights must be no less favourable than they were before taking leave (reg 18A).

*Unfair dismissal and protection from detriment*

**5.16** It is automatically unfair to dismiss an employee for a reason connected with the fact that he took or sought to take parental leave (ERA 1996, s 99; MPLR, reg 20). They are also entitled not to be subjected to any detriment on the same grounds (ERA 1996, s 47C; MPLR, reg 19). The employee may make a complaint to an employment tribunal concerning such infringements by the employer (ERA 1996, s 48).

## Maternity Rights

**5.17** Women have four rights in relation to pregnancy and childbirth. These are: the right to maternity leave; the right to maternity pay; time off for ante-natal care; and protection from detriment or dismissal on the grounds of pregnancy or childbirth.

*Maternity Leave*

**5.18** The Pregnant Workers Directive 92/85/EEC required Member States to provide women workers with at least 14 weeks' maternity. The relevant domestic law is now contained within ERA 1996, ss 71 – 75 and the MPLR, as amended by the Maternity and Parental Leave (Amendment) Regulations 2002, SI 2002/2789 (MPLAR 2002), which apply to mothers of children born on or after 6 April 2003.

*Ordinary maternity leave*

**5.19** Women are entitled to a period of ordinary maternity leave (OML) of 26 weeks (extended from 18 weeks as from 24 November 2002), without the need to accrue a qualifying period of continuous employment ): MPLR, reg 7.

## Notice requirements

**5.20** There are detailed notification requirements to be followed, failing which the maternity leave may be lost. The employee must notify her employer no later than the end of the 15th week before the expected week of childbirth (EWC) – or as soon as reasonably practicable – of the fact that she is pregnant, the expected date of childbirth and the date on which she intends to commence her OML (reg 4). This date may be varied by notifying the employer at least 28 days before the date varied or before the new date, whichever is the earlier.

**5.21** The employer must then give the woman notice of the date on which her OML will end (reg 8). If the employer fails to do this, she may return early and she is protected from detriment or dismissal if she does not return on that date (regs 10(c), 13 and 14).

## Contractual terms during absence

**5.22** With the exception of remuneration (a woman is entitled to statutory maternity pay while on maternity leave), certain other terms and conditions of employment continue to apply throughout the woman's absence (ERA 1996, s 71; MPLR, reg 17). This means that both parties are bound, inter alia, by the implied term relating to trust and confidence, notice provisions and disciplinary and grievance procedures.

## Redundancy during OML

**5.23** If the woman becomes redundant during her maternity leave, she has the right to be offered suitable alternative employment (if there is such a post) by the employer or an associated employer (reg 10).

## Right to return to work after OML

**5.24** After her OML, a woman has the right to return to the job in which she was employed before her absence, on terms no less favourable than she would have enjoyed had she not been absent (reg 18).

## Unfair dismissal and protection from detriment

**5.25** A woman is protected from detriment for exercising or seeking to exercise her rights to maternity leave, and it is an automatically unfair dismissal to dismiss a woman for a reason connected with pregnancy, childbirth or maternity leave rights (regs 19 and 20). There is one exception to this provision on automatically unfair dismissals: it is not automatically unfair to dismiss a woman (for a reason other than redundancy) if it is not reasonably practicable to allow her to return to a suitable job and she has accepted or unreasonably refused the offer of such a job made by an associated employer (reg 20(7)).

## Additional maternity leave

**5.26** A woman who is entitled to OML and who has been continuously employed for a period of 26 weeks by the 14th week before the EWC is entitled to a period of additional maternity leave (AML) of 26 weeks (regs 5 and 7). This gives qualifying female employees a total maternity leave entitlement of one year. However, maternity leave only attracts statutory maternity pay for the first 26 weeks of leave (see the section on statutory maternity pay), which means that, in practice, women will only wish to take the full 52 weeks of leave if there is a contractual entitlement covering the last half of the leave year.

## Notice requirements

**5.27** The same notice requirements apply concerning the taking of AML and dates of commencement and return as for OML.

## Right to return to work after AML

**5.28** The woman returning from AML has the same right as relates to OML to return to the job in which she was employed before her absence, on terms no less favourable than she would have enjoyed had she not been absent (reg 18), but there are two exceptions to this right to return (see the section on unfair dismissal below).

## Unfair dismissal and protection from detriment

**5.29**  As in OML, a woman is protected from detriment for exercising or seeking to exercise her rights to AML, and it is an automatically unfair dismissal to dismiss a woman for a reason connected with pregnancy, childbirth or maternity leave rights (regs 19 and 20).

**5.30**  The same exception also applies for AML, as set out in reg 20(7), ie it is not automatically unfair to dismiss a woman (for a reason other than redundancy) if it is not reasonably practicable to allow her to return from AML to a suitable job and she has accepted or unreasonably refused the offer of such a job made by an associated employer (reg 20(7)). However, there is also a small employer exception in the case of AML: it is not an automatically unfair dismissal if the employer employs five or fewer employees, including employees of any associated employer, and it was not reasonably practicable for him to offer the woman a job 'which is both suitable for her and appropriate for her to do in the circumstances' (reg 20(6)).

## Contractual and statutory maternity leave rights – OML and AML

**5.31**  Where an employee has both contractual and statutory maternity leave rights, she may not exercise the two rights separately but may choose whichever right is the more favourable (reg 21).

## Compulsory maternity leave

**5.32**  A woman may not work during the period of two weeks after the birth (ERA 1996, s 72, MPLR, reg 8).

## Statutory maternity pay

**5.33**  A woman with 26 weeks of continuous employment by the 15th week before the EWC with average earnings at or above the lower earnings limit (£79 per week from 6 April 2004) for the payment of National Insurance contributions is entitled to statutory maternity pay (SMP): see the Social Security Contributions and Benefits Act 1992, ss 164 – 171. For the first six weeks, it is paid at the rate of 90% of the woman's normal weekly earnings. For the remaining 20 weeks it is paid at the rate of statutory sick pay, which from April 2004 is £102.80 per week. A woman must give 28 days' notice of the day SMP should start.

## Time off for ante-natal care

**5.34**   A pregnant employee may request paid time off work to attend an ante-natal appointment, which may not be unreasonably refused by the employer. The employer may request written proof of the pregnancy and the appointment (ERA 1996, ss 55 and 56). The amount of pay is the normal hourly rate. The employee may complain to an employment tribunal that her employer has unreasonably refused time off or has failed to pay her for the time off. The tribunal may make a declaration and order the amount of pay due. Dismissal or subjection to a detriment because the employee has exercised her rights under these provisions will give the right to claim under the MPLR, regs 19 and 20, as well of complaining of unfair dismissal (as well as sex discrimination).

## Protection from detriment or dismissal on grounds of pregnancy

**5.35**   It is automatically unfair to dismiss a woman (or select her for redundancy) for a pregnancy-related reason, or to subject her to a detriment for such a reason (ERA 1996, ss 99 and 47C; MPLR, regs 19 and 20). As well as pregnancy itself, pregnancy-related reasons include reasons related to: childbirth; suspension on maternity grounds under ERA 1996, s 66; taking or seeking to take OML or AML; parental leave; or time off for ante-natal care. An employee who is dismissed because she is pregnant or during or after OML or AML must be provided with a written statement of the reasons for her dismissal (ERA 1996, s 92(4), for which there is no requirement of a qualifying period of employment.

## Paternity Leave

**5.36**   The Employment Act 2002 (EA 2002), s 1, introduced new rights to paternity leave (PL) by inserting new sections into the ERA 1996, ss 80A and 80B (in force from 8 December 2002). These concern the two categories of PL: one concerning the birth of a child (called 'paternity leave: birth'), and the other concerning adoption (called 'paternity leave: adoption'). Although the provisions relating to these two categories are similar, there are some differences and these two forms of PL are treated separately below. Under the ERA 1996, s 1, the Secretary of State was given power to make regulations concerning paternity leave, which was done by making the Paternity and Adoption Leave Regulations 2002, SI2002/2788 (PALR), which came into force on 8 December 2002. Where there is also a contractual right to paternity leave, an employee may not operate both rights separately but may choose whichever right is more favourable, ie he may choose either the contractual right or the statutory one, but not both (PALR, reg 30). Furthermore, PL is in addition to the 13 weeks' parental leave entitlement, discussed above.

### Paternity leave: birth

**5.37**   The PALR apply to fathers of children born on or after 6 April 2003 and who have been continuously employed for not less than 26 weeks ending with the week immediately preceding the 14th week before the expected week of the child's birth. However, it should be noted that the interpretation of "partner" in reg 2, which defines a partner as, '... a person (whether of a different or the same sex) who lives with the mother ... and the child in an enduring family relationship but is not a relative of the mother ...' is clearly wide enough for the purposes of reg 4(2) – discussed below – to apply to a woman, despite the fact that it is called paternity leave. This means, for example, the right to paternity leave could also apply (if the requirements set out in regs 2 and 4 are met) to the female partner of a woman in a lesbian relationship where that woman has had a child. However, the masculine form will be used in this description of the PALR, which should be read as also importing the feminine.

**5.38** There are a number of other requirements to be satisfied under the PALR, reg 4(2), before a father is entitled to this right. These are that he is:

● the father of the child or;

● married to or the partner of the child's mother, but not the child's father;

● and that he has (or expects to have) if he is the child's father, responsibility for the upbringing of the child; or

● if he is the mother's husband or partner but not the child's father, the main responsibility for the child's upbringing.

**5.39** The requirements in (ii) above are treated as satisfied in circumstances where the child's mother has died, and the requirements in (iii) and (iv) above are treated as satisfied even where the child has died.

**5.40** The entitlement is for up to two weeks' paid leave, which must be taken together – there is no right to take separate days of leave, although an employee may choose to take either one week's leave or two consecutive weeks' leave – and it must be taken within 56 days of the birth (PALR, reg 5(2)). The employee is entitled to Statutory Paternity Pay (SPP), which is paid at the same rate as SMP, ie from 6 April 2004, this is £102.80 per week, or 90% of average weekly earnings if this is less than that sum – these figures normally change every year (see: EA 2002, s 7; Statutory Paternity Pay and Statutory Adoption Pay (General) Regulations 2002, SI 2002/2822, reg 3); and the Statutory Paternity Pay and Statutory Adoption Pay (Weekly Rates) Regulations 2002, SI 2002/2818, reg 2). As with SMP, there are recoupment provisions which mean that employers can recover SPP paid to employees, which from April 2004 is at the rate of 92% for large employers and 104.5% for small employers, ie those with a National Insurance liability (from April 2004) of £45,000 or less (see the Statutory Paternity Pay and Statutory Adoption Pay (Administration) Regulations 2002, SI 2002/2820, reg 3).

**5.41** Employees wishing to take paternity leave must comply with certain notice requirements. Under the PALR, the employee must give notice to their employer at least 15 weeks' notice before the child's expected week (or, if that is not possible, as soon as is reasonably practicable) specifying (i) that they intend taking paternity leave and (ii) how much leave they intend to take (PALR, reg 6(1) and (2)). An employee may vary either or both (i) and (ii) above on giving at least 28 days' notice (regs 6(4). Interestingly, the employer may request that the employee provides '… a declaration, signed by the employee, to the effect that the purpose of his absence from work will be' for the purpose of caring for the child or supporting its mother and that he/she satisfies the entitlement conditions of regulation 6(3).

## Paternity leave: adoption

**5.42**  The PALR also contains provisions on PL for employees on the adoption of a child, defined as a person who is under 18 when placed for adoption (it is important to note that this right is not to be confused with adoption leave, which is discussed below). Many of the provisions concerning paternity leave relating to adoption are similar to those governing paternity leave on the birth of a child, eg those on qualifying for the entitlement, the period of leave allowed and the requirement that it must be taken within 56 days of (in this case) the date on which the child is placed with the adopter (PALR, regs 8 and 9(2)). The declaration requirements are also similar. However, the notice requirements differ from those relating to paternity leave: birth. Employees must give their employer notice of their intention to take this form of PL no more than seven days after the date on which the adopter is notified of having been matched with the child.

## Paternity leave – terms and conditions of employment while on leave

**5.43**  During the period of PL, employees are bound by all the obligations and entitled to the benefit of all the terms and conditions of their employment, apart from remuneration (ERA 1996, s 80C(5)(b)).

## Right to return after paternity leave

**5.44**  Regulation 13 of the PALR confers a right to return to work after PL, 'to the job in which he was employed before his absence'

(PALR, reg 13(1)). This right applies whether the PL was (i) taken as an isolated period of leave or (ii) whether it was the last of two or more consecutive periods of statutory leave. Employees returning after a period of PL not falling within these two categories has the right either to return to the job they were doing before their absence or, if that is not reasonably practicable, to another suitable and appropriate job. He or she is entitled to return to work on the same terms and conditions as if they had not been absent.

## Unfair dismissal and protection from detriment

**5.45**  Employees who are dismissed because they took or are seeking to take PL (or are selected for redundancy for that reason) are to be regarded as having been unfairly dismissed, ie this is an automatically unfair dismissal (PALR, reg 29). (Note that, rather strangely, unlike additional maternity leave and adoption leave, there is no small employers' exemption from these automatically unfair dismissal provisions for employees taking or seeking PL: see MPLR, reg 20(6); PALR, reg 29(4)). Employees taking or seeking to take PL, or where the employer believed that they were likely to do so, have the right not to be subjected to a detriment or any deliberate failure to act by the employer (PALR, reg 28).

# Adoption Leave

**5.46**  The EA 2002 inserted new sections 75A and 75B into the ERA 1996 concerning adoption leave (AL). The provisions concerning AL, as distinct from paternity leave on adoption, allow either adoptive parent of an adopted child born on or after 6 April, 2003 to take paid AL. There are two categories of AL: ordinary adoption leave (OAL) of 26 weeks, and additional adoption leave (AAL) of a further 26 weeks: PALR, regs 18(1) and 20(2). OAL attracts statutory adoption pay, ie it is paid leave: there is no statutory payment for AAL (although there may be contractual provisions concerning payment during this leave). Employees with 26 weeks' continuous employment who have been matched with a child by an adoption agency and agreed that the child should be placed with them are entitled to OAL. Employees completing a period of OAL are entitled to AAL, ie a total of 52 weeks' of AL. The employee may choose when this is to begin (PALR, reg 16) and there are notice and documentary proof requirements similar to those applicable in PL (PALR, reg 17). Employees failing to comply with the requirements set out in regulation 17 lose their right to take AL.

**5.47** As in PL, during OAL an employee's terms and conditions (including obligations) of the contract of employment are preserved (PALR, reg 19), but only certain terms are preserved in AAL (PALR, reg 21).

## Statutory adoption pay – ordinary adoption leave

**5.48** An adoptive parent taking OAL is entitled to statutory adoption pay (SAP) for the 26 week period: Social Security Contributions and Benefits Act 1992, s 171ZN. This is paid at the standard SMP rate (£102.80 from 6 April 2004, although these rates are likely to change every year). Employees earning less than the lower earnings limit for National Insurance contributions (£79 per week from 6 April 2004 – again, this rate changes every year) are not entitled to SAP.

## Notice requirements

**5.49** There are detailed and important notice requirements concerning the intention to take AL and the intention to return to work after AL (PALR, regs 17 and 25).

## Right to return after adoption leave

**5.50** An employee is entitled to return to his old job at the end of AL, unless there is no job to which he can return due to redundancy, in which case the employer or associated employer must offer him suitable and appropriate alternative employment on terms that are not less favourable than those of his previous contract (PALR, reg 23).

## Unfair dismissal and protection from detriment

**5.51** It is automatically unfair to dismiss an employee because he took or sought to take AL, or is selected for redundancy for that reason (PALR, reg 29). This is subject to two exemptions: (i) a small employer's exemption for AAL only (it is not applicable to OAL) whereby it is not automatically unfair for employers employing 5 or fewer employees (including those of associated employers) to refuse to allow the employee to return to work, if it is not reasonably practicable for the employer (or an associated employer) to provide suitable, appropriate work (PALR, reg 29(4)); and (ii) an exemption (irrespective of the number of employees employed) where it is not reasonably practicable (for a reason other than redundancy) for the employer to permit the employee to return to his old job but an associated employer offers him a suitable and appropriate job and the employee accepts or unreasonably refuses the offer (PALR, reg 29(5)).

**5.52** Employees are protected from detriment because he took or sought to take OAL or AAL, or the employer believed he was likely to do so, or the employee failed to return to work because of the employer's failure to satisfy him of the date on which the OAL or AAL period would end (PALR, reg 28).

## Written reasons for dismissal

**5.53** An employee who is dismissed while absent on OAL or AAL is entitled to a written statement of the reason or reasons for dismissal, without having to request it 'and irrespective of whether he has been continuously employed for any period if he is dismissed in circumstances in which that period ends by reason of the dismissal' (ERA 1996, s 92(4A)).

# Flexible Working

**5.54** In November 2001, the Work and Parents Task Force delivered a report proposing that employees who were parents of children under 6 should be able to request flexible working arrangements, and that the employer should be required to take this request seriously.

This was taken up by the Government, and a provision was inserted into the ERA 1996 by the Employment Act 2002 (see ERA 1996, ss 80F – 80I), effective from 6 April 2003. There are two sets of regulations on flexible working: the Flexible Working (Procedural Requirements) Regulations 2002, SI 2002/3207 ('the FE(PR) Regs'), and the Flexible Working (Eligibility, Complaints and Remedies) Regulations 2002, SI 2002/3236 ('the FW(ECR) regs'). The right is to request to work flexibly (ie a right to request a contractual variation), rather than an automatic right to do so. The change must relate to hours or times and place of work (ERA 1996, s 80F(1)(a)).

## Qualifying for the right

**5.55** To qualify for this right, the employee must be:

- a qualifying employee, ie with at least 26 weeks' of continuous employment (FE(PR) Regs, reg 3(1)(a);

- having or expecting to have responsibility for the upbringing of a child aged under 6 (or under 18 if the child is disabled): ERA 1996, s 80F(3) and (7);

- either the parent, foster parent, guardian, or adopter of the child, or the husband, wife or partner of such a person (FE(PR) Regs, reg 3(1)(b).

## Procedure

**5.56** The application to request the right must be made in writing, and must specify the change applied for, the date from which the employee wants it to be effective, and the effect (if any) the applicant thinks the change would have on the employer: FE(PR) Regs, reg 4; ERA 1996, s 80F. The application must be made before the fourteenth day before the day on which the child reaches the age of 6 (or 18 if disabled).

**5.57** The employer must hold a meeting within 28 days of the request, and inform the employee of the decision within 14 days of the meeting (FE(PR) Regs, regs 3 and 4). The employee may be accompanied by a fellow worker. The employee may appeal against the decision within 14 days and, if an appeal is made, an appeal meeting must be held within 14 days of the appeal being lodged, unless the appeal is upheld within 14 days of the appeal being lodged (FE(PR) Regs, regs 6 and 8).

## Grounds for refusal

**5.58**  The employer may only refuse the request on 'business grounds' (ERA 1996, s 80G(1)(b)). These are:

- burden of additional costs;

- detrimental effect of the ability to meet customer demand;

- inability to reorganise work among existing staff;

- inability to recruit additional staff;

- detrimental impact on quality or performance;

- insufficiency of work during periods that the employee proposes to work planned structural changes;

- any other ground that the Secretary of State may specify.

These grounds seem very wide, giving great scope to the employer to refuse the request.

**5.59**  Failure to follow these procedural requirements will mean that the employee may apply to an employment tribunal which can order the employer to reconsider its decision and award a maximum of 8 weeks' pay (from February 2004 this is capped at the statutory maximum of £270 per week, ie a total award of £2,160 may be made): FE(PR) Regs, reg 15.

## Unfair dismissal and protection from detriment

**5.60**  It is an automatically unfair dismissal if the reason is that the employee exercised or sought to exercise the rights to request flexible working (ERA 1996, s 104C). The employee is also protected from suffering a detriment on these grounds (ERA 1996, s 47E).

## Time off to care for dependants

**5.61** The Parental Leave Directive required Member States to introduce the right for workers to take time off for urgent family reasons. This was implemented by inserting a provision into the ERA 1996, s 57A (as amended by the Employment Relations Act 1999), giving employees a statutory right to request time off to care for dependants. No qualifying period of employment is necessary for entitlement to the right. A 'dependant' is the employee's wife, husband, child, parent, or someone living in the same household (but is not his or her employee, tenant, lodger or boarder (ERA 1996, s 57A(3)). This is wide enough to include partners of the opposite or the same sex as the employee. The definition also includes a person who reasonably relies on the employee for assistance when they fall ill, are injured or assaulted, or who relies on the employee to make arrangements for the provision of care in the event of illness or injury (ERA 1996, s 57A(4)). Where there is unexpected disruption or termination of arrangements for the care of a dependant, the definition also includes any person who reasonably relies on the employee to make arrangements for care (ERA 1996, s 57A(5).

**5.62** The right is to 'reasonable' time off, ie it is intended to allow the employee to deal with unexpected crises or emergencies. This is reflected in the range of circumstances for which time off is allowed. It is time off to take action which is necessary:

- to provide assistance on an occasion when a dependant falls ill, gives birth or is injured or assaulted;

- to make arrangements for the provisions of care for a dependant who is ill or injured;

- in consequence of the death of a dependant;

- because of the unexpected disruption or termination of arrangements for the care of the dependant; or

- to deal with an incident which involves a child of the employee and which occurs unexpectedly in a period during which an educational establishment which the child attends is responsible for him. (ERA 1996, s 57A(1)).

**5.63** The employee must inform his employer as soon as is reasonably practicable of the reason for the absence and, if he is able to inform his employer in advance of the absence, state how long he will be absent (ERA 1996, s 57A(2)).

**5.64** There is no statutory entitlement to paid time off, so the absence will be unpaid unless there are contractual provisions relating to this in the employment contract.

**5.65** The EAT in *Qua v John Ford Morrison Solicitors* (2003) gave guidance on the entitlement to time off under ERA 1996, s 57A. In determining what is a reasonable amount of time off, no account must be taken of operational disruption caused to the employer's business by the employee's absence. The employer should take account of the individual circumstances of the employee, including the number and length of previous absences and the dates on which they occurred. The EAT stated that the right is to allow the employee time off to deal with an unexpected event: they are allowed a reasonable amount of time off 'to deal with the immediate crisis' (per Mrs Recorder Cox QC at para 16).

**5.66** The employee may complain that the employer unreasonably refused time off (ERA 1996, s 57B), for which the remedies are a declaration and such compensation as the tribunal considers to be just and equitable, having regard to the employer's default and the loss to the employee.

## Unfair dismissal and protection from detriment

**5.67** As with the other rights considered in this chapter, any dismissal is automatically unfair if it relates to entitlement to time off, and the employee may make a complaint to the employment tribunal if they have been subjected to a detriment for exercising their rights under ERA 1996, s 57A.

## Part-Time Workers Directive

**5.68** Encouraging part-time work and providing the opportunity to switch from full-time to part-time working, and ensuring adequate employment protection for those wishing to do so, is a very important aspect of achieving a better work/life balance across the labour market. The protections recently introduced for part-time workers may thus be seen as part of the package of family-friendly policies. The EC Part-Time Work Directive 97/81/EC of 5 December 1997 (which was extended to apply to the UK by the Part-time Workers Directive 98/23EC) was implemented by the Part-time Workers (Prevention of Less Favourable Treatment) Regulations 2000 (SI 2000/1551) ('the PTWR') on 1 July 2000, some three months after the implementation date of 7 April 2000. The DTI has issued detailed guidance on the PTWR (Part-Time Workers – The Law and Best Practice), which encourages employers to afford opportunities for allowing workers to switch to part-time work, and to consider more flexible working. This is in line with the objectives of the Directive, although the guidance does not have legal force.

### Less favourable treatment of part-time workers

**5.69** Regulation 5(2) provides that:

> A part-time worker has the right not to be treated by his employer less favourably than the employer treats a comparable full-time worker–
> * as regards the terms of his contract; or
> * by being subjected to any other detriment by any act, or deliberate failure to act, of his employer.

**5.70** This right applies only if:

(a) the treatment is on the ground that the worker is a part-time worker, and

(b) the treatment is not justified on objective grounds.

**5.71** There must be an actual comparable full-time worker with whom the part-timer can compare himself. One person can claim parity with another if (i) he is a part-time worker, ie he is not identifiable as a full-time worker, 'having regard to the custom and practice of the employer in relation to workers employed by the worker's employer under the same type of contract' and (ii) the comparator is a comparable full-time worker (PTWR, reg 2(2)). Three conditions must be satisfied:

- the full-time worker is employed by the same employer under the same type of contract;

- that both workers are engaged in the same or broadly similar work, having regard, where relevant, to qualification, skills and experience; and

- that both workers are based at the same establishment (unless there is no full-time worker based at the same establishment as the part-time worker, but there is one based at another establishment).

**5.72** The question of whether full-time workers were employed under the same type of contract as part-timers was considered in *Matthews v Kent and Medway Towns Fire Authority* (2003), which held that retained (ie part-time) firemen could not compare themselves to full-time, regular firefighters as they were not employed under the 'same type of contract' as whole-time fire fighters, nor were they engaged in the same or broadly similar work having regard to their level of qualification, skills and experience.

## Pro Rata Principle

**5.73** Part-time workers are entitled to the same treatment pro rata as full timers doing similar work unless the less favourable treatment can be objectively justified. For the purposes of this chapter which focuses on family-friendly policies, it is important to note that part timers must have the same entitlements to maternity leave (and maternity pay), parental leave, and time-off for dependants, on a pro-rata basis, as comparable full-time workers (PTWR, reg 5).

## Family-friendly policies and changing to part-time work

**5.74** The PTWR may be particularly important in cases where a full-time worker's contract is varied, for example following a successful request under the flexible working provisions discussed above, so that they are working fewer weekly hours. In such a situation, the PTWR apply to them (reg 3). The PTWR also apply in situations where a full-time worker returns after a period of absence, eg parental leave or maternity leave, provided they are returning within a period of 12 months from the start of the absence to the same job or one at the same level (reg 4). The 'returning worker' is entitled not to be treated less favourably on the grounds of their part-time status (without objective justification) than they were before the contractual variation (PTWR, regs 4 and 5).

## Objective justification

**5.75** The right of a part-timer not to be treated less favourably than a comparable full-timer applies only if the treatment cannot be justified on objective grounds. Justification of the less favourable treatment on objective grounds means that it must be shown that it:

• is to achieve a legitimate objective, for example, a genuine business objective;

• is necessary to achieve that objective; and

• is an appropriate way to achieve the objective.

## Written reasons for less favourable treatment

**5.76** A part-time worker who considers that his employer may be treating him less favourably than a comparable full-time co-worker may require the employer to give written reasons for the difference (reg 6). If the employer fails to provide the statement within 21 days a tribunal may draw an adverse inference that the employer has infringed the right in question.

## Unfair dismissal and protection from detriment

**5.78** It is automatically unfair dismissal to dismiss a worker for a reason relating to his rights under the PTWR (reg 7(1) and (3)), and the worker has the right not to be subjected to a detriment for a reason relating to his rights under the Regulations (reg 7(2)).

## Complaint to an employment tribunal

**5.79**  A worker has the right to complain to an employment tribunal (reg 8), which may make a declaration, award compensation which the tribunal considers to be just and equitable and make recommendations (regs 8(7) and 9). There is no statutory cap on the amount of compensation that a tribunal can award, but no award can be made for injury to feelings (reg 8(11)).

## Further reading

Deakin, S, & Morris, G, *Labour Law* (3rd ed, 2001) Butterworths (chapter 6, pp. 645–658).

Smith, I, & Thomas, G, *Industrial Law* (8th ed, 2003) Butterworths (chapter 6).

## *Article*

McColgan, A, (2000) 'Family-friendly frolics?The maternity and parental leave etc regulations 1999', *Industrial Law Journal*,Vol. 29, No. 2, June, pp. 125–144.

## Self-test questions

1.    Annie has been employed for 5 years on a full-time basis as one of five designers for Poncho, a hat manufacturer. She has greatly benefited from Poncho's annual training programme in fashion trends, which includes travelling to fashion shows in Paris. Following the birth of her first child, Annie finds full-time work too exhausting.

Annie wishes to switch to working only 3 half-days per week for the next two years, but then resume full-time working. Advise Annie on any rights she may have.

2.  'Reconciling 'work life balance' is not an issue which can be resolved by the principles of labour law'. Discuss.

3.  Danny works as a solicitor. He and his wife, Mary, are about to adopt a 4 year old child. Advise Danny of his rights with regard to leave.

4.  Are family-friendly policies working in Britain? Assess the impact of these policies on the UK labour market. Give examples from case law.

# CHAPTER SIX

# Termination of employment

## Summary

This chapter considers what claims an employee whose contract is terminated by the employer may make. Consequently, this will explain how to make a claim based upon the statutory rights depending upon eligibility, as well as breach of contract. To be able to make a wrongful dismissal claim, the employee must show that the dismissal was in breach of contract. Central to both the common law and statutory rights, however, is the requirement that the employee was 'dismissed'. This chapter considers what amounts to a dismissal and the circumstances in which the dismissal will be wrongful.

## Introduction

**6.1** Those who are dismissed are likely to have two basic types of claim: they may either claim to have been dismissed in breach of contract or they may claim to have been dismissed in breach of their statutory rights. A dismissal in breach of contract is usually called a 'wrongful dismissal'. A claim for breach of statutory rights will either take the form of a complaint of unfair dismissal and/or a claim for a statutory redundancy payment. These two types of statutory claim are considered in Chapters 6 and 7. This chapter considers the concept of wrongful dismissal.

**6.2** It is common to all forms of dismissal claim that the person making it must have been dismissed. Unless a dismissal (however defined) has taken place, no claim is possible. It is important to note, however, that the common law definition of a dismissal does not necessarily coincide with the statutory definition of dismissal. This is because the common law looks solely at the agreement between the parties. Statute, on the other hand, gives an extended meaning to dismissal which means that a dismissal is deemed to have taken place for statutory purposes. An example is the expiry of a fixed term contract. So far as the common law is concerned, the expiry of a fixed term contract represents what was agreed between the parties. Thus, when the contract expires, that is an event contemplated by them and cannot therefore give rise to any claim for breach of contract. On the other hand, if the contract is held to have been 'frustrated', neither the common law nor statute will treat the event which happened as amounting to a dismissal. Similarly a termination by mutual agreement will not be treated by the common law as a dismissal.

**6.3** The critical distinction between a 'wrongful' and an 'unfair' dismissal lies in the limitations of the law of contract. If a person is dismissed in breach of contract – for example, without the notice to which he or she was entitled under the contract – then the common law is able to intervene and a claim may be made. If, however, the person is dismissed with the notice to which he or she was entitled, the common law can no longer deal with the matter since there has been no breach of contract. It is at this point that the law of unfair dismissal becomes important. The success or otherwise of a statutory claim to have been unfairly dismissed depends not upon whether there has been a breach of contract but upon whether the employer has dismissed the employee in a way which does not infringe his or her statutory rights; in other words whether the dismissal was fair or unfair. Thus, it is perfectly feasible for the situation to exist where an employee is dismissed in accordance with the contract but in a way which contravenes his or her statutory rights. In such a case, a wrongful dismissal claim will fail, whereas an unfair dismissal claim will succeed. It is important to bear in mind that the terms 'unfair' and 'wrongful' cannot be used interchangeably. They are terms of art and embody different legal concepts.

## What amounts to a dismissal?

**6.4**  This section considers various situations and examines whether they amount to a dismissal. In doing so, it compares and contrasts the position at common law and under the statutory provisions. The following situations are considered: expiry of a fixed-term contract, frustration, termination by mutual consent, dismissal with notice, dismissal without notice, resignation, resignation in breach of contract and constructive dismissal.

### Expiry of fixed term contract

**6.5**  Fixed-term contracts may take a number of forms. The contract may specify that it is to continue for a stated period (eg five years from January 1 2004). In that case, it cannot be terminated before the expiry of that period, unless its terms empower the parties to terminate it earlier or they agree to bring it to an end. See, for example, *Nelson v James Nelson & Sons Ltd* (1914). A second type of fixed-term contract is one which provides for a definite period of employment but specifies that it may be brought to a premature end by either party giving the other a stated period of notice of termination, for example six months or a year. In *Dixon v British Broadcasting Corporation* (1979) the Court of Appeal held that, in the context of employment protection legislation, such a contract is a contract for a fixed term even though it is terminable by notice on either side before the expiry of the term. Lord Denning MR emphasised that a fixed-term contract must be for a specified period.

**6.6**  A third type of fixed-term contract is one which provides that it is to continue for a stated period (eg one year) and thereafter until determined by notice. The contract cannot be terminated before the stated period expires, but it is a matter of construction of the words used in the contract whether it can be terminated at the end of the period by a notice given during that period, or whether it can only be determined after the expiry of the definite term by notice given after the end of the term. In *Costigan v Gray Bovier Engines Ltd* (1925) the contract was 'to continue for a period of 12 calendar months and thereafter until determined by three calendar months' notice in writing given by either party at any time to the other.' The court held that, although the contract could not be terminated before the expiration of the 12 months, it could be determined at the end of, or at any time after, the term by notice given either during or after the period of 12 months. See also *Morris Oddy & Co Ltd v Hayles* (1971).

**6.7** It should be noted that limitations have been placed on the use of fixed term contracts by the Fixed-Term Employees (Prevention of Less Favourable Treatment) Regulations 2002 (SI 2002/2034). The effect of these Regulations is, amongst other things, to prevent less favourable treatment of fixed-term employees by comparison with permanent employees and to convert fixed-term contracts into permanent contracts in the case of employees continuously employed for four years or more: see regs. 3 and 8.

## Frustration

**6.8** Frustration occurs when circumstances beyond the control of either party to a contract make it incapable of being performed in the form which was undertaken by the contracting parties. In that case, the contract will terminate automatically and the frustrating event will not be treated as a dismissal either for the purposes of any dismissal claim, whether at common law or under the statute. In *Davis Contractors Ltd v Fareham District Council* (1950) (at pp. 728–729), Lord Radcliffe set out the basic principle of frustration as follows:

> ... [F]rustration occurs whenever the law recognises that without default of either party a contractual obligation has become incapable of being performed because the circumstances in which performance is called for would render it a thing radically different from that which was undertaken by the contract ... [I]t is not hardship or inconvenience or material loss itself which calls the principle of frustration into play. There must be as well such a change in the significance of the obligation that the thing undertaken would, if performed, be a different thing from that contracted for.

**6.9** The doctrine of frustration applies to a contract of employment, the most common examples being illness and imprisonment. The death of either party is also best treated as a frustrating event. The effect of frustration is to terminate the contract automatically without either party having to take steps to bring it to an end. Since the employee will not be treated as having been dismissed, a complaint of unfair dismissal or a claim for a redundancy payment will fail; see *Marshall v Harland & Wolff Ltd* (1972). It should be noted that ERA 1996, s. 136(5) only protects an employee's right to a redundancy payment where the frustrating event relates to the employer, not the employee, though, if the event affects both, it will be enough that some of the effect is upon the employer: see *Fenerty v British Airports Authority* (1976).

**6.10** A permanent illness will probably frustrate the contract, as will one which is so prolonged as to prevent the employer from obtaining substantially what was bargained for. Theatrical and similar cases present peculiar problems. Cases to consider are: *Poussard v Spiers and Pond* (1876), *Bettini v Gye* (1876), *Storey v Fulham Steel Works Co* (1907) and *Condor v Barron Knights* (1966). Frustration through illness has come to be reconsidered in the last few years because of its operation in the context of the statutory rights. In *Marshall v Harland & Wolff Ltd* (1972) (at p. 106), Sir John Donaldson set out the test as follows:

> Was the employee's incapacity, looked at before the purported dismissal, of such a nature, or did it appear likely to continue for such a period that further performance of his obligations in the future would either be impossible or would be a thing radically different from that undertaken by him and accepted by the employer under the agreed terms of his employment?

**6.11** He outlined five factors to be taken into account in answering this question: the terms of the contract, including any provisions as to sick pay; how long the employment was likely to last in the absence of sickness; the nature of the employment; the nature of the illness or injury, how long it has already continued and the prospects of recovery; and the period of past employment. In relation to short-term periodic contracts, the EAT has suggested four further factors to be taken into account: the risk to the employer of incurring obligations in respect of redundancy payments or compensation for unfair dismissal to a replacement employee; whether wages have continued to be paid; the acts and statements of the employer in relation to the employment, in particular the dismissal of, or failure to dismiss, the employee; and whether in all the circumstances a reasonable employer could be expected to wait longer. See *Egg Stores (Stamford Hill) Ltd v Leibovici* (1977); see also *Hart v AR Marshall & Sons (Bulwell) Ltd* (1977).

**6.12** The EAT has returned more recently to the question of frustration of the employment contract by illness. In *Williams v Watsons Luxury Coaches Ltd* (1990) reviewed the case law and said that, in addition, two further factors should be added: the terms of the contract governing the provisions for sick pay and a consideration of the prospects for the employee's recovery. They made it clear that tribunals should be reluctant to decide that a contract of employment has been frustrated by an employee's illness and that the party alleging frustration should not be allowed to rely upon the frustrating event if that event was caused by the fault of that party. In *Collins v Secretary of State for Trade and Industry* (EAT 1460/99) the EAT held that a contract was frustrated as a result of long-term illness, even though both parties regarded the contract as continuing throughout the illness. When the employers subsequently became insolvent, the Secretary of State rejected his claim for a payment from the National Insurance Fund. The EAT upheld the tribunal's decision that, because of the frustration of his contract, he was not entitled to a payment.

**6.13** It is clear the doctrine of frustration can in appropriate circumstances be applied to a periodic contract terminable by the employer by short notice: see *Notcutt v Universal Equipment Co (London) Ltd* (1986). The facts of that case, the employee, a skilled workman, started working for the employers in 1957 under a contract which was terminable by one week's notice and which provided that no remuneration would be paid to him when he was absent from work because of sickness. In 1983 he suffered a coronary infarct and was absent from work from then on. By July 1984, when the employers were required to give him 12 weeks' notice under what is now ERA 1996, s. 86, it had become apparent that he would never be able to work again. So the employers gave him the requisite 12 weeks' notice. The employee claimed sick pay during the period of his notice, but the county court judge dismissed his claim on the grounds that his contract had been frustrated by illness before the notice was given. The Court of Appeal upheld the decision. It is not clear, however, when the court regarded the contract as having ended. Dillon LJ seems to suggest that it was when the employee had the coronary; Sheldon J said that the latest moment when the frustration could have occurred was when the medical report was presented.

**6.14** It is not entirely clear whether the imposition of a custodial sentence upon an employee frustrates the contract or terminates it by making it impossible for the employee to perform his or her part of the contract, in view of the differences of view of the members of the Court of Appeal in *Hare v Murphy Brothers Ltd* (1974). In the later case of *FC Shepherd & Co Ltd v Jerrom* (1986) the Court of Appeal did not follow its decision in that case, which it regarded as unsatisfactory. It decided that a sentence of borstal training was an event which was not foreseen or provided for by the parties at the time of contracting and that it rendered the performance of the contract radically different from that which the parties had contemplated when they entered into it. There had been no fault or default on the part of the employers and the employee was not entitled to rely on his own default. His criminal conduct, although deliberate, had no effect on the performance of the contract: the imposition of the custodial sentence was the act of the judge. The custodial sentence did frustrate the contract of apprentice-ship in this case since the imposition of the sentence meant that there would be a break in the period of training and at the end of the period of the agreement the employee would not be so well trained as the parties had contemplated he would be. Mustill LJ expressly dealt with the question of self-induced frustration and said that, by asserting that the frustration was self-induced, the employee 'asserts that he himself had repudiated the contract: and this is something which, in my judgement, he should not be allowed to do.'

## Termination by mutual consent

**6.15** At common law, the parties are free to enter into an agreement that the contract should terminate. They may also put a clause in the contract by which the employee agrees to accept a stipulated amount in satisfaction of any claims he or she may have in the event of specified events occurring, for example the premature termination of the contract. It is also open to them to agree in advance that, if certain specified events occur (eg a fixed-term contract being brought to a premature end by the employer), the employer will pay to the employee an agreed sum in satisfaction of any claims that he or she may have. Such clauses are called 'liquidated damages clauses' or 'PILON' (pay in lieu of notice) clauses. It should be noted that it is unlikely that a court or tribunal will find that there is a genuine bilateral agreement terminating the contract in cases where an employee's statutory rights are involved.

**6.16** If the courts regard the clause as a liquidated damages clause, the amount recoverable will be as stipulated in the clause without the employee having the necessity of proving the actual loss suffered. If, however, the stipulated sum is not a genuine pre-estimate of the loss but is in the nature of a penalty intended to secure performance of the contract, then it is not recoverable and the claimant must prove what damages he or she can. The essential question for the court to decide is whether the stipulated sum is a genuine pre-estimate of the loss which is likely to flow from the breach. The principles to be used in dealing with this question are set out in the speech of Lord Dunedin in the leading case of *Dunlop Pneumatic Tyre Co Ltd v New Garage and Motor Co Ltd* (1915) (at pp. 86–88: see para. 3.101 above). See also the remarks of Lopes LJ in *Law v Local Board of Redditch* (1892) (at p. 132), and *Neil v Strathclyde Regional Council* (1984), all set out in para. 3.102.

**6.17** If the clause is treated as a liquidated damages clause, the sum stipulated will be recoverable. The employee may not disregard the sum and prove that he or she has suffered greater damages, nor may the employer prove that the employee has suffered less: see *Diestal v Stevenson* (1906) and *Cellulose Acetate Silk Co Ltd v Widnes Foundry Ltd* (1933). The employee may be able to recover additional damages in respect of a default which it was not within the parties' contemplation that the agreed damages should cover. If a dispute arises between the parties, it will fall to be dealt with by the County Court or the High Court: see, for example, *Gothard v Mirror Group Newspapers Ltd* (1988), in which the issue was whether the payment in lieu of notice which was agreed between the parties should be calculated on the basis of gross pay or net pay.

**6.18** A further point to note is that a termination of employment which is within the scope of an agreed damages clause will not be a wrongful dismissal. In *Rex Stewart Jeffries Parker Ginsberg Ltd v Parker* (1988), for example, the employee's contract contained a provision that the employment could be 'determined by the giving in writing of six calendar months' notice on either side or the payment of six months' salary in lieu thereof'. He was informed that he was to be made redundant in a week's time and that he would be paid six months' salary in lieu of notice in accordance with the agreement. When he set up in competition to his former employers, they sought to enforce a non-solicitation clause against him. He argued that his dismissal was in breach of contract and that the clause was unenforceable. The Court of Appeal held that his contract entitled him to be dismissed with six months' notice or six months' salary in lieu of notice and, therefore, that his dismissal was not in breach of contract. A similar conclusion was reached by the Court of Appeal in *Abrahams v Performing Right Society Ltd* (1995). The employee was employed under a contract entitling him to two years' notice of termination, or salary in lieu of notice. The employers summarily terminated his employment. The Court of Appeal held that in doing so they were acting lawfully and were effectively electing to pay money in lieu of notice under the contract.

**6.19**  PILON clauses pose considerable problems and have led to a number of cases, which usually involve careful construction of the relevant clause. See, for example, *Skilton v T&K Home Improvements Ltd* (2000), in which the Court of Appeal said that a clause which said that the employee 'may be dismissed' with immediate effect for failing to meet sales targets did not terminate or exclude the employee's right under another clauses in the contract to three months' notice or payment of salary in lieu of three month's notice. Similarly, the differences between the approach of the High Court and the Court of Appeal in *Gregory v Wallace* (1998) show how difficult this can sometimes be. It is not appropriate to examine these problems in detail but reference should be made to Upex, *The Law of Termination of Employment* (6th ed., 2001), pp. 359–362. See also *Cerberus Software Ltd v Rowley* (2001).

**6.20**  The significance of the above discussion relates to the enforceability of restrictive covenants. As was noted in Chapter 2 (see para. 3.100) an employer who breaks the contract by wrongfully dismissing an employee cannot enforce a restrictive covenant. If, however, a liquidated damages clause or PILON clause is upheld, that will mean that the employee's dismissal will not be wrongful and thus any restrictive covenant will be enforceable.

## Dismissal with notice

**6.21** Termination occurs when either party informs the other clearly and unequivocally that the contract is to end, or the circumstances are such that it is clear that termination was intended or that it can be inferred that termination was intended. The words used to terminate the contract must be capable of being construed as words of termination. The principles are the same whether the termination consists of a dismissal by the employer or a resignation by the employee.

**6.22** A notice of dismissal by the employer must be definite and explicit and must state the date of termination (or enable it to be inferred); a mere warning of impending dismissal will not be enough. Once a notice of dismissal has been given, it cannot be withdrawn by the employer without the agreement of the employee. See *Morton Sundour Fabrics Ltd v Shaw* (1967), *Riordan v War Office* (1961) and *Harris and Russell Ltd v Slingsby* (1973). In the case of a dismissal by the employer, phrases such as 'I hereby give you notice of dismissal' are clear. Problems arise, however, where there is a row between the employer and the employee and words are used in the heat of the moment. If the words used by the employer are not ambiguous or could only be interpreted as amounting to words of dismissal, then the conclusion is clear. If, on the other hand, the words used are ambiguous and it is not clear whether they do amount to words of dismissal (eg 'You're finished with me'), it is necessary to look at all the circumstances of the case, particularly the intention with which the words were spoken, and consider how a reasonable employee would, in all the circumstances have understood them. See *BG Gale Ltd v Gilbert* (1978), *Tanner v DT Kean Ltd* (1978), *Sothern v Franks Charlesley & Co* (1981) and *J & J Stern v Simpson* (1983).

**6.23** An example of the kind of problem which can occur is *Martin v Yeoman Aggregates Ltd* (1983). The employee obtained the wrong spare part for a broken-down car. There was an angry exchange between a director and the employee. He refused to collect the correct part and was dismissed by the director. A few minutes later the director realised that he had acted in anger and that he was in breach of the correct disciplinary procedure. So he told the employee he was suspended without pay for two days. The employee treated what had happened as instant dismissal. The EAT applied the test set out in *Tanner v D.T. Kean*

*Ltd* (above) and held that there had been no dismissal, saying that it was a matter of common sense, vital to industrial relations, that either an employer or an employee should be given an opportunity of recanting from words spoken in the heat of the moment. An employee may be treated as dismissed where the employer unilaterally imposes radically different terms of employment so that, on an objective construction of the employer's conduct, there is a removal or withdrawal of the old contract. This is what happened in *Alcan Extrusions v Yates* (1996), which involved the unilateral imposition of a new shift system on a group of employees. See, to similar effect, *Hogg v Dover College* (1990). The two cases are considered more fully at para. 6.57 below.

**6.24** A further requirement in the case of dismissals with notice is that, to be valid, the notice must specify the date of termination or contain material from which the date is ascertainable. If the employer utters a warning that the employee will be made redundant at some unspecified date in the future or that, if the employee does not resign, he or she will have to be dismissed at some future date, and the employee acts on that warning, finds another job and resigns, that action will be treated as a resignation only; he or she will not be treated as having been dismissed. In *Morton Sundour Fabrics Ltd v Shaw* (1967), for example, the employers told the employee that his employment would cease when the department in which he worked was closed down, but they did not specify when that would occur. The employee made arrangements to find another job, and duly gave notice. He later applied for a redundancy payment, but his claim was rejected. Widgery J said:

> As a matter of law an employer cannot dismiss his employee by saying 'I intend to dispense with your services at some time in the coming months.' In order to terminate the contract of employment the notice must either specify the date or contain material from which that date is positively ascertainable.

**6.25** In *Rai v Somerfield Stores Ltd* (2004), the EAT said that a notice which enables an employer to terminate an employee's contract of employment only if the employee does or does not perform a particular act specified in the notice which only the employee can choose whether or not to perform is not an unequivocal notice to terminate the employment. In the case in question the employee was told that if he did not return to work by a specified date his contract would be regarded as terminated. The EAT said that this did not amount to a dismissal with notice. A final point to be noted here is that a dismissal with notice may be converted into a summary dismissal if the employer dismisses the employee on the spot during his or her notice period. Such an action would amount to a wrongful dismissal. Reference should be made to paras. 3.98 – 3.99 where notice provisions and the statutory provisions relating to notice are dealt with.

## Dismissal without notice

**6.26** A dismissal without notice – usually called 'summary dismissal' – is on the face of it a breach of contract, since the employee has been denied his or her contractual entitlement to termination of the contract by notice or to the expiry of a fixed term contract. The employer's defence in such a case is that the employee had committed a repudiation of the contract sufficiently serious to justify dismissal without notice. In effect, therefore, the issue in a summary dismissal case is not whether the employee was dismissed but whether the dismissal was in breach of contract and thus 'wrongful'. This matter is considered more fully below: see para. 6.39.

## Resignation

**6.27** The requirements in the case of a resignation by an employee are very similar to those for a dismissal. It is important for employers to know whether an employee has resigned, since if they treat the employee as having resigned when that is not in fact the case, they may be held to have dismissed the employee. If the employee's resignation is prompted by a repudiatory act or breach of contract by the employer, that may be treated as a constructive dismissal by the employer: see below, para. 6.35. A resignation does not require acceptance by the employer and, if the employee wishes to change his or her mind and withdraw the resignation, the withdrawal requires the employer's agreement. Failure to give it does not amount to a constructive dismissal: see *Denham v United Glass Ltd* (EAT 581/98).

**6.28** As with dismissal, similar questions have arisen as to what amounts to a resignation, particularly where there has been a row between the employer and the employee and it is not clear from the language used whether the employee was in fact intending to resign. If the employee's words are not ambiguous (eg 'I am resigning') or, when construed, have a clear meaning, he or she will be treated as having resigned, irrespective of whether they were intended to bear that meaning, unless the words of resignation were uttered in the heat of the moment or as a result of pressure exerted by the employer. See *Sovereign House Security Services Ltd v Savage* (1989) (at p. 116). In *Kwik-Fit (GB) Ltd v Lineham* (1992) the EAT said that there may be 'special circumstances' which may make it unreasonable for an employer to assume a resignation. The EAT held (at pp. 191–192):

> Words may be spoken or actions expressed in temper or in the heat of the moment or under extreme pressure ... and indeed the intellectual make-up of an employee may be relevant ... These we refer to as 'special circumstances'. Where 'special circumstances' arise it may be unreasonable for an employer to assume a resignation and to accept it forthwith. A reasonable period of time should be allowed to lapse and if circumstances arise during that period which put the employer on notice that further inquiry is desirable to see whether that resignation was really intended and can properly be assumed, then such inquiry is ignored at the employer's risk ... Thus where words or actions are unambiguous an employer is entitled to accept the repudiation at its face value at once, unless these special circumstances exist, in which case he should allow a reasonable time to elapse during which facts may arise which cast doubt upon that prima facie interpretation of the unambiguous words or action. If he does not investigate these facts, a tribunal may hold him disentitled to assume that the words or action did amount to a resignation ...

**6.29** On the other hand, if the words used are ambiguous, it becomes necessary to look at all the circumstances of the case, and, in particular, the intention with which the words were spoken, and to consider how a reasonable employer would, in all the circumstances, have understood the employee's words: see *Sothern v Franks Charlesly & Co* (1981) and *J & J Stern v Simpson* (1983); see also *Tanner v DT Kean* (1978), *Barclay v City of Glasgow District Council* (1983) and *Sovereign House Security*

*Services Ltd v Savage* (1989). The EAT suggested an approach to these kinds of cases in *Tanner v D.T. Kean Ltd* (1978).

**6.30** A resignation will be treated as a dismissal if the employee is invited to resign and it is made clear that, unless he or she does so, he or she will be dismissed: *East Sussex County Council v Walker* (1972) and *Jones v Mid Glamorgan County Council* (1997). In *Martin v Glynwed Distribution Ltd* (1983) (at p. 519) Sir John Donaldson MR said of these kinds of cases:

> ... Whatever the respective actions of the employer and the employee at the time when the contract of employment is terminated, at the end of the day the question always remains the same, 'Who really terminated the contract of employment?' If the answer is the employer, there was a dismissal within (section 95(2)(a)) ... If the answer is the employee, a further question may then arise, namely, 'Did he do so in circumstances such that he was entitled to do so without notice by reason of the employer's conduct?' ...

**6.31** See also *Caledonian Mining Co Ltd v Bassett* (1987), in which the EAT held that the employers had dismissed employees whom they had inveigled into resigning with the intention of depriving them of their statutory rights. The EAT held that the employees had been dismissed within what is now ERA 1996, s. 136(1)(a), applying Sir John Donaldson's dictum, above. There will be no dismissal, however, where the employee resigns and the employer invokes a contractual provision entitling him or her to terminate the contract early by making a payment in lieu of notice and, by doing so, brings the contract to an end before the expiry of the employee's notice: *Marshall (Cambridge) Ltd v Hamblin* (1994) .

## Resignation in breach of contract

**6.32** There are many cases where an employee resigns in breach of contract but it is not worth the employer's while to sue for the breach. There are also cases, however, where the employee is skilled and has been privy to confidential information. Here the failure to give the proper notice required by the contract may be significant. Employees of this type may often be subject to long notice periods of a year or more and may also have what are called 'garden leave' clauses in their contracts; such clauses are considered at paras. 3.95 above and 6.33, below. If such an employee leaves without giving correct notice, the employer may wish to enforce the contractual notice period so as to prevent him or her utilising skills or confidential information whilst they are still fresh. The question whether it is possible to do so then becomes of acute importance, since an employer is likely to have more extensive powers of restraint against someone who is still an employee than against an ex-employee.

**6.33** An example of this situation is the case of *Evening Standard Co Ltd v Henderson* (1987). The employee was employed as the production manager of the Standard. His contract required one year's notice of termination and provided that, while it lasted, he was not to engage in work outside the company without special permission. He was offered a similar position with a competitor newspaper and gave his employers two months' notice of termination. The employers sought an injunction to restrain him from undertaking employment with or providing assistance to any competitor of theirs in breach of his contract of employment. The Court of Appeal said that there was no serious issue as to liability, since the employee's contract would continue until the expiration of the one-year notice period, unless his employers accepted his repudiation. If, during that time, he were to work for the competitor, he would be in breach of contract. The Court went on to hold that the balance of convenience favoured the granting of an injunction.

**6.34** In *GFI Group Inc v Eaglestone* (1994), on the other hand, Holland J refused to hold an employee to his 20-week notice period, when he joined a competitor during the notice period. Instead, the judge granted an injunction to restrain him from joining the competitor for 13 out of the 20 weeks. The rationale for the decision was that two of the employee's colleagues, who were only on four weeks' notice, had already joined the competitor after the expiry of their notice.

## Constructive dismissal

**6.35** Different considerations arise where the employee's resignation is prompted by a breach of contract or repudiatory act committed by the employer. In that case, the resignation will be called a 'constructive dismissal'. It should be noted that this term has no statutory authority and is merely a convenient shorthand expression for a resignation on the part of the employee prompted by an action on the part of the employer which may be categorised as a repudiatory act or a breach of contract. In *Western Excavating (ECC) Ltd v Sharp* (1978) (at p. 226), Lord Denning MR said:

> If the employer is guilty of conduct which is a significant breach going to the root of the contract of employment, or which shows that the employer no longer intends to be bound by one or more of the essential terms of contract, then the employee is entitled to treat himself as discharged from any further performance ... [T]he conduct must ... be sufficiently serious to entitle him to leave at once ...

**6.36** In cases of constructive dismissal, the first question to ask is whether the employer's action is in breach of his or her contractual obligations or is a repudiation of them. That will involve ascertaining the express terms of the contract and considering whether any terms should be implied. Once the breach or repudiation has been established, it must be serious enough to entitle the employee to leave without notice. Further, the employee's resignation must have been caused by the breach. Finally, there will be no constructive dismissal if the employee waived the right to terminate the contract, for example by affirming the contract. So far as the first issue is concerned, reference should be made to paras. 3.59 and 3.110 where express and implied terms are considered. For a more detailed consideration of these issues, reference should be made to Upex, *The Law of Termination of Employment* (6th ed., 2002), pp. 135–145. See also the Court of Appeal's recent judgment in *Meikle v Nottinghamshire CC* (2004).

**6.37** The court or tribunal must be satisfied also that he or she has not waived the right to terminate by staying on too long after the conduct in question. Otherwise he or she may be taken to have elected to affirm the contract. See paras. 3.198–3.201 where this matter is considered in the context of variations of contract. In the event of a subsequent resignation, it will not be possible to claim constructive dismissal. In *WE Cox Toner (International) Ltd v Crook* (1981) (at pp. 828–829), Browne-Wilkinson J said:

Mere delay by itself (unaccompanied by any express or implied affirmation of the contract) does not constitute affirmation of the contract; but if it is prolonged it may be evidence of an implied affirmation. Affirmation of the contract can be implied. Thus, if the innocent party calls on the guilty party for further performance of the contract, he will normally be taken to have affirmed the contract since his conduct is only consistent with the continued existence of contractual obligation ... However, if the innocent party further performs the contract to a limited extent but at the same time makes it clear that he is reserving his right to accept the repudiation ... such further performance does not prejudice his rights subsequently to accept the repudiation.

**6.38**   The employee must also accept a repudiation unequivocally. An example of a failure to do so is *Harrison v Norwest Holst Group Administration Ltd* (1985) . The employers wrote to the employee stating that he would lose his directorship in two weeks' time. The employee responded with a letter headed 'Without Prejudice'. The employers later withdrew their threat to deprive him of his directorship, but the employee left anyway. The Court of Appeal treated the original threat as an anticipatory breach but said that the employee's letter was not sufficiently unequivocal to amount to an acceptance of the repudiation. Because the repudiation had not been accepted, the contract continued to run and, during the continued currency of the contract, it was open to the employers to withdraw their threat of breach.

## Wrongful dismissal

**6.39**   At common law, summary termination of the contract of employment by either party gives the innocent party the right to sue for breach of contract. The defendant may have a defence if the court is satisfied that the plaintiff was guilty of conduct which amounted to a serious breach of contract or to a repudiation of the contract. This principle is an extension of the general rule of contract, that if a party to a contract breaches an important term of the contract or evinces an intention no longer to be bound by one or more of its essential terms, the innocent party has a choice: he or she may either waive the breach or repudiation and choose to treat the contract as continuing or may accept the breach or repudiation and treat himself or herself as discharged from the performance of any further obligations under the contract, which is thus at an end. As a general rule, the breach or repudiation, whether by employer or employee, requires to be accepted by the other party before the contract comes to an end. This issue has been the subject of considerable discussion and debate, particularly in relation to the summary dismissal of an employee by an employer, and is considered more fully below: see paragraph 6.50.

**6.40** A contract of employment is terminable by notice, express or implied, unless the contract is for a fixed term or for the completion of a specific task or contains an exhaustive enumeration of the grounds upon which it may be terminated. If, therefore either party terminates the contract summarily, ie without notice, the other party has the right at common law to sue for breach of contract. If the defendant's summary termination of the contract was a response to an action on the part of the plaintiff, a defence may be available. But he or she must be able to show that the plaintiff's behaviour amounted to a breach of a serious term of the contract or a repudiation of the contract which entitled him or her to terminate the contract summarily. The plaintiff's breach need not have been known at the time of the summary dismissal: *Boston Deep Sea Fishing & Ice Co v Ansell* (1888) and *Cyril Leonard & Co v Simo Securities Trust Ltd* (1972).

**6.41** If the summary dismissal by the employer is not justified, the employee will be treated as having been wrongfully dismissed; if the employer's conduct causes the employee to resign and that conduct is held to be repudiatory or in breach of contract, the employee's contract will be treated as having been breached. An action for wrongful dismissal or breach of contract is heard in the County Court or High Court; the employment tribunals also now have jurisdiction in such cases where damages are claimed.

## Breach by employer

**6.42** A summary dismissal takes place where the employer fails to observe the provisions in the contract relating to notice or a fixed term of employment. This type of case effectively brings the employment to an end and in practical terms does not give the employee the opportunity of choosing whether to affirm the contract or accept the repudiation. In such a case, the employer may be able to justify the action on the grounds of the employee's breach: see below at para. 6.46. Otherwise, the question is principally one of how much the employee should receive by way of damages, since the remedies of injunction and specific performance are unlikely to be available.

**6.43** The employer may also commit a breach of an express or implied term. For a fuller discussion, see Chapter 3. In the case of an alleged breach of an implied term, the term and its breach must be established. It must then be established that the breach was sufficiently serious to be repudiatory. Finally, the employee must have accepted the repudiation. The case law, much of which has been considered in Chapter 3, shows the problems that can arise. An example is *Bliss v South East Thames Regional Health Authority* (1987), where the employers acted in a way which the Court of Appeal held to be a repudiation of the employee's contract, by requiring him to submit to a medical examination and suspending him when he refused. They held that the employer's action was in breach of contract by requiring the employee, without reasonable cause, to submit to the medical examination and, when he refused, by suspending him. That was a breach of the implied term that they would not without reasonable cause conduct themselves in a manner likely to damage or destroy the relationship of trust and confidence between employer and employee. The breach was so serious as to go to the root of the contract and to entitle the employee to treat the contract as at an end. The breach was a continuing breach until the employers lifted the suspension. After the employers withdrew the requirement and lifted the suspension, they offered to give him time to make up his mind about his future intentions and to pay him while he did so. They then tried to argue that his acceptance of his salary affirmed the contract so as to preclude him from accepting their repudiation, as he purported to do. The Court of Appeal held that he had not affirmed the contract by his conduct in accepting the salary payments and he was entitled to accept the repudiation. The Court took the view that the cardinal factor was that the employer was prepared to give the employee time to make up his mind and to pay while he was doing so. See also *Dietmann v London Borough of Brent* (1988), where the employee's acceptance of the offer of employment was held to amount to acceptance of the employer's repudiation so as to preclude her from injunctive relief. This point was made at first instance, but did not arise in the Court of Appeal.

**6.44** The employee must accept the employer's breach or repudiation unequivocally. A failure to do so may lead to the consequence that the employer withdraws the repudiation before it has been unequivocally accepted. If the employee then purports to accept the repudiation after it has been withdrawn and resigns, he or she will not succeed in an action for breach of contract. An example of this is *Harrison v Norwest Holst Group Administration Ltd* (1985). The employers wrote to the employee stating that he would lose his directorship in two weeks' time. The employee responded with a letter headed 'Without Prejudice'. The employers later withdrew their threat to deprive him of his directorship, but the employee left anyway. The Court of Appeal treated the original threat as an anticipatory breach but said that the employee's letter was not sufficiently unequivocal to amount to an acceptance of the repudiation. Because the repudiation had not been accepted, the contract continued to run and, during the continued currency of the contract, it was open to the employers to withdraw their threat of breach. See *also Lewis v Motorworld Garages Ltd* (1986) and *Shook v London Borough of Ealing* (1986).

**6.45** A problem associated with the foregoing discussion is the extent to which the employer may change the employee's job duties without committing a breach of contract. This matter has been discussed in Chapter 3. See, for example, *Cresswell v Board of Inland Revenue* (1984), which concerned the introduction of computerisation of the PAYE system within the Inland Revenue. The judge upheld this as a permissible change, despite the fact that considerable changes in the employees' jobs were entailed. In *Royle v Trafford Borough Council* (1984), on the other hand, an employee who continued to teach a class of pupils but refused to take extra pupils because of industrial action, was held to have had his breach of contract affirmed by his employers, who did not suspend or dismiss him. But, because of his imperfect performance of his contract, the judge held that there was no reason why he should receive his full salary. The Court was entitled to make a reduction from his salary representing the notional value of the services he did not render.

## Breach by employee

**6.46** A dismissal will be wrongful, if the employer dismisses the employee without giving him or her the notice he or she is entitled to, or, in the case of a fixed term contract with no notice provision, allowing him or her to see out the fixed term. In this kind of case, the employer's defence will rest upon breaches of contract alleged to have been committed by the employee. There must be a breach by the employee of the express or implied terms of the contract, and the breach must amount to a repudiation or be sufficiently fundamental: see, for example, *Laws v London Chronicle (Indicator Newspapers) Ltd* (1959) (at p. 700, Lord Evershed MR), considered at para. 3.132, above. In this context, however, the remarks of Edmund-Davies LJ in *Wilson v Racher* (1974) ( at p. 430), should be noted:

> Reported decisions provide useful, but only general guides, each case turning upon its own facts ... [A] contract of service imposes upon the parties a duty of mutual respect.

**6.47** This means that opposite conclusions may be reached on similar facts, as in *Pepper v Webb* (1969) and *Wilson v Racher* (1974) and that, whilst in one context one single, relatively minor, breach may be sufficient to justify summary dismissal, the same will not be true of other, different contexts: see, for example, *Sinclair v Neighbour* (1967). The most common instances of breaches of contract giving rise to summary dismissals are misconduct, disobedience to lawful orders and negligence. For cases involving misconduct or alleged misconduct, see *Clouston & Co Ltd v Corry* (1906), *Sinclair v Neighbour* (1967), and *Wilson v Racher* (1974). In *Laughton and Hawley v Bapp Industrial Supplies Ltd* (1986), the EAT held that an employee's expressed intention of setting up in competition with the employer was not in itself a breach of the implied duty of loyalty to the employer and did not amount to misconduct. Misconduct is sometimes given the epithet 'gross'. In *Willson v Brett* (1843), at p. 115–6, Rolfe B. said that he 'could see no difference between negligence and gross negligence – that it was the same thing, with the addition of a vituperative epithet.' For cases involving disobedience to lawful orders, see *Laws v London Chronicle (Indicator Newspapers) Ltd* (1959) and *Pepper v Webb* (1969); for cases involving negligence, see *Baster v London & County Printing Works* (1899), *Power v British India Steam Navigation Co Ltd* (1930), and *Jupiter General Insurance Co Ltd v Shroff* (1937). Negligence sometimes has the epithet 'gross' added to it but in *Dietmann v Brent London Borough Council* (1987) (at p. 748) Hodgson J. characterised this usage as unhelpful. Most of the cases mentioned here have already been considered in detail in Chapter 3.

**6.48** Although every case turns upon its own facts, a single act is less likely to justify summary dismissal than a series of actions; the quality of the breach is what counts, not the consequences flowing from it. The more serious the breach the more likely it is that it will be held to justify summary dismissal. An example of the problem of deciding what amounts to misconduct or gross misconduct is *Dietmann v London Borough of Brent* (1988). The council's disciplinary procedure provided that, in the case of more serious offences, the employees should be invited to a formal disciplinary meeting but that certain types of gross misconduct 'may lead to a recommendation to the council for instant dismissal ...' Clause 7 of the contract of employment provided: 'Any breach of disciplinary rules will render you liable to disciplinary action, which will normally include immediate suspension followed by dismissal, or instant dismissal, for offences of gross misconduct unless there are mitigating circumstances ...' 'Gross misconduct' was defined as 'misconduct of such a nature that the authority is justified in no longer tolerating the continued presence at the place of work of the employee who commits an offence of gross misconduct.' Examples of gross misconduct were given and the clause continued: 'this list is neither exclusive nor exhaustive, and in addition there may be other offences of a similar gravity which would constitute gross misconduct.' The Court of Appeal held that the Council were not entitled to dismiss her summarily without giving her a hearing under the disciplinary procedure. The correct construction of Clause 7 of her contract was that, if the alleged breach of a disciplinary rule amounted to gross misconduct, this would normally mean immediate suspension, pending the outcome of the disciplinary hearing; the hearing might result in a recommendation of either instant dismissal without notice or ordinary dismissal on proper notice. The Court rejected the employers' argument that the relevant words meant that for offences of gross misconduct, instant dismissal, not preceded by suspension, and without the need for the delay caused by a formal disciplinary hearing, was permissible. The Court of Appeal agreed with Hodgson J's view that, on the council's argument, 'the more serious the offence ... the less procedural protection the employee charged with misconduct would have': see p. 851. The Court of Appeal also upheld the judge's decision that Mrs Dietmann's admitted gross negligence did not constitute 'gross misconduct' as defined by the contract, but added that they were not prepared to say that gross negligence can never amount to gross misconduct.

**6.49**   At common law the employer is not obliged to give a reason for the dismissal, provided that grounds for dismissal exist: see *Ridgeway v Hungerford Market Co* (1835). It will be a complete defence in an action for wrongful dismissal if the employer can establish that, unknown to him or her at the time of dismissal, the employee had committed breaches of contract which, had they been known, would have justified summary dismissal: see *Boston Deep Sea Fishing and Ice Co Ltd v Ansell* (1888), approved in *Cyril Leonard & Co Ltd v Simo Securities Trust Ltd* (1972). The most likely remedy in a wrongful dismissal action is damages; the measure of damages will be the loss suffered by the employee until such time as the contract could have been lawfully terminated. Prima facie, therefore, the measure of damages will be the loss of earnings and other contractual benefits during the notice period to which the employee was entitled or for the unexpired part of a fixed-term contract. Injunctions are rarely available, except for the purpose of enforcing restrictive covenants or 'garden leave' clauses.

## Effect of breach or repudiation on the contract

**6.50**   The most likely question of the effect of a breach or repudiation on the contract of employment has given rise to considerable discussion. It has not always been clear whether a distinction should be drawn between a summary dismissal or termination, on the one hand, and breach or repudiation, on the other. It is arguable that a distinction should be made between conduct which actually terminates the contract and therefore amounts to a wrongful dismissal and conduct which amounts to a failure to observe a basic term of the employment relationship (eg a reduction by the employer of the employee's wages). In the former case, the conduct arguably terminates the contract without more. This question was left open by the House of Lords in *Rigby v Ferodo Ltd* (1988), considered at paras. 3.215 and 3.217. Lord Oliver of Aylmerton said that the question did not arise on the facts of the case. In the case of a failure to observe a basic term, the question is whether the conduct in question automatically terminates the contract or whether it gives the innocent party the choice of affirming the contract or accepting the breach as a repudiation and treating the contract as at an end.

**6.51**   A repudiation, or repudiatory breach, generally requires acceptance by the innocent party before there is a termination, but it has been argued that contracts of employment are an exception. The argument is often put on the basis that a contract of employment cannot be ordered by the courts to be performed, by means of an order of specific performance. In *Decro-Wall International S.A. v Practitioners in Marketing Ltd* (1971) (at p. 369), Salmon LJ said:

> I doubt whether a wrongful dismissal brings a contract of service to an end in law, although no doubt in practice it does. Under such a contract a servant has a right to remuneration ... in return for services. If the master, in breach of contract, refuses to employ the servant, ... the contract will not be specifically enforced ... [T]he only result is that the servant, albeit he has been prevented from rendering services by the master's breach, cannot recover remuneration under the contract because he has not earned it ... His only money claim is for damages for being wrongfully prevented from earning his remuneration.

**6.52** In the later case of *Gunton v Richmond-upon-Thames London Borough Council* (1980) (at p. 771), Buckley LJ developed this view of wrongful dismissal further. He said:

> ... [C]ases of wrongful dismissal in breach of a contract of personal service have certain special features. In the first place, as the term 'wrongful dismissal' implies, they always occur after the employment has begun and so involve an immediate breach by the master of his obligation to continue to employ the servant. Secondly, a wrongful dismissal is almost invariably repudiatory in character ... Thirdly, the servant cannot sue in debt under the contract for remuneration in respect of any period after the wrongful dismissal, because the right to receive remuneration and the obligation to render services are mutually interdependent. Fourthly, the servant must come under an immediate duty to mitigate his damages and so must almost invariably be bound to seek other employment in fulfilment of that obligation ... It follows ... that at least as soon as the servant finds, and enters into, other employment he must put it out of his power to perform any continuing obligations on his part to serve his original employer. At this stage, if not earlier, the servant must ... be taken to have accepted his wrongful dismissal as a repudiatory breach leading to a determination of the contract of service.

**6.53** In the same case, Brightman LJ said, at p. 778:

It is clear beyond argument that a wrongfully dismissed employee cannot sue for his salary or wages as such, but only for damages. It is also ... equally clear that such an employee cannot assert that he still retains his employment under the contract. If a servant is dismissed and excluded from his employment, it is absurd to suppose that he still occupies the status of a servant.

**6.54** These principles were followed in the later case of *Marsh v National Autistic Society* (1993), in which the principal of a school established by the Society was dismissed in breach of contract by them. The employee argued that, in the absence of any notice terminating his employment in accordance with his contract, the dismissal amounted to a repudiatory breach of contract, which was only capable of bringing his contract to an end if he accepted it, which he did not, and that the contract therefore remained in force until he either accepted the repudiation or was given proper notice by the Society. He sought an interlocutory injunction to restrain the Society from dismissing him or purporting to dismiss him otherwise than in accordance with the provisions of his contract of employment and an order that he should continue to be paid his remuneration. Both were refused by the judge. Ferris J reviewed the authorities quoted above, and went on to say, at p. 459:

[T]hey [ie the authorities] show ... that where ... a contract of employment has been wrongfully terminated by the employer the ordinary contractual principles relating to acceptance of repudiatory breach apply and to some extent at least the authorities show that the contract continues to subsist ... The very same authorities show, however, ... that, although it is the employer who in those circumstances is in breach of contract by having committed a repudiatory breach, the employee is not thereafter entitled to remuneration as a matter of debt.

**6.55** In the later case of *Boyo v Lambeth London Borough Council* (1994), the Court of Appeal reviewed the authorities dealing with this issue, particularly *Gunton's* case and *Sanders v Ernest A Neale Ltd* (1974). They felt constrained to follow *Gunton*, but it is clear, particularly from the judgements of Ralph Gibson and Staughton LJJ, that the majority would have preferred to decide the case unconstrained by the decision in that case. Ralph Gibson LJ's view was that a wrongful dismissal requires a real acceptance by the employee and that the court should not easily infer acceptance, as suggested by Buckley L.J.in *Gunton*: see at p. 743. Staughton L.J.'s view was that a direct repudiation, whether by employer or employee, determines a contract of employment and that, in that respect, such contracts are in a class of their own: see at p. 747. In the later case of *Cerberus Software Ltd v Rowley* (2001), Sedley LJ in his dissenting judgement supported the elective theory but his remarks were obiter. For the moment, therefore, the principle is that a wrongful dismissal requires acceptance by the employee, but that acceptance will be easily inferred. Clearly, however, this area is ripe for re-examination by the House of Lords.

**6.56** The alternative type of case is that in which the employer does not dismiss the employee but engages in actions which seek to change 'the nature of the work required to be done or the times of employment', as Shaw LJ said in *Gunton*'s case, above, at p. 459. An example of such a case is the House of Lords decision in *Rigby v Ferodo Ltd*, above. This case has been fully considered: see para. 3.215. The dispute arose from the unilateral imposition by the employers of wage reductions. The employee continued to work at the reduced rate but instituted proceedings for damages to recover the difference between the wages to which he was entitled under his contract and the wages actually paid to him by his employers. It was agreed that the employers' action amounted to a fundamental and repudiatory breach. The first point dealt with by the House of Lords was the employers' argument that the breach constituted the giving of the necessary 12 weeks' notice required under the contract to terminate the employment. The House of Lords rejected this, on the footing that it was an impossible contention on the facts of the case, since the employers were concerned to keep their workforce and never purported to give such a notice. The main argument was that contracts of employment are an exception to the general rule that an unaccepted repudiation leaves the contractual obligations of the parties unaffected and that the wrongful repudiation of the fundamental obligations of either party not only brings to an end the relationship of employer and employee but also terminates the contract immediately without the necessity of any acceptance by the party not in default. It followed, therefore, according to this argument, that the unilateral reduction in the employee's wages amounted to a termination of the contract and his sole remedy was damages limited to the shortfall from his original contractual wage over a 12-week period. Lord Oliver of Aylmerton, who gave the main speech in the House of Lords, rejected this argument and said that there was no reason why a contract of employment should be on any different footing from any other contract. He did appear, however, to make a distinction between a repudiatory breach and a wrongful dismissal. Although he was at pains to point out that the case was not one of wrongful dismissal and said that it would not be appropriate to decide that question, which, on the facts, did not arise, he did say this, at p. 34:

> Whatever may be the position under a contract of service where the repudiation takes the form either of a walk-out by the employee or of a refusal by the employer any longer to regard the employee as his servant, I know of no principle of law that any breach which the innocent party is entitled to treat as repudiatory of the other party's obligations brings the contract to an end automatically.

**6.57**  The decisions of the EAT in *Hogg v Dover College* (1990) and *Alcan Extrusions v Yates* (1996) are difficult to reconcile with this statement, however. In the first case, the employee was demoted and paid a reduced salary. The EAT held that the effect of this action was to dismiss him, despite the fact that he continued to work for the employers. In the second case, the facts were that a group of employers unilaterally imposed a variation on the employees, in circumstances which amounted to a repudiation of the contract. The employees chose not to resign but to continue to work the new terms under protest; they also complained of unfair dismissal. The EAT upheld the tribunal's decision that there had been a dismissal, taking the view that, where an employer unilaterally imposes radically different terms of employment, there is a dismissal if, on an objective construction of the relevant letters on the part of the employer, there is a withdrawal or removal of the old contract.

**6.58**  If these decisions are correct, then an employee affected by a unilateral variation could stay on and continue to work for the employer under protest but could also complain of unfair dismissal or, if appropriate, claim a redundancy payment. From a contractual point of view, however, they seem to fly in the face of Lord Oliver's statement above in suggesting that, where the employer commits a repudiatory act such that it can be said that there is a removal or withdrawal of the old contract, that contract ends automatically. If Lord Oliver's statement of the law is accepted as correct, it is possible to say that an employee who is a victim of a repudiatory act is effectively confined to a claim for damages (if the repudiation takes the form of a wrongful dismissal) or unpaid, or under-paid, wages (if the repudiation takes the form of a unilateral reduction in wages, as in *Rigby v Ferodo Ltd*). In other cases, such as a unilateral change in non-financial terms of the employee's contract, the choice is between waiving the breach and thus affirming the contract, or accepting the repudiation and resigning. In all these cases, it is highly unlikely that the court will grant injunctive relief.

**6.59** On the other hand, if the act of termination or repudiatory act is the *employee's*, there are circumstances in which, despite the impossibility of forcing the employee to work in accordance with the contract, nevertheless the court is prepared to treat the contract as subsisting for the purposes of restraining him or her from committing breaches of the contract. The breaches in question are often breaches of a clause in the contract governing competition or the use of confidential information and the like. In *Thomas Marshall (Exports) Ltd v Guinle* (1978), for example, the employee purported to resign when his fixed-term contract still had 4 years to run. The contract had clauses in it dealing with competition and the use of confidential information. Megarry V-C. held that the employee's wrongful termination of the contract required acceptance by the employer and did not automatically terminate it. He accepted that the court was powerless to compel the employee to continue to work in accordance with his contract, but said that his repudiation did not release him from his obligations. These were more extensive than they would have been had the repudiation been treated as effective to terminate the contract and had the employee been in the position of an ex-employee. The injunctions sought against the employee in this case were to restrain solicitation of the employer's customers and to restrain the disclosure or use of confidential information.

**6.60** This may be contrasted with the more recent case of *Evening Standard Co Ltd v Henderson* (1987), which was considered earlier in the chapter. The employee was obliged to give one year's notice of termination, but purported to give two months' notice. There was a clause in his contract to the effect that, during its duration, he was not to engage in work outside the company without special permission. His purpose in giving shorter notice than he was obliged to was to enable him to accept a position on a rival newspaper which would be in competition with his employer's newspaper. In this case, the injunctions sought were to restrain him from undertaking or continuing employment with any competitor of the employers and from disclosing confidential information relating to them for the duration of the contractual notice period. The employers gave an undertaking to the trial judge to continue to pay the employee's salary until his contract lawfully expired but without requiring him to continue working for them, although in fact they were also willing to allow him to continue working for them. In those circumstances, the Court of Appeal granted the injunctions sought, on the footing that the employee would not be forced to work for the employers or be reduced to a condition of starvation or idleness.

**6.61** Although there are perceptible differences between the two cases, the important point about both, at least for present purposes, is that the courts held that there are circumstances in which, and purposes for which, an employer may be allowed to refuse to accept a repudiation. In the Evening Standard case, however, Lawton LJ stressed that the hearing of an interlocutory appeal is not the time to examine these issues in depth.

## Further reading

Deakin, S, & Morris, G, *Labour Law* (3rd ed, 2001) Butterworths (chapters 4 & 5).

Smith, I, & Thomas, G, *Industrial Law* (8th ed, 2003) Butterworths (chapter 7).

Upex, R, *The Law on Termination of Employment* (6th ed) Jordans 2001.

### Article

Brodie, D, (1998) 'Beyond exchange: the new contract of employment', *Industrial Law Journal*, Vol. 27, No. 2, June, pp. 79–102.

## Self-test questions

1.  Arnold, Bruce and Clive work for Kings Ltd, which is in financial difficulties.

    A cheque for £1000 has been fraudently cashed by an employee of the company, and Mr P the managing director believes the employee to have been Arnold. When confronted by Mr P, Arnold denies the offence, but Mr P is convinced that only Arnold would have been in a position to do such a thing and dismisses him without consulting the other directors. Bruce, who is a senior foreman and has worked for the company's headquarters where he has always worked, is told that he will be moved to a small factory some ten miles distant. When Bruce refuses to move, he too is dismissed. Clive is told that in order to effect economies, the company will not be giving him his annual pay rise to which he is contractually entitled. Clive remonstrates and two days later hands in his notice.

    Advise Arnold, Bruce and Clive.

2.  'The right to wrongful dismissal is no longer relevant in the twenty-first century'. Discuss.

3.  Assess the impact of the term relating to mutual trust and confidence (see Chapter 3) on the termination of employment, with particular reference to remedies.

4.  Colin alleges that he is being harassed at work by his line manger, Marlene. He has reported this to Marlene's manager, Bob. Bob has ignored Colin's grievance. Colin has complained to the managing Director, Linda, who has told Colin to 'grow up'. Marlene continues to harass Colin.

    Advise Colin.

# CHAPTER SEVEN

# Unfair Dismissal

## Summary

One of the rights which arise when an employee is dismissed is the statutory right not to be unfairly dismissed. This chapter considers that right. The key points are:

- the general rules of unfair dismissal applying to employees who have been continuously employed for one year; and

- certain types of dismissal for which there are special rules and which often do not have a requirement of a minimum period of employment.

Overall, this statutory right provides a floor of protection for employees, but is it adequate?

**7.1** Until the introduction of the right not to be unfairly dismissed in 1972, employees enjoyed limited statutory protection. Indeed, until the Contracts of Employment Act 1963 (now transformed into Part 1 of the Employment Rights Act 1996), employees had no statutory rights at all. The Redundancy Payments Act 1965 was the first attempt to provide a floor of rights and gave rise to a large volume of case-law on the meaning of 'redundancy' but, looking back at it from the perspective of 2004, one can say that the level of protection it offered was limited. So it is fair to say that the introduction of the right not to be unfairly dismissed by the Industrial Relations Act 1971 – the only part of that controversial piece of legislation to survive – represents a significant advance for the rights of employees. The basic structure of the original legislation has been retained over the years of its life, albeit that there have been numerous additions and alterations. The qualifying length of employment has fluctuated according to political fashion, ranging from two years at the height of the Conservative era to 6 months during the life of the Labour Government in the 1970's; the limitation period for presenting claims was originally one month and is now three. But what we have in 2004 is still recognisable as the creature which struggled to life in 1972.

**7.2**  As was mentioned in Chapter 6, those who are dismissed are likely to have two basic types of claim: a wrongful dismissal claim, in other words a claim that they have been dismissed in breach of contract, or a claim that they have been dismissed in breach of their statutory rights. The latter type of claim will either be an unfair dismissal claim – considered in this chapter – or a claim for a redundancy payment, considered in Chapter 7. In general, an employee who is dismissed by reason of redundancy is better advised to complain of unfair dismissal rather than to claim a redundancy payment, since he or she stands to be awarded a higher level of compensation if the claim is successful. Pure redundancy payments claims are for this reason fairly uncommon.

**7.3**  Potential claimants must fulfil certain requirements before being able to make a complaint of unfair dismissal. These are:

1.  they must be an employee;

2.  they must have been 'continuously employed' for one year;

3.  they should not be in one of the excluded classes;

4.  they must present their complaint of unfair dismissal within three months of the 'effective date of termination'; and

5.  they must have been 'dismissed'.

**7.4**  If the special rules apply, the requirement of one year's continuity of employment does not apply; nor does the rule that an employee must be under the age of 65. So, for an example, an employee claiming to have been dismissed for reasons related to trade union membership may be over 65 and may only have been continuously employed for three months. In the case of a dismissal to which the general rules apply, where the employee qualifies for the right and has been dismissed, the two main questions are (1) what was the reason for the dismissal, and (2) whether the employer followed a fair procedure when deciding to dismiss. It is fair to say that in most cases of unfair dismissal, the main issue is whether the employer acted fairly.

## Qualifications

### Status of the claimant

**7.5** ERA 1996, s 94(1) provides that an employee has the right not to be unfairly dismissed by his or her employer. This right is made subject to other provisions of the ERA 1996, such as the provision excluding those who have reached 'normal retiring age' or who are over 65: see s 109(1). Thus, the right not to be unfairly dismissed only extends to employees; it is not available to those who are self-employed. The distinction between employees and self-employed persons was examined in Chapter 3, to which reference should be made.

### Excluded categories

**7.6** The following categories of employee are excluded from the legislation:

1. employees employed under illegal contracts;

2. those covered by diplomatic or state immunity;

3. employees of international organisations or the Commonwealth Secretariat;

4. Crown employees;

5. parliamentary staff;

6. employees over retirement age;

7. short-term and casual employees;

8. employees affected by national security;

9.   share fishermen; and

10.  those in police service and members of the armed forces.

**7.7**  It is not intended to go into most of these categories in any detail. Reference should be made to Upex, *The Law of Termination of Employment* (6th ed, 2001), pp. 29–48. Illegal contracts have already been considered in Chapter 3. The only category to be considered here is those over retirement age. The relevant provision governing the exclusion from the unfair dismissal right of employees over retirement age is section 109. Employees are excluded from the right not to be unfairly dismissed if they satisfy one of two conditions: either they have reached the 'normal retiring age' for an employee holding that position in that undertaking or, if there was no normal retiring age, the age of sixty-five. This exclusion to employees dismissed, or selected for dismissal for redundancy, for certain types of what are called 'inadmissible reasons'. These are set out in para. 7.108 below.

**7.8**  In *Nothman v Barnet London Borough Council* (1979) the House of Lords held, by a majority, that s 109(1) 'sets up only one barrier to be overcome by the class of employee whose conditions of employment specify a normal retiring age, and another and entirely different barrier to be overcome by the class of employee whose conditions of employment specify no retiring age.' So it is necessary to decide first whether there is a normal retiring age; if there is, the second barrier will not apply; if, on the other hand, there is no normal retiring age, the second barrier will then operate.

**7.9**  In *Waite v Government Communications HQ* (1983) the House of Lords said that the phrase 'normal retiring age' means the retiring age laid down in the terms and conditions upon which the employee was employed ('the contractual retiring age'). The presumption that the contractual retiring age is the normal retiring age may be displaced by evidence that there is in practice some higher age at which employees holding the position are regularly retired, and which they have reasonably come to regard as their normal retiring age. This test was applied in *Hughes and Coy v Department of Health and Social Security* (1985), in the context of retirement policy in the civil service. When the employees in question were recruited, the policy was to allow them to remain until 65, subject to continued efficiency. This policy was changed in 1981, when both employees were over 60. They were both compulsorily retired in accordance with the policy. The House of Lords rejected their claims to present complaints to the employment tribunal. Applying the Waite test, Lord Diplock said that the presumption that the contractual retiring age is the normal retiring age is rebutted only as long as the policy in question remains in force. See also *Brooks v British Telecommunications plc* (1992) and *Barclays Bank plc v O'Brien*, in which the Court of Appeal reviewed the authorities. In *Wall v British Compressed Air Society* (2004), the Court of Appeal applied the decision in Waite and said that an employee who holds a unique position can have a normal retirement age and, if he or she has a contractual retirement age that is the normal retiring age. The word 'normal' in s 109(1)(a) does not require the existence of one or more comparators.

**7.10** A further question is whether the normal retiring age may be below the contractual retiring age. In *Bratko v Beloit Walmsley Ltd* (1996) the EAT said that the employer cannot reduce the normal retiring age below the contractual age of retirement, without going through the normal steps necessary to change a contractual term. They said that the decision of the House of Lords in *Waite's* case contemplates only the possibility of a normal retiring age higher than the contractual retiring age, and not lower. An employee who is taken on after the age of 65 may be held to have a normal retiring age which is later than 65, but it remains necessary to look at the terms of the contract. The fact that an employee is taken on when over 65 does not mean that there must be implied a later retiring age: see *Dixon v London Production Tools Ltd and Phildon Instrumentation (London) Ltd* (1980).

## Continuity of employment

**7.11** Continuity of employment is important in the present context because the statutory rights considered in this and the next chapter are available only to employees who have been 'continuously employed' for the requisite period of time. In the case of the unfair dismissal rights, that period is one year: see ERA 1996, s 108(1), as amended by the Unfair Dismissal and Statement of Reasons for Dismissal (Variation of Qualifying Period) Order 1999 (SI 1999/1436). Continuity of employment is also used to compute the amount of a redundancy payment and of a basic award of compensation for unfair dismissal.

**7.12** The main rules for determining continuity are in sections 210 to 219. It should be noted that any week during which the employee has a contract of employment with the employer counts towards the period of continuous employment, irrespective of his or her weekly hours of work. Continuity of employment involves two elements: first, the existence of a continuous (ie unbroken) relationship between employer and employee; and secondly, an unbroken relationship which lasts the requisite length of time. The length of the employee's period of employment is normally computed in months and years, but if a question arises as to whether continuity has been broken, the employment must be looked at week by week in accordance with the statutory provisions: ERA 1996, s 219(3).

**7.13** The date at which the employee must have the minimum period of employment is the 'effective date of termination', defined by ERA 1996, s 97 as either the date when the notice given to the employee expires or, in the case of a summary dismissal, the date of the summary dismissal. The starting date for the calculation is the day on which he or she started work: ERA 1996 s 211(1). That means the day on which the employment under the contract began, not the day on which the employee started to perform the duties: see *General of the Salvation Army v Dewsbury* (1984).

**7.14** The effect of these rules is that the tribunal should decide the starting-date of the employment and the effective date of termination. If the effective date of termination is less than one year after the starting-date, the employee will have insufficient continuity. Thus, an employee whose contract starts on September 1 2003 and whose effective date of termination is August 26 2004 will not qualify for the right not to be unfairly dismissed. The provisions of sections 97(2) and 145(5) should be noted in this context, however. Their effect is to postpone the effective date or termination or relevant date in cases where the employer gives less notice than the employee is entitled to under section 86. The effect is that, if an employee on the verge of qualifying for the statutory rights is dismissed summarily, the effective date of termination or relevant date may be extended by one week, which may be sufficient to carry him or her over the threshold of the qualifying period. The one-year qualifying period does not apply, however, to the same groups of employees as were mentioned at para. 7.7 above.

**7.15** Provided that the employee is employed by the same employer, continuity of employment is not affected by the fact that he or she may have a number of consecutive contracts of employment with that employer involving different types of work or different terms of working in different places: see *Re Mack Trucks (Britain) Ltd* (1967), *Wood v York City Council* (1978) and *Bradford Metropolitan District Council v Dawson* (1999).

**7.16** Sections 210 to 219 set out the rules for determining whether a week counts. The general rule is that a week which does not count under these provisions will break continuity: ERA 1996, s 210(4). If continuity is broken, the employee's period of previous employment will be destroyed, and the qualification process will have to start all over again. There are, however, specific provisions which prevent this result occurring, particularly in the case of strikes and lockouts: see para. 7.30, below. If a period (a week or longer) does not count but does not break continuity (eg because the employee is on strike during that period), the beginning of the period of continuous employment will be treated as postponed by the length of the period which does not count; thus a month's strike will mean that the start of continuous employment will be taken to have been a month later: ERA 1996, s 211(3).

**7.17** The following weeks count: (1) weeks 'during the whole or part of which an employee's relations with his employer are governed by a contract of employment'; and (2) weeks in which the employee is absent from work for certain specified reasons: see ss 212(1) and 210(4) and para. 7.18 below. Employees who are absent may be covered either by section 212(1) or (3). Section 212(1) protects them during absence on holiday, for example, since their relations with their employer during their absence remain governed by a contract of employment. The weeks of absence will count under ERA 1996, s 212(1).

**7.18** The question is when section 212(3) applies. A week of absence only counts under this provision if it is caused by the events specified in that paragraph and the employee's relations with the employer are not governed by a contract of employment. The events are: (1) absence because of sickness or injury; (2) absence on account of a temporary cessation of work; and (3) absence 'in circumstances such that by arrangement or custom, (the employee) is regarded as continuing in the employment of his employer for all or any purposes'. It is important to bear in mind that the employee's absence, and the fact that the contract may cease during the absence, will not break continuity, provided that the absence is covered by section 212(3).

**7.19** The first situation, which falls within ERA 1996, s 212(3)(a), arises where the employee is incapable of work in consequence of sickness or injury, but only if the employee's relations with the employer are not governed by a contract of employment. The employee will be covered by section 212(1) if the contract continues during his or her absence, though there may come a stage when the illness causes the contract to be frustrated. An employee off sick for a long time may at some stage be dismissed, in which case both section 212(1) and (3)(a) would apply. But section 212(3)(a) only applies to absence for up to 26 weeks by virtue of ERA 1996, s 212(4). After that, continuity is broken. Although the dismissal need not be expressly because of sickness or injury, there must be some causal connection between the two: see *Scarlett v Godfrey Abbott Group Ltd* (1978), *Green v Wavertree Heating and Plumbing Co Ltd* (1978) and *Pearson v Kent County Council* (1993).

**7.20** The second situation, where the employee is absent from work on account of a temporary cessation of work, falls within ERA 1996, s 212(3)(b). The three main questions which arise here are: (a) whether there is a cessation of work; (b) whether the cessation is temporary; and (c) whether the employee is absent on account of that temporary cessation. See *Bentley Engineering Co Ltd v Crown and Miller* (1976).

**7.21** The House of Lords held, in *Fitzgerald v Hall, Russell & Co Ltd* (1970), that the phrase 'cessation of work' means a cessation of work for the employee to do, because there is no longer any work for him or her to do; it is not necessary that the employer should cease operations in the factory or the section of it in which the employee works. On the other hand, the provisions of s 212(3)(b) will not apply in situations such as those where an employee is a member of a pool of workers amongst whom the employer distributes work and is not allocated work for some time, the work being given to another member of the pool: see *Byrne v Birmingham City District Council* (1987) and *Letheby & Christopher Ltd v Bond* (1988).

**7.22** Arguably, the best approach to questions of this sort is to treat an employee's absence from work, whether caused by resignation or dismissal, as a cessation of work, so that the only question which then arises is whether the absence was temporary, looking at the matter with hindsight. The reported cases have not followed this simple approach, however. It has been held, for example, that an employee who leaves voluntarily and then returns, or is dismissed and then re-engaged, may not fall within section 212(3)(b): see *Bunt v Fishlow Products Ltd* (1970). In *Roach v CSB (Moulds) Ltd* (1991) the EAT decided that there was insufficient continuity of employment in the case of an employee who was dismissed by his employers, went to work for another employer for about 12 days, and then returned to his previous employers at a lower grade for some seven months before being finally dismissed by them. See also *Ryan v Shipboard Maintenance Ltd* (1980). On the other hand, it has been held that an employee who takes another job during the period of cessation may still be within section 212(3)(b), but the job must clearly be a stop-gap: see *Thompson v Bristol Channel Ship Repairers and Engineers Ltd* (1970). Absence caused by a resignation or by a dismissal regarded as permanent (for example, because the dismissal followed a row between employer and employee) has also been held not to count. It is difficult to see why such absences should not be regarded as temporary. It should be noted that an employee who works for the same employer in two successive weeks but with a gap between the two periods of work, for example because he or she resigned to go to work for another employer but then left and was re-engaged by the previous employer, will be held to fall within section 212(1): see *Carrington v Harwich Dock Co Ltd* (1998) and *Sweeney v J & S Henderson (Concessions) Ltd* (1999).

**7.23** The cessation of work must also be temporary, a question which must be determined with hindsight, looking retrospectively at the circumstances of the absence from work. In doing so, the whole period of employment is relevant. Evidence of the intention of the parties at the time is relevant, but absence of such evidence is not conclusive. The test is objective. The question whether a cessation of work is temporary is one of fact and degree in each case. Although there is no limit on the length of the absence, if it is lengthy the question will arise whether it is to be regarded as temporary or permanent.

**7.24** Attempts to decide whether any particular absence is or is not 'temporary' have given rise to an extensive body of cases which are not easy to reconcile with each other. The first question is what is meant by the word. In *Ford v Warwickshire County Council* (1983), Lord Diplock said: '... (T)he whole scheme of the Act appears to me to show that it is in the sense of 'transient', ie lasting only for a relatively short time, that the word 'temporary' is used (in section 212(3)(b)) ...' Subsequently, the use of the word 'transient' has been deprecated and judges have preferred the phrase 'lasting only for a relatively short time': see Woolf LJ in *Flack v Kodak Ltd* (1986) and *Sillars v Charrington Fuels Ltd* (1989). What is a short time in one employment is not necessarily a short time in another employment. The whole matter is one of relativity.

**7.25** The problems posed by section 212(3)(b) have led to two basic approaches: the 'mathematical' approach and the 'broad' approach. The first approach concentrates on comparing the length of the periods of employment with the length of the intervening gaps. The second approach involves looking at all the circumstances over the whole period of employment (including the intentions of the parties) to see whether the break in question is a temporary cessation. The decisions of the Court of Appeal mentioned above suggest that the mathematical approach is appropriate where there is a regular seasonal pattern of employment and non-employment and that the broad approach is preferable where the pattern of work is irregular. In this respect the two Court of Appeal decisions may usefully be contrasted with each other. The essential difference between the two approaches is that the mathematical approach is objective in its concentration upon comparing the periods during which the employee was in work and out of work. Because the broad approach, on the other hand, enables the tribunal to look at all the factors, including the intention of the parties, it gives far greater flexibility.

**7.26** The third situation is catered for by ERA 1996, s 212(3)(c), where the employee is 'absent from work in circumstances such that, by arrangement or custom, he is regarded as continuing in the employment of his employer for all or any purposes.' It is necessary to establish both that there existed an arrangement or custom and that, by virtue of that arrangement or custom, the employee was regarded as continuing in the employment of the employer for all or any purposes; these should be regarded as strict requirements which cannot be made retrospectively: see *Wishart v National Coal Board* (1974), *Lane v Wolverhampton Die Testing Ltd* (1967) and *Rhodes v Pontins Ltd* (1971). But an agreement to reinstate a dismissed employee and, on reinstatement, to preserve accrued continuity appears to satisfy section 212(3)(c): see *Ingram v Foxon* (1984). In *Curr v Marks and Spencer plc* (2003), the Court of Appeal said that it cannot be said that an employee is regarded as 'continuing in the employment' where she participates in a child break scheme by which she is required to resign with the option of re-employment at the end of the child break. They said that the arrangement in question could not be said to be one by which both parties regarded her as continuing in the employment of the employer for any purpose during the weeks of the child break.

**7.27** In *Lloyds Bank Ltd v Secretary of State for Employment* (1979), the EAT held that ERA 1996, s 212(3)(c) covered an employee who worked on a 'week on, week off' basis, and said that the weeks when the employee did not work and was not required to work were periods not governed by her contract, and that, accordingly, she was absent by arrangement within section 212(3)(c). In the later case of *Corton House Ltd v Skipper* (1981), the EAT took the view that 'absent from work' has two possible meanings: either simply not working or not at the work-place, or absent from work when under the contract the employee should normally be present. Slynn J. (as he then was) favoured the latter interpretation, on the basis of which section 212(3)(c) would not have been satisfied since the employee was not required to be there. Even if the former meaning were applied, as Slynn J. felt bound to, in view of the Lloyds Bank case, the provision would still have applied, since no special custom or arrangement had been established.

**7.28** Arguably, however, the better way of interpreting section 212(3)(c) is that it only applies where an employee has no contract (where the contractual relationship has ceased temporarily or permanently) between two periods during which he or she works full-time under a contract of employment. It should not be used to protect employees whose hours fluctuate, nor should it be used as a safety net provision to catch hours of work, or periods of employment, which cannot be accommodated within the other paragraphs of Part XIV, Chapter 1 of the 1996 Act. This view is supported by some of the dicta of the House of Lords in *Ford v Warwickshire County Council*, above, albeit in the context of section 212(3)(b). If it is correct, the cases discussed above should be regarded as wrongly decided.

**7.29** In *Letheby & Christopher Ltd v Bond* (1988), the EAT refused to apply the provisions of section 212(3)(c) to a casual worker who was absent from work for a week when she was on holiday. They said that the tribunal should have asked whether, when the absence took place, the parties regarded the employment as continuing. Since she was employed under single separate contracts, it was not possible to say that her employment was continuing after the cessation of the previous contract. A similar conclusion was reached in the later case of *Booth v United States of America* (1999). The employees worked under a series of fixed-term contracts, which in total exceeded the qualifying period of employment, but between each contract there was a gap of two weeks. At the end of the two-week gap the employees were re-engaged. The EAT upheld the tribunals' decisions that the employees were not protected by section 212(3)(c) as there was no arrangement.

**7.30** Special rules operate for weeks during all or part of which an employee takes part in a strike or is absent from work because of a lockout by the employer. The two most important are: (1) the week will not count but the employee's continuity will not be broken; and (2) the beginning of the employee's period of continuous employment will be postponed by the amount of time the dispute lasts; ie a dispute lasting two months will cause the starting date of the period of continuous employment to be treated as two months later than it actually was: see ERA 1996, s 216(1)–(3). It is immaterial whether the strike is unlawful (ie without proper strike notice), unconstitutional (in breach of a procedure agreement) or unofficial (not given official union backing). A period of time after the end of the strike but before an employee returns to work will probably be treated as a 'temporary cessation of work' and covered by section 212(3)(b): see *Clarke Chapman-John Thompson Ltd v Walters* (1972). Employees laid off because of a strike or lockout at another plant will probably also be covered by section 212(3)(b).

*Claims out of time*

**7.31** An employee will lose the right to complain of unfair dismissal if the complaint is presented out of time. ERA 1996, s 111(2) provides that an employment tribunal may not consider a complaint of unfair dismissal unless it is presented to the tribunal within three months of the 'effective date of termination' or such further period as the tribunal considers reasonable in a case where it is satisfied that it was not reasonably practicable for the complaint to be presented within three months. This provision goes to the tribunal's jurisdiction. This means that the tribunal cannot hear the complaint unless it has considered as a preliminary issue whether to allow the complaint to proceed: see *Porter v Bandridge Ltd* (1978).

**7.32**  The main question for the tribunal to consider in a case of this kind is whether it was reasonably practicable for the complaint to be presented within three months of the effective date of termination. If it concludes that it was reasonably practicable, the tribunal must go on to consider within what period it was reasonable for the complaint to have been presented. The approach of the Court of Appeal in *Dedman v British Building & Engineering Appliances Ltd* (1974) is still followed, although that case was decided under provisions whose relevant wording was 'practicable', and in the context of a 28-day limitation period. This approach has been affirmed in subsequent Court of Appeal decisions, and it has been stressed that employment tribunals should be fairly strict in enforcing the time limits and that questions of reasonable practicability are questions of fact: see *Wall's Meat Co Ltd v Khan* (1979). In *Palmer v Southend-on-Sea Borough Council* (1984), May LJ said that 'reasonably practicable' means more than what is reasonably capable physically of being done and that to construe the words as 'reasonable' would be to take a view too favourable to the employee. He also emphasised that, since the issue is pre-eminently one of fact, the EAT and the Court of Appeal should be slow to interfere with the employment tribunal's decision. See *Consigna plc v Sealy* (2002), which considered this issue in relation to a complaint delayed in the post.

**7.33**  The decision that it was not reasonably practicable for a complaint to be presented within the time limit is not the end of the matter. The tribunal must go on to decide upon the period within which it was reasonable to present the complaint. In *James W. Cook & Co (Wivenhoe) Ltd v Tipper* (1990), for example, which involved employees who delayed making applications because they were led to believe that work would pick up, the Court of Appeal took the view that it would not be right to fix a date earlier than two weeks after the expiry of the limitation period as the date when the employees should have realised that hope has gone; they then allowed a further two weeks after that as a reasonable period within which to make an application. Two employees, whose complaints were presented outside that period, had their complaints dismissed for want of jurisdiction. In *Schultz v Esso Petroleum Co Ltd* (1999) the Court of Appeal reversed the tribunal's decision that a complaint presented almost six months out of time was time-barred. This is a surprisingly long time outside the time limit, but the explanation for the Court of Appeal's decision probably lies in the unusual facts of the case.

**7.34** The conclusion to be drawn from the above cases is that, in general, a tribunal should be careful about extending the time for presenting a complaint much beyond a month, except in exceptional circumstances. Clearly, too, the longer the period that elapses after the expiry of the limitation period, the less likely becomes an extension of time.

## Dismissal

**7.35** It is fundamental to a complaint of unfair dismissal or a claim for a redundancy payment that the employee should have been dismissed. Unless the tribunal is satisfied that there has been a dismissal, the case will fail. In the case of unfair dismissal complaints, ERA 1996, s 95 1996 contains the definition of dismissal; the statutory provision is exhaustive. The combined effect of the statutory provisions and judicial interpretations of them is that some situations clearly fall within them, for example, an actual dismissal; some situations are deemed to be a dismissal, for example, a resignation prompted by a repudiatory breach on the employer's part or the expiry of a fixed-term contract. Some situations (for example, a frustrating event or a voluntary resignation unprompted by action on the employer's part) are outside the definition.

**7.36** It is important when determining whether an action falls within the definition of dismissal to start with the statutory language and then to examine the relevant judicial decisions. This is different from the common law position involving wrongful dismissal, to which the statutory definition does not apply. It is also important to bear in mind that an event which is treated as a dismissal by the statute may not be a dismissal at common law. For example, the expiry of a fixed-term contract is expressly treated as a dismissal by ERA 1996, s 95(2)(b). At common law, however, it will not amount to a dismissal.

**7.37** The basic statutory definition of dismissal in ERA 1996, s 95(1) is as follows:

> ... an employee is dismissed by his employer if (and ... only if)–
>
> (a) the contract under which he is employed is terminated by the employer (whether with or without notice),
>
> (b) he is employed under a contract for a fixed term and that term expires without being renewed under the same contract, or
>
> (c) the employee terminates the contract under which he is employed (with or without notice) in circumstances such that he is entitled to terminate it without notice by reason of the employer's conduct.

**7.38** The statutory definition set out above is the basic definition used in both the unfair dismissal and (with a slight difference of wording) the redundancy payments provisions in the Employment Rights Act 1996. The third type of dismissal in the definition is usually called a 'constructive dismissal', but that is not a term to be found in the legislation. For a discussion of the first and third concepts – actual and 'constructive' dismissals – reference should be made to Chapter 6, where they are examined.

## Reason for dismissal

**7.39** Once it has been established that the employee has been dismissed, an unfair dismissal claim will fall to be decided in two stages. The first stage consists of establishing what was the reason for the dismissal; at the second stage the tribunal must be satisfied that the employer acted reasonably in dismissing for the given reason.

**7.40** Reasons may be divided into two categories: (1) what may be called 'potentially fair' reasons; and (2) reasons which, subject to certain exceptions, make a dismissal automatically unfair (eg dismissals for reasons relating to trade union membership or activities, or relating to leave for family reasons). The second category is discussed in later in this chapter: see para. 7.108. Where a dismissal falls within that category, it will be automatically unfair.

**7.41** The 'potentially fair' reasons are so called because they can potentially justify dismissal, but they do not necessarily justify dismissal, since ERA 1996, s 98(4) obliges the tribunal to decide whether the employer acted reasonably or unreasonably in treating the reasons as sufficient for dismissing the employee. In a complaint of unfair dismissal involving the potentially fair reasons, ERA 1996, s 98(1) places the burden on the employer to show the reason (or, if there was more than one, the principal reason) for the dismissal. He or she must then show that the reason falls within one of the five specific categories set out in s 98(2) and (1)(b). These are set out below: see para. 7.49.

**7.42** As part of the process of establishing the reason for the dismissal ERA 1996, s 92 entitles an employee to be given a written statement of reasons for the dismissal by the employer. This right is considered first, after which the 'potentially fair' reasons will be considered.

## Written statement of reasons under ERA 1996 s 92

**7.43** ERA 1996 s 92 gives to a dismissed employee the right to be given a written statement giving particulars of the reasons for the dismissal by his or her employer. The employee's entitlement is to be provided with a written statement giving particulars of the reasons for the dismissal. But the employee must first ask for the written statement, which should be given by the employer within 14 days of the employee's request. In addition, an employee who is dismissed, either while she is pregnant, or after childbirth in circumstances in which her ordinary or additional maternity leave period ends by reason of her dismissal, will be entitled to be provided with a written statement. The entitlement is irrespective of length of employment and does not depend upon the employee first making a request: see ERA 1996, s 92(4), as amended.

**7.44** If the employer unreasonably fails to provide a written statement in either of the cases set out in the preceding paragraph or provides one containing inadequate or untrue particulars, the employee may present a complaint to the employment tribunal within three months of the date of termination: s 93. If the tribunal finds the complaint well-founded, it may make a declaration as to what it finds to have been the employer's reasons for dismissing the employee; it must also award the employee two weeks' pay: s 93(2).

**7.45** The EAT has held that ERA 1996, s 93 should be rigidly construed and that there should be clear evidence that there has been an unreasonable failure: see *Charles Lang & Sons Ltd v Aubrey* (1978). A failure cannot be said to be unreasonable where it is based upon a conscientious belief that there has been no dismissal: *Brown v Stuart Scott & Co* (1981). A statement of reasons is not untrue if the employer genuinely believes that the reason given is the reason for the dismissal. It is not necessary for the employment tribunal to embark upon a consideration of whether the reason was good or bad: see *Harvard Securities plc v Younghusband* (1990).

**7.46** It is not enough merely to rely upon the answer put in to the employee's original application; the statute clearly contemplates an independent and separate document: see *Rowan v Machinery Installations (South Wales) Ltd* (1981). The document must be of such a kind that the employee, or anyone to whom he or she may wish to show it, can know from reading the document itself why the employee has been dismissed, and it may refer to other documents provided that the document the employee receives contains a simple statement of the essential reasons for the dismissal: *Horsley Smith & Sherry Ltd v Dutton* (1977) and *Gilham v Kent County Council (No 1)* (1985).

**7.47** The employment tribunal may only hear complaints relating to statements issued in response to an employee's request; if the employer voluntarily gives a written statement, the employee will not be able to complain about it unless the employer refers to it and effectively adopts it in response to the employee's request. See *Catherine Haigh Harlequin Hair Design v Seed* (1990) and *Marchant v Earley Town Council*, above.

**7.48** Written statements are admissible in evidence in any proceedings, by virtue of ERA 1996, s 92(5). If the employer gives another reason in subsequent litigation, the tribunal would either ignore that other reason and hold the employer to the original statement or treat the change of reason as going to the employer's credibility.

## General rules

**7.49** In a complaint of unfair dismissal involving the so-called 'potentially fair' reasons, ERA 1996, s 98(1) places the burden on the employer not only to show the reason (or, if there was more than one, the principal reason) for the dismissal but also to show that the reason falls within one of the five categories set out in section 98(2) and (1)(b), which are: (1) capability or qualifications; (2) the employee's conduct; (3) redundancy; (4) statutory requirements; or (5) 'some other substantial reason of a kind such as to justify the dismissal of an employee holding the position which that employee held'. The burden of establishing the reason, or principal reason, for the dismissal lies upon the employer. If he or she fails to do so, the dismissal will be unfair.

**7.50** In *Abernethy v Mott, Hay and Anderson* (1974) (at p. 330), Cairns LJ said:

> A reason for the dismissal is a set of facts known to the employer, or it may be beliefs held by him, which cause him to dismiss the employee. If at the time of his dismissal the employer gives a reason for it, that is no doubt evidence, at any rate as against him, as to the real reason, but it does not necessarily constitute the real reason. He may knowingly give a reason different from the real reason out of kindness or because he might have difficulty in proving the facts which actually led him to dismiss; or he may describe his reasons wrongly through some mistake of language or of law.

**7.51** So an incorrect label will not be fatal to the employer's case. See also *Clarke v Trimoco Motor Group Ltd* (1993) and *Ely v YKK Fasteners (UK) Ltd* (1994). In this last case, the Court of Appeal said that Abernethy's case could be applied by analogy 'to enable resort to be had to a state of facts known to and relied upon by the employer, for the purpose of supplying him with a reason for dismissal, which, as a consequence of his misapprehension of the true nature of the circumstances, he was disabled from treating as such at the time.' The Court upheld the tribunal's decision that the employee's late notification to his employers that he had changed his mind about resigning could amount to 'some other substantial reason' within ERA 1996, s 98(1)(b).

**7.52** If, however, the employer relies upon one particular reason and the reason is not established, it is not possible to try to rely upon an entirely different reason either at the tribunal hearing or upon appeal, though it may, of course, be possible to apply for leave to amend the notice of appearance: see *Nelson v BBC (No 1)* (1977), in which the reason given was redundancy, but the Court of Appeal held that the tribunal was wrong in deciding that he had been dismissed for redundancy, and that the EAT was not entitled to apply the facts found to a possible but unpleaded defence of 'some other substantial reason'. An error of characterisation of the reason for the dismissal by the tribunal is an error of law, since it is a question of legal analysis to determine under which part of section 98 the reason given by the employer falls: see *Wilson v Post Office* (2000) and *Burkett v Pendletons (Sweets) Ltd* (1992). The House of Lords' decision in *Smith v Glasgow City District Council* (1987) makes it clear that an employment tribunal must be careful in making its finding as to the reason or principal reason for the dismissal.

**7.53** The House of Lords decision in *W Devis & Sons Ltd v Atkins* (1977) (applied by the EAT in *Vauxhall Motors Ltd v Ghafoor* (1993)) established the principle that an employer may not bring in evidence of what happened after the dismissal or of events which occurred before the dismissal but which did not come to his or her knowledge until afterwards. In such a case, the consequence is likely to be a decision that the employee was unfairly dismissed, but the evidence of the misconduct will be relevant to the question of remedies.

**7.54** Finally, it should be noted that ERA 1996, s 107 prevents a tribunal from taking into account any industrial pressure exerted on the employer to obtain the dismissal, when determining the reason for the dismissal: see para. 7.162, below.

## General rules: capability and qualifications

**7.55**  ERA 1996, s 98(3) defines 'capability' means 'capability assessed by reference to skill, aptitude, health or any other physical or mental quality', and 'qualifications' means 'any degree, diploma or other academic, technical or professional qualification relevant to the position which the employee held'. In *Shook v Ealing London Borough Council* (1986) the EAT stressed that under ERA 1996, s 98(2)(a) the reason for dismissal must relate to the employee's capacity and to the performance of his or her duties under the contract of employment. It is not necessary to show that the employee's incapacity (in this case disabilities caused by back trouble) would have affected the performance of all that he or she might be required to do under the contract.

**7.56**  This category of reason also embraces lack of capability. It should be viewed relatively narrowly as applying mainly to cases where the employee is incapable of satisfactory work; cases where a person has not come up to standard through his or her own carelessness, negligence or idleness, are better dealt with as cases of conduct rather than capability. The difference is between 'sheer incapability due to an inherent incapacity to function' and 'a failure to exercise to the full such talent as is possessed': see *Sutton & Gates (Luton) Ltd v Boxall* (1978). See also *James v Waltham Holy Cross Urban District Council* (1973) and *Cook v Thomas Linnell & Sons Ltd* (1977).

## General rules: conduct

**7.57**  There is no statutory definition of 'conduct'. Apart from the overlap between conduct and capability, conduct itself has been held to embrace a wide range of actions. Its scope includes gross misconduct, such as theft, violence, negligence and working in competition with the employer, and lesser matters, such as clocking offences or swearing. What may be called 'off-duty' conduct will fall within this head, if it in some way bears upon the relationship between the employer and the employee, particularly where criminal offences are involved: see *Singh v London Country Bus Services Ltd* (1976), *Nottinghamshire County Council v Bowly* (1978), *Norfolk County Council v Bernard* (1978), *Moore v C & A Modes Ltd* (1981) and *P v Nottinghamshire County Council* (1992).

## General rules: redundancy

**7.58**  The definition of 'redundancy' is considered Chapter 8, at para. 8.5.

## General rules: statutory requirements

**7.59**  ERA 1996, s 98(2)(d) provides that the fourth potentially fair reason is that 'the employee could not continue to work in the position which he held without contravention (either on his part or that of his employer) of a duty or restriction imposed by or under an enactment'. An example would be the loss of a driving licence in the case of a person employed as a driver, or a teacher declared unsuitable by the Department for Education and Skills: see *Sandhu v Department of Education and Science and London Borough of Hillingdon* (1978) and *Sutcliffe & Eaton Ltd v Pinney* (1977). The EAT has held, however, that the fact that the employers genuinely but erroneously believe that they will contravene a statutory requirement cannot be a reason falling within ERA 1996, s 98(2)(d), though it might be 'some other substantial reason': *Bouchaala v Trusthouse Forte Hotels Ltd* (1980). The fact that the continued employment of the employee contravenes a statutory requirement does not exonerate the employer from acting reasonably in accordance with ERA 1996, s 98(4).

## General rules: some other substantial reason

**7.60**  The fifth category of reason is stated in ERA 1996, s 98(1)(b) to be 'some other substantial reason of a kind such as to justify the dismissal of an employee holding the position which the employee held'. This is a fairly wide category of reasons. The most common examples relate to the business needs of the employer and have tended to involve a refusal by the employee to agree to a change in contractual terms or a refusal to agree to a reorganisation falling short of redundancy: see *RS Components Ltd v Irwin* (1973) and *Hollister v National Farmers' Union* (1979). But this category is wide enough to embrace other reasons, for example the dismissal of one spouse as a result of the dismissal of the other: see *Kelman v Oran* (1983) and *Scottish and Newcastle Retail Ltd v Stanton and Durrant* (EAT 1126/96).

**7.61** The Court of Appeal has considered this category of reason in a number of cases. It has held that it includes dismissals instigated by a third party, the expiry and non-renewal of a fixed-term contract, the imposition of a sentence of imprisonment, and a mistake as to the employee's intentions (brought about by his late notification to the employers that he had changed his mind about resigning): see *Dobie v Burns International Security Services (U.K.) Ltd* (1984), *North Yorkshire County Council v Fay* (1986), *Kingston v British Railways Board* (1984) and *Ely v YKK Fasteners (UK) Ltd* (1994). In *Kent County Council v Gilham (No 2)* (1985), the Court of Appeal said the burden on the employer of showing a substantial reason is designed to deter employers from dismissing employees for some trivial or unworthy reason.

**7.62** The Transfer of Undertakings (Protection of Employment) Regulations 1981 (as amended) (TUPE), reg. 8(2) also provide that where, either before or after a relevant transfer, the employee is dismissed because of economic, technical or organisational reasons entailing changes in the workforce of either the transferor or transferee, the dismissal will be treated as being for some other substantial reason; the tribunal will then have to consider section 98(4). Transfers of undertakings are considered more fully in Chapter 9.

## Procedure leading to dismissal

**7.63** Once a potentially fair reason under the ERA 1996 has been established, it is then necessary to consider whether the employer acted fairly in dismissing for that reason. Section 98(4) states as follows:

> ... the determination of the question whether the dismissal is fair or unfair (having regard to the reason shown by the employer)–
> (a)  depends on whether in the circumstances (including the size and administrative resources of the employer's undertaking) the employer acted reasonably or unreasonably in treating it as a sufficient reason for dismissing the employee, and
> (b)  shall be determined in accordance with equity and the substantial merits of the case.

**7.64** The effect of section 98(4) is that there is no burden of proof on either the employer or the employee. It is therefore wrong for an employment tribunal to place the burden on the employer of satisfying them that he or she acted reasonably: *Post Office (Counters) Ltd v Heavey* (1990), *Boys and Girls Welfare Society v McDonald* (1996) and *Hackney LBC v Usher* (1997).

**7.65**   In this context it is worth reflecting upon what Aristotle had to say about the meaning of 'equity'.

... Equity, though just, is not legal justice, but a rectification of legal justice. The reason for this is that law is always a general statement, yet there are cases which it is not possible to cover in a general statement. In matters therefore where, while it is necessary to speak in general terms, it is not possible to do so correctly, the law takes into consideration the majority of cases, although it is not unaware of the error this involves. And this does not make it a wrong law; for the error is not in the law nor in the lawgiver, but in the nature of the case: the material of conduct is essentially irregular ... This is the essential nature of the equitable: it is a rectification of law where law is defective because of its generality ...

(See Aristotle, *Nicomachean Ethics*, V.x.3 7.)

**7.66**   A question which is beginning to arise is whether, and in what circumstances, the consideration of the fairness or otherwise of the dismissal requires the tribunal to take into account an employee's rights under the European Convention on Human Rights. In one case, *X v Y* (2003), the EAT declined to interpret s 98(4) in a way compatible with the Convention rights, since it took the view that there was no engagement of any relevant articles. Another factor in that case was that the employer was a private sector employer. Subsequently, in *Pay v Lancashire Probation Service* (2004), another division of the EAT, said that, at least in relation to a public sector employer, a tribunal should interpret s 98(4) having regard to the employee's Convention rights. They said: 'we accept ... that a public sector employer will not act reasonably under section 98(4) if it violates its employee's Convention rights.' They went on to say that the 'circumstances' envisaged by s 98(4) should include all those matters weighed in the balance in assessing whether there has been an interference with a Convention right and those matters advanced as justification under the relevant article of the Convention.

## The correct approach to reasonableness

**7.67** The Court of Appeal has stressed that appeals to the EAT and beyond only lie on points of law and has discouraged attempts to dress up questions of fact as questions of law. But it is clear that the question of fairness cannot be considered solely as one of fact, and therefore unappealable. It is best described as a mixed question of fact and law. The tenor of the Court of Appeal decisions is to restrict considerably the circumstances in which appeals may be made to the EAT from employment tribunals' decisions and to discourage the EAT from reversing the tribunal's decisions because it would have reached a different conclusion. The case law in this area is extensive, but the main cases to be considered are: *Bailey v BP Oil (Kent Refinery) Ltd* (1980), *Thomas & Betts Manufacturing Ltd v Harding* (1980), *W & J Wass Ltd v Binns* (1982), *Woods v WM Car Services (Peterborough) Ltd* (1982), *O'Kelly v Trusthouse Forte plc* (1983), *Martin v Glynwed Distribution Ltd* (1983), *Dobie v Burns International Security Services (U.K.) Ltd* (1984), *Gilham v Kent County Council (No 2)* (1985) and *Piggott Brothers & Co Ltd v Jackson* (1992).

**7.68** In *Neale v Hereford and Worcester County Council* (1986) (at p. 483) May LJ in the Court of Appeal said:

> Their (ie the employment tribunal's) job is to find the facts, and to apply the relevant law and to reach the conclusion to which their findings and their experience lead them. It will not ... be often that when an employment tribunal has done just that, and with the care, clarity and thoroughness which the employment tribunal in the present case displayed, that one can legitimately say that their conclusion 'offends reason', or that their conclusion was one to which no reasonable employment tribunal could have come. Deciding these cases is the job of employment tribunals and when they have not erred in law neither the appeal tribunal nor this court should disturb their decision unless one can say in effect: 'My goodness, that was certainly wrong.'

**7.69** This approach may be characterised as the 'reasonable decision' approach. It was summarised by Browne-Wilkinson J. (as he then was) in *Iceland Frozen Foods Ltd v Jones* (1983) (at pp. 24–25), in words quoted with approval by the Court of Appeal in Neale's case, above:

The correct approach ... is as follows:

(1) the starting point should always be the words of section (98(4)) themselves;

(2) in applying the section an employment tribunal must consider the reasonableness of the employer's conduct, not simply whether they (the members of the employment tribunal) consider the dismissal to be fair;

(3) in judging the reasonableness of the employer's conduct an employment tribunal must not substitute its decision as to what was the right course to adopt for that of the employer;

(4) in many, though not all, cases there is a band of reasonable responses to the employee's conduct within which one employer might take one view, another quite reasonably take another;

(5) the function of the employment tribunal, as an industrial jury, is to determine whether in the particular circumstances of each case the decision to dismiss the employee fell within the band of reasonable responses which a reasonable employer might have adopted. If the dismissal falls within the band the dismissal is fair: if the dismissal falls outside the band, it is unfair.

**7.70** In *Foley v Post Office* (2000), Mummery LJ robustly endorsed the *Iceland Frozen Foods* approach saying that the decision itself, which had been approved and applied by the Court of Appeal, 'remains binding on this court, as well as on the employment tribunals and the Employment Appeal Tribunal'. He described the disapproval by the EAT of that approach as 'an unwarranted departure from authority'.

**7.71** The tribunal must not substitute its own view for that of the employer. This point has been emphasised by decisions of the EAT, in *Beedell v West Ferry Printers Ltd* (2000), and the Court of Appeal, in *Foley v Post Office* (2000). This means that it is permissible for the tribunal to look at the employer's honest and genuine belief, but the belief must be upon reasonable grounds: see *St Anne's Board Mill Co Ltd v Brien* (1973), *W Devis & Sons Ltd v Atkins* (1977) and *Alidair Ltd v Taylor* (1978).

**7.72** The appellate courts have stressed that the relevant question is whether it was reasonable of the employer to dismiss the employee and that in many cases there may be a range of courses of action open to the employer, all of which fall within the band of reasonableness; for an employment tribunal to prefer one course of action to another will cause it to apply the test of what it would have done itself and not the test of what a reasonable employer would have done: see *British Leyland (U.K.) Ltd v Swift* (1981), *NC Watling & Co Ltd v Richardson* (1978), *Iceland Frozen Food Ltd v Jones* (1983) and *Neale v Hereford and Worcester County Council* (1986). See also *Whitbread & Co plc v Mills* (1988).

**7.73** In deciding upon the fairness or otherwise of the dismissal, the tribunal must take into account any relevant provision of the Code of Practice on Disciplinary Practice and Procedures in Employment. In *W Devis & Sons Ltd v Atkins* (1977), Viscount Dilhorne said that non-compliance with the Code does not necessarily make a dismissal unfair, but that a failure to follow a procedure prescribed in the Code may lead to the conclusion that a dismissal was unfair, which, if that procedure had been followed, would have been held to have been fair. The decision of the EAT in *Lock v Cardiff Railway Company Ltd* (1998) appears to go further by suggesting that a failure by an employment tribunal to take into account the Code of Practice and to examine whether it has been complied with will vitiate the tribunal's decision. This cannot be right.

**7.74** As the case-law has developed over the years, adherence to the notion of procedural fairness has gained ground and considerable importance has been attached to it. It means that a dismissal may be made unfair by the use of an unfair procedure (eg lack of warnings or opportunity for the employee to state his or her side of the case), even where the reason is a perfectly good one. This was stressed by the House of Lords in its decision in *Polkey v AE Dayton Services Ltd* (1988), which has a particularly important bearing on the whole area of procedural fairness. The case involved the question whether a dismissal which would be unfair because of a failure to follow a fair procedure can be held to be fair if the employer is able to establish that following a fair procedure would have made no difference to the outcome. The House of Lords said that the correct question is whether the employer has been reasonable or unreasonable in deciding that the reason for dismissing the employee was a sufficient reason, not whether the employee would nevertheless have been dismissed even if there had been prior consultation or warning. Whether the employer could reasonably have concluded that consultation or warning would be useless so that the failure to consult or warn would not necessarily render the dismissal unfair was a matter for the employment tribunal to consider in the light of the circumstances known to the employer at the time of the decision to dismiss.

**7.75**  Lord Mackay of Clashfern LC, who gave the main speech, adopted the approach suggested by Browne-Wilkinson J. in *Sillifant v Powell Duffryn Timber Ltd* (1983). In that case, the judge stressed that the only test of the fairness of a dismissal is the reasonableness of the employer's decision to dismiss, judged at the time at which the dismissal takes effect. He said:

> An employment tribunal is not bound to hold that any procedural failure by the employer renders the dismissal unfair: it is one of the factors to be weighed by the employment tribunal in deciding whether or not the dismissal was reasonable within section (98(4)). The weight to be attached to such procedural failure should depend upon the circumstances known to the employer at the time of dismissal, not on the actual consequence of such failure. Thus in the case of a failure to give an opportunity to explain, except in the rare case where a reasonable employer could properly take the view on the facts known to him at the time of dismissal that no explanation or mitigation could alter his decision to dismiss, an employment tribunal would be likely to hold that the lack of 'equity' inherent in the failure would render the dismissal unfair.

**7.76**  He did suggest, however, that there may be rare cases 'where the offence is so heinous and the facts so manifestly clear that a reasonable employer could, on the facts known to him at the time of dismissal, take the view that whatever explanation the employee advanced it would make no difference ...' Browne-Wilkinson J. went on to say that, if the decision to dismiss was unfair in the circumstances, but the observance of fair procedure would have made the dismissal fair, the correct approach would be for there to be a finding of unfair dismissal but a reduction in the employee's compensation. He said:

> An employee dismissed for suspected dishonesty who is in fact innocent has no redress: if the employer acted fairly in dismissing him on the facts and in the circumstances known to him at the time of dismissal the employee's innocence is irrelevant. Why should an employer be entitled to a finding that he acted fairly when, on the facts known and in the circumstances existing at the time of dismissal, his actions were unfair

but which facts subsequently coming to light show did not cause any injustice? The choice in dealing with section [98(4)] is between looking at the reasonableness of the employer or justice to the employee. *Devis v Atkins* (1977) shows that the correct test is the reasonableness of the employer ...

**7.77** Lord Bridge of Harwich also considered the effect on compensation of taking the procedural steps and quoted a further passage from Browne-Wilkinson J.'s judgment in *Sillifant's* case:

There is no need for an 'all or nothing' decision. If the employment tribunal thinks there is a doubt whether or not the employee would have been dismissed, this element can be reflected by reducing the normal amount of compensation by a percentage representing the chance that the employee would still have lost his employment.

**7.78** The emphasis on procedural fairness, which is highlighted by this case, should not be allowed to distract the commentator from observing that it is as much about compensation as about procedural fairness. Effectively, the House of Lords is drawing attention to the fact that the observance of procedure is important but that, if the tribunal's judgment is that the outcome would have been a fair dismissal even had a fair procedure been observed, the issue becomes one of correctly reflecting that judgment in the measure of compensation.

**7.79** This reflection makes one wonder whether the introduction of ERA 1996, s 98A(2) by the EA 2002, s 34(2), which was supposed to reverse the effect of the decision in *Polkey*, actually makes any difference. This new provision states that a failure by an employer to follow a procedure in relation to the dismissal of an employee 'shall not be regarded for the purposes of section 98(4) as by itself making the employer's action unreasonable if he shows that he would have decided to dismiss the employee if he had decided to follow the procedure.' This inelegant piece of drafting is largely meaningless and does not affect the position so far as compensation is concerned.

## The effect of the Employment Act 2002

**7.80** Section 34(1) of the 2002 Act has introduced a new provision into the ERA 1996, s 98A(1), which links the new procedures enacted in the 2002 Act to the unfair dismissal provisions. It comes into play where one of the procedures set out in EA2002, Sch 2, Part I (relating to dismissal and disciplinary procedures) applies. In that case, an employee is to be treated as unfairly dismissed if the procedure has not been completed and the non-completion is 'wholly or mainly attributable to failure by the employer to comply with its requirements'. Part I sets out two alternative dismissal and disciplinary procedures, the 'standard' procedure and the 'modified' procedure. The latter applies in cases of alleged misconduct.

These provisions are due to come into effect on 1 October 2004.

## Statutory right to be accompanied at disciplinary and grievance hearings

**7.81**   The Employment Relations Act 1999 (ERA 1999) gives a worker (as defined in s 13(1)–(3) of that Act) the right to be accompanied at a disciplinary or grievance hearing. Section 10 applies where a worker is 'required or invited' by the employer to attend a disciplinary or grievance hearing and 'reasonably requests' to be accompanied at the hearing. The employer must allow the worker to be accompanied by a single companion chosen by the worker. The companion must either by a trade union official, an official of a trade union reasonably certified in writing by the union as having experience of, or as having received training in, acting as a worker's companion at disciplinary or grievance hearings, or another of the employer's workers. In this last case, the employer should allow the fellow-worker reasonable time off during working hours to accompany the worker.

**7.82**   The employer must allow the companion to address the hearing (but not answer questions on the worker's behalf) and to confer with the worker during the hearing. ERA 1999, s 10(4) and (5) provide for the situation where the companion will not be available at the time chosen by the employer for the hearing. In that case the employer must postpone the hearing to the time proposed by the worker provided that it is reasonable and is within five working days beginning with the first working day after the day proposed by the employer. A worker who complains that the right has been infringed may present a complaint to an employment tribunal within three months of the date of the infringement or threatened infringement: ERA 1999, s 11(1) and (2). If the tribunal finds the complaint well-founded it must order the employer to pay compensation of up to two weeks' pay.

**7.83** The final point to note is that the right not to be unfairly dismissed is extended to workers who exercise or seek to exercise their rights under section 10(2) or (4) and to workers who accompany or seek to accompany another worker: s 12(3). Further, the exclusions relating to length of employment and age (considered above at paras. 7. 11 and 7.7) do not apply. Section 12(6) specifically applies the unfair dismissal provisions to workers.

## Procedural fairness: capability and qualifications

**7.84** In cases involving unsatisfactory work performance, the employer must satisfy the employment tribunal that he or she honestly believed on reasonable grounds that the employee was incapable. A full and careful investigation of the facts should be undertaken; if, however, that is done, the employer does not have to satisfy the tribunal that he or she drew the correct conclusion, only that he or she had sufficient evidence upon which he or she could reach that conclusion. See *Alidair Ltd v Taylor* (1978) and *Cook v Thomas Linnell & Sons Ltd* (1977). It is necessary for the employer to follow a reasonable procedure, and, in particular, to give the employee a warning and an opportunity to improve, but a failure to do so will not automatically make the dismissal unfair, particularly if it can be shown that the employee is incapable of improving or already knows clearly what is expected, or that the giving of a warning would have made no difference to the result. See *Hollister v National Farmers' Union* (1979), *James v Waltham Holy Cross Urban District Council* (1973) and *AJ Dunning & Sons (Shopfitters) Ltd v Jacomb* (1973). In exceptional cases, it may not be necessary to follow a procedure. But that is only likely to be an option where the employee can be shown to be clearly incapable of improving or to know already what is expected: see *Cook v Thomas Linnell & Sons Ltd*, above.

**7.85** When cases involving ill-health occur, particularly if the employee suffers from long-term or severe illness, the contract may be frustrated, in which case there will be no dismissal. This aspect has already been considered: see chapter 3. The case law makes it clear that the employer must deal with ill employees carefully, particularly if the employee is suffering from mental illness, as in *O'Brien v Prudential Assurance Co Ltd* (1979). In cases of prolonged absence, the question is whether the employer can be expected to wait any longer, and, if so, how much longer: *Spencer v Paragon Wallpapers Ltd* (1977). Except in exceptional circumstances, the employee should be consulted and the employer should take reasonable steps to find out the true medical position, preferably by means of a sufficiently detailed medical report to enable an informed decision to be made: *East Lindsey District Council v Daubney* (1977), *Williamson v Alcan (UK) Ltd* (1978), *A. Links & Co v Rose* (1991) and *Eclipse Blinds Ltd v Wright* (1992). The EAT has stressed that the decision to dismiss is managerial, not medical, but the employer should consider the possibility of offering alternative work within the employee's capabilities, if it is available: *Merseyside and North Wales Electricity Board v Taylor* (1975).

**7.86** In cases of persistent, intermittent absence for minor illness, the employer should conduct a fair review of the employee's attendance record and the reasons for it, and give the employee appropriate warnings and an opportunity to make representations. This type of situation was considered by the EAT in *Lynock v Cereal Packaging Ltd* (1988), in which the employee had a poor attendance record. See also *International Sports Co Ltd v Thomson* (1980).

**7.87** A final point to note concerns claims made both under the Disability Discrimination Act 1995 and the unfair dismissal provisions. The EAT has pointed out that a tribunal should not hold a dismissal which is contrary to the DDA to be automatically unfair. They pointed out that it should be possible to have a disability-related dismissal which is not necessarily unfair, since the criteria applying under the DDA and the unfair dismissal provisions are different. See *HJ Heinz Co Ltd v Kenrick* (2000).

## Procedural fairness: conduct

**7.88** As with cases of unsatisfactory work performance, the employer must show that his or her view of the facts stemmed from an honest belief based upon reasonable grounds; it is also important to undertake a careful investigation which provides sufficient evidence for the conclusion reached: see *Trust House Forte Leisure Ltd v Aquilar* (1976), *Cook v Thomas Linnell & Sons Ltd* (1977) and *Laughton and Hawley v Bapp Industrial Supplies Ltd* (1986). In *British Home Stores Ltd v Burchell* (1980) the EAT set out the following guidelines for tribunals to apply when dealing with cases of alleged misconduct:

> First ... there must be established by the employer the fact of that belief; that the employer did believe it. Secondly, that the employer had in his mind reasonable grounds upon which to sustain that belief. And thirdly ... that the employer at the stage at which he formed that belief on those grounds, had carried out as much investigation into the matter as was reasonable in all the circumstances of the case.

**7.89** This approach was approved by the Court of Appeal in *W. Weddel & Co Ltd v Tepper* (1980). The *Burchell* case involved alleged dishonesty, but the test to which it has given its name is generally applied to those cases where the reason for the employee's dismissal is the employer's belief that there has been misconduct of some kind. The Court of Appeal has re-affirmed that the *Burchell* test 'remains binding on this court, as well as on employment tribunals and the Employment Appeal Tribunal. Any departure from that approach ... is inconsistent with binding authority': see *Foley v Post Office* (2000).

**7.90** It is particularly important to remember, when looking in detail at aspects of dismissal for conduct, that the overriding consideration for an employment tribunal is to decide whether the employer acted reasonably or unreasonably in dismissing the employee, within the requirements of ERA 1996, s 98(4). It is easy to allow decided cases and principles that are thought to be deducible from them to obscure the words used by the statute. It is also easy to forget that the decision in many cases depends on the facts as found by the tribunal. It is tempting to argue that, because a tribunal or another division of the EAT has decided a factual issue in a particular way, a subsequent tribunal should decide a similar factual issue in the same way. It is seldom that the facts of two different cases arising from different contexts are identical. It follows that two different tribunals may reach opposite conclusions on similar sets of facts, without either committing an error of law, simply because it is for each tribunal to decide, on the facts in front of it, whether that employer's decision to dismiss that employee in those circumstances was reasonable or unreasonable. It is essential to concentrate upon the necessarily general words of s 98(4) and the Code of Practice. A tribunal should not allow itself 'to be diverted into the channels created by judicial decisions' but should 'drink at the pure waters of the section': see Waite J in *Siggs and Chapman (Contractors) Ltd v Knight* (1984). In *Walls Meat Co Ltd v Khan* (1979), Lord Denning MR complained that 'if we are not careful, we shall find the (employment) tribunals bent down under the weight of the law books or, what is worse, asleep under them.'

**7.91** In considering an employer's conduct of an investigation, an employment tribunal will generally follow the three-stage approach set out in *Burchell*'s case above, and widely followed. In *Scottish Daily Record & Sunday Mail (1986) Ltd v Laird* (1996) IRLR 665, for example, the Court of Session said that the employment tribunal had not erred in holding that the employee's dismissal was unfair because the employers had failed to satisfy the *Burchell* test. The Court pointed out that, although there is no burden on the employer to satisfy the tribunal that it acted reasonably, the employer is still required to produce some evidence to show that the requirements described at each of the three stages of the test were satisfied. In *Sainsbury's Supermarkets Ltd v Hitt* (2003) the Court of Appeal emphasised that the range of reasonable responses test applies as much to the question whether an investigation is reasonable in all the circumstances as it does to the reasonableness of the decision to dismiss. See also *Panama v London Borough of Hackney* (2003), in which the Court of Appeal held that the tribunal had not properly applied the second and third limbs of the *Burchell* test.

**7.92** Problems of procedural fairness arise where an employer conducts an investigation but cannot identify the persons responsible for the acts in question. In such a case, the issue is whether it is reasonable for the employer to engage in 'blanket dismissals' and dismissal all the possible suspects even if some of them are innocent. The dismissal may be fair, but the employment tribunal must be satisfied that the employer conducted a proper investigation: see *Whitbread & Co plc v Thomas* (1988), in which the EAT applied *Monie v Coral Racing Ltd* (1981) (CA). See also *Parr v Whitbread plc, t/a Threshers Wine Merchants* (1990).

**7.93** Other issues which have arisen in the context of investigations have been the use of anonymous informants and the withholding of witness statements from the employee under threat of dismissal. In these, as in other, types of case, the overriding consideration, which has been emphasised regularly by the higher courts, is that the employer must have acted reasonably. See, for examples, the following cases: *Morgan v Electrolux Ltd* (1991), *A v Company B Ltd* (1997) IRLR 405 and *Louies v Coventry Hood & Seating Co Ltd* (1990), distinguished by the Court of Appeal in the later case of *Hussain v Elonex plc* (1999). In *Louies* the substance of the case was contained in statements which the employee had asked to see but which had not been shown to him, with no good reason being shown, and on which substantial reliance had been placed by the employers in reaching the decision to dismissed him; in the *Hussain* case, on the other hand, although the employers failed to disclose to the employee the existence of statements obtained from independent witnesses in relation to the incident which led to his dismissal, nevertheless he was told of the accusations against him and given a full opportunity to respond to them. Mummery L.J. pointed out that 'there are no hard and fast rigid rules to be adopted in these cases ... What matters is fairness and reasonableness.'

**7.94** Issues of fairness also arise where the employer treats employees differently (for example, by dismissing one and not another). In that case the dismissal will not be held to be unfair provided that the decision was one which a reasonable employer could reach. In such a case, however, the tribunal will commit an error of law if it substitutes its own view of the facts and the conclusions to be drawn from them for those of the employer: see *Securicor Ltd v Smith* (1989), which involved two employees one of whom was dismissed (his appeal being disallowed by the employers' appeal panel) whereas the other was reinstated by the appeal panel with a final warning, and *Cain v Leeds Western Health Authority* (1990), *Frames Snooker Centre v Boyce* (1992) and *London Borough of Harrow v Cunningham* (1996). Similar considerations arise where the employee in question is dismissed for an offence (eg assaulting another employee) but there is evidence that in the past other employees have not been dismissed for a similar offence: see *Procter v British Gypsum Ltd* (1991) and *Paul v East Surrey District Health Authority* (1995). In this last case the Court of Appeal stressed that in cases of this kind ultimately the question for the employer is whether in the particular case dismissal is a reasonable response to the misconduct; it warned that tribunals should scrutinise arguments based upon disparity of treatment with particular care.

**7.95**  Procedural fairness is particularly important in cases of conduct, though the requirements are not absolute. Generally, the employer should go through a procedure appropriate to the nature and size of the organisation and a failure to do so, except in the exceptional cases considered below, will cause the dismissal to be unfair. A failure to apply a procedure, however, will not cause the dismissal to be unfair, for example if the employee shows himself to be 'determined to go his own way' or has taken up a position which is unlikely to be altered by being given a hearing: see *Retarded Children's Aid Society Ltd v Day* (1978) and *James v Waltham Holy Cross Urban District Council* (1973). But it is important to bear in mind that the decision in *Polkey's* case means that in most cases such questions are not generally relevant.

**7.96**  The procedure will probably involve the application of the employer's disciplinary rules, which should make clear what amounts to an offence and what the result of a breach of the rules will be, and they should have been brought sufficiently to the employee's notice. If there are no rules, or the rules make no provision for the particular offence, the provisions of the Code of Practice will be relevant. In most cases (with the exception of a dismissal for a single act of gross misconduct), the employer should employ a warnings system, eg an oral warning followed by a written warning and then by a final written warning specifying that a further recurrence will lead to dismissal. The employee should also be interviewed and given the opportunity to state his or her case; he or she should also be told of any right to appeal.

**7.97**  In cases involving allegations of criminal offences, the employer does not have to prove the employee's guilt and, provided his or her belief is genuine and reasonable, the dismissal of the employee will not be made unfair by the latter's subsequent acquittal: see *Da Costa v Optolis Ltd* (1977). This is likely also to be the case where an employee accused of a crime pleads guilty and the employer refuses to accept the explanation that he or she was not guilty but had bowed to pressure to plead guilty to avoid a prison sentence. In such a case, the question is whether on the facts which were known or ought to have been known to the employers, they genuinely believed on reasonable grounds that the employee was guilty. If the procedure by which the employers reached their conclusion was faulty, they will have failed to act reasonably. In the absence of any lapse of procedure, it is an error of law for the employment tribunal to seek to reopen the factual issues on the basis of which the employers reached their conclusion: see *British Gas plc v McCarrick* (1991). See also *P. v Nottinghamshire County Council* (1992).

## Procedural fairness: redundancy

**7.98** There are two possible types of complaints of unfair dismissal for redundancy. The first, and most common, type occurs where the employee complains that the way the redundancy dismissal was handled was unfair and therefore contrary to ERA 1996, s 98(4). The second type of complaint occurs where an employee dismissed for redundancy argues that he or she was selected for redundancy for an 'inadmissible' reason. This second type of dismissal is considered below at para. 7.108.

**7.99** If the tribunal is satisfied that the reason was redundancy, it is likely that the dismissal will be held to be fair, unless the employer acts with blatant unfairness. Although in recent years the EAT has shown greater preparedness to hold a dismissal for redundancy unfair, by emphasising standards of good industrial relations practice, it has expressed the view that, provided the selection process is fair, an employment tribunal should scrutinise critically a complaint that the dismissal was unfair on some other grounds: see *Williams v Compair Maxam Ltd* (1982), *Freud v Bentalls Ltd* (1983), *Grundy (Teddington) Ltd v Plummer and Salt* (1983) and *Stacey v Babcock Power Ltd (Construction Division)* (1986). Further, if the employee would still have been made redundant had the employer taken reasonable steps to consult with the employee or find him or her other employment, the tribunal may either find that the dismissal was fair or order that (if it was unfair) no compensation, other than the basic award, should be paid. In such a case, in view of the House of Lords' decision in *Polkey v A.E. Dayton Services Ltd*, above, the tribunal would normally find the dismissal unfair and award no compensation, though it is open to them to find that the employer could reasonably have concluded that consultation or warning would be useless so that the failure to consult or warn in the light of the circumstances known to the employer at the time the decision to dismiss was taken was not unreasonable. A tribunal may also conclude that, on the facts as found by it, the dismissal was unfair, but that, had a fair procedure been followed, the employee could have been fairly dismissed within a given period of time. In that case, it may confine the period of loss, for the purposes of assessing compensation, to that period of time.

**7.100**   A further alternative is that the tribunal may conclude that the dismissal was unfair, but that, had the employer gone through a fair procedure, the employee would have stood a chance of being fairly dismissed at the end of the procedure. If the tribunal reaches such a decision, it may go on to reduce the compensation by the relevant percentage. It is important, however, that the tribunal should consider what would have been the result if the proper procedure had been followed: see *Red Bank Manufacturing Co Ltd v Meadows* (1992).

**7.101**   The two main obligations laying upon an employer proposing to dismiss an employee for redundancy are to make reasonable efforts, where practicable, to find him or her suitable alternative employment in the undertaking, or, where appropriate, with an associated employer and to consult with him or her and give reasonable warning of impending redundancy: see *Vokes Ltd v Bear* (1974), *Thomas & Betts Manufacturing Ltd v Harding* (1980), and *Williams v Compair Maxam Ltd* (1982), which contains a particularly useful discussion of this area. In *Langston v Cranfield University* (1998) the EAT said that an employment tribunal should consider the two questions of failure to seek alternative employment on the part of the employee and lack of consultation; it should also consider the fairness of the selection. A failure to do so will amount to an error.

**7.102**   The important decision of the House of Lords in *Polkey v A. E. Dayton Services Ltd* is the general starting-point for a consideration of the employer's obligations when dismissing for redundancy. It was considered above, at para. 7.74. The principles considered in *Polkey* were followed by the Court of Appeal in *Duffy v Yeomans & Partners Ltd* (1995). It said that the test of reasonableness under what is now section 98(4) is objective and it is not necessary for an employer to have applied his or her mind to the question of consultation for a dismissal without consultation to be within the range of reasonable responses under section 98(4). Although normally a dismissal will be unfair where there has been no consultation, the effect of a failure to consult is a matter of fact and degree for the employment tribunal. This view is consistent with the House of Lords decision in *Polkey's* case and, it is submitted, is correct in taking the view that each case must be decided on its own facts, bearing in mind the general proposition that normally an employer will not act reasonably unless he or she goes through the appropriate procedure. This decision is in accord with the decision in *Polkey's* case.

**7.103**  The courts have thus continued to emphasise the need for prior consultation and warning, and have been reluctant to find exceptional circumstances which would obviate this requirement. These requirements are not avoided by the fact that the employers are a small company or that immediate decisions needed to be made: see *Heron v Citilink-Nottingham* (1993). More recently, in *Mugford v Midland Bank plc* (1997), the EAT reviewed the position regarding consultation and said this:

(1)  Where no consultation about redundancy has taken place with either the trade union or the employee the dismissal will normally be unfair, unless the employment tribunal finds that a reasonable employer would have concluded that consultation would be an utterly futile exercise in the particular circumstances of the case.

(2)  Consultation with the trade union over selection criteria does not of itself release the employer from considering with the employee individually his being identified for redundancy.

(3)  It will be a question of fact and degree for the employment tribunal to consider whether consultation with the individual and/or his union was so inadequate as to render the dismissal unfair. A lack of consultation in any particular respect will not automatically lead to that result. The overall picture must be viewed by the tribunal up to the date of termination to ascertain whether the employer has or has not acted reasonably in dismissing the employee on the grounds of redundancy.

## Procedural fairness rules: statutory requirements

**7.104**  The fact that the employer shows that it is not possible to continue to employ the employee in the particular job he or she does, without contravening a statutory requirement, does not mean that there is no need to go through a fair procedure before dismissing the employee: see *Sutcliffe and Eaton Ltd v Pinney* (1977) and *Sandhu v Department of Education and Science and London Borough of Hillingdon* (1978).

## Procedural fairness: some other substantial reason

**7.105**  The two main areas which have evolved through the cases are reorganisations which fall short of redundancy, and changes in the employee's terms of employment though this category of reason is wide enough to embrace other matters, for example the dismissal of one spouse as a result of the dismissal of the other: see *Kelman v Oram* (1983) and *Scottish and Newcastle Retail Ltd v Stanton and Durrant* (EAT 1126/96). They show the difficulty of drawing the line between fairness and unfairness where there is a clear conflict between the employer's legitimate business interests and the employee's contractual rights, since the employee's contract is static and, prima facie, he or she can insist upon continued performance of it as it stands.

**7.106**  In *Hollister v National Farmers' Union* (1979) the Court of Appeal said that, provided that the employment tribunal has found that there was a substantial reason justifying dismissal, it is not necessary for the employers to consult the employee about the reorganisation of the business. All that needs to be shown is a sound commercial reason for making the reorganisation. In *Labour Party v Oakley* (1988), by way of contrast, the Court of Appeal held that the dismissal of an employee because of a reorganisation was unfair. Although the reorganisation was a substantial reason of a kind to justify the dismissal, what made the dismissal unfair was that the employers used the reorganisation as a pretext for her dismissal when they had already decided not to renew her fixed-term contract. See also *Bowater Containers Ltd v McCormack* (1980), *Genower v Ealing, Hammersmith and Hounslow Area Health Authority* (1980), *Ladbroke Courage Holidays Ltd v Asten* (1981), and *Richmond Precision Engineering Ltd v Pearce* (1985).

**7.107**  Often, but not always, allied with reorganisations are unilateral changes in the terms of the employee's contract, which raise difficult issues of law and practice. It is clear that the rules of procedural fairness apply here too, despite the apparent tendency of the EAT and

Court of Appeal to favour employers. See, for example, *RS Components Ltd v Irwin* (1973) and *St John of God (Care Services) Ltd v Brooks* (1992).

## Automatically unfair dismissals

**7.108** In the preceding two sections, the general rules of unfair dismissal were considered. These are the rules which generally apply to dismissals for what have been called the 'potentially fair' reasons. In this section, 'automatically unfair' dismissals are considered. They are so called because they are dismissals in circumstances such that statute has decreed that the ordinary considerations of fairness are overridden and thus do not arise. The cases where this happens are essentially cases where the legislature has taken the view that their importance is such as to justify treating them as special cases and to dispense with the usual qualifications of length of employment and age. It is interesting to note that the categories of automatically unfair dismissal have been regularly expanded over the years. In the early days of the unfair dismissal right, the only type of dismissal to be treated as automatically unfair was a dismissal in relation to trade union membership and activities. The thinking behind the development of these categories is not obvious.

**7.109** In this chapter, the following types of dismissal will be treated as automatically unfair:

1. dismissals in connection with trade union membership and activities, or trade union recognition;

2. dismissal for participation in official industrial action;

3. dismissal of an employee in connection with leave for family reasons including paternity and adoption leave);

4. dismissal for reasons connected with health and safety;

5. dismissal of a shop or betting worker for refusing Sunday work;

6. dismissal in connection with an employee's rights under the Working Time Regulations;

7. dismissal for reasons relating to an employee's performance of his or her duties as an occupational pension fund trustee;

8. dismissal for reasons relating to an employee's performance of his or her duties as an employee representative;

9. dismissal for making a 'protected disclosure';

10. dismissal for assertion of a statutory right;

11. dismissal of an employee in connection with the national minimum wage legislation;

12. dismissal in connection with an employee's rights under the Tax Credits Act 1999;

13. dismissals of employees arising under paragraph 28 of the Transnational Information and Consultation of Employees Regulations 1999;

14. dismissals arising under regulation 7 of the Part-time Workers (Prevention of Less Favourable Treatment) Regulations 2000;

15. dismissals arising under regulation 6 of the Fixed-term Employees (Prevention of Less Favourable Treatment) Regulations 2002;

16. dismissal of a worker in connection with the statutory right to be accompanied at a disciplinary or grievance hearing.

**7.110** In cases 1–15, a selection for redundancy for one of those reasons may also make the dismissal for redundancy automatically unfair: see TULRCA 1992, s 153, and ERA 1996, s 105 (as amended). The first, fourth, ninth and tenth cases will be considered in more detail since they have given rise to such case-law as there is. For a more detailed analysis of the statutory provisions relating to all the cases, reference should be made to Upex, *The Law of Termination of Employment* (6th ed, 2001), pp. 195–238.

## Dismissals in connection with union membership or activities and recognition of unions

**7.111** In this section two types of dismissal will be considered: dismissals in connection with trade union membership and activities; and (ii) dismissals in connection with trade union recognition. This second type of dismissal arises as a result of the introduction of procedures relating to union recognition by the Employment Relations Act 1999.

**7.112** Section 152(1) of the Trade Union and Labour Relations (Consolidation) Act 1992 (TULRCA) provides that a dismissal, or a selection for dismissal for redundancy, will be automatically unfair if the reason for it is one of the following:

1. membership, or proposed membership, of an 'independent trade union';

2. participation, or proposed participation, in its 'activities' at an 'appropriate time'; and

3. non-membership of any trade union, or of a particular trade union, or of one of a number of particular trade unions, or refusal or proposed refusal of such membership.

**7.113** The reasons set out above are called 'inadmissible reasons' In the case of a dismissal, or a selection for redundancy, for one of these reasons, employees are protected whether or not they have been continuously employed for one year or have reached retirement age: TULRCA 1992, s 154(1). Further, they may be entitled to higher compensation and interim relief.

**7.114** A trade union will be an 'independent trade union', and thus within section 152, if it satisfies the definition set out in section 235(1) of the ERA 1996. Two requirements need to be satisfied: (1) the trade union is not under the domination or control of an employer or a group of employers or of one or more employers' associations; and (2) the trade union 'is not liable to interference by an employer or any such group or association (arising out of the provision of financial or material support or by any other means whatsoever) tending towards such control'. See *Blue Circle Staff Association v Certification Officer* (1977), *Association of HSD (Hatfield) Employees v Certification Officer* (1978), *Squibb United Kingdom Staff Association v Certification Officer* (1979) and *Government Communications Staff Federation v Certification Officer* (1993). See chapter 10 for further detail.

**7.115** Section 152(3) of the 1992 Act treats as falling within section 152(1) (c), above: (a) an employee's refusal, or proposed refusal, to comply with a requirement (whether or not imposed by the contract or in writing) that, in the event of a failure to become or ceasing to remain a member of a trade union or one of a number of trade union, he or she must make one or more payments; and (b) an objection, or proposed objection, to the operation of a provision under which, in the event mentioned in (a), the employer is entitled to deduct one or more sums from his or her pay.

**7.116** The Court of Appeal has said that section 152 is not concerned with an employer's reactions to a trade union's activities but with the employer's reactions to an individual employee's activities. If, therefore, a dismissal has nothing to do with anything the employee has personally done or proposed to do, section 152 will not apply: see *Carrington v Therm-a-Stor Ltd* (1983) and *Discount Tobacco & Confectionery Ltd v Armitage* (1990).

**7.117** The provisions of section 152 apply only to dismissals for the reasons set out above. A distinction, not always easy to draw, needs to be made between such dismissals and dismissals for industrial action. In *Drew v St Edmundsbury Borough Council* (1980), for example, the employee, who was a trade union member, was dismissed after he had been employed for less than the qualifying period of continuous employment (at the material time, 26 weeks) for repeatedly complaining to his employers about health and safety matters. Although he purported to be following a trade union directive to go slow, the directive was not concerned with health and safety matters. The employment tribunal decided that he was not dismissed for taking part in trade union activities but for taking part in industrial action. He therefore had not been continuously employed for long enough. The EAT upheld their decision.

**7.118** The first type of dismissal falling within section 152(1) is one where the reason for the dismissal is that the employee 'was ... a member of an independent trade union'. In *Discount Tobacco & Confectionery Ltd v Armitage* (1990) Knox J. said:

> ... (T)he activities of a trade union officer in negotiating and elucidating terms of employment is ... the outward and visible manifestation of trade union membership. It is an incident of union membership which is, if not the primary one, at any rate, a very important one and we see no

genuine distinction between membership of a union on the one hand and making use of the essential services of a union, on the other. Were it not so, the scope of section (152(1)(a)) would be reduced almost to vanishing point, since it would only be just the fact that a person was a member of a union, without regard to the consequences of that membership, that would be the subject matter of that statutory provision and, it seems to us, that to construe that paragraph so narrowly would really be to emasculate the provision altogether.

**7.119** This approach was described by the Court of Appeal as 'unquestionably correct' in *Associated British Ports v Palmer* (1994). See also *Speciality Care plc v Pachela* (1996).

**7.120** Section 152(1)(b) uses the phrase 'activities of an independent trade union'. This should not be interpreted restrictively but should be interpreted reasonably; it embraces an employee's participation in trade union activities during the course of his or her previous employment: see *Dixon v West Ella Developments Ltd* (1978) and *Fitzpatrick v British Railways Board* (1992). In *Britool Ltd v Roberts* (1993) the EAT said that actual participation in a strike, whether as a leader or otherwise, will rarely if ever constitute an activity within section 152(1)(b). But, since leading a strike involves not only leading the strike when it is in operation but a preliminary planning and consultation stage, those preliminary activities may be within the provision. In *Lyon v St James's Press* (1976), Phillips J. said of acts claimed to come within the protection: '. . wholly unreasonable, extraneous or malicious acts done in support of trade union activities might be a ground for a dismissal which might not be unfair' See also *Bass Taverns Ltd v Burgess* (1995), which involved the dismissal of an employee who had made disparaging remarks about the company at an induction course for trainee managers, and *Chant v Aquaboats Ltd* (1978), in which the EAT said that 'activities of an independent trade union' do not include an individual's independent activities as a trade unionist and held that the organising of a petition about safety standards, which was vetted by the local branch of the union before being handed to the employers, was not a trade union activity within the Act.

**7.121** TULRCA 1992, s 152(2) defines 'appropriate time' as a time which is either outside an employee's working hours or 'is a time within his working hours at which, in accordance with arrangements agreed with or consent given by his employer, it is permissible for him to take part' in the activities. 'Working hours' means any time at which an employee is required to be at work in accordance with the contract of employment. See *Marley Tile Co Ltd v Shaw* (1980) and *Zucker v Astrid Jewels Ltd* (1978). See Chapter 10 for further detail.

**7.122** The second type of dismissal considered here is dismissal in connection with trade union recognition. Employees dismissed or selected for redundancy for one of the reasons set out below will be treated as automatically unfairly dismissed. Further, in the case of a dismissal, or a selection for redundancy, for one of these reasons, employees are protected whether or not they have been continuously employed for one year or have reached retirement age. See TULRCA 1992, Sch A1, paras. 161 and 164. The reasons are as follows:

(a)    the employee acted with a view to obtaining or preventing recognition of a union or unions by the employer under Schedule A1 of the TULRCA 1992;

(b)    the employee indicated that he or she supported or did not support recognition of a union or unions;

(c)    the employee acted with a view to securing or preventing the ending under the Schedule of bargaining arrangements;

(d)    the employee indicated that he or she supported or did not support the ending of bargaining arrangements;

(e)    the employee influenced or sought to influence the way in which votes were to be cast by other workers in a ballot arranged under Schedule A1;

(f)    the employee influenced or sought to influence other workers to vote or abstain from voting in such a ballot;

(g)    the employee voted in such a ballot;

(h)    the employee proposed to do, failed to do, or proposed to decline to do, any of the things referred to above.

**7.123** A reason will not fall within the above list if it constitutes an unreasonable act or omission by the employee: see TULRCA 1992, Sch A1, para. 161(3). The dismissal of an employee selected for redundancy will be automatically unfair, by virtue of TULRCA 1992, Sch. A1, para. 162, if it is shown that

(a) the circumstances constituting the redundancy applied equally to one or more other employees in the same undertaking who held positions similar to that held by the employee and who have not been dismissal by the employer; and

(b) the reason why the employee was selected was one of the reasons listed above.

## Dismissals in health and safety cases

**7.124** ERA 1996, s 100 governs these types of dismissal. As with the other types of automatically unfair dismissals, for employees covered by this provision there is no minimum qualifying period of continuous employment; nor are they excluded if they are over the normal retirement age: ERA 1996, ss 108(3) and 109(2). A preliminary point to note is that the person claiming unfair dismissal in these circumstances must be an employee of the employer: see *Costain Building & Civil Engineering Ltd v Smith and Chanton Group plc* (2000), considered at para. 3.25 The claimant was an engineer who was supplied by an agency to Costains. He claimed that he had become an employee of Costains and, when his services were dispensed with, that he had been unfairly dismissed by them contrary to ERA 1996, s 100(1)(b). The EAT held that he did not become an employee of Costain and that therefore he could not complain of unfair dismissal.

**7.125** It should be noted that selection for redundancy for any of the reasons set out in this section will also be automatically unfair: s 105(1) and (3). An employee dismissed for one of the reasons set out below may apply to the employment tribunal for interim relief under section 128. It should be noted that the statutory limit for a compensatory award of compensation will not apply to these types of unfair dismissal: s 124(1A).

**7.126** Section 100(1) provides that the dismissal of an employee will be automatically unfair if the reason (or principal reason) for it is one of the five reasons specified in that subsection. The burden of proving that a dismissal was for health and safety reasons is on the employee: see *Tedeschi v Hosiden Besson Ltd* (EAT 959/95). Where there is more than one possible reason for the dismissal, the tribunal must determine what was the principal reason for the dismissal. The six reasons set out in section 100(1) are as follows:

1.  The employee carried out, or proposed to carry out activities in connection with preventing or reducing risks to health and safety at work, after being designated by the employer to do so.

2.  The employee, as a workers' representative on health and safety matters or member of a safety committee, performed, or proposed to perform, any functions as such a representative or committee member, in accordance with arrangements established under or by virtue of any enactment or by reason of being acknowledged as representative or committee member by the employer.

3.  The employee took part (or proposed to take part) in consultations with the employer pursuant to the Health and Safety (Consultation with Employees) Regulations 1996 or in the election of safety representatives (whether as a candidate or otherwise).

4.  In the case of employees at a place where there was no workers' representative or safety committee or, where there was a representative or a committee, but it was not reasonably practicable for the employees to raise the matter by those means, they brought to the employer's attention by reasonable means circumstances connected with their work which they reasonably believed were harmful or potentially harmful to health and safety.

5.  There were circumstances of danger which the employee reasonably believed to be serious and imminent, and which he or she could not reasonably be expected to avert, and he or she left, proposed to leave, or (while the danger persisted) refused to return to, the place of work or any dangerous part of it.

6.  There were circumstances of danger which the employee reasonably believed to be serious and imminent and he or she took, or proposed to take, appropriate steps to protect himself or herself or other persons from the danger. Whether the steps were appropriate is to be judged by reference to all the circumstances including, in particular, his or her knowledge and the facilities and advice available to him or her at the time:

s 100(2). In the case of a dismissal for this reason, the dismissal will not be automatically unfair if the employer shows that it was (or would have been) so negligent for the employee to take the steps which he or she took, or proposed to take, that a reasonable employer might have dismissed him or her for taking, or proposing to take them: s 100(3).

**7.127** The first two cases set out above relate only to the defined activities of safety representatives, employees with designated health and safety functions and members of safety committees. An employee will only be protected by these provisions, however, if he or she is a representative in respect of the area where the health and safety complaint arises: see *Shillito v Van Leer (UK) Ltd* (1997). In *Goodwin v Cabletel Ltd* (1998), the EAT said that it is open to a tribunal to consider whether the manner in which the employee approached the health and safety problem took him or her outside the scope of his or her health and safety activities. They said:

> The protection afforded to the way in which a designated employee carries out his health and safety activities must not be diluted by too easily finding acts done for that purpose to be a justification for dismissal; on the other hand, not every act, however malicious or irrelevant to the task in hand, must necessarily be treated as a protected act in circumstances where dismissal would be justified on legitimate grounds.

**7.128** The fourth case covers any employee, provided that he or she has gone through any safety committee or representative where possible, unless it is not reasonably practicable to do so. Employees who take the issue into their own hands run the risk, therefore of falling outside section 100(1)(c). In a case covered by this provision, the employee must show that he or she reasonably believed that the circumstances were harmful or potentially harmful to health or safety. In *Kerr v Nathan's Wastesavers Ltd* (EAT 91/95), which involved an employee who was dismissed for refusing to drive a vehicle which, in his opinion, might become overloaded by the end of the working day, the EAT said that the duty placed on the employee to show reasonable belief should not be too heavy, since the purpose of the legislation is to protect employees who raise matters of health and safety. The EAT nevertheless upheld the tribunal's decision that the case should be dismissed on the grounds that, although the employee's belief was genuine, it was not based on reasonable grounds. In *Balfour Kilpatrick Ltd v Acheson* (2003), the EAT held that taking industrial action is not a 'reasonable means' of bringing health and safety concerns to the employer's attention.

**7.129** *Harvest Press Ltd v McCaffrey* (1999) is a decision on the fifth type of health and safety dismissal above, under section 100 (1)(d). The employee left his workplace in the middle of a shift because of the abusive behaviour of a fellow-employee which made him fear for his safety. He was dismissed for walking out in the middle of a shift. The EAT upheld the employment tribunal's decision the dismissal fell within section 100(1)(d) and said that dangers caused by fellow-employees are within the wider scope of that provision. They said that 'danger' is used in the provision without any limitation and is intended to cover any danger, however arising.

**7.130** Employees who are tempted to report a health and safety matter to an outside body such as the Health and Safety Executive again run the risk of putting themselves outside section 100. In such a case, the question would be whether the case was covered by section 100(1)(e) and whether the steps taken by the employee were 'appropriate steps to protect himself or other persons from the danger'. Again, the question would arise as to whether the employee should have raised the issue internally with a safety official or the employer before taking more serious action. In *Masiak v City Restaurants (UK) Ltd* (1999), a chef who was dismissed for refusing to cook food which he considered unfit for human consumption complained of unfair dismissal under section 100(1)(e). The tribunal said that the phrase 'other persons' relates only to fellow-employees. The EAT allowed his appeal and said that the statutory provisions are not limited in this way.

## Dismissals and protected disclosures

**7.131** Section 103A provides that a dismissal will be automatically unfair if the reason (or principal reason) is that the employee made a 'protected disclosure'. It is not necessary for employees covered by this provision to serve a minimum qualifying period of employment; nor are employees over the normal retiring age excluded: ss 108(3) and 109(2). Selection for redundancy on these grounds is also automatically unfair: s 105(1) and (6A). The present legislation derives from the Public Interest Disclosure Act 1998, which inserted the unfair dismissal provisions discussed in this section into the ERA 1996 1996.

**7.132** An employee dismissed for a reason set out above may apply to the employment tribunal for interim relief under s 128(1). It should be noted that the statutory limit for a compensatory award of compensation will not apply to this type of unfair dismissal, by virtue of s 124(1A).

The phrase 'protected disclosure' means 'a qualifying disclosure (as defined by section 43B) which is in accordance with any of sections 43C to 43H' of the ERA 1996. A disclosure made before the Public Interest Disclosure Act came into force may be a 'protected disclosure': see *Milaszawicz v Stolt Offshore Ltd* (2002).

**7.133** An employee will be protected by the provisions of the Act if both the following requirements are satisfied:

(a)  he or she makes a disclosure in relation to one of the specified categories of subject-matter and

(b)  he or she uses one of the specified manners of procedure to make the disclosure.

There are six categories of subject-matter and six procedures by means of which a disclosure may be made. Once the circumstances fall within one subject-matter category and one procedure, then the employee is protected.

**7.134** A 'qualifying disclosure' is defined by ERA 1996, s 43B as 'any disclosure of information which, in the reasonable belief of the employee making the disclosure, tends to show one or more' of the following:

(a)  that a criminal offence has been committed, is being committed or is likely to be committed;

(b)  that a person has failed, is failing or is likely to fail to comply with any legal obligation to which he or she is subject;

(c)    that a miscarriage of justice has occurred, is occurring or is likely to occur;

(d)    that the health or safety of any individual has been, is being or is likely to be endangered;

(e)    that the environment has been, is being or is likely to be damaged;

(f)    that information tending to show any matter falling within any of the preceding paragraphs has been, is being or is likely to be deliberately concealed.

**7.135**   The following points should be noted, however:

(1)    the employee's belief must be 'reasonable';

(2)    a disclosure will not qualify for protection if the person making it commits an offence by doing so;

(3)    a disclosure will not qualify if it is one in respect of which legal professional privilege would apply;

(4)    it is irrelevant where the alleged failure takes place, eg that alleged environmental damage has taken place in Brazil.

**7.136**   In *Darnton v University of Surrey* (2003), the EAT said that, for there to be a qualifying disclosure, it must have been reasonable for the employee to believe that the factual basis of what was disclosed was true and that it tends to show a relevant failure, even if the employee was wrong, but reasonably mistaken. In relation to the second type of qualifying disclosure above, relating to a failure by a person to comply with a legal obligation, the EAT has said that the word 'likely' in s 43B(1)(b) requires more than a possibility or risk that an employer might fail to comply with a relevant legal obligation. The information disclosed should, in the reasonable belief of the worker at the time it was disclosed, tend to show that it is probable or more probable than not, that the employer will fail to comply with the relevant legal obligation.

**7.137**   The protection only applies to the employee if he or she follows one of the specified procedures to disclose the matter in question. The aim of the legislation is to encourage employees to disclose the information through the appropriate channels first, rather than going directly to an outsider. The Act makes it easier for employees to gain protection by making a disclosure to their employer rather than disclosing information to the press, for example.

**7.138** Six procedures are specified: see ERA 1996, s 43C. The first applies where the employee makes a qualifying disclosure in good faith to the employer or another responsible person. Disclosure may only be made to that other person, however, where the employee reasonably believes that the failure relates solely or mainly to the conduct of that person or any other matter for which that other person has legal responsibility. If the disclosure is made to another person in accordance with a procedure whose use by the employee is authorised by the employer, he or she will be treated as making the disclosure to the employer.

**7.139** The second procedure applies to a qualifying disclosure made to disclosure to a legal adviser; if it is made in the course of obtaining legal advice: s 43D. The third procedure applies where the qualifying disclosure is made in good faith to a Minister of the Crown. The procedure applies where the employee's employer is an individual appointed under an enactment by a Minister of the Crown or a member of the Scottish Executive or is a body any of whose members are appointed in this way: s 43E.

**7.140** The fourth procedure applies to a qualifying disclosure made in good faith to a 'prescribed person': s 43F. A list of prescribed persons is to be found in the Public Interest Disclosure (Prescribed Persons) Order 1999 (SI 1999/1549). The disclosure will be protected if the employee reasonably believes that the relevant failure falls within any description of matters in respect of which the person to whom he or she makes disclosure is prescribed and that the information disclosed, and any allegation contained in it, are substantially true. It is not proposed to set out the complete list here, but it should be noted that the Schedule to the Order contains both a list of prescribed persons and a description of the matters which may be disclosed to them. Thus, for example, the Chief Executive of the Criminal Cases Review Commission is included and the description of matters in respect of which disclosure may be made is 'actual or potential miscarriages of justice'.

**7.141** The fifth procedure, set out in section 43G, relates to qualifying disclosures in cases other than those set out above. Such disclosures must comply with the following conditions:

(a)    the employee must make the disclosure in good faith;

(b)    the employee must reasonably believe that the information disclosed, and any allegation contained in it, are substantially true;

(c)    the employee must not make the disclosure for the purposes of personal gain;

(d)    it must be reasonable in all the circumstances of the case for him or her to make the disclosure.

**7.142** In *Street v Derbyshire Unemployed Workers' Centre* (2004), the EAT said that good faith involves the deployment of an honest intention and there is nothing inconsistent in an employee holding a belief that material disclosed was true and yet promoting it for reasons based on personal antagonism. They held that it was open to the tribunal to conclude that the employee's belief was vitiated by her personal antagonism and added that the purpose of the PIDA is not 'to allow grudges to be promoted and disclosures to be made in order to advance personal antagonism.

**7.143** Section 43G(2) sets out a further list of conditions which must be satisfied and section 43G(3) sets out the factors which should be considered when determining whether it is reasonable for the employee to make the disclosure. The further conditions are as follows:

1.    at the time of making the disclosure the employee must reasonably believe that he or she will be subjected to a detriment by the employer if he or she makes a disclosure to the employer or to a prescribed person in accordance with section 43F;

2.    if there is no prescribed person in relation to the relevant failure, the employee must reasonably believe that it is likely that evidence relating to the relevant failure will be concealed or destroyed if he or she makes a disclosure to the employer;

3.    the employee must have previously made a disclosure of substantially the same information to the employer or in accordance with section 43F.

**7.144**  The factors relating to whether it is reasonable to make the disclosure are:

(a)   the identity of the person to whom the disclosure is made;

(b)   the seriousness of the failure;

(c)   whether the failure is continuing or is likely to occur in the future;

(d)   whether the disclosure is made in breach of a duty of confidentiality owed by the employer to any other person;

(e)   any action which the employer or the person to whom the previous disclosure was made has taken or might reasonably be expected to have taken as a result of the disclosure; and

(f)   whether in making the disclosure to the employer the employee complied with any procedure whose use was authorised by the employer.

The last two factors only come into play, if at all, in cases relating to previous disclosures under section 43G(2)(c).

**7.145**  The sixth procedure is available where the subject-matter of the disclosure is sufficiently serious to merit the employee bypassing the other procedures. For this to apply, ERA 1996, s 43H requires the employee to show:

(i)    the disclosure was made in good faith;

(ii)   he or she reasonably believed that the information disclosed, and any allegation contained in it, were substantially true;

(iii)  he or she did not make the disclosure for personal gain;

(iv)   the matter disclosed was of an exceptionally serious nature;

(v)    in all the circumstances, it was reasonable for him or her to make the disclosure.

**7.146**  Section 43H(2) provides that, in determining whether it is reasonable for the employee to make the disclosure, regard must be had to the identity of the person to whom the disclosure is made.

## Dismissals for assertion of a statutory right

**7.147**   These types of dismissal are governed by ERA 1996, s 104. It is not necessary for employees covered by this provision to serve a minimum qualifying period of employment; nor are employees over the normal retiring age excluded: ss 108(3) and 109(2). Selection for redundancy on these grounds is also automatically unfair: s 105(1)( and (7).

**7.148**   The dismissal of an employee will be automatically unfair if the reason (or principal reason) for it was that the employee brought proceedings against the employer to enforce a 'relevant statutory right' or alleged that the employer had infringed a 'relevant statutory right', as defined by s 104(4). In both cases the right must be a right of the dismissed employee, but it is immaterial whether the employee has the right or not and whether it was infringed or not, provided that the claim to the right and its infringement are made in good faith: s 104(2). It is sufficient for this section to apply that the employee made it reasonably clear to the employer what the right claimed to have been infringed was; it is not necessary to specify the right: s 104(3).

**7.149**   The following statutory rights are stated by s 104(4) to be 'relevant statutory rights':

1.   any right conferred by the 1996 Act, for which the remedy for its infringement is by way of a complaint or reference to an employment tribunal;

2.   the right conferred by section 86 to a minimum period of notice; and

3.   the right conferred by sections 68, 86, 146, 168, 169 and 170 of the Trade Union and Labour Relations (Consolidation) Act 1992, relating to deductions of union dues, action short of dismissal on grounds related to trade union membership and activities, and time off for trade union duties and activities; and

4.   the rights conferred by the Working Time Regulations.

**7.150**   In *Mennell v Newell & Wright (Transport Contractors) Ltd* (1996) the EAT said that a dismissal of an employee because of his refusal to sign a new contract permitting his employer to make deductions from his wages could fall within section 104. They said that a threat of dismissal in order to impose a variation of the contract to enable the employer to make deductions from wages may amount to an infringement of the employee's statutory right under Part II of the ERA 1996 not to have deductions made from his or her wages without consent. It is not necessary for the employee to have brought proceedings; it is enough that he or she has alleged in good faith that the employer has infringed a relevant statutory right. When the case reached the Court of Appeal, however, that Court allowed the employers' appeal on the grounds that, on the facts, the reason for the employee's dismissal was his refusal to sign the new contract, not his allegation that a statutory right had been infringed. It is clearly important for tribunals hearing cases under this provision to make a clear finding of fact as to the reason for the dismissal. In *Armstrong v Walter Scott Motors (London) Ltd* (EAT 766/02), the EAT held that an employee had been unfairly dismissed for asserting his statutory right to paid holiday under the Working Time Regulations.

## Special cases

**7.151**  The types of dismissal discussed in this section are different from automatically unfair dismissals in that they do not share the two features common to that type of dismissal: that the dismissal was automatically unfair, and that the requirements relating to qualifying length of employment and age exclusion do not apply. These are cases which have special rules relating to the type of dismissal in question. Two cases are considered here: dismissal and industrial action and dismissals of replacement employees.

### Dismissals and industrial action

**7.152**  Three types of dismissal fall to be considered here:

1.  dismissals of employees taking part in unofficial industrial action under TULRCA 1992, s 237;

2.  dismissals in connection with strikes and lockouts;

3.  dismissals caused by industrial pressure, under ERA 1996 s 107.

**7.153** The first type of dismissal is governed by TULRCA 1992 s 237(1), whose general effect is to deprive of the right to complain of unfair dismissal employees who, at the time of dismissal, were taking part in an unofficial strike or other industrial action. The circumstances in which a strike will be considered to be unofficial are set out in TULRCA 1992 s 237(2). That provision operates in such a way as to place the burden on the employee of showing that the industrial action was not unofficial. The two circumstances in which industrial action is not unofficial are: (1) where the dismissed employee is a member of a trade union and the action is authorised or endorsed by that union; and (2) where the employee is not a member of a trade union but amongst those taking part in the industrial action are members of a trade union which has authorised or endorsed the action. The industrial action is not to be regarded as unofficial if none of those taking part in it are members of a trade union: see proviso to s 237(2). See *Balfour Kilpatrick Ltd v Acheson* (2003).

**7.154** Dismissals in connection with strikes and lockouts are covered by TULRCA 1992, s 238 which removes from the employment tribunal the jurisdiction to hear a complaint of unfair dismissal where, at the date of dismissal (as defined by s 238(5)), the employer was conducting or instituting a lockout, or the employee (complainant) was taking part in a strike or other industrial action. But its jurisdiction will be restored if one or more 'relevant employees' (as defined: see para. 7.160 below) of the same employer either have not been dismissed or have been offered re-engagement within three months of their dismissal, but the complainant has not been offered re-engagement. See *Williams v National Theatre Board Ltd* (1982), *Highland Fabricators Ltd v McLaughlin* (1985), and *Bolton Roadways Ltd v Edwards* (1987).

**7.155** The consequences of section 238 are that, if the employer dismisses all the strikers and re-engages none of them, the tribunal has no jurisdiction. Once, however, there is selectivity, either in dismissing or re-engaging, the saving provisions in section 238 will be triggered and the employer will have to beware of the various pitfalls they contain. If jurisdiction is given to the tribunal, it will proceed to hear the case in the ordinary way, subject to the amendments made to section 98(4) in cases of non-re-engagement. In such cases also, the limitation period for a complaint is extended to six months from the complainant's date of dismissal: TULRCA 1992, s 239(2).

**7.156** There may be borderline cases in which the tribunal will have to decide whether the dismissal is for trade union membership or activities (and falls within TULRCA s 152) or is in connection with industrial action (and falls within s 238): see *Winnett v Seamarks Brothers Ltd* (1978) and *Drew v St Edmundsbury Borough Council* (1980). An employee dismissed for trade union membership or activities does not have to have been employed for the qualifying period, whereas an employee dismissed for industrial action does.

**7.157** The Court of Appeal has stressed that the question what are the necessary elements of a lockout, strike or other industrial action is not one of law, but of fact: see *Express & Star Ltd v Bunday* (1988). In *Tramp Shipping Corporation v Greenwich Marine Inc* (1975), Lord Denning MR said:

> ... (A) strike is a concerted stoppage of work by men done with a view to improving their wages or conditions, or giving vent to a grievance or making a protest about something or other. It is distinct from a stoppage which is brought about by an external event such as a bomb scare or by apprehension of danger.

**7.158** In *Coates v Modern Methods & Materials Ltd* (1982) ICR 763 Eveleigh LJ said:

> ... (F)or a person to take part in a strike he must be acting jointly or in concert with others who withdraw their labour, and this means that he must withdraw his labour in support of their claim. The fact that a man stays away from work when a strike is on does not lead inevitably to the conclusion that he is taking part in a strike.

The main question in fact is whether a person was 'taking part' in the strike at the date of dismissal. This is part of the definition of 'relevant employees' and is considered below. See Chapter 12 for further detail.

**7.159** Examples of 'other industrial action' have been held to be a refusal to work overtime, taking part in a decision to impose an overtime ban, a refusal to carry out a lawful instruction given by the employer without extra pay, and a threat of withdrawal of labour. See *Power Packing Casemakers Ltd v Faust* (1983), *Naylor v Orton & Smith Ltd* (1983), *Lewis and Britton v E. Mason & Sons Ltd* (1994). In *Rasool v*

*Hepworth Pipe Co Ltd* (1980) the EAT held that attendance at an unauthorised mass meeting for the purpose of ascertaining the views of the workforce with regard to impending wage negotiations fell short of industrial action.

**7.160**   In relation to a lockout, 'relevant employees' means employees who were directly interested in the dispute in contemplation or furtherance of which the lockout occurred; in relation to a strike or other industrial action, it means those employees at the establishment who were taking part in the action at the complainant's date of dismissal: s 238(3). The provisions of section 237, which deal with the dismissal of those taking part in unofficial industrial action (considered above), do not affect the question of who are relevant employees for the purposes of section 238.

**7.161**   The main question which arises here is what constitutes 'taking part' in a strike or other industrial action. In *Coates v Modern Methods & Materials Ltd* (1982) the Court of Appeal stressed that the words 'taking part in a strike' are ordinary words the meaning of which the employment tribunal is best fitted to decide. It is the employee's actions, and not the reasons or motives behind the actions, that determine whether an employee is taking part in a strike. So if an employee stops work when other employees come out on strike and neither says nor does anything to indicate disagreement with the strike or indicate a refusal to join the strike, the employee is taking part in a strike. See also *McCormick v Horsepower Ltd* (1981) and *Bolton Roadways Ltd v Edwards* (1987). In *Manifold Industries Ltd v Sims* (1991), the EAT emphasised that the question whether or not an employee is taking part in a strike is to be determined by what he or she was in fact doing; the employer's knowledge of the employee's actions is not a relevant consideration.

**7.162**   Finally, ERA 1996, s 107 requires the tribunal to ignore certain kinds of pressure from third parties and to decide upon the reason for the dismissal and its fairness as if there had been no pressure. 'Pressure' is defined as 'any pressure which, by calling, organising, procuring or financing a strike or other industrial action, or threatening to do so, was exercised on the employer to dismiss the employee.' See *Trend v Chiltern Hunt Ltd* (1977), *Hazells Offset Ltd v Luckett* (1977), *Ford Motor Co Ltd v Hudson* (1978), and *Colwyn Borough Council v Dutton*

(1980). If the pressure was exercised because the employee was not a trade union member, the employer or the employee may ask the employment tribunal, under TULRCA 1992, s 160, to join as a party to the proceedings the person claimed to have exerted the pressure. That person may have to make a total or partial contribution to any compensation awarded against the employer.

## Replacement employees

**7.163** In view of the fact that the qualifying period for the right not to be unfairly dismissed is one year, the provisions of ERA 1996, s 106 are not likely to be needed very often. Section 106 specifically applies to employees engaged to replace employees absent because of pregnancy or childbirth or on adoption leave. The replacement must be told in writing that the employment will be ended when the absent employee returns. When he or she is dismissed, the dismissal will be treated as being for some other substantial reason, but the employer will still need to satisfy the requirements of section 98(4), which should not be difficult.

## Remedies

**7.164** The remedies available to an employee whose complaint of unfair dismissal succeeds are a re-employment order or compensation. In a limited number of cases, interim relief may be asked for. Employment tribunals do not have the power to grant injunctions, which in any case are most likely to be appropriate to enforce a restrictive covenant. It is worth bearing in mind that, at the end of the day, the only real question for an employer is how much it will be necessary to pay an employee, since non-compliance with a re-employment order or an order following on from an interim relief application will mean a larger compensation bill. For a full discussion of these remedies, see Upex, *The Law of Termination of Employment* (6th ed, 2001), chapters 7 and 8.

### Reinstatement and re-engagement orders

**7.165** The main remedies for unfair dismissal were intended to be reinstatement and re-engagement orders, and the whole tenor of the statutory provisions is to suggest that the employment tribunal should apply those remedies first: see ss 112–116. In reality, though, few re-employment orders are made.

**7.166** A reinstatement order is an order to the employer to treat the applicant as if he or she had not been dismissed. In deciding whether to make an order, the tribunal must comply with the requirements of section 116(1), and take into account the following factors: the complainant's wishes; the practicability for the employer of compliance with the order; and, where the complainant caused or contributed to some extent to the dismissal, whether it would be just to order reinstatement.

**7.167** If the tribunal decides not to order reinstatement, it should then consider whether to order re-engagement: s 116(2). A re-engagement order is an order that the employee should be engaged by the employer, or by a successor of the employer or an associated employer, in employment comparable to that from which he or she was dismissed, or 'other suitable employment': s 115(1). In deciding whether to make the order, the tribunal must have regard to the requirements of section 116(3). The three factors it must take into account are similar to those mentioned above in relation to reinstatement orders. In relation to the second factor (practicability), however, the tribunal must consider the practicability of re-engagement with a successor of the employer or an associated employer.

**7.168** The first step the tribunal should take is to explain to the employee the re-employment orders it may make and to ask whether he or she wishes the tribunal to make an order; if the employee asks for a re-employment order to be made, the tribunal may then make an order, but is not obliged to do so: s 112(2) and (3). If the tribunal decides to consider making a re-employment order, it must first consider whether to make a reinstatement order; if it decides not to do so, it must then consider whether to make a re-engagement order. If it decides not to make any order, it must make an award of compensation: s 112(4).

**7.169** The effect of an order of reinstatement is to give the employee his or her old job back; it will include an ancillary order for arrears of pay between the date of dismissal and the date of reinstatement. There is no statutory maximum to the amount which may be ordered to be paid under section 114(2)(a). The effect of a re-engagement order will be to give the employee a job similar to the one from which he or she was dismissed. Section 115(2) requires the tribunal when making the order to specify the terms of re-engagement, again including arrears of pay.

**7.170** If the employer does not comply fully with the terms of a reinstatement or re-engagement order, the tribunal must award such an amount of compensation as it thinks fit having regard to the loss sustained by the employee, subject to the maximum permissible: s 117(1) and (2). If the employer totally fails to comply, then the tribunal must go on to award compensation in the usual way and it must also make an additional award of compensation in accordance with s 117(3)(b). In cases of total non-compliance, the employer may escape the consequences of non-compliance by showing that it was not 'practicable' to comply with the re-employment order: s 117(4).

## Compensation

**7.171** An employment tribunal will award compensation if it makes no order for re-employment, or if it makes such an order but the employer totally fails to comply with it. Compensation may consist of the following elements: a basic award; a compensatory award; and an additional award.

**7.172** If the employment tribunal makes a finding of unfair dismissal, it must first consider whether to make an order for the re-employment of the applicant. If he or she does not wish such an order to be made or if the tribunal decides against making an order, it will proceed to award compensation. If it does make an order, but the employer totally fails to comply with it, the tribunal will make an additional award and then go on to award compensation in the usual way. In most cases, compensation usually consists of a basic award and a compensatory award.

**7.173** The basic award is calculated in the same way as a redundancy payment. It is necessary to take the complainant's age, length of continuous employment on the effective date of termination and the amount of gross weekly pay. Reductions in the basic award may be made where the employee is near retirement, where the employee unreasonably refuses an offer of reinstatement, where the employee's conduct before dismissal makes it just and equitable to make a reduction, where the employee has already received a redundancy payment, and where the employee has received an ex gratia payment from the employer.

**7.174** The compensatory award should be 'such amount as the tribunal considers just and equitable in all the circumstances having regard to the loss sustained by the complainant in consequence of the dismissal in so far as that loss is attributable to action taken by the employer': see s 123(1). The maximum amount of compensatory award that may be awarded was £55,000 as from 1 February 2004. The heads of loss which the compensatory award may cover were set out in *Norton Tool Co Ltd v Tewson* (1972) and are: (1) immediate loss of wages; (2) manner of dismissal; (3) future loss of wages; and (4) loss of protection in respect of unfair dismissal or dismissal by reason of redundancy. A fifth head of loss was subsequently added: loss of pension rights.

**7.175** It is important to note that in two types of unfair dismissal the amount of the compensatory awards is unlimited. These are cases in which the dismissal is automatically unfair because it was a health and safety case and covered by s 100 or because the employee made a 'protected disclosure' and the dismissal fell within s 103A, or because the employee was selected for reasons falling within either of those provisions: see paras. 7.124 and 7.131 above. This is an exception to the general rule that the compensatory award is subject to a limit, the current limit being £55,000 as from 1 February 2004.

**7.176** The compensatory award is subject to deductions, the main ones being deductions in respect of mitigation and deductions for 'contributory fault' under s 123(4) and (6) respectively. It is also subject to adjustments by virtue of the provisions of the Employment Act 2002 in relation to non-completion of statutory procedures. Additional awards may also fall to be made.

## Futher reading

Collins, H, *Justice in Dismissal* (1992) Oxford.

Deakin, S, & Morris, G, *Labour Law* (3rd ed, 2001) Butterworths (chapter 5).

Smith, I, & Thomas, G, *Industrial Law* (8th ed, 2003) Butterworths (chapters, 8 & 9 ).

Upex, R, *The Law on Termination of Employment* (6th ed, 2001) Jordans.

### Article

Hepple, B, & Morris, G, (2002) 'The Employment Act 2002 and the Crisis of Individual Employment Rights', *Industrial Law Journal*, Vol. 31, No. 2, September, pp. 245–269.

## Self-test questions

1. Harry has worked for Speedy Co as an HGV driver for 10 years. Over the last six months Harry's attendance record has been poor; he has frequently been absent for at least one day each week and claims to have been suffering from back trouble. Speedy Co is suspicious about the absences and warns Harry that it cannot tolerate the situation indefinitely. In March 1994, Speedy's personnel manager, Graham, arranged for Harry to see Sheila, the company's medical officer, but Sheila is unable to confirm or deny whether the back trouble is genuine. On 1 April Harry failed to attend work and no explanation was received by the company. Graham thereupon telephoned Harry and told him that unless he apologised he need not turn up for work the next day. Harry retorted that he had no intention of apologising as he had left a message with Graham's secretary Flo, that his back was bad again. Flo denies this.

   Advise Speedy Co of the liabilities that arise in this scenario.

2. The Employment Act 2002 does much to protect employers, little for employees. Explain this statement in relation to procedural fairness in unfair dismissal.

3. Emma is the owner of Posh's Garage. Robbie and Kylie are employed as mechanics and David is the petrol pump attendant. Recently Emma decided she was overdoing things and has agreed to sell the garage to Geri who already owns Spice Sports Cars Showroom. Geri tells Emma that David's services will not be required as his younger brother Liam is unemployed and looking for a job. Emma dismisses David two days before the sale is completed. One month after taking over Posh's Garage Geri decides there is not enough work there for two mechanics and asks Robbie to move to Spice Sports Cars Showroom. Robbie refuses since Spice Sports Cars Showroom is five miles further from his home than Posh's Garage, and he is therefore dismissed. The following week, Kylie is replaced by Noel, in order to service fuel-injection engines in high performance motor cars.

   Advise David, Robbie and Kylie.

4. 'There is no justice in dismissal'. Critically evaluate Collin's theory, using case law examples to support your arguments.

# CHAPTER EIGHT

# Redundancy

## Summary

This chapter considers the law relating to redundancy. Employees dismissed for redundancy have two main statutory rights: (1) the right to complain of unfair dismissal and (2) the right to claim a redundancy payment. The advent of the unfair dismissal right has meant that there are fewer claims for redundancy payments, for two main reasons: the qualifying period of employment is shorter and the levels of compensation are potentially higher. In addition, the statutory provisions relating to unfair dismissal are less complex than those relating to redundancy payments.

This chapter will consider:

- the definition of redundancy; and

- redundancy payments claims.

At the end of this chapter, the right to time off during the notice period to look for new employment or make arrangements for training for further employment will be discussed briefly.

## Redundancy

**8.1**   The statutory provisions relating to redundancy payments originated in the Redundancy Payments Act 1965. That Act was the first attempt to provide a floor of rights and its provisions gave rise to a large number of cases, many of them trying to apply the definition of 'redundancy' to a variety of different situations. Much of that case law is now of historical interest only, but it gave rise to interesting and intricate discussions, for example, about the nature of pastry cooking. Nevertheless, looking back at the legislation, one can say that it was a notable milestone on the road to the creation of a floor of rights.

**8.2**  Employees are generally only entitled to the right not to be unfairly dismissed, as has been seen, if they have been continuously employed for one year, though that requirement is sometimes lifted: see ERA 1996, s 108, as amended by the Unfair Dismissal and Statement of Reasons for Dismissal (Variation of Qualifying Period) Order 1999 (SI 1999/1436) and Chapter 6. In the case of the right to claim a redundancy payment, the employee must have been continuously employed for two years: ERA 1996, s 155. In both cases, the employee must have been dismissed. The definition of 'dismiss' is considered in Chapter 5. It should be noted that, in the case of claims under Part XI (ie the provisions relating to redundancy payments claims), the definition is extended in cases where the employee is offered alternative employment: see ERA 1996, ss 136(5) and 139(1) and (4). The definition of 'redundancy', which is the first matter to be considered in this chapter, is common to both the unfair dismissal and redundancy payments rights. Apart from the definition of redundancy, however, the two Parts governing the separate rights are completely self-contained. This means that the provisions of Part XI are not applicable to unfair dismissal claims, nor are those of Part X applicable to redundancy payments claims. It will be an error of law if a tribunal applies the wrong provisions to the wrong type of claim: see *Hempell v WH Smith & Sons Ltd* (1986) and *Jones v Governing Body of Burdett Coutts School* (1997). See also *Shawkat v Nottingham City Hospital NHS Trust* (1999).

**8.3**  In general, an employee dismissed for redundancy will be advised to complain of unfair dismissal or make a dual claim. This is because a complaint under the unfair dismissal provisions enables the employment tribunal to decide whether the employer's decision to dismiss was reasonable in all the circumstances, whereas the redundancy payments provisions merely enable the tribunal to decide whether the statutory presumption of redundancy has or has not been rebutted.

Further, the unfair dismissal provisions give an employee the possibility of receiving greater compensation, in the form of the basic award, which is calculated in the same way as a redundancy payment, plus a compensatory award, which is not available under the redundancy payments provisions. In the case of a dual claim, the successful employee will either receive a basic award or a redundancy payment, but not both, since ERA 1996, s 122(4) contains set-off provisions.

## The definition of redundancy

**8.4** As was mentioned above, the definition of redundancy serves a dual purpose: redundancy is one of the potentially fair reasons in unfair dismissal cases, and an employee who is dismissed by reason of redundancy is also entitled to a redundancy payment: ERA 1996, s 135(1).

**8.5** Redundancy is defined in s 139(1) as follows:

... An employee who is dismissed shall be taken to be dismissed by reason of redundancy if the dismissal is wholly or mainly attributable to —

(a)  the fact that his employer has ceased or intends to cease
    (i)   to carry on the business for the purposes of which the employee was employed by him, or
    (ii)  to carry on that business in the place where the employee was so employed, or
(b) the fact that the requirements of that business
    (i)   for employees to carry out work of a particular kind, or
    (ii)  for employees to carry out work of a particular kind in the place where the employee was employed by the employer,
have ceased or diminished or are expected to cease or diminish.

**8.6** Section 139(6) makes clear that 'cease' and 'diminish' mean cease and diminish either permanently or temporarily and for whatever reason.

**8.7** In cases involving only a claim for a redundancy payment, section 163(2) enacts a presumption of redundancy. This means that the burden is on the employer who wishes to dispute liability to make the payment to prove that the employee was not redundant. In cases involving a complaint of unfair dismissal and a claim for a redundancy payment, however, the presumption will not operate in relation to the unfair dismissal complaint: see Employment Tribunals Act 1996, s 7(6). In unfair dismissal cases, the burden is on the employer to show what the reason (or principal reason) for the dismissal was. If an employer fails to discharge that burden, the dismissal will be automatically held to be unfair. It is therefore possible for an employer to fail to rebut the presumption of redundancy in the redundancy payment claim and thus become liable for a redundancy payment, and to fail to establish the reason for the dismissal in the unfair dismissal claim and thus be held to have dismissed the employee unfairly: see *Midland Foot Comfort Centre v Moppett* (1973).

**8.8** The first question to determine is whether the dismissal is by reason of the particular circumstances which constitute a redundancy. In *Hindle v Percival Boats Ltd* (1969), the Court of Appeal held that, provided that the employer honestly believes that the dismissal of the employee is due to some reason other than redundancy (however mistaken the belief may be), the dismissal will not be by reason of redundancy. But it emphasised that employment tribunals must be wary of dishonest employers or employers who misdirect themselves into thinking that they were influenced by the employee's deficiencies, when the main factor was that the requirements of the business had declined.

## Mobility and redundancy

**8.9** The definition of redundancy in section 139(1) uses the phrase 'in the place where the employee was ... employed.' In earlier cases, the issue was regarded as being one determined by reference to the employee's contract, in other words whether the employer had contractual authority, express or implied, to order the employee to move; or, put in another way, what degree of contractual mobility the employee was subject to. The effect was that if the employee was required to move to another factory within the radius of the mobility obligation because of the closure of the factory where he or she worked, it would not be possible to claim a redundancy payment, since there had not been a cessation of the business in the place where he or she was employed: see *United Kingdom Atomic Energy Authority v Claydon* (1974), *Sutcliffe v Hawker Siddeley Aviation Ltd* (1973) and *Rank Xerox Ltd v Churchill* (1988). This has been called the 'contractual test'.

**8.10** In *Bass Leisure Ltd v Thomas* (1994), on the other hand, what has been called the 'factual' test was used. There, the EAT said that 'the place' where an employee is employed does not extend to any place where the employee may be contractually required to work; the question is primarily a factual one and the only relevant contractual terms are those which define the place of employment and its extent.

**8.11** The question whether the 'contractual' or 'factual' test is to be preferred has been considered by the Court of Appeal, in *High Table Ltd v Horst* (1997). Peter Gibson LJ reviewed the case law and distinguished the earlier cases on the ground that the issue considered there by the Court of Appeal was whether the employees in question were in breach of contract in refusing an instruction to work further afield than they had previously been accustomed to. He preferred the conclusion of the EAT in the later case of *Bass Leisure Ltd v Thomas* (above) that the place where the employee is employed 'is to be established by a factual inquiry, taking into account the employee's fixed or changing place or places of work and any contractual terms which go to evidence or define the place of employment and its extent, but not those (if any) which make provisions for the employee to be transferred to another.'

**8.12** This is an important decision, but it should be remembered, however, that Peter Gibson LJ emphasises that it goes merely to the question whether the employee was redundant and not whether the employer acted reasonably. Equally it will not affect the question whether the employee should lose the entitlement to a redundancy payment because he or she is held to have unreasonably refused a suitable offer of alternative employment: see para. 8.39 below.

## Applying the definition

**8.13** Of the two definitions of redundancy given in section 139(1), that relating to cessation of a business has caused little difficulty. It is not necessary to show that the employer is the legal owner of the business in question, only that that person is in control of the business:

see *Thomas v Jones* (1978). The other definition, in section 139(1)(b), that there is a cessation or diminution in the requirements of a business for work of a particular kind, is by no means straightforward and has caused considerable difficulties. In a series of cases, the Court of Appeal has held that the fact that there has been a reorganisation of the business does not necessarily mean that there has been a redundancy; it is part of the factual background. The fundamental question is whether the requirement for employees to carry out work of a particular kind has ceased or diminished. So, for example, in *Carry All Motors Ltd v Pennington* (1980), the employee was dismissed from his job as a transport clerk when his employers decided that the work of the transport manager and transport clerk could be carried out by one employee only. The tribunal decided that he had not been dismissed by reason of redundancy because the same work remained. The EAT reversed their decision and held that the question was whether the requirement for employees to do that work had diminished. Since one employee was doing the work formerly done by two, there was a redundancy.

**8.14** A reorganisation does not of itself mean that there is a redundancy situation, particularly if the amount of work remains the same or increases: In *Johnson v Nottinghamshire Combined Police Authority*, above, Lord Denning MR said:

> An employer is entitled to reorganise his business so as to improve its efficiency and, in doing so, to propose to his staff a change in the terms and conditions of their employment: and to dispense with their services if they do not agree. Such a change does not automatically give the staff a right to a redundancy payment. It only does so if the change in the terms and conditions is due to a redundancy situation.

**8.15** Subsequent decisions have tended to espouse the idea that, in considering whether there has been a diminution in the requirements of the business for employees to carry out work of a particular kind, the tribunal must look at the terms of the employee's contract. This is called the 'contract test'. An example of this is *Cowen v Haden Ltd* (1983), where an employee was employed as a divisional contracts surveyor and was 'required to undertake, at the direction of the company, any and all duties which reasonably fall within the scope of his capabilities.' The Court of Appeal held that the requirement that the

351

employee should perform the duties within the scope of his capabilities was restricted to the duties of a divisional contracts surveyor; the employers therefore had no right to require him to transfer from that work to assume the job of a quantity surveyor.

**8.16** The authorities in this area were carefully and critically reviewed by the EAT in *Safeway Stores plc v Burrell* (1997), which contains a valuable analysis of the approaches propounded by the courts in recent years. The employee's dismissal arose from a reorganisation or 'delayering' of the employers' management structure, with the result that there were less management positions than before, which gave rise to redundancies. The tribunal decided that he had not been dismissed by reason of redundancy, since the work done by the employee still had to be done and, therefore, the requirements of the employers' business for employees to carry out work of a particular kind had not ceased or diminished. The EAT reversed this decision and said that he had been dismissed by reason of redundancy. They said that a three-stage process is involved in determining whether a dismissal for redundancy has taken place: (1) was the employee dismissed? (2) had the requirements of the employer's business for employees to carry out work of a particular kind ceased or diminished? If so (3) was the dismissal of the employee caused wholly or mainly by the state of affairs identified in stage 2? They said that at stage 2, the only question to be asked is whether there is a cessation or diminution in the employer's requirements for employees (not the applicant) to carry out work of a particular kind and that, at this stage, it is irrelevant to consider the terms of the employee's contract. At stage 3, the tribunal is concerned with causation. This decision is important and should prompt a re-evaluation of the meaning of a dismissal for redundancy. It is also notable for its emphasis on the words of the statute.

**8.17** The *Safeway* decision was approved by the House of Lords in *Murray v Foyle Meats Ltd* (1997), Lord Irivine of Lairg LC said:

> The language of s. 139(1)(b) ... asks two questions of fact. The first is whether one or other of various states of economic affairs exists. In this case, the relevant one is whether the requirements of the business for employees to carry out work of a particular kind have diminished. The second question is whether the dismissal is attributable, wholly or mainly, to that state of affairs. This is a question of causation ... The key

word in the statute is 'attributable' and there is no reason in law why the dismissal of an employee should not be attributable to a diminution in the employer's needs for employees irrespective of the terms of his contract or the function which he performed.

**8.18** In the light of this decision, the decision of the EAT in *Church v West Lancashire NHS Trust* (1998) should be treated with caution. Further, the reasoning of the EAT in *Shawkat v Nottingham City Hospital NHS Trust* (1999) (which was not cited in *Murray v Foyle Meats Ltd*) seems in some respects to be inconsistent with the Murray decision, although the decision they arrived at could have been reached by means of the reasoning used in *Safeways Stores Ltd v Burrell* and *Murray v Foyle Meats Ltd*. In that case, the employee was employed as a staff grade doctor in thoracic surgery. Following the establishment of a cardio-thoracic unit, he was required to perform both cardiac and thoracic surgery. He refused and was dismissed. The tribunal rejected his claim that his dismissal was for redundancy, but the EAT allowed his appeal and remitted the case to the tribunal, on the footing that it was not clear that a tribunal could only have reached one conclusion. They said that the tribunal should have asked itself whether in the particular circumstances the requirements of the trust's business, the business for the purposes of which the employee was employed, for employees to carry out work of a particular kind had ceased or diminished. By excluding consideration of what the employee actually did and what he was employed to do, the tribunal had erred. They distinguished the Safeways case on the grounds that it was a 'bumping' case, although 'bumping' does not seem to have been involved there; in any case, in the light of the decision in Murray, that would seem to be irrelevant.

**8.19** It should be borne in mind that a reorganisation which does not fall within the statutory definition of redundancy may amount to 'some other substantial reason,' the fifth potentially fair reason in an unfair dismissal case: see para. 7.60 above.

## Redundancy consultation

**8.20** S. 188 TULRCA 1992 provides a duty to consult with trade unions in respect of redundancy situations. This collective right arises from the EU law, under the auspices of the Collective Redundancies

Directive 75/129 (as amended by a further revising Directive (92/56)). Consequently, redundancy consultation is governed by the Collective Redundancies and Transfer of Undertakings (Protection of Employment) (Amendment) Regulations 1999 (SI 1999/1925).

## Duty to Consult

**8.21**  Under the 1999 Regulations where an employer is 'proposing' to make 20 or more redundancies 'at one establishment', the employer must consult with trades unions, elected representatives or individually with the employees affected with a minimum of 30 days (see *Governing Body of the Northern Ireland Hotel and Catering College and North Eastern Education and Library Board v National Association of Teachers in Further and Higher Education* (1995)). Where the employer is proposing to dismiss 100 or more employees within a 90-day period under s.188(1) TULRCA 1992, the duty to consult arises where an employer is 'proposing to dismiss as redundant' (see *R v British Coal Corporation ex p Vardy* (1993)).

## Elected representatives

**8.22**  Where no trades unions are recognised (see Chapter 11), the 1999 Amendment Regulations provide a set of default provisions, requiring the election of employee representatives for the purposes of consultation in relation to the proposed redundancies. Where nobody comes forward for election, then the consultation may be undertaken on an individual employee basis (*R v Secretary of State for Trade and Industry ex p UNISON* (1996)).

## General duty to consult

**8.23**  S.188(2) TULRCA 1992 sets out a general duty to consult with those affected, through their union or by their elected representatives, about the redundancies. Consequently, s 188(4) TULRCA 1992 sets out the information to be provided by the employer regarding the redundancies, including the methods of selection, the criteria for the redundancies and the consequences, including the redundancy payments.

## Failure to Consult

**8.24**  Where an employer fails to consult with the affected workforce, s 189(1) TULRCA 1992 provides for complaint to an employment tribunal. The grounds for such a complaint can be for failure in relation to the election, or the withholding of information or lack of consultation overall. Where a tribunal upholds a complaint, it is obliged to make a declaration to that effect and may also make a protective award.

**8.25**  Protective awards are defined in s.189(3) and require the defaulting employer to pay compensation to the employees affected, normally no more than 90 days pay. The amount of the award is calculated on the basis of a week's pay of each employee for each week of the protected period.

**8.26**  Where 'special circumstances' exist which render it reasonably impracticable for an employer to comply with the requirements of consultation, such as consequential immediate closure of the business on death of the employer (*AEEU GMB v Clydesdale Group plc* (1995)), then a defence arises and the requisite sanctions would not apply. But the application of such a defence is a rarity and requires 'out of the ordinary' circumstances to have prevailed giving rise to such an exception.

## Mass redundancies

**8.27**  If an employer is proposing to dismiss a group of employees (usually more than 100 at any one time), there is an obligation to inform the Department of Trade & Industry (DTI), at least 90 days in advance of these redundancies taking place (see s 193 TULRCA 1992). Failure to notify the Secretary of State is a criminal offence which is punishable on summary conviction by a fine not exceeding £5,000. In these situations, the Government may provide guarantee payments, as it does so in insolvency redundancies.

## Claim for redundancy payment

**8.28**  The provisions governing offers of re-engagement and alternative employment operate in two separate ways: either they affect the question whether or not the employee is to be treated as having been dismissed; or they operate to disentitle him or her from receiving a redundancy payment which would otherwise be payable.

**8.29** There is the additional complicating factor of the trial period: this comes into operation in both cases where the offer of new employment differs at all from the terms of the previous employment. The trial period provisions are considered separately in the next section. The statutory provisions also apply where there is a change of employer: ss 141 and 146(1).

## Dismissal and offer of alternative employment

**8.30** Section 138 deals with the situation where an employee who is under notice of redundancy (or who has been constructively dismissed) is offered alternative employment. As will be seen from the discussion below, there are circumstances in which an employee will be treated as not having been dismissed. In such circumstances, there will be no entitlement to a redundancy payment, simply because entitlement to a payment depends upon having been dismissed for redundancy and, therefore, if there is no dismissal, there can be no entitlement. Once, however, the employee is found to have been dismissed, he or she may be disentitled from receiving the payment which would otherwise be payable if there is held to have been an unreasonable refusal of a suitable offer: see ss 141 and 146. The trial period provisions in section 138 build on the basic structure of section 136 by setting out the circumstances in which a trial period will come into operation. If an employee unreasonably terminates the employment during the trial period, that act will disentitle him or her from the right to receive a payment.

**8.31** Section 138 deals with the situation where an employee who is under notice of redundancy (or who has been constructively dismissed) is offered alternative employment. The point of its provisions, which follow on from the basic definition of dismissal in s 136 (which is very similar to the definition of dismissal in s 95 in relation to the unfair dismissal provisions), is to determine in what circumstances the employee is to be treated as having been dismissed.

**8.32** Section 138 caters for two alternative possibilities: either that the terms and conditions of the new employment are the same as those of the old, or that they are different. In both cases, there must be an offer of a renewal of the contract or of re-engagement under a new contract; an offer of re-engagement must be made before the ending of the employment under the previous contract. The renewal or re-engagement must take effect immediately on the ending of the previous employment, or within four weeks. If any of the conditions are not complied with, there will be a dismissal. Where the new contract is the same as the old, and all the conditions of section 138(1) are complied with, there will be no dismissal and section 213(2) will preserve continuity of employment. In *SI (Systems and Instruments) Ltd v Grist and Riley* (1983), the EAT said that, on a proper construction of what is now section 138(1), a distinction is to be drawn between cases of renewal and re-engagement. In cases of renewal, the offer need not be made before the termination of the contract of employment, but in cases of re-engagement under a new contract, the offer must be made before termination. 'Renewal' includes 'extension': ERA 1996, s 235(1).

## Trial period

**8.33** Where the provisions of the new contract differ at all from the provisions of the previous contract, section 138(2) brings a trial period into operation. If the employee leaves or is dismissed during the trial period, he or she will be treated as having been dismissed under the previous contract. An employee whose termination of the contract during the trial period is held to be unreasonable will be disentitled from receiving a redundancy payment: see para. 8.38 below.

**8.34** The coming into operation of the trial period occurs in all cases whether the old contract is renewed or the employee is re-engaged under a new contract and where there is a difference between the terms and conditions of the new contract and the corresponding provisions of the previous contract, unless it is one to which the de minimis rule applies: see *Rose v Henry Trickett & Sons Ltd* (1971). The trial period generally starts with the ending of the previous contract and ends four weeks from the date on which the employee starts work under the new contract, by virtue of section 138(3). In *Benton v Sanderson Kayser Ltd* (1989) the question arose as to the meaning 'period of four weeks', used by s 138(3)(b). The Court of Appeal held that 'period of four weeks' means a period of four consecutive weeks calculated according to the calendar, rather than the period of time actually worked.

**8.35** The trial period may only be extended, by agreement between the parties, for the purpose of retraining the employee and the agreement must comply with the requirements of s 138(6). An extension for any other reason will have no effect. This means that an employee who decides to leave during the period of the extension will be held to have resigned: see *Meek v J Allen Rubber Co Ltd and Secretary of State for Employment* (1980).

**8.36** An employee who leaves during the trial period or who is dismissed by the employer (for a reason connected with or arising out of the change in the contract) will be treated as having been dismissed on the date on which the previous contract ended and for the reason for which that contract was ended: s 138(4). Similar considerations apply where there is more than one renewal of the original contract or the employee is again re-engaged under a new contract. Section 138 applies also to offers of re-engagement with associated employers: s 146(1). It may be noted that a refusal to offer an employee a trial period may cause the dismissal to be unfair: see *Elliot v Richard Stump Ltd* (1987).

**8.37** In cases of constructive dismissal, the rules set out above will apply, but with the added complication that a so-called common law trial period will come into existence. This means that if, in breach of the contract, the employee is transferred to another department and takes the job there on trial, he or she has a reasonable period in which to decide whether to take the new job or leave (the 'common law' trial period). If he or she decides to take it, the statutory trial period then comes into operation: see *Air Canada v Lee* (1978) and *Turvey v CW Cheyney & Son Ltd* (1979). The difficulty with this is that, since the employee is granted a reasonable time under the common law trial period to make up his or her mind, it is not easy to know when the statutory trial period has started and whether, when the employee left the employment, the statutory period had ended or not. If it had, there will have been no dismissal and the employee will be held to have resigned.

**8.38** If the employee leaves during the trial period, entitlement to a redundancy payment will be lost if the new employment was suitable, and the termination of the employment during the trial period was unreasonable: s 141(4). For a consideration of what is unreasonable, see para. 8.39 below.

## Offers of re-engagement or alternative employment

**8.39** The provisions of ERA 1996, s 141 affect an employee treated as dismissed for redundancy by virtue of s 138. An employee will be disentitled from receiving a redundancy payment where he or she unreasonably refuses an offer of suitable new employment. Section 141(1) applies to an offer made before the ending of the previous employment to renew the contract or re-engage him or her under a new one, the renewal or re-engagement taking effect no more than four weeks after the ending of the previous contract. If the provisions of the new contract are the same as those of the old, the employee will be disentitled, if he or she unreasonably refuses the offer: s 141(2) and (3)(a). Where the provisions of the new contract differ, the first question is whether the offer is an offer of 'suitable employment in relation to the employee', since section 141(2) will only disentitle the employee in the case of an unreasonable refusal of a suitable offer: see 141(3)(b). If he or she actually gives the new contract a try, the statutory trial period will come into operation; if he or she then leaves during it, entitlement will be lost if the new employment was suitable, and the termination of the employment during the trial period was unreasonable: s 141(4). Whether there has been an offer is essentially an issue of fact for the tribunal to decide.

**8.40** The two significant questions here concern what is meant by 'suitable' and 'unreasonable'. They must be kept separate and dealt with separately by the tribunal: see *Carron Co. v Robertson* (1967), *Hindes v Supersine Ltd* (1979) and *Taylor v Kent County Council* (1969). The suitability of the offer is to be looked at objectively by the employment tribunal and is regarded by the appellate courts as being a matter of fact and degree for it to decide. In *Taylor v Kent County Council Lord Parker CJ* said that suitability 'means employment which is substantially equivalent to the employment which has ceased', but there are suggestions in later cases that an objectively unsuitable offer may be made suitable (or vice versa) by the employee's attitude towards it: see, for example, *Hindes v Supersine Ltd*, and *Executors of J F Everest v Cox* (1980).

**8.41** In the case of an offer found not to be suitable, it will not be necessary to go on to consider the reasonableness of the employee's refusal. If, however, the offer is found to be suitable, the tribunal must then consider the reasonableness of the refusal by looking at the personal reasons that relate to the employee. This is a subjective matter to be considered from the employee's point of view: see *Cambridge & District Co-operative Society Ltd v Ruse* (1993). This must be judged as at the time the offer is made and not with hindsight, taking account of the personal circumstances of the individual employee, and also his or her reaction in those circumstances; all the relevant factors should be considered as a whole: see *Thomas Wragg & Sons Ltd v Wood* (1976), *Paton Calvert & Co. Ltd v Westerside* (1979), and *Executors of JF Everest v Cox*, above. In looking at the two separate factors of suitability and reasonableness, the employment tribunal is entitled to look at factors which may be common to both questions: see *Spencer v Gloucestershire County Council* (1985).

## Change of employer

**8.42** The statutory provisions discussed in the preceding sections apply equally to associated employers of the original employer. This means that an offer of employment made by an associated employer is as good as an offer made by the original employer and the provisions of section 141 apply in the same way to an employee who is offered employment by an associated employer: see s 146(1). Provided that the person offering employment is within the definition of 'associated employer', it does not matter that the associated employer has no employees at the time of the offer of employment and is a dormant company reactivated especially for the purpose of offering employment to the redundant employee(s): see *Lucas v Henry Johnson (Packers & Shippers) Ltd* (1986).

**8.43** In other cases, the transferee of the business may incur liability. This will depend upon whether there has been a transfer of an undertaking within the Transfer of Undertakings Regulations 1981: see the next chapter, Chapter 9.

## The effect of misconduct

**8.44**  If an employee is dismissed for misconduct, albeit in a redundancy situation, the presumption of redundancy will be rebutted and the dismissal will not have been by reason of redundancy. In such a case, the tribunal should scrutinise the employer's reason carefully, to ensure that it is not a reason trumped up to defeat a legitimate claim. If, on the other hand, the employer dismisses the employee for redundancy, but discovers misconduct on his or her part, ERA 1996, s 140(1) must be complied with. This provision operates so as to disentitle an employee where the employer, 'being entitled to terminate his contract of employment by reason of the employee's conduct', terminates it in one of three ways: (1) without notice, or (2) by giving shorter notice than the employee is entitled to, or (3) by giving the correct notice but also stating in writing that the employer would be entitled to terminate the contract summarily because of the employee's conduct.

**8.45**  The EAT has expressed the view that what is now section 140(1) applies where there is a single dismissal (ie a dismissal for redundancy and not explicitly for misconduct) as well as a double dismissal (ie a dismissal for redundancy followed by a dismissal for misconduct): see *Simmons v Hoover Ltd* (1977). So if, for example, the employer gives the employee less notice than he or she is entitled to and subsequently misconduct on the part of the employee comes to light, section 140(1) will relieve the employer of liability; if, on the other hand, the employer gives the correct notice, liability to pay a redundancy payment will not be extinguished unless the employee is dismissed a second time.

**8.46**  Section 140(1) uses the phrase 'where the employer, being entitled to terminate his contract ...' The effect of the italicised words was considered by the EAT in *Bonner v H Gilbert Ltd* (1989). It held that where the employer raises a defence to a redundancy payments claim based on s 140(1), the question of whether or not he or she is entitled to terminate the employee's contract must be determined according to the 'contractual' approach propounded in *Western Excavating (ECC) Ltd v Sharp* (1978). In other words, the employer must show that the employee was guilty of conduct which was a significant breach of contract or which showed that he or she no longer intended to be bound by one or more of the essential terms of the contract. A reasonable belief that the employee has committed a breach of contract will not be enough.

**8.47**  Section 140(3) gives the employment tribunal power to award all or part of the redundancy payment, where the employer terminates the contract in accordance with s 140(1) and the second dismissal takes place 'at any relevant time'. This phrase is defined in s 140(5) as 'any time within the obligatory period'; 'obligatory period' is defined in section 136(4). In *Simmons v Hoover Ltd (1977)* the EAT expressed the view that what is now section 140(3) applies only where there are two dismissals. If their analysis of section 140(1) and (3) is correct, the result is that some serious anomalies exist, which tend to favour employers who act wrongfully.

**8.48**  Special considerations apply in the case of strikes. The employee's action in taking part in a strike has been held to be 'employee's conduct' within section 140(1): see *Simmons v Hoover Ltd (1977)* above. If the dismissal provokes a strike, section 140(2) operates to negate the effect of s 140(1), so that the employee does not lose the entitlement to a redundancy payment. Section 140(2) will not operate, however, if the strike came first. In that case, s 140(1) will operate. It is a moot point whether section 140(3) will operate, but it is submitted that it does not, since its terms exclude termination by reason of taking part in a strike.

## Calculation of redundancy payment

**8.49**  The calculation of a redundancy payment is based on the following factors: the employee's age at the relevant date (in most cases, the same date as the effective date of termination in unfair dismissal cases; the number of years of continuous employment; and the amount of gross weekly pay (calculated in accordance with ss 220–229). The calculation is subject to the following limits: (1) the number of years used in the calculation may not exceed 20: s 162(3); and (2) the amount of a week's pay may not exceed a figure set annually by the Secretary of State, the amount being currently £250: s 227(1), as amended by the Employment Rights (Increase of Limits) Order 2003 (SI 2003/3038).

**8.50** Redundancy payments are calculated in accordance with ERA 1996, s 162 and the total amount arrived at may be subject to a deduction in certain cases, mainly in the case of misconduct or where employees are near retirement age. Social security benefits paid to the employee are not deductible.

**8.51** The method of calculation is to take each year of continuous employment, working backwards from the relevant date. For each year of continuous employment the amount of the redundancy payment is assessed on the basis of the employee's age at the beginning of the year. For each year in which the employee was aged 41 or more (but not more than 64), one and a half week's pay is payable; for each year in which he or she was between 22 and 41, one weeks' pay; for each year over the age of 18 between the time he or she started work and 22, half a week's pay: ss 162(2) and 211 (2). Thus, an employee employed for 20 years and made redundant at 62 will receive a redundancy payment reckoned on the basis of the years of continuous employment from 62 going back to 42. The maximum redundancy payment that can be awarded at present is thus £7,500. Employment before the age of 18 may not be counted: s 211(2). The employee's period of continuous employment will be treated as starting on his or her 18th birthday if that date is later than the starting date. The employment tribunal may use its discretion to award all or part of a redundancy payment in cases involving misconduct by the employee: see para. 8.44.

## Right of employee to time off

**8.52** Employees given notice of dismissal by reason of redundancy are entitled by section 52(1) to reasonable time off during the notice period to look for new employment or make arrangements for training for further employment. They must have been continuously employed for two years. They need not provide evidence that they have an appointment, though it may be relevant to the reasonableness of the employer's conduct to ask whether the employee has an appointment and to make some enquiries about it: see *Dutton v Hawker Siddeley Aviation Ltd* (1978). The amount of time off is not statutorily defined, but the employee is not entitled to be paid more than 40 per cent of a week's pay: s 53(1) and (5). That does not mean, however, that it would not be reasonable for the employer to allow more time off, though the employee would not be entitled to be paid. Disputes about this entitlement are heard by the employment tribunal: s 54.

**8.53** It should be noted that only those made redundant are entitled to the right to time off, and not other employees who are dismissed, and that the entitlement to time off does not depend upon the employee's eventual entitlement, or otherwise, to a redundancy payment: see *Dutton v Hawker Siddeley Aviation Ltd*, above.

## Futher reading

Deakin, S, & Morris, G, *Labour Law* (3rd ed, 2001) Butterworths (chapter 5).

Smith, I, & Thomas, G, *Industrial Law* (8th ed, 2003) Butterworths (chapters 8 & 9).

Upex, R, *The Law on Termination of Employment* (6th ed, 2001) Jordans.

### Article

Hall, M, & Edwards, P, (1999) 'Reforming the statutory redundancy consultation procedure', *Industrial Law Journal*, Vol. 28, No. 4, December, pp. 299–318.

## Self-test questions

1.  Violetta is a professional singer and is employed by Manc Operatics Company. Two weeks ago, Violetta overheard at a post-concert party that Aled, the Musical Director, would have to reorganise the Company due to financial pressures.

    Last week, Violetta was offered a lead singing part in the next touring musical, to be played in the USA, Europe and Australia. However, yesterday Violetta learnt that she is pregnant and decided that the travelling will be too much. When she informed the Company's managing director, Diana, of her news, Violetta was added to Aled's 'redundancy list'. The next day, Isolde was given Violetta's role on tour.

Figaro, the company's pianist does not like overseas travel and has asked if he might be found alternative work in the UK, whilst the others go on tour. Diana, has informed him that '... it is part of your contract and if you don't go you are effectively resigning from your post'. Figaro formally resigned earlier today. Though, the Management Team has today announced that 'It was intending to make all the Company's musicians redundant, since its future overseas tours would not require them any longer, as it would employ musicians in the various places during the tour'.

Advise Violetta and Figaro.

2.    'Redundancy payments fail to reflect an employee's loyalty to their employer'. Discuss.

3.    Explain the legal significance of consultation in redundancy situations.

4.    Talk-francais, a French multinational company, makes mobile phones and has 70% of the European market. Recently technological innovation in camera-mobiles has appeared and Talk-francais is competing with its main market rival, Hellenic-Speak. Hellenic-Speak purchases the innovation and announces plans to manufacture camera-mobiles within the next 6 months. Consequently Talk-francais sales fall and as a result Talk-Francais announces the closure of its UK subsidiary and informs its French workforce that 20% of the 1,100 workers will be dismissed and the remainder must accept a 30% cut in pay. Simultaneously, Talk-Francais sells its Marketing Division to Hellenic-Speak.

Advise the employees of Talk-francais of any dismissial and/or redundancy rights which they may have?

# CHAPTER NINE

# Transfers of Undertakings

## Summary

Business reorganisations are widespread. To that end, the law seeks to regulate them under TUPE. TUPE provides a complex blend of both EU and UK legal principles. In this chapter we consider the regulation of business transfers, the sale of the ownership of a business and the consequential changing from employer A to new employer B, and its effects upon the contract of employment and the employee subjected to the transfer.

This chapter will consider:

- the definition of a transfer;

- the concept of 'relevant transfer';

- what transfers and does not;

- whether unfair dismissal claims can be brought; and

- what changes can be made to terms and conditions post-transfer.

At the end of this chapter, the right to consultation will be discussed.

## TUPE

**9.1** The law relating to Transfers of Undertakings derives from EEC Council Directive 187 of February 14 1977, on the Approximation of the Laws of the Member States relating to the Safeguarding of Employee's Rights in the Event of Transfers of Undertakings, Businesses or Parts of Businesses (77/187/EEC). The 1977 Directive was subsequently amended by Directive 98/59/EC and both directives have now been consolidated into Council Directive 2001/23/EC, whose provisions are quoted in the text below. The original directive was transposed into domestic law by the Transfer of Undertakings (Protection of Employment) Regulations 1981 (as amended) (TUPE). The 2001 Directives awaits transposition into UK Law. That event is expected to happen in 2005.

## Directive 2001/23/EC

**9.2** The provisions of the Directive have (which, as already seen, derive from the 1977 Directive) have been considered in a considerable number of decisions in the European Court of Justice. In *Foreningen af Arbejdsledere i Danmark v Daddy's Dance Hall A/S* (1988), one of the cases of lasting significance in this area, the Court said:

> ... The objective of Directive 77/187 is to ensure as far as possible the safeguarding of employees' rights in the event of a change of proprietor of the undertaking and to allow them to remain in the service of the new proprietor on the same condition as those agreed with the vendor. The Directive therefore applies as soon as there is a change, resulting from a conventional sale or a merger, of the natural or legal person responsible for operating the undertaking who, consequently, enters into obligations as an employer towards employees working in the undertaking, and it is of no importance to know whether the ownership of the undertaking has been transferred.

**9.3** Article 1(1)(a) of the Directive states that it is to apply to 'any transfer of an undertaking, business or part of an undertaking or business to another employer as a result of a legal transfer or merger.' Article 1(1) goes on to state:

(b)     ... there is a transfer within the meaning of this Directive where there is a transfer of an economic entity which retains its identity, meaning an organised grouping of resources which has the objective of pursuing an economic activity, whether or not that activity is central or ancillary.

(c)   This Directive shall apply to public and private undertakings engaged in economic activities whether or not they are operating for gain.

**9.4**   These new provisions were substituted by Council Directive 98/50/EC and are intended to clarify the legal concept of transfer in the light of the previous case law of the ECJ.

**9.5**   Article 3 provides for the automatic transfer to the transferee of the transferor's rights and obligations arising from a contract of employment or from an employment relationship existing on the date of the transfer. In *Katsikas v Konstantinidis* (1993) the European Court of Justice held that this provision does not preclude an employee employed by the transferor from objecting to the transfer to the transferee of the contract of employment or employment relationship. It said that in such cases it is for the Member States to decide what the fate of the contract of employment or employment relationship with the transferor should be.

**9.6**   Article 4(1) (as substituted) states:

> The transfer of the undertaking, business or part of the undertaking or business shall not in itself constitute grounds for dismissal by the transferor or the transferee. This provision shall not stand in the way of dismissals that may take place for economic, technical or organisational reasons entailing changes in the work force.

**9.7**   Article 4(2) goes on to provide that if the contract of employment or the employment relationship is terminated because the transfer involves a substantial change in working conditions to the detriment of the employee, the employer is to be regarded as having been responsible for the termination. The relationship between Article 3(1) as interpreted in the *Katsikas* case (above) and Article 4(2) was considered by the ECJ in *Merckx and Neuhuys v Ford Motors Co Belgium SA* (1997). The distinction made by the Court is between the employee of his or her own accord deciding not to continue with the employment relationship with the transferee, in which case the *Katsikas* case will apply, and terminating the contract because the transfer involves a substantial change in working conditions, such as a change in the level of remuneration; in the latter case, Article 4(2) will apply. Much will depend upon the facts of any given case.

**9.8** The following matters will be considered: (1) the meaning of 'undertaking' and 'business'; (2) what amounts to a 'transfer'; (3) the effect of article 4 in relation to dismissals.

## The meaning of 'undertaking' and 'business'

**9.9** The question is important since it relates to the coverage of the Directive and the sorts of transfers which are embraced by it. In *Allen v Amalgamated Construction Co Ltd* (2000) the Court said:

> It is ... clear that the Directive is intended to cover any legal change in the person of the employer ... and ... it can, therefore, apply to a transfer between two subsidiary companies in the same group, which are distinct legal persons each with specific employment relationships with their employees. The fact that the companies in question not only have the same ownership but also the same management and the same premises and that they are engaged in the same works makes no difference in this regard.

Thus a transfer between subsidiary companies in the same corporate group is covered by the Directive.

**9.10** Decisions of the ECJ in the early 1990s suggested that the court was prepared to take a broad view of activities which were to be treated as a business or part of a business. In *Stichting v Bartol* (1992), the ECJ said that 'activities of a special nature' may be regarded as comparable to a business or part of a business. The case arose in the context of the switch of a grant from one foundation to another, neither being profit-making organisations. In *Rask and Christensen v ISS Kantineservice A/S* (1993), which involved the outsourcing of a staff canteen, the ECJ took the matter a stage further and said that the Directive can apply to a situation where the owner of an undertaking entrusts to the owner of another undertaking, by means of a contract, the responsibility of providing a service for employees, which it had previously operated directly, and which is ancillary to its economic activities. The Court developed this view further in *Schmidt v Spar- und*

*Leihkasse der Früheren Ämter Bordesholm, Kiel und Cronshagen* (1995), when it decided that the Directive may apply to an ancillary activity where the transfer involves a single employee and does not involve the transfer of any tangible assets. See also *EC Commission v United Kingdom* (1994), in which the ECJ said: '... The Court has already accepted, at least implicitly, in the context of competition law ... or social law ... that a body might be engaged in economic activities and be regarded as an 'undertaking' for the purposes of Community law even though it did not operate with a view to profit.'

**9.11**  Recent decisions of the European Court of Justice suggest that the Court is taking a more cautious approach to interpretation of the Directive. Thus, for example, in *Ledernes Hovedorganisation (Acting on behalf of Rygaard) v Dansk Arbejdsgiverforening (Acting on behalf of Strø Mølle Akustik A/S) (Rygaard's case)* (1996), which involved the taking over by a sub-contractor of completion of a building contract, together with the workers and materials assigned to it, the ECJ decided that the Directive did not apply. The Court reiterated that the decisive criterion is whether the business in question retains its identity and went on to say that the transfer should relate to 'a stable economic entity whose activity is not limited to performing one specific works contract'. They said that the directive does not apply where the transferor undertaking merely makes available to the new contractor certain workers and material for carrying out the works in question.

**9.12**  The decision in *Rygaard's* case may be contrasted with the decision in *Merckx and Neuhuys v Ford Motors Co Belgium SA* (1997), decided some six months later. The case involved the transfer of a car dealership without a transfer of tangible assets from Ford dealers to independent dealers. More than three-quarters of the Ford dealer's staff were dismissed but the employees in question were told that they would be transferred to the new dealers; after the transfer the Ford dealers discontinued their activities. The ECJ ruled that Article 1(1) of the Directive applied to the transfer of the dealership, emphasising that the decisive criterion is whether the entity in question retains its economic identity. The Court reiterated its view that the transfer of tangible assets is not conclusive of whether the entity in question retains its economic identity and said: 'The purpose of an exclusive dealership for the sale of motor vehicles of a particular make in a certain sector remains the same even if it is carried on under a different name, from different premises and with different facilities.'

## The meaning of 'transfer'

**9.13** The starting-point for a consideration of this question is *Spijkers v Gebroeders Benedik Abattoir* (1986). In that case, the ECJ emphasised that the aim of the Directive is to ensure 'the continuity of employment relationships existing within a business, irrespective of a change of owner' and said that the decisive criterion is 'whether the business in question retains its identity.' It went on to say:

> ... It is necessary to consider all the facts characterising the transaction in question, including the type of undertaking or business, whether or not the businesses tangible assets, such as buildings and movable property are transferred, the value of its intangible assets at the time of the transfer, whether or not the majority of its employees are taken over by the new employer, whether or not its customers are transferred and the degree of similarity between the activities carried on before and after the transfer and the period, if any, for which those activities were suspended. It should be noted, however, that all those circumstances are merely single factors in the overall assessment which must be made and cannot, therefore, be considered in isolation.

**9.14** This approach has been articulated in very similar language in the cases which have followed this decision and the emphasis of the Court has been on whether an undertaking retains its identity: see *Schmidt v Spar- und Leihkasse der Früheren Ämter Bordesholm, Kiel und Cronshagen* (1995), *Ledernes Hovedorganisation* (*Acting on behalf of Rygaard*) v *Dansk Arbejdsgiverforening* (*Acting on behalf of Strø Mølle Akustik A/S*) (*Rygaard's case*) (1996), *Merckx and Neuhuys v Ford Motors Co Belgium SA* (1997) and *Süzen v Zehnacker Gebdudereinigung GmbH Krankenhausservice, Lefarth GmbH* (*Party joined*) (1997).

**9.15** In *Dr Sophie Redmond Stichting v Bartol* (1992), the ECJ ruled that a transfer within Article 1(1) of the Directive may take place where a public body decides to terminate a subsidy paid to one legal person, as a result of which the activities of that legal person are terminated, and to transfer it to another legal person with similar aims. The Court said that the decision by a public body to alter its policy on subsidies is as much a unilateral decision as the decision of an owner to change its lessee.

**9.16** In recent years, this issue has given rise to a number of significant cases. The first, *Merckx and Neuhuys v Ford Motors Co Belgium SA* (1997), involved the transfer of a car dealership without a transfer of tangible assets from Ford dealers to independent dealers. The employees advanced a number of arguments to the Court, saying that the transfer was outside the Directive: (1) because there had been no transfer of either tangible or intangible assets and no preservation of the undertaking's structure and organisation; (2) because the transferor dealer ceased trading and was put into liquidation after the transfer; (3) because the majority of the staff were dismissed upon the transfer; and (4) because the notion of a legal transfer within Article 1(1) of the Directive required the existence of a contractual link between the transferor and the transferee. The Court rejected all these arguments.

**9.17** In *Süzen v Zehnacker Gebdudereinigung GmbH Krankenhausservice, Lefarth GmbH (Party joined)* (1997), case the question was whether the termination of a cleaning contract with one contractor and the grant of the contract to another contractor amounts to a transfer within the Directive. As in the *Merckx* case, there was no transfer of tangible or intangible assets. The Court reiterated what it had said in previous cases, that the decisive question is whether the entity in question retains its identity. It said that, although the absence of a contractual link between the transferor and the transferee or (as here) the two undertakings successively granted the cleaning contract might point to the absence of a transfer, it was not conclusive. It added the transfer may take place in two stages, through the intermediary of a third party such as the owner or the person putting up the capital, and stressed that the transfer must relate to a stable economic entity whose activity is not limited to performing one specific works contract (as in *Rygaard*'s case). It said, at pp. 670–671:

> The term entity thus refers to an organised grouping of persons and assets facilitating the exercise of an economic activity which pursues a specific objective ... The mere fact that the service provided by the old and the new awardees of a contract is similar does not therefore support the conclusion that an economic entity has been transferred. An

entity cannot be reduced to the activity entrusted to it. Its identity also emerges from other factors, such as its workforce, its management staff, the way in which its work is organised, its operating methods or indeed, where appropriate, the operational resource available to it ... The mere loss of a service contract to a competitor cannot therefore by itself indicate the existence of a transfer ... In those circumstances, the service undertaking previously entrusted with the contract does not, on losing a customer, thereby cease fully to exist, and a business or part of a business belonging to it cannot be considered to have been transferred to the new awardee of the contract.

**9.18** The Court pointed out that the absence of a transfer of assets does not necessarily preclude the existence of a transfer and that, in considering the various criteria which have identified as relevant to the question whether the business has retained its identity, the degree of importance to be attached to each criterion 'will necessarily vary according to the activity carried on, or indeed the production or operating methods employed in the relevant undertaking.'

**9.19** A similar approach may be detected in *Francisco Hernández Vidal SA v Gomez Perez* (1999) and *Sánchez Hidalgo v Asociacion de Servicios ASER* (1999). The first group of cases involved contracting-in, where cleaning work was brought back in-house after being contracted out; the second group involved a change of contractor. In both groups of cases, the ECJ concentrated on whether an 'economic entity' had been transferred and said it had.

**9.20** This approach was followed in the later decision of *Allen v Amalgamated Construction Co Ltd* (2000), which involved the transfer of an employee between subsidiary companies in the same corporate group. Both companies shared the same management and premises and also shared administrative and support functions. The ECJ held that there was a transfer within article 1 of the Directive. It is worth noting here that the Court approached this case on the basis that it was one involving an activity based essentially on manpower. This was because, although the activity in question (the driving of underground tunnels) required a significant amount of plant and equipment, the mine owner provided those assets and not the contractors. The ECJ pointed out that the fact that ownership of the assets required to run the undertaking do not pass to the new owner does not preclude a transfer.

**9.21** The most recent decision of the ECJ in this area is *Oy Liikenne AB v Liskojärvi and Juntunen* (2001). The facts of the case were that the operation of seven bus routes was awarded to Oy Liikenne AB; they had previously been operated by Hakunilan Liikenne Oy. Hakunilan dismissed 45 drivers, of whom 33 were re-engaged by Oy Liikenne; no vehicles or other assets connected with the operation of the bus routes were transferred, although Oy Liikenne bought uniforms from Hakunilan for some of the drivers who entered its service. The applicants were amongst the 33 drivers who were taken on by Oy Liikenne. They claimed that there had been a transfer of an undertaking and that they were entitled to enjoy the more favourable terms and conditions applied by their previous employer. The Court said:

> ... In a sector such as scheduled public transport by bus, where the tangible assets contribute significantly to the performance of the activity, the absence of a transfer to a significant extent from the old to the new contractor of such assets, which are necessary for the proper functioning of the entity, must lead to the conclusion that the entity does not retain its identity. Consequently, in a situation such as that in the main proceedings, Directive 77/187 does not apply in the absence of a transfer of significant tangible assets from the old to the new contractor.

**9.22** This approach suggests that the decisive criterion in such cases is whether the tangible assets 'contribute significantly' to the activity and does not seem to take into account the possibility that there may be factors pointing towards the conclusion that the entity retains its identity.

## The effect of Article 4 in relation to dismissals

**9.23** Article 4(1) contains two propositions. The first is that a transfer of an undertaking 'shall not in itself constitute grounds for dismissal ...' The second is that the the previous statement 'shall not stand in the way of dismissals that may take place for economic, technical or organisational reasons entailing changes in the workforce.' The first is transposed into UK law by TUPE reg. 8(1), the second by reg. 8(2): see para. 9.45 below.

**9.24**   The ECJ has made it clear that it is for national law to decide upon the appropriate remedy for a dismissal which contravenes article 4(1), but that art. 4(1) of itself does not make a dismissal brought about by a transfer a nullity: see *Wendelboe v LJ Music APS* (1985) and *Foreningen af Arbedsledere I Danmark v A/S Danmols Inventar* (1985). The House of Lords has subsequently decided that TUPE reg. 8(1), which declares a dismissal brought about by a transfer to be automatically unfair, gives effect to and is consistent with the Directive: see *Wilson v St Helens Borough Council* (1998). It is not therefore necessary to go so far as to say that a dismissal in such circumstances is a nullity.

## The Transfer of Undertakings Regulations 1981 (TUPE)

**9.25**   The effect of the Regulations is that they afford protection to employees where there is a 'relevant transfer' of an 'undertaking'. Where there is a relevant transfer, an employee's contract will be automatically transferred to the person to whom the undertaking is transferred. The importance of the decisions of the ECJ considered above lies in the fact that courts and tribunals in the United Kingdom are required to interpret the Regulations so that, as far as possible, they conform to the Directive.

**9.26**   The following matters are considered here: (1) the meaning of 'undertaking'; (2) the meaning of 'relevant transfer'; (3) the effect of a relevant transfer.

**9.27**   It should be noted that, as a general rule, a tribunal considering whether there has been a relevant transfer of an undertaking should consider as separate issues, first, whether the entity in question was an undertaking and, second, whether there was a relevant transfer. The EAT has made it clear that these two issues should be considered as separate questions and has said that, although it is not invariably an error of law not to raise the two questions as separate questions or to fail to deal with them in that order, a tribunal which fails in this way runs a real risk of error: see *Cheesman v R Brewer Contracts Ltd* (2001) and *Whitewater Leisure Management Ltd v Barnes* (2000).

## The meaning of 'undertaking'

**9.28** The definition of 'undertaking' is to be found in regulation 1(1): ''undertaking' includes any trade or business.' Recent decisions in the Court of Appeal and the EAT have drawn heavily on the case-law of the ECJ when considering whether a particular entity amounts to an undertaking. In *Whitewater Leisure Management Ltd v Barnes* (2000) the EAT said that there are two formulations which can be used to identify whether there is an economic entity. The first asks whether there is 'a stable and discrete economic entity'; the alternative version asks whether the entity is 'sufficiently structured and autonomous'. The EAT suggested that the expression 'distinct cost centre' might be helpful. Had the EAT considered the ECJ decision in *Allen v Amalgamated Construction Co Ltd*, above, it might have reached a different conclusion. That case, it will be recalled, said that there may be a transfer of an economic entity even where there is no transfer of the plant and equipment necessary to carry out the activity because they are supplied by the person granting the contract.

**9.29** The Whitewater decision also appears to be inconsistent with the later decision of another division of the EAT, presided over by the President (Lindsay J.), in *RCO Support Services and Aintree Hospital Trust v UNISON and others* (2000). There, the EAT held that there may be an undertaking and a transfer of that undertaking despite the fact that neither significant assets nor a majority of the workforce moves over. He took a similar approach in *Argyll Training Ltd v Sinclair and Argyll & The Islands Enterprise Ltd* (2000) when deciding that a training contract and the arrangements made for its performance amounted to an undertaking. Yet the Court of Appeal in *RCO Support Services and Aintree Hospital Trust v UNISON and others* (2002) upheld the EAT's decision, rejecting *Suzen*'s approach, finding it not necessary for there to be a transfer of employees and/or assets in order for TUPE to apply. This cases is subject to appeal before the *House of Lords* (see *also Wynnwith Engineering v Bennett* (2002); *P & O Transport European Ltd; v Initial Transport Services Ltd* (2003)).

**9.30** In *Cheesman v R Brewer Contracts Ltd* (2001), which involved the loss of a maintenance contract, Lindsay J said:

> (i) As to whether there is an undertaking, there needs to be found a
> stable economic entity whose activity is not limited to performing one

specific works contract, an organised grouping of persons and of assets enabling (or facilitating) the exercise of an economic activity which pursues a specific objective ...; (ii) In order to be such an undertaking it must be sufficiently structured and autonomous but will not necessarily have significant assets, tangible or intangible ...; (iii) In certain sectors such as cleaning and surveillance the assets are often reduced to their most basic and the activity is essentially based on manpower ... ; (iv) An organised grouping of wage-earners who are specifically and permanently assigned to a common task may in the absence of other factors of production, amount to an economic entity ...; (v) An activity of itself is not an entity; the identity of an entity emerges from other factors such as its workforce, management staff, the way in which its work is organised, its operating methods and, where appropriate, the operational resources available to it ...

**9.31**  The approach taken in these cases by Lindsay J lays emphasis on the social objectives of the Directive, the safeguarding of employees' rights. That approach leads to the conclusion that tribunals should be ready to find that an entity is an undertaking and that that undertaking has been transferred.

## The meaning of 'relevant transfer'

**9.32**  A 'relevant transfer' is defined in regulation 3(1) as 'a transfer from one person to another of an undertaking situated immediately before the transfer in the United Kingdom or a part of one which is so situated.' Regulation 3(2) applies the Regulations to transfers by sale or other disposition or by operation of law, but transfers of share capital (eg as in takeovers) and dispositions of physical assets are excluded. Regulation 3(4) provides that a transfer may be effected by a series of two or more transactions and that it may take place whether or not any property is transferred to the transferee by the transferor.

**9.33**  The starting-point of any discussion of whether there has been a transfer of an undertaking is the ECJ decisions in *Süzen v Zehnacker Gebdudereinigung GmbH Krankenhausservice, Lefarth GmbH (Party joined)* (1997), *Francisco Hernández Vidal SA v Gomez Perezi* (1999) and *Sánchez Hidalgo v Asociacion de Servicios ASER* (1999): see para. 9.17 above. What falls to be considered here is how the Courts and tribunals in the United Kingdom have approached the ECJ's decisions.

**9.34** Very soon after the decision in *Süzen*, the Court of Appeal heard the appeal from the High Court in *Betts v Brintel Helicopters Ltd* (1997). The case involved the loss by one company (Brintel) of a contract to provide helicopter services and its transfer to another (KLM). KLM only took over rights associated with the contract and engaged none of Brintel's employees. The main issue in the Court of Appeal was whether there was a transfer of an undertaking, in other words whether the undertaking had retained its identity in the hands of the transferee. Kennedy LJ reviewed the relevant case-law of the European Court of Justice and said that the limited transfer of assets (the right to land on oil rigs and use oil rig facilities) could not lead to the conclusion that the undertaking had retained its identity. He said:

> The real distinction ... is between (1) labour-intensive undertakings, in which if the staff combine to engage in a particular activity which continues or is resumed with substantially the same staff after the alleged transfer the court may well conclude that the undertaking has been transferred so that it has retained its identity in the hands of the transferee; and (2) other types of undertaking in relation to which the application of the Spijkers test involves a more wide-ranging inquiry.

**9.35** This decision may be contrasted with the decision of another division of the Court of Appeal, about a year later, in *ECM (Vehicle Delivery Service) Ltd v Cox* (1999). A contract to distribute cars ('the VAG contract') was lost by one contractor and awarded to ECM. They chose to organise the contracted service in a different way; they dispensed with the previous contractor's base and refused to engage any of the staff employed on the vehicle delivery contract because they had asserted that their employment was protected by TUPE. The Court of Appeal upheld the decision of the tribunal and the EAT that there had been a relevant transfer. The argument of ECM in the Court of Appeal was that there was no transfer of an undertaking, although it accepted that there was an undertaking carried on by the previous contractor. The basis of their argument was that *Süzen* signalled a change of emphasis in the ECJ and that the position on transfers of undertakings following that decision was that, where the only continuing feature is the nature of the activity itself and all that continues is the service itself, it is impossible to find that an undertaking has been transferred. So in the case in question, it was argued, all that continued was the activity of delivering cars under the VAG contract. Mummery LJ, with whom the other lords justices agreed, rejected that argument and held that the employment tribunal had applied the correct test, as laid down in *Spijkers* and subsequent cases. He also observed that the tribunal was entitled to have regard, as a relevant circumstance, to the reason why the employees were not taken on by ECM. He suggested that the importance of *Süzen* had been overstated and pointed out that the ECJ had not overruled its previous interpretative rulings. He also observed that the criteria laid down by the ECJ still involve consideration of 'all the facts characterising the transaction in question' as identified in *Spijkers*.

**9.36**  The first of these is *RCO Support Services and Aintree Hospital Trust v UNISON* (2002). The case involved cleaners and caterers. The cleaners were employed by Initial Hospital Services Ltd at Walton Hospital, one of two hospitals run by the Aintree Hospitals NHS Trust. Initial tendered for the cleaning contract at Fazakerley, the other hospital run by the Trust, but it was won by RCO None of the Walton cleaners applied for jobs with RCO and none were taken on. Subsequently the employment of cleaners at Walton ended and a number of them brought unfair dismissal proceedings. The catering staff were employed at Walton by the Trust itself. Three of the support staff were dismissed for redundancy. Applications were invited by RCO, who held the catering contract at Fazakerley. One applicant was not offered a job and another declined the job offered to her. The ET held that there was a relevant transfer from Initial to RCO in respect of the cleaners and from the Trust to RCO in respect of the caterers. The EAT dismissed the appeals. They said that the absence of movement of significant assets or of a major part of the workforce does not necessarily deny the existence of a relevant transfer and expressed the view that *Süzen* can no longer be safely relied upon. The Court of Appeal upheld the EAT's decision, favouring the approach taken by the Court of Appeal in ECM over that taken by the earlier CA in *Betts v Brintel*. Lindsay J. emphasised the safeguarding of employees' rights as the being crucial objective.

**9.37**  The second decision from the EAT is again of a division presided over by Lindsay J., in *Cheesman v R. Brewer Contracts Ltd* (2001).

379

The case again involved the loss of a maintenance contract. The previous contractor, Onyx, took over the contract from a district council; it acquired as part of the contract use of the council's yard, its equipment and its office accommodation. It took on 14 employees who had previously been allocated by the council to the contract. When it lost the contract to Brewer, Onyx dismissed the 14 staff; none of them were taken on by Brewer and no tangible or intangible assets passed from Onyx to Brewer, either directly or indirectly by way of the council. The dismissed employees claimed that there had been a transfer of an undertaking to Brewer and brought claims against it. After considering the question of what amounts to an undertaking, Lindsay J. addressed the question of what constitutes a transfer. He said:

> As for whether there has been a transfer:
> (i) As to whether there is any relevant sense a transfer, the decisive criterion for establishing the existence of a transfer is whether the entity in question retains its identity, as indicated, inter alia, by the fact that its operation is actually continued or resumed ...
> (ii) In a labour-intensive sector it is to be recognised that an entity is capable of maintaining its identity after it has been transferred where the new employer does not merely pursue the activity in question but also takes over a major part, in terms of their numbers and skills, of the employees specially assigned by his predecessors to that task. That follows from the fact that in certain labour-intensive sectors a group of workers engaged in the joint activity on a permanent basis may constitute an economic entity ...
> (iii) In considering whether the conditions for existence of a transfer are met it is necessary to consider all the factors characterising the transaction in question but each is a single factor and none is to be considered in isolation ... However, whilst no authority so holds, it may, presumably, not be an error of law to consider 'the decisive criterion' in (i) above in isolation; that, surely, is an aspect of its being 'decisive', although, as one sees from the 'inter alia' in (i) above, 'the decisive criterion' is not itself said to depend on a single factor.
> (iv) Amongst the matters thus falling for consideration are the type of undertaking, whether or not its tangible assets are transferred, the value of its intangible assets at the time of transfer, whether

or not the majority of its employees are taken over by the new company, whether or not its customers are transferred, the degree of similarity between the activities carried on before and after the transfer, and the period, if any, in which they are suspended ...

(v)  In determining whether or not there has been a transfer, account has to be taken, inter alia, of the type of undertaking or business in issue, and the degree of importance to be attached to the several criteria will necessarily vary according to the activity carried on ...

(vi)  Where an economic entity is able to function without any significant tangible or intangible assets, the maintenance of its identity following the transaction being examined cannot logically depend on the transfer of such assets ...

(vii)  Even where assets are owned and are required to run the undertaking, the fact that they do not pass does not preclude a transfer ...

(viii)  Where maintenance work is carried out by a cleaning firm and then next by the owner of the premises concerned, that mere fact does not justify the conclusion that there has been a transfer ...

(ix)  More broadly, the mere fact that the service provided by the old and new undertaking providing a contracted-out service or the old and new contract-holder are similar does not justify the conclusion that there has been a transfer of an economic entity between predecessor and successor ...

(x)  The absence of any contractual link between transferor and transferee may be evidence that there has been no relevant transfer but it is certainly not conclusive as there is no need for any such direct contractual relationship ...

(xi)  When no employees are transferred, the reasons why that is the case can be relevant as to whether or not there was a transfer ...

(xii)  The fact that the work is performed continuously with no interruption or change in the manner or performance is a normal feature of transfers of undertakings but there is no particular importance to be attached to a gap between the end of the work by one subcontractor and the start by the successor ...

**9.38**  More generally the cases also show:

(i)  The necessary factual appraisal is to be made by the national court ...

(ii) The Directive applies where, following the transfer, there is a change in the natural person responsible for the carrying on of the business who, by virtue of that fact, incurs the obligation of an employer vis-à-vis the employees of the undertaking, regardless of whether or not ownership of the undertaking is transferred ...

(iii) The aim of the Directive is to ensure continuity of employment relationships within the economic entity irrespective of any change of ownership ... and our domestic law illustrates how readily the courts will adopt a purposive construction to counter avoidance ... (see *Bowers v Stevens & Marc* (2004)).

## The effect of a 'relevant transfer'

**9.39** The effect of regulation 5(1) is that a relevant transfer does not of itself terminate the employee's contract, so that the transferor will not be liable for a redundancy payment; the contract will be treated as if it had been made between him or her and the transferee (ie the new employer). It applies to the transfer of an undertaking or a part of an undertaking.

**9.40** On the completion of the relevant transfer, regulation 5(2) provides that all the transferor's (ie old employer's) rights, powers, duties and liabilities 'under or in connection with' the employee's contract of employment are transferred and anything done before the transfer is completed by the transferor in relation to the contract is treated as done by the transferee. The wording of this regulation suggests that, when a relevant transfer takes place, liability passes to the transferee and the transferor drops out of the picture. It should be noted, however, that a transfer under regulation 5 will be effective irrespective of whether the employees knew of the transfer and the identity of the transferee: see *Secretary of State for Trade and Industry v Cook* (1997). The notable exception is pensions (see *Beckmann v Dynamco Whicheloe Macfarlane Ltd* (2002)). Yet recent case suggests that this may not be so (see *Martin v South Bank University* (2003). See also cl. 35, Pensions Bill 2004).

**9.41** Regulation 5(2) has been held to embrace an employee's accrued right not to be unfairly dismissed, the transferor's right to enforce a restrictive covenant in an employment contract and an employee's complaint of sex discrimination arising from an act of the transferor before the transfer: see *BSG Property Services v Tuck* (1996), *Morris Angel & Son Ltd v Hollande* (1993) and *DJM International Ltd v Nicholas* (1996). An employer's contractual obligations arising from a collective agreement incorporated into employees' individual contracts will also transfer under regulation 5: see *Whent v T. Cartledge Ltd* (1997). In *Bernardone v Pall Mall Services, Martin v Lancashire County Council* (2001) the Court of Appeal held that regulation 5(2) is wide enough to transfer to the transferee the transferor's tortious liability towards an employee injured at work and thus liability in negligence may pass to the transferee. The Court also held that the transferor's rights under an employer's liability insurance policy transferred to the transferee. In *Unicorn Consultancy Services Ltd v Westbrook* (2000) the EAT held that the payment of sums due to employees under the transferor's profit-related pay scheme was a liability which passed to the transfer on the transfer of the undertaking.

**9.42**  It should be noted, however, that regulation 5 protects the rights which the employee had against the transferor so that they cannot be varied on a transfer to the transferee. In *Crédit Suisse First Boston (Europe) Ltd v Lister* (1999) the Court of Appeal refused to allow a transferee employer to enforce a restrictive covenant which it had introduced into the employee's contract (with the consent of the employee) when it took over the undertaking. The Court said that, since the transferor employer could not have prevented the employee from working for a competitor after the termination of his employment, the transferee could not do so either. It was irrelevant that the new contract also gave the employee a compensating benefit in return for agreeing to the imposition of the restriction. See also *Crédit Suisse First Boston (Europe) Ltd v Padiachy* (1999). In *Kerry Foods Ltd v Kreber* (2000) the EAT held that liability for a failure to consult under regulation 10 was a liability arising 'in connection with' an individual worker's contract and so fell within regulation 5(2).

**9.43**  The general position is subject to two provisos. First, regulation 5(5) preserves the employee's right to resign and claim constructive dismissal where a substantial change is made in the working conditions to his or her detriment; but a mere change in the identity of the employer will give the employee no rights unless he or she can show that in all the circumstances the change is significant and is to his or her detriment. Second, regulation 5(1) and (2) are made expressly subject to regulation 5(4A). The effect of this provision is that regulation 5(1) and (2) will not operate to transfer employees' contracts of employment and the rights, powers, duties and liabilities under or in connection with them, if they inform the transferor or the transferee that they object to becoming employed by the transferee. The effect will be the same as if they had resigned before the transfer.

**9.44** Regulation 5 applies to persons employed 'immediately before' the transfer: see reg. 5(3). In *Secretary of State for Employment v Spence* (1986), the Court of Appeal held that regulation 5 was concerned with contracts of employment subsisting at the moment when the undertaking was transferred. As the employees' contracts were not subsisting at the moment of transfer, they had been dismissed before the relevant transfer. This question was subsequently considered by the House of Lords, in *Litster v Forth Dry Dock & Engineering Co Ltd (in receivership)* (1989). The House of Lords held that the Regulations should be given a purposive construction in a manner which would accord with the decisions of the European Court of Justice on the Directive and, where necessary, words should be implied to achieve that effect. There should be implied into regulation 5(3) after the words 'immediately before the transfer' the words 'or would have been so employed if he had not been unfairly dismissed in the circumstances described by regulation 8(1)'. In reaching this decision, the House of Lords followed the decision of the European Court of Justice in *P. Bork International A/S v Foreningen af Arbejdsledere i Danmark (1989) and Marleasing v LA Comercial* (1992).

## Dismissals and Regulation 8

**9.45** Dismissals on the transfer of an undertaking are governed by reg. 8. Regulation 8(1) sets out the general rule, that an employee dismissed either before or after a relevant transfer will be treated as automatically unfairly dismissed, if the transfer or a reason connected with it is the reason or principal reason for the dismissal. The rule applies to employees both of the transferor and the transferee. The general rule does not apply, however, when there is an 'economic, technical or organisational reason entailing changes in the workforce or either the transferor or transferee either before or after a relevant transfer' and that is the reason or principal reason for dismissing the employee: reg. 8(2). In that case, the reason will be treated as 'some other substantial reason' within ERA 1996, s 98(1)(b) and the fairness of the reason must then be considered by the tribunal under section 98(4): see *McGrath v Rank Leisure Ltd* (1985). The correct approach is to consider first whether regulation 8(1) applies so as to make the dismissals automatically unfair; if it does not, then the tribunal should consider whether regulation 8(2) applies.

**9.46** One issue which has now been resolved by the House of Lords concerned the effect of a dismissal which is brought about by the transfer of an undertaking. In *Wilson v St. Helens Borough Council and Meade v British Fuels Ltd* (1998) two groups of dismissals were involved. The group involved in the *Wilson* case were dismissals for an economic or technical reason and thus within regulation 8(2); the group involved in the *Meade* case were dismissals for a reason connected with the transfer and thus within regulation 8(1). Lord Slynn of Hadley gave the main speech. It centred round the issue whether a dismissal of an employee brought about by a transfer of an undertaking is or is not a nullity. He took the view that the provisions of regulation 8(1) and (2) point to a dismissal being effective and not a nullity and do not create an automatic obligation on the part of the transferee to continue to employ employees who have been dismissed by the transferor. He then went on to consider whether TUPE complies with the Directive. Having considered the relevant case-law of the ECJ, he concluded that the Directive does not create a community law right to continue in employment which does not exist in national law and that TUPE gives effect to and is consistent with the Directive. Thus, if an employee is dismissed by the transferor and re-engaged by the transferee, the latter will assume any liability for dismissals incurred by the transferor. The employee will not be able to insist on the observance by the transferee of his or her previous terms or conditions and will be bound by the terms and conditions agreed with the transferee. The dismissal will thus be unfair by virtue of regulation 8(1) but not ineffective.

**9.47** The relationship between regulation 8(1) and 8(2) was considered by the Court of Appeal in *Warner v Adnet Ltd* (1998). In that case, the argument on behalf of the employee was that the two paragraphs are mutually exclusive and that, if the tribunal concludes that the dismissal was for a reason falling within regulation 8(1), it is precluded from considering the case under regulation 8(2). The Court of Appeal rejected that argument. Mummery LJ said that the regulations must be read as a whole and that the drafting of regulation 8(2) is such that it expressly contemplates circumstances in which regulation 8(1) will be disapplied and where a view formed by a tribunal under regulation 8(1) is not final or conclusive. This approach was followed by another division of the Court of Appeal in the later case of *Whitehouse v Charles A. Blatchford & Sons Ltd* (2000).

**9.48** The words 'economic, technical or organisational' in regulation 8(2) have been considered in a number of cases. The preferred approach now seems to be that of the EAT in *Wheeler v Patel* (1987). They said that the word 'economic' is to be construed *ejusdem generis* with the other two adjectives and is to be given a limited meaning relating to the conduct of the business. They said that it does not include broad economic reasons for a sale, such as the desire to obtain an enhanced price or a desire to achieve a sale. See also *Gateway Hotels Ltd v Stewart* (1988) and *Ibex Trading Co Ltd v Walton* (1994). It should be noted, however, that the reason will not fall within regulation 8(2) unless it also entails changes in the workforce: see *Delabole Slate Ltd v Berriman* (1985).

# TUPE and Consultation

**9.48** As with redundancy in chapter 8, TUPE contains provisions which facilitate for consultation between employers (both transferor and transferee) and trade unions/elected representatives. The effect of Regulations 6, 9 and 10 of TUPE is to preserve the existing collective arrangements on sale of the business and to inform all of its happening, as well as consult on its consequences.

- Regulation 6 requires that any collective agreement made between the transferor and a trade union shall have effect as if it had been made with the transferee.

- Regulation 9 provides that any trade union which was recognised by the transferor shall be deemed to be recognised by the transferee.

- Regulation 10 obliges the transferor and transferee to consult with recognised trade unions or elected representatives (in the absence of a recognised trade union) for the purposes of collective consultation under TUPE.

**9.49**  Following the enactment of the Employment Relations Act 1999 and the establishment of trade union recognition, where there are sufficient members of the workforce who are trade union members, then Regulation 9 may become more complex and may have to respond to the pace of change brought about by this new legal framework (see Chapter 11).

## Information and consultation rights

**9.50**  Regulation 10 of TUPE sets an obligation to collectively consult before a business transfer. Under Regulation 10 the transferor must inform and consult with 'appropriate representatives' of affected employees, ie those employees subjected to the transfer or by measures taken in connection with the transfer. This means that all those being transferred should be consulted/informed, but also other employees who are not transferring but are affected should be consulted. Regulation 9 provides on who is consulted regarded a transfer – recognised trade unions. However, where no trade unions are recognised, then elected representatives must be in place (this is to be discussed below at para. 9.52).

## Trades unions

**9.51**  Central to consultation is the requirement that the transferee provide information to the transferor to inform the workforce. Where recognised trade unions are in place the consultation process should be relatively straightforward. However, where no such unions exist, identifying 'appropriate representatives' is crucial. Since July 1999, the Collective Redundancies and Transfer of Undertakings (Protection of Employment) (Amendment) Regulations 1999, to be discussed below, set out new requirements for consultation for transfers post 1 November 1999 where no recognised unions exist.

## Employee representatives

**9.52** Following the ECJ's ruling in *EC Commission v United Kingdom* (1994), which found that the UK government had violated the right to consultation, the Collective Redundancies and Transfer of Undertakings (Protection of Employment) (Amendment) Regulations 1995 (SI 1995/2587) were enacted. These were later to be found in breach of EU law and the Collective Redundancies and Transfer of Undertakings (Protection of Employment) (Amendment) Regulations 1999 (as discussed in Chapter 10) were passed. The 1999 Regulations came into force from 1 November 1999. They provide that where no such trade union exists or applies, the transferor can choose whether to inform/consult with employee representatives who have been elected and hold the authority to receive information and be consulted on behalf of affected employees, or to hold elections for ad hoc representatives for the purposes of the TUPE transfers.

## TUPE's general consultation requirements

**9.53** Regulation 10(2) provides that the transferor should provide the elected representatives with information on: the facts of the transfer (date and reasons); the 'legal, social and economic' implications (as perceived by the transferee) for the affected employees; what measures are envisaged, post-transfer; and any other information provided or measures envisaged by the transferee. Regulation 10(3) requires the transferee to notify the transferor of any information appropriate to be given to the elected representatives. Regulation 10(3) requires the transferee to notify the transferor of any measures envisaged taking affect after the transfer, so as to enable this information to be given to the affected employees. Though, the transferee is not obliged to consult prior to the transfer with those affected by the transfer. It is important that under the 1999 Regulations at all times the transferor should consider that 'proper' informing and consulting is taking place in relation to the transfer.

**9.54** Regulation 10(5) requires that consultation should be conducted 'with a view to seeking the (elected) representatives agreement to measures to be taken'. To that end, consultation only commences following information which leads to the transferor/transferee envisaging taking measures in connection with the transfer (ie redundancies, changes to contracts, changes to working conditions/practices, union derecognition or union recognition, or any changes whatsoever). Once consultation commences TUPE implies that all proposed measures should be discussed in good faith and every effort is made to accommodate views and differences and reach agreement where possible.

### *Sanctions*

**9.55** Any breach of Regulation 10 gives right to complain to an Employment Tribunal under Regulation 11 on the grounds of failure to comply (ie electoral defects; no or lack of information; no, limited or lack of consultation; lack of trade union recognition; or any other case affecting employees). Where an ET upholds the complaint, a Declaration is given and the transferor will be required to pay 13 weeks pay to each employee affected. Note that the week's pay is NOT subject to the maximum limit of £260 per week for these purposes.

## Futher reading

Deakin, S, & Morris, G, *Labour Law* (3rd ed, 2001) Butterworths (chapter 5).

Hardy, S, *Understanding TUPE* (2001) Chandos Publishing, Oxford.

Smith, I, & Thomas, G, *Industrial Law* (8th ed, 2003) Butterworths (chapters, 8 & 9).

McMullen, J, *Business Transfers and Employee Rights* (2001) Butterworths.

### *Articles*

McMullen, J, (1996) 'Atypical transfers, atypical workers and atypical employment structures – a case for greater transparency in transfer of employment issues', *Industrial Law Journal*, Vol. 25, No. 4, December, pp. 286–307.

Sargeant, M, (2002) 'New Transfer Regulations', *Industrial Law Journal*, Vol. 31, No. 1, March, pp. 35–54.

## Self-test questions

1. Wessex County Council has decided to apply 'best value' tendering for its secretarial services. Dolly, Flo, Joe and Bert are currently administrative staff providing secretarial services at Wessex County Council's offices. To improve service performance, a contracting-out exercise, with tenders from private contractors, to provide photocopying, typing and filing were undertaken. Quicktype, a private provider, were awarded the contract. Dolly, Joe and Bert were transferred. Flo, who was on maternity leave, was not transferred, as Quicktype claimed that she was not in the part of the business subject to the transfer. Dolly, due to her long service is paid more than the other staff, but Quicktype now wish to harmonise terms and are offering her a new contract on less pay. Joe has been told that he is to be dismissed due to his recent absence and Bert is complaining that his pension has not been transferred across.

   Advise Dolly, Flo, Bert and Joe.

2. 'The Transfer of Undertaking (Protection of Employment) Regulations 1981 have provided a fertile source of litigation and legal difficulties concerning their application.' Evaluate this statement, providing examples from case law.

3. Explain the legal significance of consultation in TUPE situations.

4. The University of Dorchester has a dining room for its staff. Anna, Betty, Mark and Henry are the kitchen staff employed to service the staff dining area room. Following complaints from lecturers, the University decides to provide them with an improved service and therefore invited tenders from private contractors to provide staff lunches. The University also realises that the service is overstaffed and makes Henry redundant. A week later a bid by a rival catering to run the staff dining room is accepted by the University. UK catering interview the existing kitchen staff and tell the University that in view of her disciplinary record they do not wish Mark to work with them. Betty

does not want to be transferred to the new catering company because she has heard that their overtime rates are less attractive then the University's. The new catering company has now told Anna, who does most of the cooking, that in view of the fact that there is to be a completely new menu, they will probably need to replace her with someone more experienced in vegetarian cooking.

Advise Anna, Betty, Mark and Henry.

# CHAPTER TEN

# Trade Unions and their Members

## Summary

This chapter considers the legal definition of a trade union, how unions govern their internal affairs, the right to join a trade union and trade union disciplinary matters (ie the rights not to be unjustifiably disciplined or expelled by a trade union).

In this chapter we have shown:

- S. 1 of TULRCA 1992 defines a trade union as 'an organisation wholly or mainly of workers ...whose principal purposes include the regulation of relations between workers ...'..

- Unions are NOT corporate bodies (s 10, TULRCA 1992).

- Freedom of Association protects trade unions from discrimination.

- The union contract of membership is set by the union's rules.

- Statutory rules on exclusion, expulsion and other disciplinary actions have existed since 1984. These rules protect union members from arbitrary action by their union's governing bodies and officials (ss 174, 64–66).

- Political funds are expenditure for political objects (Osborne ruling (1911) and are subject to strict rules.

# Defining a trade union

**10.1**  It was the advent of the industrial revolution which produced organised labour. However, the initial reaction to trade unions in Britain was hostile. Strict measures resulted, including exile (for example, the Tolpuddle Martyrs). Trade unions, or the combining of workers, remained illegal associations because they restricted the terms on which each member would sell his labour (*Hornby v Close* (1867)) until 1900. Since their creation and legal acceptance, trade unions have held a unique legal status in UK law.

**10.2**  A trade union is defined in s 1 of the Trade Union and Labour Relations (Consolidation) Act 1992 (hereinafter referred to as TUL-RCA 1992) as 'an organisation (whether temporary or permanent) ... which consists wholly or mainly of workers of one or more descriptions and whose principal purposes include the regulation of relations between workers of that description or those descriptions and employers or employers' associations.'

## Employer associations

**10.3**  The same applies to employer associations. Employers' Associations are defined by s 122 TULRCA 1992 as organisations (whether or not they are temporary or permanent) consisting wholly or mainly of employers or individual owners of undertakings and having amongst their principal purposes the regulation of relations between those employers and workers or trade unions. Though, unlike a trade union, an employers' association can be either an incorporated or unincorporated body. Where an association is unincorporated, it has the same rights and obligations as a trade union.

## Reform – Employment Relations Bill 2003

**10.4**  The Employment Relations Bill 2003, before Parliament, seeks to implement measures to improve the operation of individual employment rights, which ensure that union members have clear rights to use their union's services, and cannot be influenced by employers to relinquish essential union rights. Furthermore, the Bill clarifies the role of the companion in grievance and disciplinary proceedings. Lastly, it grants greater powers to strike out weak and vexatious claims.

## Trade unions and legal status

**10.5** With regard to trade unions legal status, at common law they are unincorporated associations (ie they are not corporate bodies with separate legal 'personality'), but they are given quasi-corporate status by s 10 TULRCA 1992. The effect of this is that unions are able to make contracts, sue and be sued in relation to contract, tort or other matters, hold property via trustees, and have criminal proceedings taken against them, but for all other purposes they are treated as unincorporated associations. It has been held by the High Court (somewhat controversially), that a union cannot be defamed because it does not have any legal personality beyond that of its members (*Electrical, Electronic Telecommunications and Plumbing Union v Times Newspapers Ltd* (1980)).

### Independence

**10.6** The grant of a certificate of independence is of fundamental importance to a trade union, because most statutory rights enjoyed by unions (eg those relating to disclosure of information, consultation, discrimination against union members, time off for union members and officials, and most recently, the right to use the statutory recognition procedures), require that the union must be independent. The requirement of independence as a precondition for the grant of union rights is to ensure that collective rights are exercised by bodies that are not mere staff associations over which an employer may have control.

**10.7** The test of independence in s 5 TULRCA 1992 is in two parts: it requires that a union 'is not under the domination or control of an employer or group of employers or of one or more employers' associations, and is not liable to interference by an employer or any such group or association (arising out of the financial or material support or by any other means whatsoever) tending towards such control ...'. Such requires no onerous control by their employer. This was considered in *Blue Circle Staff Association v The Certification Officer*

(1977). Consequently, the Certification Officer must consider in respect of each application by a trade union the following:

(a)    the history of the trade union/organisation;

(b)    its membership base;

(c)    its organisation and structure;

(d)    its finance;

(e)    employer provided facilities; and

(f)    its negotiating record.

**10.8**  In *News Group Newspapers Ltd v Society of Graphical and Allied Trades* (SOGAT 1982) the question to be determined was whether assets in the name of branches of the SOGAT 82 trade union belonged to the trade union or to the individual branches. Consequently, whilst each branch was not a separate trade union, the fact that it had the status of unincorporated association meant that its fund belonged to the branch rather than the union. The statutory definition also expressly includes federations or confederations of unions, 'an organisation which comprises wholly or mainly of employers or individual proprietors ...and whose principal purposes include the regulation'.

## Union amalgamations

**10.9**  There are two ways of proceeding under the 1992 Act, which also applies to unincorporated employers' associations (s 133), that is either:

(a)    by amalgamation which must be supported by a separate ballot of both transferor and transferee union; or

(b)    a transfer of engagements which requires approval only by a vote of the transferor's membership.

## Certification

**10.10**  The Certification Officer certifies and makes periodic checks that a union is maintaining its independence since he may withdraw certificates if the characterisation of the union changes. An appeal from the Certification Officer to the EAT takes the form of a full re-hearing and 'the parties are not limited to the material presented to or considered by the Certification Officer in the course of his enquiries.'

## Certification Officer

**10.11** The role of Certification Officer (as previously defined in para. 1.18) is largely an adjudicative role on the political fund, trade union amalgamations and principal executive committee elections. The Certification Officer is given specific power to regulate his own procedure. The Certification Officer may also make provision for expenses to be paid for the purpose of or in conjunction with their attendance at hearings before the Certification Officer. In addition, the Certification Officer has jurisdiction to hear complaints by members that their trade union (or any branch or section of the union) is in breach, or threatens to be in breach, of its own rules in respect of any of the following matters:

- regarding the appointment or election of a person to a union;
- union disciplinary proceedings;
- the constitution of proceedings of any executive committee.

Furthermore, any such other matters as may be specified by the Secretary of State.

Mr David Cockburn is currently the Certification Officer.

## Employer interference

**10.12** The second limb is forward-looking, and therefore more speculative. The test posed by the Act is whether the union is 'liable to interference' by an employer 'tending towards' control. In *The Certification Officer v Squibb UK Staff Association* (1979) it was decided that the phrase meant 'vulnerable to interference' or 'exposed to the risk of interference', eg the possibility of an employer withdrawing facilities that it might have granted to a union at some point in the future. The likelihood of such interference actually occurring is irrelevant.

## Trade union registration

**10.13** A list of trade unions is maintained by the Certification Officer, an independent office established in 1975, and now enjoying wide-ranging administrative and judicial functions in relation to trade unions. Listing is a voluntary and largely mechanical administrative process which nevertheless has significant advantages for a trade union. A body claiming to be a union may submit an application for listing (together with the appropriate fee, and a copy of its rules) to the Certification Officer. The Certification Officer is bound to list the body as a union provided it does not have the same name as an existing or de-listed body. The union will be entitled to tax benefits in respect of its provident benefits fund. It will also be allowed to take advantage of the special procedure for transferring property to the union's trustees. However, the most important advantage of being listed is that a union can apply for a certificate of independence. The decision in *Taff Vale Railway Company v Amalgamated Society of Railway Servants* (1901) concluded from the fact that they were registered under the Trade Union Acts 1871 and 1876 that unions could be sued in tort in their registered name. Yet a trade union cannot be sued for libel, as it lacks sufficient legal personality for those purposes in law (see *Electrical, Electronic Telecommunications and Plumbing Union v Times Newspapers* (1980)).

## Listing of trade unions

**10.14** A list of trade unions is maintained by the Certification Officer, an independent office established in 1975, and now enjoying wide-ranging administrative and judicial functions in relation to trade unions. Listing is a voluntary and largely mechanical administrative requirement. In *Bonsor v Musicians' Union* (1956), Lord Morton said that a union was 'a body distinct from the individuals who from time to time compose it'.

**10.15** At common law trade unionism itself is in unreasonable restraint of trade, since unions restrict the freedom of contract between employer and employee, most particularly in the taking of strike action and the closed shop. EAT in *Blue Circle Staff Association v Certification Officer* (1977).

## Bridlington principles

**10.16**   The Bridlington principles were adopted by the TUC in 1939 to govern inter-union disputes, so as to police the 'poaching' of members. The agreement is non-binding. Yet all trade unions in the UK subscribe to them, although it establishes a strict regime. For instance, Regulation G of the principles allows the General Secretary of the TUC to appoint a legally qualified individual as Chair of the Committee (Professor Lord Wedderburn QC). Further, Principle 4 concerns the avoidance of inter-union disputes. This establishes a requirement that unions involve the TUC before any industrial action is taken. The TUC's Disputes Committee may also make an award with which the parties are obliged to comply (TUC Rule 12(b)). All of these principles set out basic rules to prevent inter-union rivalry and disputes.

## Internal Union Governance

**10.17**   The basis for trade union governance is the rulebook. Union rulebooks set out the terms of which the contract to which membership must comply. To that end, the union's rulebook allows its officials to work and provide power to them, in order to perform their function. For example, in *Heaton's (St Helens) Transport Ltd v Transport and General Workers' Union* (1973), the Court of Appeal construed that the respondent union was generally liable for its officials. Yet, on appeal, the House of Lords saw the union steward's authority as depending on the rule book and custom and practice. Consequently, whether union officials are liable for their actions depends on whether they complied with their own rulebook or not.

## The Union rule book

**10.18**   The Court of Appeal in *Iwanuszezak v General Municipal Boilermakers and Allied Trades Union* (1988) stated that since unions exist, primarily, to promote the interests of the membership as a whole rather than the interests of individual members, it is permissible for a union to give priority to the collective interest of the membership as a whole over the individual interest. Consequently, union rulebooks exist to fulfil this task. In *Thomas v National Union of Mineworkers (South Wales Area)* (1985), it was established that it would be ultra vires for union officials to finance a form of picketing that would be bound to involve criminal acts, it was not ultra vires if the picketing were merely capable of involving criminal acts, as the union officials had acted within the agreed rules. Consequently, the union rulebook provides the basis upon which the institutions that govern the union, can operate. Since 1952, the Court of Appeal in *Lee v Showmen's Guild of GB*, held that whilst the courts would normally not seek to interfere in the business of voluntary legal bodies, it was proper to protect the rights of trade union members. As a result, the courts hold certain grounds for judicial review against trades unions. This means that members can potentially complain to the courts about the processes adopted by any union, if they have grounds to believe that it breaches the union's own rulebook and it is in the public interest. Yet Vinelott J summarised the situation in *Taylor v National Union of Mineworkers (Derbyshire Area)* (1985) when he stated: 'The courts are in principle reluctant to intervene in the internal affairs of any association, corporate or (otherwise). If they do intervene, they take the view that the affairs of the association should generally be conducted with the will of the majority, and they will decline to interfere if (the action being brought) could be overturned by a simple majority of the members'.

## Union funds

**10.19** Duty to maintain accounts is found in s 28, TULRCA 1992 which sets down detailed rules for the carrying on of unions' and employers' associations' financial affairs, similar to those obligations imposed on companies. Trade unions accounts must be audited and submitted to the Certification Officer, s 32 TULRCA 1992. Furthermore, subject to s 32A TULRCA 1992 (inserted by TURERA 1993), every union member must receive a statement on the accounts submitted to the Certification Officer.

**10.20** Section 15 of TULR(C)A 1992 renders it unlawful for a union's property to be applied for the purposes of indemnifying individuals for any penalty imposed by a court for:

(a)     contempt of court, or

(b)     a criminal offence.

Therefore, union officials in general owe a fiduciary duty to the member of their union. By s 16 of TULRCA 1992, members of trade unions have powers to act against trustees of the union's property in respect of unlawful application of such assets, or trustees who comply with any unlawful direction given to them under the rules of the union.

## The Political Fund

**10.21** The House of Lords in its landmark ruling in *Amalgamated Society of Railway Servants v Osborne* (1910), the 'Osborne judgment' as it is more familiarly known, ruled that the use of union funds for political purposes was illegal, since they were only empowered to pursue those objects permitted in the Trade Union Act 1871 and this was not one of them (ie fund political parties). However, subsequently, the Trade Union Act of 1913 allowed trade unions to use trade union monies for 'political objects', where its members approved of it by ballot. The later 1984 Trade Union Act tightened up the rules, particularly allowing members to opt-out of this 'political levy'.

**10.22** Under s 71 TULRCA 1992, unions must now seek approval for their 'political objects' and cannot expend on these without the consent of voting members, by majority.

S 72 TULRCA 1992, defines 'political objects' as:

●     contributions to a political party;

●     any service or property donated or provided to a political party;

●     maintenance of a holder of political office;

●     publication of materials persuading people to vote for a particular political party.

This ballot must take place every 5 years.

## Union Elections

**10.23** By s 46 of TULRCA 1992, every member of the principal executive committee of a trade union has to be elected every five years by all members of the union. Unions are subject to strict rules in relation to elections, as follows:

- balloting must be held in secret and preferably by postal voting;

- there should be non-interference by 'the union or any of its members, officials or employees'; and

- unions should finance all elections.

As an alternative to a postal vote, a union used to be able to conduct a semi-postal ballot or workplace ballot if the union was satisfied that there were no reasonable grounds to believe that this would not result in a free election as required by ss 2 and 3 of the Trade Union Act 1984.

**10.24** Each union must appoint a qualified independent scrutineer, and give him the duties set out in s 49(3) or s 75(3). He may also be given 'additional functions'. The union should ensure that it would be unreasonable for any person to call the scrutineer's independence into question by reason of:

- anything in the terms of the scrutineer's appointment;

- interference with the carrying out of his function.

**10.25** Any breach of these statutory election requirements can result in a complaint to the Certification Officer, seeking an enforcement order, requiring the trade union concerned to take remedial action and comply with the correct process. Should the Certification Officer fail to act, only thereafter can action be sought in the High Court.

## Discipline

**10.26** All union rulebooks should set out clear rules in relation to disciplining its members. Therefore, any such disciplinary action must be carried out in accordance with the union's own rule book. As the Court of Human Rights in Strasbourg ruled in *Cheall v UK* (1986), unions should decide all matters in accordance with their own rules, particularly in relation to disciplinary proceedings. Clearly, the judges are reluctant to allow a domestic union tribunal to be final adjudicators of questions of fact on their own rulebook, and also intervene if there is no evidence to support a finding of fact found by any disciplinary committee (*Lee v Showmen's Guild* (1952), also *Partington v National and Local Government Officers' Association* (1981)).

**10.27** Consequently, trade unions must comply with the rules of natural justice because 'although the jurisdiction of a domestic tribunal is founded on contract, express or implied, nevertheless the parties are not free to make any contract they like' (*Breen v Amalgamated Engineering Union* (1971). For example, in *Roebuck v National Union of Mineworkers (Yorkshire Area) (Yorkshire Area)* (1977), where the union president both brought the complaint and heard the complaint, it was held that such a situation breached the principles of natural justice, since it made no difference that the union rules generally required the president to chair the meeting since he could vacate it in special circumstances and should have done so here.

**10.28** A union is prohibited from disciplining a member for not taking part in industrial action notwithstanding that a majority of that member's colleagues voted in favour of the action in a properly held ballot, and this is naturally seen by the unions as a threat to traditional union concepts of solidarity.

## *Unjustifiable action*

**10.29** S. 64 TULRCA 1992 establishes the right of each trade union member not to be unjustifiably disciplined. To that end, the most important grounds (TULRCA 1992, s 65(2)) on which discipline of a trade union member is to be taken as unjustifiable are:

- failure to support a strike or industrial action;

- failure to participate in a strike or industrial action;

- indication of opposition to a strike;

- indication of lack of support for a strike;

- failure to contravene a contract of employment;

- the making of an assertion that the union, or any official, the representative or trustee thereof, has contravened or is proposing to contravene a requirement imposed;

- consulting the Certification Officer or asking him to provide advice or assistance;

- failure to agree to the making of a deduction of subscriptions arrangement;

- resigning from one union to join another.

**10.30** The central term 'discipline' is given a broad definition. S 64(2) TULRCA 1992 includes:

- expulsion;

- a sanction (usually, a fine);

- deprivation of benefits afforded to other members;

- union dues/subscriptions;

- subjecting the individual to any detriment (eg, dissuading another union from allowing membership. See for example *National and Local Government Officers Association v Killorn and Simm* (1990)).

**10.31** Aggrieved trade union members, claiming unjustifiable discipline, may complain to an ET and seek a declaration within 3 months of the date of the alleged act by the union. An order of compensation can be awarded, capped up to £61,300.

## Expulsion

**10.32** The House of Lords in *Cheall v Association of Professional, Executive, Clerical and Computer Staff* (1983) ruled that there was no right for an individual to associate with those who did not want to associate with them. The later Thatcher Government Employment Act 1980 enacted a right not to be unreasonably expelled or excluded from a trade union where a closed shop agreement was in operation.

The provisions were modified by the Trade Union Reform and Employment Rights Act 1993, which removed the link with closed shop employment. The modified right currently exists as s 174 TULRCA 1992.

**10.33** Compensation can also be awarded, the amount depending upon whether the union has rescinded the decision to impose discipline. Damages can be recovered by a member where it is reasonably foreseeable that loss will flow as a result of breach of the contract of membership (*Bonsor v Musicians' Union* (1955) ). In awarding damages, the court will not be required to take into account any injury to feelings that the member may have suffered. Further, a member will be required to take reasonable steps to mitigate losses (see *Edwards v Society of Graphical and Allied Trades* (1971)). Compensation is awarded on a just and equitable basis, subject to a statutory maximum of £56,900. If a claim is heard by the EAT there is a minimum award of £5,300.

## The right to join a trade union

**10.34** With the repeal of the Combination Acts in 1824, trade unions were legalised and the freedom to associate prevailed. This right has long been protected under international and European law – ILO Conventions No. 87 (Association and the Right to Organise) and 98 (Right to Organise and bargain Collectively); Article 11, ECHR (1950); and, Article 5, European Social Charter. All of these labour standards provide the positive right to join a trade union.

### Freedom of Association

**10.35** Notwithstanding these standards, the UK has been long troubled with this right. In the first instance, until relatively recently, unions were banned at GCHQ (a Government security intelligence unit) in Cheltenham. Furthermore, Lord Diplock in *Cheall v Association of Professional, Executive, Clerical and Computer Staff* (1983), regarded the positive nature of the right, to imply a mutuality of the negative:

'... there can be no right of an individual to associate with others who are not willing to associate with him ....'. In general terms, the freedom to associate means:

- The right to peaceful assembly and to freedom of association with others, including the right to join trade unions for the protection of their interests;

- No restrictions shall be placed on the exercise of these rights other than as are prescribed by law and are necessary in a democratic society, in the interests of national security or public safety, for the prevention of disorder or crime, for the protection of health or morals or for the protection of the rights and feedoms of others (Article 11, ECHR (1950)).

**10.36** In *Wilson and Palmer* (2002), their respective employers had offered pay increases on the relinquishing of their trade union rights. The House of Lords held that such action did not deprive the employees, who desired to exercise their freedom of association and remain in their trade unions, of their statutory rights and protection. The European Court of Human Rights in Strasbourg, took a different view, upholding that the UK law had failed to protect trade union members and that the British employers concerned had violated the freedom to associate.

**10.37** S. 2 of the Employment Relations Act 1999, contained a change of wording to s 146 TULRCA 1992, so as to effectively reverse the ruling in *Wilson and Palmer* (above). S 2 ERelA 1999, makes it unlawful for an employee to be 'subjected to any detriment' for trade union reasons.

## Refusal of employment

**10.38** Where a person is refused employment because of a requirement to join a trade union or to cease to become a trade union member, s 137 TULRCA 1992 makes such conditions unlawful. Although, an important distinction must be made between trade union membership and activities (see *Harrison v Kent CC* (1995))), since s 137 only provides protection in situations regarding membership.

## Closed shop

**10.39** The 'closed shop' (a requirement to join a certain trade union to gain and/or retain employment) thrived in Britain between 1974and 1980. It characterised some 1.8 million workplaces. Following the European Court of Human Rights ruling in the 'railwaymen's' case (*Young, James & Webster* (1981)), where the closed shop was declared a violation of the freedom to associate (Article 11) since it forced labour to join a trade union (thus enhancing the right to dissociation) Mrs Thatcher's first administration abolished it, making it almost an illegal practice, save where on religious grounds it was necessary and justifiable (Employment Act 1988, now s 152(1)(c), TULRCA 1992, see para. 10.40, below).

## Action short of dismissal

**10.40** Under s 146 TULRCA 1992, where a trade union member is subjected to any detriment attributable to such membership, for example where an employer prevents or deters membership of a trade union, whether by an act or omission of his employer, the employee (only regarding events during his employment) can complain to an ET on grounds of discrimination (see *Robb v Leon Motors Ltd* (1978), *National Coal Board v Ridgway* (1987), *Gallacher v Department of Transport* (1994) & *Wilson v United Kingdom* (2002), for examples).

## Dismissal due to trade union association

**10.41** Under s 152 TULRCA 1992, where a trade union member is dismissed because of his trade union membership, such a dismissal (as seen previously in chapters 5 and 6) will be automatically deemed unfair (see *Fitzpatrick v British Railways Board* (1991)). Higher levels of compensation are also available in such cases with a minimum award of £3,500 being set and additional award up to £13,500 being also available in such cases. The special award was abolished in 1999.

## Blacklisting

**10.42** The Employment Relations Act 1999 gives the Secretary of State a power to make regulations prohibiting the compiling of blacklists of trade unions. Yet no regulations have been made to-date.

## Dissociation rights?

**10.43** It was the Donovan Commission (1968) which observed that the right to dissociation must also exist, but that a negative right did not necessarily rely upon the existence of a positive right. To that end, the right to dissociate was reinforced in the early 1980s, by the then newly elected Conservative Government, so as to protect those individuals who did not desire to join a trade union.

**10.44** The *Young, James and Webster* (1981) case highlights the case in favour of a parallel right of dissociation. These railway workers were being forced to join the railway union, effectively then a closed shop (see para. 10. 36, above). They sought to legally challenge this require-ment and succeeded in the European Court of Human Rights in Strasbourg. However, nowadays, s 152(1)(c ) TULRCA 1992, provides the requisite protection for those individuals who do not wish to join a trade union and suffer a detriment as a result. Notably it will be automatically unfair to select a worker for dismissal due to non-membership of a particular trade union. Furthermore, s 146(1)(c) also protects the worker from discrimination for action short of dismissal.

## Further reading

Deakin, S, & Morris, G, *Labour Law* (3rd ed, 2001) Butterworths (chapters 8 & 10).

Smith, I, & Thomas, G, *Industrial Law* (8th ed, 2003) Butterworths (chapters 2 & 10).

## Articles

Davies, P, & Kilpatrick, C., 'UK worker representation after single channel', *Industrial Law Journal*, 2004, Vol. 33 (2), pp. 95–120.

Ewing, K, 'Freedom of association and the Employment Rights Act (1999)', *Industrial Law Journal*, 1999, Vol. 28 (4), pp. 283–298.

Ewing, K, 'The Implications of Wilson and Palmer', *Industrial Law Journal*, 2003, Vol. 32 (1), pp. 1–22.

## Self-test questions

1. Statutorily define a British trade union. What are the legal implications of such a definition?

2. Freedom Association is fundamental to collective organization in the UK. Discuss.

3. Arthur has been a member of his union, ACTNOW, since 1982 and has been a shop steward for the last 4 years. Two months ago, he stood for re-election and was beaten by Bill, a work colleague, losing by 8 votes. However, a week after the election it transpired that Bill has stolen some ballot papers from the lockers of some of colleagues and it is alleged that Bill used these votes to get elected. Arthur confronted Bill about this, and consequently a fight broke out. Subsequently, Arthur was disciplined by his union's regional representative, Colette, and it was decided that Arthur is banned from standing for a position in his union for the next five years. Arthur appealed to the union's National Executive, of which Colette is a member, but it was dismissed. Apparently, at the appeal hearing Colette did not make any representations, but voted to dismiss Arthur's appeal.

    Advise Arthur on any rights and remedies he may have with regard to his union's disciplinary action against him.

4. Assess the impact of the provisions of the Employment Relations Bill 2003 on trade unions from 2004 onwards.

# CHAPTER ELEVEN

# Collective Bargaining

## Summary

This chapter considers trade union membership, rights and activities, voluntary and statutory recognition, and collective bargaining rights.

In this chapter we have shown:

- Collective bargaining is the process by which a trade union negotiates with an employer on issues relating to the terms and conditions of employment.

- S. 178(1) TULRCA 1992 defines collective bargaining as 'negotiations relating to ....terms & conditions, physical conditions at work, engagement or non-engagement or suspension of employment, allocation of duties, matters of discipline and union membership or non-membership of a trade union'.

- Collective bargaining results in collective agreements and requires the duty to disclose information for collective bargaining (s 182, TULRCA 1992).

- The right of association is protected by UK law and ensures that workers are not refused employment on grounds of either trade union membership or non-membership.

- Trade unions are protected against dismissal on trade union grounds or are subjected to a detriment as a result of being a trade union member or involved in trade union action and/or activities.

- Recognition, can be voluntary and statutory. The statutory basis is governed by the Employment Relations Act 1999, as amended, and requires the CAC to adjudicate on applications. The voluntary system is underpinned by the common law, requiring the parties to intend such bargaining to take place. The statutory process requires compliance with a complicated set of rules, comprising the establishment of a level of support in an agreed bargaining unit. Following a ballot, should 50% of the balloted bargaining unit support recognition, then recognition ensues and collective bargaining with the newly recognised trade union follows.

## Trade union membership, rights and activities

11.1  Collective bargaining evolved in the UK as a post-war initiative, as a means of regulating pay and other terms and conditions of employment. Following the success of Joint Industrial Councils, works councils, a growth in trade unions prevailed. Underpinned by International Labour Organisation (ILO) Conventions, these bodies became organised and collective bargaining began. ILO No. 87 of 1948 provides for the freedom of association and the right to organise, and No. 98 of 1949 provides for the right to bargain collectively. However, since 2000 under the 1998 Human Rights Act, the now incorporated European Convention on Human Rights (ECHR) of 1950, Article 11 ensures the right to freedom of peaceful assembly and to freedom of association with others.

### Trade union membership

11.2  Article 1(1) of ILO Convention No. 88 of 1948 secures that 'workers shall enjoy adequate protection against acts of anti-union activities'. In the context of the UK, since 1971 and now under the Trade Union & Labour Relations Consolidation Act 1992 (TULRCA) trade union rights are protected (see Chapter 10).

## Trade union rights

**11.3**  The provisions of the TULRCA 1992 provide three distinct trade union rights:

- a trade union member has the right not to be subjected to any detriment (s 146, TULRCA 1992);

- dismissal of a trade union member is automatically regarded as unfair, particularly those affected employees who hold functions cognate to trade union duties (eg health and safety representatives or worker representative) (s 152, TULRCA 1992); and,

- trade union officials and members are allowed 'reasonable' time-off, without pay, to undertake their duties (s 168, TULRCA 1992). Note trade union officials involved in collective bargaining receive paid time-off to execute these duties.

## Trade union activities

**11.4**  The exact scope of activities of trade unions is open to interpretation. Phillips J provides guidance in his judgment in *Lyon v St James Press* (1976) stating that: 'The special protection afforded to trade union activities must not be allowed to operate as a cloak for conduct which ordinarily justify dismissal'. The ACAS Code of Practice on Time Off for Trade Union Duties provides further advice, yet is more prescriptive in so far as it details 'voting in union elections, executive meetings and annual conferences' (paras. 21–22) as union duties. However, case law has further expanded this rather narrow approach to include:

(a)  seeking union recognition (*Taylor v Butler Machine Tool* Ltd (1976));

(b)  discussing union matters (*Zucker v Astrid Jewels Ltd* (1978));

(c)  seeking advice from union officials (*Stokes v Wheeler-Green Ltd* (1979)); and,

(d)  seeking to recruit new members (*Bass taverns Ltd; v Burgess* (1995)).

## Time-off for trade union activities

**11.5** Reasonable time should be given to such activities, including the holding of a meeting during the employers' time (see *Marley Tile Co Ltd; v Shaw* (1980), per Goff LJ). The appropriate time for trade union activities is defined as not only occasions 'outside the employee's working hours' but also time 'within working hours at which, in accordance with arrangements agreed with, or consent given by his, it is permissible for him to take part in those activities' (TULRCA 1992, s 146(2), 170(2)). In *Post Office v Union of Post Office Workers* (1974), Lord Reid declared that, 'it does not include periods when in accordance with his contract the worker is on his employer's premises, but not actually working'. The time taken off must be reasonable as to amount and the circumstances when it is taken. For example, in *Wignall v British Gas Corporation* (1984) the applicant had already been granted 12 weeks' leave for union business when he sought a further 10 days for the preparation of a union district monthly magazine. The EAT upheld the tribunal's decision that it was reasonable for the employers to refuse the further time.

**11.6** Yet the EAT in *Marley Tile Co Ltd v Shaw* (1980) held that a meeting of maintenance men to protest about the shop steward's lack of credentials during working hours was 'at an appropriate time', because the legislation had to be construed in the light of 'actual industrial practice'. On appeal, their Lordships took a more narrow view and agreed that whilst consent might be implied, it could not arise by way of extension from custom and practice elsewhere, only at the factory in question.

## Time off by trade union officials

**11.7** Where his union is recognised, an official is entitled to time off with pay 'to carry out those duties ...which are concerned with industrial relations between his employer and any associated employer and their employees' (s 168(1), TULR(C)A 1992, and this is in accordance with ILO Convention No. 135. This is restricted to those duties concerned with negotiations about matters within s 244, TULR(C)A 1992 'in relation to which the trade union is recognised by the employer' or 'any functions related to or connected with any (such) matters ...and the employer has agreed may be so performed by the trade union'. If the employer refuses, the official can complain to the employment tribunal and seek a declaration and compensation; however, he should not ignore the employer's refusal and take the time off regardless, since 'Official' is defined as any officer of the union or branch and any such other person elected under the union rules to represent the members or some of them (TULR(C)A 1992, s 119).

**11.8** The ACAS Code of Practice on Time Off gives some indication of the duties for which time off should be granted:

(a)   collective bargaining with the appropriate level of management;

(b)   informing constituents about negotiations or consultations with management;

(c)   meetings with other lay officials or with full-time officials;

(d)   interviews with and on behalf of constituents on grievance and disciplinary matters;

(e)   appearing on behalf of constituents before an outside body.

**11.9** It may be argued, however, that 'duties' in s 168, TULR(C)A 1992 is used in the everyday sense of 'business, office or function', rather than inflexibly associating them with an official's duties.

## Union learning representatives

**11.10** By s 168 A, TULR(C)A 1993, introduced in 2002, an employer must permit an employee who is a union learning representative time off for the purposes of carrying on these activities in relation to qualifying members of the trade union: analysing learning or training needs; providing information and advice about learning or training matter; arranging learning or training and promoting the value of learning or training; consulting the employer about carrying on such activities, or preparing for these matters. The representative must have undergone sufficient training to enable him to carry on these activities and the union must give the employer notice of this fact. The amount of time off and the purposes for which it is taken are those that are reasonable in all the circumstances.

**11.11**  By s 170, TULR(C)A 1992, a trade union member is to be allowed reasonable time off during working hours without pay to take part in the activities of an independent trade union recognised by the employer for the purposes of collective bargaining. The Employment Relations Act 1999 replaces the term 'action short of dismissal' with the broader term 'detriment', bringing this part of the TULR(C)A 1992 into line with other measures to protect union and employee representatives, who are not permitted reasonable time-off by their employers. 'Detriment' can be suffered as a result of 'any act, or any deliberate failure to act, by his employer' (s 146, TULR(C)A 1992).

## Time- off for health and safety representatives

**11.12**  A duly appointed health and safety representative has a right to reasonable time off with pay to perform his function and to be trained (Safety Representatives and Safety Committee Regulations 1977 (SI 1977/1500), regulation 4, para. 2).

## Strike action?

**11.13**  There is no general right to strike in Britain. In fact, strike action is positively discouraged by both the criminal and civil law. Essentially, the effect of industrial action impacts upon the contract of employment. As Donovan LJ said in *Rookes v Barnard* (1963) in the majority of strikes no such notice to terminate the contract is either given or expected. The law relating to industrial action is dealt with in detail in the next chapter, Chapter 12.

## Collective bargaining and agreements

**11.14**  Collective agreements are contracts resulting from the process of collective bargaining between unions and employers, for the purposes of regulating the procedures that will be adopted by the union and employer, and/or determining the terms and conditions under which workers will work. Most collective agreements are likely to fall within the statutory definition of a collective agreement. Such collective agreements can either be legally enforceable as contracts or non-contractual, depending upon the intentions of the parties, as well as the content of the agreement. They are usually not legally enforceable. However, their provisions can become part of the contract of employment of individual employees.

**11.15** The statutory definition of collective agreement can be found in s 178 TULRCA 1992. It defines a collective agreement as 'any agreement or arrangement made by or on behalf of one or more trade unions and one or more employers or employers' associations' and relating to one or more of the following matters:

• machinery for negotiation or consultation relating to the above, including recognition;

• terms and conditions of employment;

• engagement or non-engagement, or termination or suspension of employment or the duties of employment, of one or more workers;

• matters of discipline;

• a worker's membership or non-membership of a trade union;

• facilities for trade union officials;

• pay, including pensions, has been emphasised and added to the list (see *UNIFI v Union Bank of Nigeria plc* (2001)).

**11.16** Due to having such a wide scope, it is possible for most agreements to fall outside its parameters (see eg *Universe Tankships Inc. of Monrovia v International Transport Workers Federation* (1982), which involved a dispute over a 'goodwill payment' to the union's welfare fund). Whilst collective agreements are unlikely to be legally binding, the legal position is complex. Traditionally, collective agreements can fall under one of three regimes: the first covers agreements concluded before 1 December 1971 (ie fall outside the statutory definition in s 178 TULRCA 1992); the second covers agreements concluded under the Industrial Relations Act 1971 regime; and, the third covers agreements made under the regime that replaced it.

• Agreements prior to 1 December 1971

The common law governs these contracts. In particular the law focuses upon what was intended by the parties to the agreement and whether they intended that the agreement should be legally binding (see *Ford Motor Co Ltd v Amalgamated Union of Engineering and Foundry Workers* (1969), where it was held that the collective agreement was not intended by the parties to be legally binding).

● Agreements under the Industrial Relations Act 1971

Agreements entered into between 30 November 1971 and 16 September 1974 fall under the Industrial Relations Act 1971. The Act requires that collective agreements entered into during this period should be automatically deemed to be binding on the parties to it, unless a clause stating the contrary exists, so making it non-binding. Most agreements entered into during that period routinely included such a clause, commonly known as the 'TINALEA' clause – 'This is not a legally enforceable agreement'.

● Agreements made (after 16 September 1974) under TULRCA

Any collective agreements entered into after this date were governed by the provisions introduced by the Trade Union and Labour Relations Act 1974, now contained in s 179 TULRCA 1992. The new Act presumes that, unless an agreement is in writing and contains a clause stating that it is intended to be binding as between the parties to it, it is deemed not to be a legally enforceable contract. However, under the 1999 Employment Relations Act, under the statutory recognition procedure any collective bargaining procedures imposed by the CAC will take effect as a legally binding contract enforceable before the courts.

11.17 It should be noted, even if a collective agreement is binding as between the parties, some clauses contained in it may not be enforceable by a court. Such clauses fall into two categories: 'no-strike' clauses, and clauses which are discriminatory. For instance, a clause in a collective agreement which prohibits or restricts the right of workers to engage in a strike or other industrial action will not be binding as between the employer and individual employees unless the following requirements under s 180 TULRCA 1992 are satisfied:

(a)    the collective agreement which contains the clause must be in writing;

(b)     the agreement must contain a provision expressly stating that the clause to be incorporated into individual contracts;

(c)     the agreement must be reasonably accessible to employees at their place of work and available for them to consult during working hours;

(d)     the clause must in fact be incorporated into the individual contracts of employment.

**11.18**     Further, the extent that a clause in a collective agreement discriminates against a person on grounds of sex, race or disability, it is void under the provisions of, respectively, s 77 Sex Discrimination Act 1975, s 72 Race Relations Act 1976 and s 9 Disability Discrimination Act 1995. As to when the provisions of a collective agreement become incorporated into individual contracts of employment, this is determined by fact. Incorporation may be express (as in *Robertson v British Gas Corporation* (1983), where the contract of employment stated that 'the collective agreement will apply to you'), or implied. In any event, procedural agreements (eg on recognition) are unlikely to be held appropriate for incorporation (see generally, *Cadoux v Central Regional Council* (1986), *Marley v Forward Trust Group Limited* (1986), *Whent v T Cartledge Limited* (1997) and *Burke v Royal Liverpool University Hospital NHS Trust* (1997)).

## Trade union recognition

**11.19**     Recognition is accepting a trade union as the representative of the workforce. In effect, recognition is defined in s 178 TULRCA 1992 as meaning '… recognition of the union by an employer, or two or more associated employers, to any extent, for the purpose of collective bargaining …'. At time of writing the Employment Relations Bill 2003 is before Parliament. This Bill, which is expected to become law by Autumn 2004, comes about due to a review of the 1999 Employment Relations Act which introduced a new framework for statutory recognition and derecognition of trade unions into the UK. Part 1 of this proposed new law seeks to amend the Schedule to the 1999 Act, clauses 1 and 4 of the new Bill clarify how a bargaining unit is to be determined by the Central Arbitration Committee (CAC). Clauses 2 and 3 extend existing powers, including the right of the CAC to reduce the 20 days period of negotiation of the parties to agree a bargaining unit and places a duty on the employer to supply information to the unions to assist this process. Clause 5 provides a right for trade unions to communicate with the workforce in the bargaining unit from the point of the CAC's acknowledgement and acceptance of the union's application for statutory recognition.

**11.20** Clearly, the legal significance of recognition lies in the increased rights that a trade union derives as a result of recognition. Historically in the UK, union recognition has not been a compulsory process, but voluntary. The Employment Relations Act 1999 changed that and formally introduced a controversial new statutory recognition procedure, under which a union may claim recognition against the employer's wishes. However, the exception lies in situations relating to a transfer of an undertaking, where the former (transferor) employer recognised a union or unions, the new (transferee) employer is also bound to afford recognition to the union or unions (Regulation 9, Transfer of Undertakings (Protection of Employment) Regulations 1981). Yet, currently there is no legal provision which prevents the new employer from subsequently derecognising the union post-transfer, where recognition by the former employer was voluntary (ie not under the new statutory procedures).

## Voluntary recognition

**11.21** Under common law, recognition is an entirely voluntary process. In such circumstances, recognition occurs by agreement, as a matter of custom and practice and/or good employment relations, rather than through law. The established principles governing voluntary recognition are that pre-existing collective bargaining occurred expressly or impliedly, albeit evidenced (see *National Union of Tailors and Garment Workers v Charles Ingram & Co Ltd* (1977)). For example, in *National Union of Gold, Silver and Allied Trades v Albury Bros Ltd* (1978), the Court of Appeal held that recognition means negotiating with a view to striking a deal on an issue: a discussion over rates of pay was not sufficient to amount to representational rights or consultation (per Eveliegh LJ). Furthermore, once an employer is taken to have recognised a union, it cannot, in the absence of the formal withdrawal of recognition, argue that it did not intend to recognise, such is supported in *Union of Shop, Distributive and Allied Workers v Sketchley Ltd* (1981). Lastly, the recognising of a trade union by an employers' association does not bind all of its members to bargain with that union, as noted in *National Union of Gold, Silver and Allied Trades v Albury Bros Ltd* (1978), above.

**11.22** Part II of the 1999 Act points out that in general the statutory provisions do not apply to voluntary recognition. However, where the employer and the union have previously reached a voluntary recognition agreement, but that agreement is not being honoured, or the parties have not been able to agree a method of collective bargaining, the union can apply to the CAC to determine a method of collective bargaining. The imposed method will be enforceable in the same way as if the CAC had declared the union to be recognised under the statutory procedures.

## Statutory Recognition

**11.23** The Employment Relations Act 1999, which received Royal Assent on 27 July 1999 enacted a new statutory recognition procedure, whereby an employer has a legal duty to recognise an independent trade union (or trade unions) where a majority of the relevant workforce seeks it. The Employment Relations Act and its provisions (inserting a new s 70A and a Schedule A1 into the TULRCA 1992) on recognition came into force on 6 June 2000. These provisions are further amplified by a statutory instrument (The Trade Union Recognition (Method of Collective Bargaining) Order 2000 (SI 2000/1300)) which sets out the method by which collective bargaining might be carried out in the absence of any agreement between the union and the employer on the matter, and by a DTI Code of Practice on Access to Workers during Recognition and Derecognition Ballots, which give practical guidance about the steps employers should take to allow unions reasonable access to workers during recognition ballots. As noted above, this Act is subject to revision under the Employment Relations Bill 2003, due to become an Act in 2004.

### New process

**11.24** Under the statutory procedure, a new process is born where an independent trade union may apply to an employer for recognition in relation to a particular group of workers (a 'bargaining unit'). If the employer does not agree to recognise the union, or disputes the appropriate bargaining unit for the purposes of recognition, the union may apply to the CAC to decide the appropriate bargaining unit and/or whether the union should be recognised. Subject to the circumstances, recognition can be automatic, or a ballot may need to be held. Where it is shown that a majority of the workers in the bargaining unit are members of the union, the CAC can declare the union recognised without a ballot; otherwise, a secret ballot of all the workers in the bargaining unit must be held. The recognition procedures do not apply where the employer employs fewer than 21 workers.

**11.25** The scope of compulsory recognition under the new statutory procedures is restricted to collective bargaining over pay, hours of work and holidays, although the parties are free to extend the scope of collective bargaining by agreement. The Act does not require collective bargaining over training, but instead imposes a separate obligation on the employer to consult union representatives periodically on the employer policy, actions and plans on training. The statutory recognition procedures are intended for use only if attempts to reach a voluntary agreement have failed. Strong emphasis is placed on the desirability of reaching agreement. The procedures are subject to strict time limits, but additional time is permitted at every stage for the parties to negotiate. Where the parties fail to reach agreement and the CAC imposes a method of collective bargaining, the imposed method has effect as a legally binding contract between the employer and the union, enforceable in the courts. The new procedures also enable the employer or the workers to apply to the CAC for derecognition in certain circumstances. The procedures for derecognition are similar to those for recognition. In most circumstances, derecognition is not possible until at least three years from the time when recognition was awarded.

### Applying for recognition

**11.26** The statutory recognition procedure begins with a formal request for recognition to an employer. Two or more unions can apply jointly, but in such a case it must be shown that the unions will co-operate effectively in collective bargaining and, if the employer wishes, conduct single-table bargaining. The request must be in writing, must specify the union or unions and the bargaining unit in respect of which recognition is claimed, and must state that the request is made under Schedule A1, TULRCA 1992. The request will not be valid unless the union (or each of the unions) has a certificate of independence, and the employer (together with any associated employers) employs at least 21 workers on the day of the request, or an average of at least 21 workers in the 13 weeks leading up to that day.

**11.27** Once an application has been received, the statutory procedure will end if, within 10 working days, the parties agree both the bargaining unit and that the union should be recognised for collective bargaining in respect of that bargaining unit. If the employer agrees to negotiate, either in relation to the bargaining unit or the union, the employer is then entitled to a further period of 28 days for negotiation, extendable by mutual agreement. If the parties subsequently reach agreement, the statutory procedure ceases to apply.

**11.28** If the employer rejects the application, or negotiations are unsuccessful, the union may apply to the CAC to decide the appropriate bargaining unit and/or whether there is majority support for recognition amongst the workers in the bargaining unit. No such application may be made where the employer has agreed to negotiate and the union has rejected or failed to respond to a timely proposal by the employer to seek the assistance of ACAS.

## The CAC's test

**11.29** Where an application is made to the CAC, the CAC has 10 days to decide whether the application is valid and admissible. The CAC cannot consider an application unless, in addition to the requirements already noted, it is satisfied that at least 10 per cent of the proposed bargaining unit are members of the union, and that a majority of workers in the proposed bargaining unit would be likely to favour recognition. If the CAC receives more than one application, and the proposed bargaining units overlap (ie at least one worker is a member of all the bargaining units), then unless the unions agree to make a joint bid, or all but one of the unions withdraws, each application will be subject to the '10 per cent test' to see whether at least 10 per cent of the bargaining unit are members of the union. If only one application passes the test, it may proceed; if more than one application passes, or none of them passes, none of the applications will be allowed to proceed. Furthermore, the application must not cover any workers in respect of whom the CAC has already accepted an application, or in respect of whom an independent union is already recognised. No application may be made within 3 years of a previous unsuccessful application by that union in respect of the same (or substantially the same) bargaining unit, and an application must not be substantially the same as an application accepted by the CAC within the previous 3 years.

## Bargaining Unit?

**11.30** If the CAC has been asked to decide on the appropriate bargaining unit, it must initially give the parties a further 28 days to agree the bargaining unit. If the parties are still deadlocked, the CAC must determine the appropriate bargaining unit within 10 days, taking into account the need for the bargaining unit to be compatible with effective management, and, so far as is consistent with that need, the following factors:

(a) the views of the employer and the union (or unions);

(b) existing national and local bargaining arrangements;

(c) the desirability of avoiding small fragmented bargaining units within an undertaking;

(d) the characteristics of the workers falling within the bargaining unit and of any other employees of the employer whom the CAC considers relevant;

(e) the location of the workers.

paras. 18 & 19 of CAC Guidance.

**11.31** In *R v CAC ex p Kwik Fit (GB) Ltd* (2002), the Court of Appeal advised the CAC to take a 'light touch' approach, including a primary consideration of the geographical scope of the workers concerned. However, once the appropriate bargaining unit has been established, the CAC must consider whether there is majority support for recognition among the workers in the bargaining unit. If the CAC is satisfied that a majority of the workers in the bargaining unit are members of the union, the CAC must issue a declaration of recognition, without the need for a ballot, unless one of the following conditions is met:

(a)   the CAC is satisfied that a ballot should be held in the interests of good industrial relations;

(b)   a significant number of the union members within the bargaining unit inform the CAC that they do not want the union to conduct collective bargaining on their behalf;

(c)   membership evidence is produced which leads the CAC to conclude that there are doubts whether a significant number of the union members within the bargaining unit want the union to conduct collective bargaining on their behalf. This evidence must either be evidence about the circumstances in which union members became members (eg were incentives provided to members to join?), or evidence about the length of time for which union members have been members (eg was there a membership drive prior to a recognition application?).

## Ballots for recognition

11.32   If any of the above conditions is met, or if the CAC is not satisfied that a majority of the workers in the bargaining unit are members of the union, the CAC must arrange for the holding of a secret ballot of the workers in the bargaining unit. Detailed rules exist in connection with the conduct of a ballot on recognition. The ballot must be conducted by a qualified independent person appointed by the CAC. The ballot must normally be held within 20 working days of the appointment of the independent person. It must be secret, and may be held at the workplace or by post at the CAC's discretion (ie a postal ballot is not compulsory). The costs of the ballot are split equally between the union and the employer. The employer is under a legal duty to co-operate with the ballot, to give the union reasonable access to the workers in the bargaining unit to campaign for recognition, and to provide information to the CAC concerning the workers in the bargaining unit (eg their names and home addresses). If the employer does not co-operate with the ballot, the CAC may order the employer to take specific steps to remedy that failure, and if the employer still fails to co-operate, the CAC may cancel the ballot and declare the union recognized. Where the result of the ballot indicates that recognition is supported by the majority of those who vote and at least 40% of all the workers in the bargaining unit, the CAC must declare the union to be recognised by the employer for collective bargaining over the pay, hours of work and holidays of all the workers in the bargaining unit.

**11.33** If the union is unsuccessful in the ballot, the CAC must declare that the union is not recognised. No further application for recognition may be made by the same union in respect of the same (or substantially the same) bargaining unit for the next 3 years.

## CAC recognition

**11.34** If the CAC declares a union to be recognised, and the employer and union cannot agree on a method for conducting collective bargaining over pay, hours and holidays, either party can ask the CAC for assistance. The CAC must allow a 42-day negotiation period for the parties to try to reach a voluntary agreement before intervening. After that period has elapsed, the CAC will try for a further 28 days (or longer, if all agree) to help the parties reach agreement. If that attempt is unsuccessful, the CAC must impose the method of collective bargaining on the parties.

**11.35** Where the CAC imposes a method of collective bargaining, the imposed method has effect as a legally binding contract between the employer and the union, enforceable in the courts by an order of specific performance ordering the other party to comply with the method. Failure to comply with such an order could constitute contempt of court. Once the CAC has imposed a bargaining method, the parties can vary it (including the fact that it is legally binding) by agreement in writing.

## Changes Affecting the Bargaining Unit

**11.36**  Part III of the Schedule, annexed to the 1999 Act contains provisions where bargaining arrangements may need to be varied over time to reflect changes in the employer's business (eg in its structure, scope or size). Where recognition has been imposed under the statutory procedures, there is a further statutory procedure for altering the recognition arrangements. The employer or the union may apply to the CAC to determine whether the original bargaining unit is no longer appropriate because the organisation, structure, nature or size of the business has changed.

**11.37**  On such an application, the parties have 10 working days in which to attempt to agree a new bargaining unit. If they do so, the CAC must declare the union recognised for the new bargaining unit. If they fail to agree, the CAC must decide whether the original bargaining unit is still appropriate, and if not, what other unit (if any) would be appropriate, applying the same criteria as in an original application. If the CAC decides that no unit is appropriate, the union will be derecognised. The employer may also seek derecognition on the grounds that the bargaining unit has ceased to exist. As before, the parties have 10 working days to agree a new bargaining unit, failing which the CAC must decide whether the original bargaining unit is still appropriate, and if not, what other unit (if any) would be appropriate. Again, if the CAC decides that no unit is appropriate, the union will be derecognised.

**11.38**  If the CAC decides that a new bargaining unit would be appropriate, it must then decide whether the union should be recognised for that unit. In particular, it must consider whether the difference between the original bargaining unit and the new bargaining unit is such that the level of support for recognition needs to be reassessed in a fresh ballot. If the changes are minor, the CAC may decide that support does not need to be reassessed, and will declare the union recognised for the new unit. If support does need to be reassessed, the same procedures apply as in an original application (ie the 10 per cent test, likelihood of majority support, automatic recognition if over 50 per cent membership, etc). If a ballot is required, it must follow the same procedures as the original ballot.

## Derecognition?

**11.39**  As noted already above, the Employment Relations Act also contains procedures for derecognition which mirror those for recognition. Parts IV, V and VII provide statutory derecognition procedures, where the CAC has made a declaration of recognition or has imposed a method of collective bargaining. Derecognition may not take place until at least three years after the CAC declared the union recognised or specified a method of collective bargaining. It is possible for an employer to apply to the CAC to de-recognise where, after the three year period has elapsed:

- the employer (together with any associated employers) has employed an average of fewer than 21 workers over a 13 week period;

- the employer believes that the majority of workers in the bargaining unit support the end of the bargaining arrangements;

- the employer applies for de-recognition in relation to a union that was previously automatically recognised.

**11.40**  The detailed procedures differ according to the reason for derecognition. Where the basis for derecognition is the fact that the employer has fewer than 21 workers, the employer can give notice to the union that it is to be derecognised from a given date at least 35 working days after the notification. The union may appeal to the CAC if it wishes to contest the employer's claim. If the CAC finds that the employer still has 21 or more workers, the collective bargaining arrangements will remain in place; otherwise they will end on the date specified in the employer's notice.

**11.41**  Where the employer believes that the union is no longer representative of the bargaining unit, the employer must first write to the union requesting the end of the bargaining arrangements. The union has 10 working days in which to accept or reject the employer's notice or, if the union agrees to negotiate, a further 28 days to reach agreement. If no agreement is forthcoming, the employer may apply to the CAC to decide whether a majority of workers support derecognition. Just as with applications for recognition, a threshold '10 per cent test' must be satisfied before the CAC can consider an application for derecognition, ie there must be prima facie evidence that at least 10 per cent of the bargaining unit favour an end to the collective bargaining arrangements, and that a majority of the bargaining unit would be likely to do so. Where these requirements are satisfied, the CAC must hold a secret ballot to decide whether the majority of workers support derecognition. If the ending of the bargaining arrangements is supported by the majority of those who vote and at least 40% of all the workers in the bargaining unit, the CAC must declare that the bargaining arrangements will cease to have effect from a specified date.

**11.43** Similar requirements apply where workers in the bargaining unit request an end to the collective bargaining arrangements. Where the union was automatically recognised on the grounds of more than 50 per cent union membership in the bargaining unit, the employer may request the end of the bargaining arrangements on the grounds that fewer than half the workers in the bargaining unit are members of the union. Again, time is allowed for negotiation, and if no agreement is reached the CAC will hold a ballot of the workers in the bargaining unit. In addition to the above, workers may apply to the CAC for de-recognition of a union which does not have a certificate of independence. Such an application may be made at any time after a non-independent union is recognised (ie the usual three year limit does not apply). Again, the CAC cannot consider the application unless there is prima facie evidence that at least 10 per cent of the bargaining unit favour an end to the bargaining arrangements and a majority of them are likely to do so.

## Recognition Rights

**11.44** The main rights accruing to an independent, recognised trade union in relation to consultation and the provision of information are:

(a)  to receive relevant information for the purposes of collective bargaining;

(b)  to be consulted in respect of collective (ie large scale) redundancies; and

(c)  to be consulted in relation to a transfer of an undertaking.

## Disclosure of Bargaining Information

**11.45** The duty to disclose information to a recognised trade union for the purposes of collective bargaining was introduced by the Industrial Relations Act 1971, and is now contained in ss 181–185 TULRCA 1992. Complaints of a failure to disclose information lie to the CAC. Prior to the Act, the duty to disclose information could be circumvented by an employer either refusing initially to recognise, or by subsequently de-recognising, a union. This has changed following the introduction of the statutory recognition procedure by the Employment Relations Act 1999, although where recognition is voluntary the position is unchanged.

## Extent of the Duty to Disclose Information

**11.46** The duty to disclose is contained in s 181(2) TULRCA 1992, which creates a two-limb test for deciding whether information needs to be disclosed. An employer must disclose to representatives of a recognised, independent trade union, on request, all information relating to the employer's undertaking which is in the employer's possession, and is information:

(a) without which the union would be impeded to a material extent in carrying on collective bargaining with the employer; and

(b) which it would be in accordance with good industrial relations practice for the employer to disclose.

**11.47** Requests to an employer for information must be in writing, if the employer so requests (s 181(3)). The employer must disclose or confirm the requested information in writing, if the union representatives so request (s 181(5)). The duty is a duty to disclose information for the purposes of collective bargaining. It follows that an employer may only be required to disclose information under these provisions for collective bargaining about matters, and in relation to descriptions of workers, for which the union is in fact recognised by the employer. If recognition is partial, the employer need not provide information which falls outside the scope of that recognition. The CAC has indicated that what must be considered is whether the union would be significantly hampered without the provision of a particular type of information (ie would the absence of the information be a 'significant impediment' to the union in carrying on collective bargaining).

**11.48**  The CAC must also consider whether it would be in accordance with good industrial relations practice to release the requested information. In considering this issue, s 181(4) states that regard must be had to the ACAS Code of Practice on Disclosure of Information ('the Code'). The CAC has stated that 'good industrial relations practice' reflects the actual practice of good employers.

## Exceptions to the duty

**11.49**  Whilst s 181 TULRCA 1992 creates a general duty to disclose collective bargaining information to independent recognised unions, the duty can be avoided in the circumstances set down in s 182(1), which lists seven categories of cases in which disclosure will not be ordered against an employer:

(a)   where it would be against the interests of national security to disclose;

(b)   where disclosure would contravene an enactment;

(c)   where the information requested was communicated to or obtained by the employer in confidence (eg tenders issued in confidence);

(d)   where the information requested relates specifically to an individual;

(e)   where disclosure of the requested information would cause substantial injury to the employer's undertaking (other than any effect which it might have on collective bargaining);

(f)   where the information has been obtained by the employer for the purpose of bringing, prosecuting or defending any legal proceedings;

(g)   where the compiling or assembling of the information would involve a amount of work or expenditure out of reasonable proportion to the value of the information in the conduct of collective bargaining.

## Complaints of Failure to Disclose Information

**11.50** If an employer fails to comply with the duty to disclose, a union can bring a complaint under the procedure set out in s 183 TULRCA 1992. A complaint lies to the CAC. Upon receipt of a claim, the CAC is required to consider whether the complaint is reasonably likely to be settled by conciliation. If so, the CAC must refer the matter to ACAS and notify the union and the employer of the referral (s 183(2)). If ACAS cannot resolve the complaint, the dispute is referred back to the CAC. If the CAC is to deal with the claim, it proceeds to hear and determine the complaint, and makes a declaration stating whether or not the complaint is well-founded, in whole or in part, giving reasons for its findings (s 183(3)).

# Central Arbitration Committee (CAC)

**11.51** The Industrial Arbitration Board was replaced in 1975 by the Central Arbitration Committee (CAC) (as discussed previously in para. 1.17). Its purpose is to act as an independent machinery for arbitration, as well as exercise its statutory jurisdiction under the 1999 Employment Relations Act (s 259, TULRCA 1992) to :

- review collective agreements;

- determine applications for statutory recognition/derecognition; and,

- adjudicate on complaints under ss 183–186, TULRCA 1992 (failure to disclose information).

**11.52** The CAC is headed by a President (currently Burton J.) and comprises of a chairman, assisted by lay panel members, representing both employers and employees. See www.cac.go v.uk.

# Remedies for non-cooperation in collective bargaining

**11.53** The remedies for non-cooperation on collective bargaining include declaration and arbitration.

## Declaration

**11.54** If the CAC finds in favour of the union, s 183(5) requires that the CAC's declaration must specify the following matters:

(a)    the information which should have been disclosed;

(b)    the date on which the employer refused to supply the requested information or refused to confirm the information in writing; and

(c)    a period of time within which the employer is bound to make good the failure to disclose that information. In specifying a time limit, the CAC must allow a period of at least one week from the date of the declaration.

**11.55** The CAC cannot specify what matters it thinks ought to be disclosed in the future as between the parties.

## Arbitration

**11.56** The ultimate remedy for a failure to disclose in accordance with the statutory provisions is unilateral arbitration. If the employer fails to comply with the terms of the declaration, the union may present a further complaint to the CAC under s 184. If the CAC finds wholly or partly in favour of the union, it must make a declaration to that effect. After such a declaration has been granted, it is possible for the union to make a further claim, in writing, that those employees specified in the claim should have their terms and conditions of employment modified in accordance with the claim (s 185(1)). The power of the CAC to award amended terms and conditions is restricted to employees and to terms and conditions which relate to matters within the scope of the employer's recognition of the union (s 185(4)). Therefore, if a union is only partially recognised by an employer, eg for the purposes of dealing with the employer's pension scheme, the union cannot seek an order modifying terms and conditions in respect of matters such as pay, hours of work, etc. Secondly, the CAC cannot impose an order in respect of terms fixed by statute (s 185(7)).

## Future reforms

**11.57** At the EU Council of Ministers meeting on 17 December 2001, the latest EU laws on collective bargaining were agreed. The National Consultation and Information (NIC) Directive is based upon the social partnership approach. That is, workers should have the basic right to consultation, but a mechanism for bargaining should be agreed between the parties and utilised accordingly. This new law requires companies with 50 or more employees to regularly inform on the enterprises' economic situation and to consult with workers on key decisions regarding the organisation's future. These include situations where jobs are threatened and where any anticipatory measures, such as training, skill development and other measures increasing the adaptability of employees, are planned. Consultation is also compulsory for decisions that are likely to lead to substantial changes in work organisation or in contractual relations. National governments will enact their own implementing measures, with sanctions for breaches, and are free to extend further these minimal information and consultation rights. From 2005 this law will apply to those organisations with 150 or more workers, from 2007 for those businesses with over 100 workers and from 2008 for those with more than 50 workers.

### National consultation?

**11.58** The UK Government opposed the NIC Directive on the grounds of subsidiarity, in so far as it believes it to be an unnecessary measure. Under the new NIC Directive, consultation is required where an employer proposes to dismiss 20 or more workers as redundant at one establishment within 90 days or less. Where 100 or more redundancies are proposed, consultation must commence at least 90 days before the first dismissal. However, these rules duplicate existing legal arrangements required under the Collective Redundancy Directive, discussed previously. The information that must be disclosed is a statement of the proposed dismissals and reasons for such, the numbers affected and the proposed method of selection and what payments are available.

## Worker involvement?

**11.59** After a record thirty-one years of EU negotiation, on 8 October 2001 the EU's Employment and Social Policy Council adopted a Regulation for a European Company Statute and a related Directive on Employee Involvement. Both these legal instruments take effect from 2004. This adoption arises after many years of controversy surrounding both the Fifth Directive on Company Law, which proposed worker representatives on company boards, and the failed Vredling Directive which proposed compulsory worker representatives in multinationals. The Regulation provides for companies located in the EU and operating in more than one Member State registering as a Societas Europea (SE) (a so-called 'European company') and to adopt one set of national rules and adopt a single management reporting system as a means of governance. More importantly, this Regulation permits trading within the EEA without having to register in each Member State in which they operate, on condition that the SE has a minimum capital of 120,000 euros. On the other hand, the Directive provides further regulation of information and consultation on matters concerning the SE itself and allows for employee participation in the supervisory or administrative body of the SE. The purpose of this Directive is to ensure that when an SE is established no reduction in employee involvement occurs. These additional workplace democracy provisions are modelled on those contained in the EWC Directive. They again include a 'default' set of rules whereby if no agreement on employee involvement can be reached, a consequential works council is established consisting of between 3 and 30 employees.

**11.60** The passing of the European Company Statute Regulation, as well as the Employee Involvement and NIC Directives, with their potential impact to establish EU-wide frameworks for collective bargaining, are highly significant for the future development of a fully participative European social partnership model. However, the actual take up rate of these new initiatives is uncertain, given the low level of establishment of European Works Councils since 1993. If such reluctance applies to EU-wide national bargaining, then it is clear that the NIC Directive is also doomed to fail.

## Further reading

Deakin, S, & Morris, G, *Labour Law* (3rd ed, 2001) Butterworths (chapters 7 and 9).

Smith, I, & Thomas, G, *Industrial Law* (8th ed, 2003) Butterworths (chapter 2).

### Article

Simpson, B, 'Trade union recognition and the law : a new approach', *Industrial Law Journal*, 2000, Vol. 29 (3), pp. 193–222.

## Self-test questions

1.  Outline the statutory procedure for trade union recognition, as enacted by the 1999 Employment Relations Act? What alternatives exist for trade union bargaining?

2.  How has the House of Lord's judgment in the Wilson/Palmer case changed the protection afforded to trade union members? And, is the law now adequate in dealing with potential discrimination against trade union officials?

3.  Vernon is the elected representative of TEACHU, the lecturers union recognised and New Learn College. Last week, Vernon's manager, Mr Stickler, told him that he could not rearrange three lectures to attend a branch meeting and rejected his application for a day residential course on first aid.

    Advise Vernon on his rights to time-off as a trade union official.

4.  EasyClean Ltd; provide cleaning services throughout the UK, with eight branches nationwide, employing some 610 people. Easy-Clean does not recognise any trade union, nor does it desire to do so. Recently, Sweepers Unite, a UK union, has recruited new members at several of EasyClean's branches. Out of 165 staff at its Muncaster area branch office, some 83 staff have joined Sweepers Unite. Bob, the Muncaster Area Manager, has recently declined a request by Sweepers Unite, upon the advice of EasyClean's Head Office, for voluntary recognition.

Advise EasyClean Limited on the procedure to be followed, the potential outcomes and likely result of Sweepers Unite's application for statutory recognition.

# CHAPTER TWELVE

# Industrial Action

## Summary

This chapter considers the right to strike, the tortious liabilities of unions, trade unions statutory immunities, as well as individual liability for industrial action.

In this chapter we have shown:

- A trade dispute is defined as 'a dispute between workers and their employer which relates wholly or mainly to ...: terms and conditions, engagement or otherwise of workers, matters of discipline and membership of trade unions' (s 244, TULRCA 1992).

- Strikes are defined as 'any concerted stoppage of work' (s 246, TULRCA 1992).

- The economic torts are: inducement to breach of contract, intimidation, conspiracy and interference with trade or business.

- The 'golden formula' in 'contemplation and furtherance of a trade dispute' statutory immunity prevails.

- Limitations on statutory immunity include secondary action and unlawful picketing.

## Industrial Action

**12.1** According to Labour Market Trends (June 2004) in 2003 UK work stoppages fell to 133 (compared with 146 in 2002). 499,100 working days were lost and days lost through strike action accounted for 1 in 10,300 (compared with 1 in 3,900 in 2002). More significantly, some 150,600 workers were involved in industrial action.

**12.2** 'Industrial action' is defined as a strike or withdrawal of labour. The basic principle in relation to industrial action is as Lord Watson puts it in *Allen v Flood* (1898) : '... strikes are only effective when undertaken lawfully'. The Employment Relations Bill, currently before Parliament, in Part 3 amends the law relating to industrial action, including measures to simplify the law relating to ballots for industrial action and ballot notices. Moreover, it strengthens the protection against the dismissal of workers taking official and lawful industrial action. The latter reform involves the exempting of employer 'lock-outs' for an 8 week period.

### Strikes and contracts of employment

**12.3** A 'strike' is defined in s 246 of TULRCA 1992 as 'any concerted stoppage of work'. In *Connex South Eastern Ltd v Rail Maritime and Transport Workers* (1999), the Court of Appeal held that the definition of 'strike' is wide enough to cover any refusal to work for periods when the workers would normally work. In most, if not all, strike action, contracts of employment are affected. However, no notice to terminate the contract is given. Even though, strike action amounts to a repudiation of contract. For instance, the EAT in *Simmons v Hoover Ltd* (1977) provided guidance: '... it seems to us to be plain that it was a repudiation for here there was a settled, confirmed continued intention on the part of the employee not to do any of the work which under contract he had been engaged to do; which was the whole purpose of his contract'. Consequently, the employer has a choice whether or not to accept the repudiation by the strikers. Such an acceptance results in dismissal. Yet some industrial action is non-contractual based (see for examples *Secretary of State for Employment v Associated Society of Locomotive Engineers and Firemen (No 2)* (1972); *Cresswell v Board of*

Inland Revenue (1984); *Miles v Wakefield Metropolitan District Council* (1987); and *Ticehurst v British Telecommunications plc* (1992)).

## Pay and strike action

**12.4**  Action short of dismissing strikers, is that the employer is clearly not obliged to pay the striking workers during the industrial action itself. Most notably, the employee must show that he/she is available and willing to work (*Henthorn and Taylor v Central Electricity Generating Board* (1980)). The general principle is that deductions from pay are regulated by agreement between parties and by a statutory exception under s 14(5) of ERA 1996.

**12.5**  Alternatively, an employer may take legal action and sue striking employees for damages instead on account of a breach of contract. However, the major legal dilemma in this scenario is how to calculate the damages concerned. For example, the courts have rejected a proportionate share of overhead expenses during lost days as the appropriate measure. Courts have a tendency to award only a proportional amount of the claim sought by the suing employers.

## Forms of industrial action

**12.6**  Strike action is not the only form of industrial action. Other forms include work-to-rule and go-slow, as well as overtime bans. In addition, employees may work normally but refuse to perform the particular duty about which they are protesting. Sit-ins are another form of industrial action.

## Industrial action by the employer

**12.7**  An employer may also resort to industrial action, since an employer holds the right to make changes in their business. Consequently, employers may have cause to 'lock-out' their workforce.

## Legality of industrial action

**12.8** Industrial action is lawful where it conforms to the well-enunciated two-fold test of Lord Diplock in *Dimbleby & Sons Ltd v National Union of Journalists* (1984):

(a)  Whether the employers have a cause of action at common law; and,

(b)  Whether those taking industrial action are acting in 'contemplation or furtherance of a trade dispute against the employer'. If so, s 219 of TULR(C)A 1992 gives immunity from action which:
* induced a person to breach a contract of employment;
* threatened that a contract of employment will be breached;
* interferes with the trade, business or employment of a person; or
* constitutes an agreement by two or more persons to procure the doing of any such act.

This means that the normal torts are removed, where this test is satisfied.

## The economic torts

**12.9** As noted above (9.8), there are several different ways of committing this tort during industrial action:

(a)  direct inducement;

(b)  indirect inducement by unlawful means;

(c)  procuring breach of contract by unlawful means.

**12.10** Most commonly during industrial action, a relevant tort is committed when a trade union official directly persuades a worker to breach their contract of employment. Similarly, where trade unions organise action against suppliers or distributors of the employer with whom it is in dispute and as a result induce a breach of the employer's commercial contracts. Alternatively, a tort is committed if the strikers unlawfully interfere with any contract by actually preventing performance.

## Inducement

**12.11** Inducement means more than the fact that a trade union official informs the workforce that the employer is intending to make redundancies and/or change working methods and the workforce goes on strike in protest. Now s 219 of the TULRCA 1992, provides that an act done by a person in contemplation of furtherance of a trade dispute shall not be actionable in tort on the ground only:

(a)   that it induces another person to breach a contract or interferes or induces any other person to interfere with its performance; or

(b)   that it consists of his threatening that a contract (whether one to which he is a party or not) will be broken or its performance interfered with, or that he will induce another person to break a contract or to interfere with its performance.

The tort of direct inducement to breach a contract was recognized in *Lumley v Gye* (1853).

## Interference

**12.12** Lord Diplock in *Merkur Island Shipping Corporation v Laughton* (1983) regarded the tort of 'interfering with the trade or business of another person by doing unlawful acts' as a 'genus of torts' of which procuring breach of contract is a 'species'. Therefore, the tort of interference may include such interference with future contracts not yet in existence (*Stratford (JT) & Son Ltd v Lindley* (1965) and *Union Traffic Ltd v TGWU* (1989). This was not made out by the distribution of leaflets outside supermarkets urging members of the public to boycott the employer's mushrooms (*Middlebrook Mushrooms Ltd v Transport and General Workers Union* (1993)). Consequently, to be tortious the persuasion had to be directed at one of the parties to the commercial contract in issue (see *Falconer v ASLEF & NUR* (1986) ).

## Breach of contract

**12.13** The previous torts are required as a precondition to the commission of breach of contract, normally by unlawful means of indirect inducement and procuring breach of contract.

## Intimidation

**12.14**    The tort of intimidation includes threat of a breach of contract or other unlawful act as well as threats of violence. Now s 219(1)(b), TULRCA 1992, 'where it consists in threatening that a contract (whether one to which he is a party or not) will be broken or its performance interfered with, or that he will induce another person to break a contract or interfere with its performance' immunity arises.

## Conspiracy

**12.15**    A conspiracy to commit a crime or a tort is also included. A conspiracy to injure consists of an agreement to cause deliberate loss to another without cause or excuse with the intention of injuring the claimant (eg *Huntley v Thornton* (1957) ). The unlawful means of pursuing the strike must, however, be integral to the aims of the conspirators and not peripheral to them. In most cases, immunity against liability for conspiracy is unnecessary because the cause is continued would amount to justification in itself at common law. Immunity is therefore provided by s 219(2), TULRCA 1992, where an 'agreement or combination by two or more persons to do or procure the doing of any act in comtemplation or furtherance of a trade dispute shall not be actionable in tort if the act is one which, if done without any such agreement or combination, would not be actionable in tort'.

## Trade Dispute Immunity

**12.16**    As noted above, when these torts emerged at common law and later statute, Parliament decided to provide protection to trade unions, so as to give them immunity from legal action against them. To that effect, it did not allow trade unions and their officials as well as members the right to break the law, but to neutralise the normal effect of actions pursued for the torts listed above, when trade unions undertook legitimate industrial action (*Express Newspapers Ltd v McShane* (1980)). The latter immunity became known as the 'Golden Formula'.

## The 'Golden Formula'

**12.17** The 'Golden Formula' provides that to be protected and be given immunity from suit, the individual must be acting 'in contemplation or furtherance of a trade dispute' (s 219(2) TULRCA 1992). The words in 'contemplation' meant, according to Lord Loreburn in *Conway v Wade* (1909): 'that either a dispute is imminent and the act is done in expectation of and with a view to it, or that the dispute is already existing and the act is done in support of one side to it'. The formula has three parts to be satisfied:

(i)  there must be a temporal relationship between the action to be taken and a trade dispute;

(ii)  the trade dispute must be between workers and their employer; and

(iii)  the dispute must be over one or more of the matters listed in s 244 TULRCA 1992, which defines a trade dispute.

## Trade dispute

**12.18** S. 244(1), TULRCA1992 defines a trade dispute as: 'A dispute between workers and their employer, that is to say, which relates wholly or mainly to one of the following:

(a)  terms and conditions of employment, or the physical conditions in which any workers are required to work;

(b)  engagement or non-engagement, or termination of suspension of employment or the duties of employment, of one or more workers;

(c)  allocation of work or the duties of employment as between workers or groups of workers;

(d)  matters of discipline;

(e)  the membership or non-membership of a trade union on the part of a worker;

(f)  facilities for officials of trade unions; and

(g)     machinery for negotiation of consultation, and other procedures, relating to any of the foregoing matters, including the recognition by employer or employers' association of the right of a trade union to represent workers in any such negotiation or consultation or in the carrying out of such procedures'.

**12.19**  Consequently, a trade dispute must relate wholly or mainly to one or more of the matters set out above in s 244 of TULRCA 1992. Yet, Lord Denning ruled in (*Beetham v Trinidad Cement Ltd* (1960) that a dispute '... exists whenever a difference exists, and a difference can exist long before the parties become locked in combat ...It is sufficient that they should be sparring for an opening'.

**12.20**  The Court of Appeal in *P v The National Association of School Masters/Union of Women Teachers* (2001) held that there was a trade dispute when employees refused to teach a particular pupil, who, it was claimed, was disruptive in class.

## Losing immunity

**12.21**  The statutory immunities under s 219 will be removed in the following situations:

(a)     secondary action;

(b)     unlawful picketing;

(c)     action to enforce union membership;

(d)     action to impose union recognition;

(e)     action in support of dismissed unofficial strikers;

(f)     action without proper notice to an employer;

(g)     action without a valid strike ballot.

## Dismissal and post-termination protection

**12.22**  Section 244(5), TULRCA 1992, excludes a person who has ceased to be employed unless:

(a) his employment was terminated in connection with the dispute; or

(b) was one of the circumstances giving rise to it.

**12.23** The rules relating to the dismissal of employees during industrial action are set out in ss 237 – 238A TULRCA 1992. The Employment Relations Act 1999 made important amendments, in force since April 2000, to the well-established principles on dismissal for industrial action by creating an eight week 'protected period' during which a dismissal for taking part in industrial action will be automatically unfair. Consequently, employees are only protected if it is official action, and would be covered by the statutory immunities against liability in tort under s 219 TULRCA 1992 having complied with the relevant law.

**12.24** Under s 237 TULRCA 1992, an employee cannot bring an unfair dismissal complaint if at the time of the dismissal the employee was taking part in an unofficial strike or other unofficial industrial action. Unofficial industrial action is when it is taken without the authorisation or endorsement of a union engaged in the action.

**12.25** The Court of Appeal's conclusion in *University College London Hospital NHS Trust v UNISON* (1999) was that a dispute will relate to employees' terms and conditions only where it concerns their relationship with their current employer. Such might be fraught with difficulties when applied to TUPE situations. For example, in *Westminister City Council v UNISON* (2001), a dispute about a proposal to transfer an undertaking, including its employees, from the local authority to a private company was a trade dispute, the Court of Appeal held that the dispute was predominantly about the change in the identity of the employer and not about public policy issues.

## Secondary action

**12.26** Section 17(2) of EA 1980 first defined 'secondary action' as:

when, and only when, a person -

(a)   induces another to break a contract of employment or interferes or induces another to interfere with its performance, or

(b)   threatens that a contract of employment under which he or another is employed will be broken or its performance interfered with, or that he will induce another to break a contract of employment or to interfere with its performance, if the employer under the contract of employment is not a party to the trade dispute.

**12.27**   Section 4 of the Employment Act 1990 finally removed all immunity for secondary action other than secondary picketing where it is peaceful.

## Strike Ballots

**12.28**   Sections 226–234, TULRCA 1992 removed the immunity of unions and individual strike organisers from certain actions in tort unless a majority of union members likely to be called out in industrial action have approved that action in a properly held ballot.

**12.29**   A ballot is required only in respect of 'an act done by a trade union'; that is, if it is authorised or endorsed by the Principal Executive Committee, the President or General-Secretary of the trade union concerned. As a general rule, the first authorisation or endorsement of the strike or other industrial action must be given within four weeks from the date the ballot is taken. Since 1999, the union and the employer may extend this period by agreement for up to another four weeks. These ballot rules are strictly applied and a minor failure can negate industrial action and remove the relevant immunities. For example, in *National Union of Rail, Maritime and Transport Workers v Midland Mainline Ltd* (2001), it was held that this meant that the union had not accorded entitlement to vote in the ballot equally to members who it was reasonable, at the time of the ballot, for the union to believe would be induced to take part in the industrial action.

**12.30**   A union intending to organise industrial action must conduct separate ballots for each place of work, subject to certain important exceptions. By s 228 of TULRCA 1992, in so far as the union believes, and it is a reasonable belief, that the persons to be induced to take part in a strike or other industrial action are engaged at different places of work, it must hold a ballot at each such place of work.

**12.31**  The High Court held, in *University of Central England v National and Local Government Officers' Association* (1993) that it is not necessary for entitlement to vote in a ballot to be restricted to employees of only one employer. Furthermore, in *British Telecommunications plc v Communication Workers Union* (2004), the High Court stated that not everyone balloted need be affected, where the union had mistakenly advised its members that strike action included action short of a strike. This too did not invalidate the ballot. But it had not given the information required under the TULRCA 1992 on the categories of workers who would be balloted, and this was grounds for an injunction.

**12.32**  New provisions contained in the Employment Relations Act 1999 established important exceptions to the above principles. The new s 228A of TULRCA 1992 provides that the union need not ballot different workplaces separately because of s 228 in any of the following situations:

(a)  at least one union member in a workplace is directly affected by the dispute in question;

(b)  entitlement to vote is restricted to union members who have an occupation (or occupations) of a particular kind and are employed by a particular employer (or any of a number of employers) with whom the union is in dispute;

(c)  entitlement to vote is restricted to union members who, according to the union's reasonable belief, have an occupation (or occupations) of a particular kind and are employed by a particular employer (or any number of employers) with whom the union is in dispute.

**12.33**  By s 234A to TULRCA 1992, the union must give advance notice of industrial action to the affected employer(s). In fact, the trade union concerned must 'take such steps as are reasonably necessary to ensure that the employer receives' a specified notice of industrial action.

## Ballot papers

**12.34**  Under s 229(3) TULRCA 1992, an industrial action ballot paper must specify who is authorised for the purposes of calling members to take part or continue to take part in industrial action. There will be no immunity for the trade union if action supported by a ballot is not in fact called by the person named in the ballot paper. The union must give the employer seven days' notice of its intention to hold a ballot. The Employment Relations Act 1999 removed the duty to 'name names', and replaced it with a duty to provide information to an employer so that the employer can make plans in relation to the industrial action. The union must also provide the employer, not less than three days before the ballot, with a sample voting paper (s 226A TULRCA 1992).

## Picketing

**12.35**  The central justification of peaceful picketing lies in the right to freedom of speech and peaceful protest. Article 11 of the 1950 European Convention on Human Rights establishes the right to freedom of association and peaceful assembly, which applies to the law on picketing.

**12.36**  Pickets may not commit the following crimes:

(a)  Obstruction of the highway:

Subject to s 132 of the Highways Act 1980, '… if a person without lawful authority or excuse in any way wilfully obstructs the free passage along the highway, he shall be guilty of an offence…'. The illegality of an obstruction is a question of fact, and depends on 'the length of time the obstruction continues, the place where it occurs, the purpose for which it is done, and of course whether it does in fact cause an actual obstruction as opposed to a potential obstruction' (*Nagy v Weston* (1965)).

(b)  Obstructing a police constable:

Section 51(3) of the Police Act 1964 makes it a criminal offence to obstruct a police constable in the execution of his duty and that duty is to prevent trouble where he reasonably apprehends a breach of the peace as a 'real possibility'.

(c)  Assaults:

While assaults may be committed on a picket-line, there is no such crime or tort unless the capacity to carry into effect the intention to commit a battery is present at the time of the over act indicating an immediate intention to commit a battery. *Thomas v National Union of Mineworkers (South Wales Area)* (1985) since the threats uttered by the picketing striking miners were made from the side of the road to working miners who were in vehicles which the pickets could not reach.

(d)  Public Order Act Offences:

By s 4 of the Public Order Act 1986, a person is guilty of an offence if the picketeer:

(a)  uses towards another person threatening, abusive or insulting words or behaviour, or

(b)  distributes or displays to another person any writing, sign or other visible representation which is threatening, abusive or insulting with intent to cause that person to believe that immediate unlawful violence.

(e)  Unlawful assembly:

An unlawful assembly consists of the assembly of three or more persons with the intention of fulfilling a common purpose in such a manner as to endanger the public peace. It is an offence at common law to obstruct the public in the exercise or enjoyment of rights common to all, including free passage along the highway. In *J. Lyons & Sons v Wilkins* (1899) Lindley LJ thought it did, since it constituted an attempt to persuade, regardless of any obstruction. Lord Denning MR in *Hubbard v Pitt* (1975) considered that this view 'has not stood the test of time ...'.

(f)  Harassment:

The Protection from Harassment Act 1997, Section 1 establishes that it will be an offence for someone to pursue a course of conduct that amounts to harassment or another and which he knows, or ought to know, amounts to harassment. 'Harassment' is not defined in the Act, but can include 'alarming the person or causing the person distress' (s 7).

**12.37** Picketing is not actionable per se but only if a tort is committed by the pickets (*News Group Newspapers Ltd v Society of Graphical Allied Trades* (1982)).

## Nuisance

**12.38** Private Nuisance is an unlawful interference with an individual's enjoyment or use of his land. To sue for the tort, the claimant must have some proprietary interest in the land and this action is most likely to be relevant where pickets block an access route. Picketing accompanied by violence, or even merely noise, may be a private nuisance. Scott J in *Thomas v National Union of Mineworkers* (*South Wales Area*) (1985) held that mass picketing at the gates of five collieries in South Wales during the miners' strike of 1984/85 was tortuous and could be restrained at the suit of the plaintiffs who were working miners.

**12.39** The immunity for picketing is found in s 220 of TULRCA 1992, which reads:

> It shall be lawful for a person in contemplation of furtherance of a trade dispute to attend
> (a)  at or near his own place of work, or
> (b)  if he is an official of a trade union, at or near the place of work of a member of that union whom he is accompanying and whom he represents.

## Secondary pickets

**12.40** A secondary picket is not liable for economic torts, like inducing breach of contract, where he pickets his own place of work and his employer is:

(a)  an immediate supplier or customer of the employer in dispute, and the aim is to disrupt services between them; or

(b)     an associated employer of the employer in dispute and the aim is to cut off dispute (TULRCA 1992, s 224).

**12.41** Even if the picketeer fulfils all the other requirements of secondary action, the picket must be at or near his place of work to attract immunity (see *Mersey Dock and Harbour Co v Verrinder* (1982). According to the Code of Practice on Picketing, the 'place of work' means 'an entrance to or an exit from the factory, site or office at which the picket works'.

**12.42** The immunity has also been narrowly applied by the courts. For example, *Broome v DPP* (1974): 'The section gives no protection in relation to anything the pickets may say or do whilst they are attending if what they say or do is unlawful … The section therefore gives a narrow but nevertheless real immunity to pickets.

**12.43** In contrast, the statute contains no specific restriction on the number of pickets, but clearly large numbers may intimidate more easily than the actions of the few. Lord Reid's opinion has already been reviewed. The Code of Practice describes mass picketing as 'obstruction if not intimidation' and para 31 recommends ensuring that 'in general the number of pickets does not exceed six at any entrance to a workplace: frequently a smaller number will be appropriate'.

## Remedies

**12.44** Most employers will not seek damages against striking employees. More likely, the employers desire the return of their workforce to full employment capacity. As a result, employers will often seek injunctions to enable this.

### Injunctions

**12.45** The principles determining whether injunctions are to be granted are found in *Cyanamid Co v Ethicon Ltd* (1975), where the House of Lords postulated that it was only necessary that the plaintiff have an arguable case and that there was a serious issue to be tried. The court should not at this stage express a concluded opinion as to the law unless it is reasonably clear (*Associated British Ports plc v Transport and General Workers Union* (1989)). In *Associated British Ports plc v Transport and General Workers Union* (1989) the Court of Appeal stated that the status quo was to be understood in the sense that work was still proceeding at the time the writ was issued, so that was the status quo position.

**12.46** S. 221 TULRCA1992, provides that if there might be a 'trade dispute' defence to an injunction, the court must not grant without notice relief unless all reasonable steps have been taken: (a) to notify the other side of the application; and (b) to give them an opportunity of putting their case.

**12.47** The primary methods of enforcement on the breach of injunctive orders are committal for contempt, up to a maximum of 2 years. Sequestration is an alternative remedy which is only granted as a last resort to enforce a judgment requiring a person to do an act within a specified time or to abstain from doing a specified act. It operates by sequestrating all the real and personal property of the union or persons subject to the order, and is cumulative to other methods of enforcing an order such as committal.

## Damages

**12.48** The amount of damages that can be awarded against a union is limited by s 22 TULRCA 1992. S 22 grades liability in bands, from a maximum of £10,000 in the case of a union with less than 5,000 members, up to a maximum of £250,000 for a union with 100,000 or more members. Consequently, certain property belonging to trade unions is protected from awards of damages, such as the personal property of the union's trustees, officials and members and the union's political fund (provided its rules prevent the fund from being used to finance strikes or other industrial action).

## Further reading

Bowers, J, Duggan, M, & Reade, D, *The Law on Industrial Action and Trade Union Recognition* (2004) Oxford University Press.

Deakin, S, & Morris, G, *Labour Law* (3rd ed, 2001) Butterworths (chapter 11).

Ewing, K, *The Right to Strike* (1991) Clarendon Press: Oxford.

Smith, I, & Thomas, G, *Industrial Law* (8th ed, 2003) Butterworths (chapter 11).


*Articles*

Simpson, B, 'The Labour Injunction, Unlawful Means and a right to strike', *Modern Law Review*, 1987, Vol. 50, pp. 506–516.

Simpson, B, 'Code of Practice on Industrial Action Ballots', *Industrial Law Journal*, 2001, Vol. 30, pp. 194–198.

## Self-test questions

1. The legal framework governing strike action is so unworkable, as to be irrelevant in the twenty-first century. Discuss.

2. What must unions do to ensure that any industrial action taken is lawful?

3. Bumpy Cars Ltd is a leading manufacturer of sports cars. Currently it is in dispute with its workforce, whose union, Stand Firm, has held a ballot and is involved in a trade dispute with Bumpy Cars Ltd in relation to overtime pay and working hours. Last week, 2-day strike action took place, during which Bumpy Cars Ltd's management found it difficult to enter the premises due to the 11 employees on the picket line. It also observed 4 delivery lorries being turned away, hearing one driver being threatened that 'if he entered, his truck would be overturned'. Lastly, it was reported to Bumpy Cars Ltd that some of their regular customers had received letters in the post, advising them not to purchase any Bumpy Cars Ltd's vehicles in future.

   Advise Bumpy Cars Ltd on any available remedies its management have against its employees and Stand Firm, their recognized workforce union.

4. What liabilities do unions and individual union members hold when taking industrial action?

# Index